Crisis of Leadership in Public Education

JOSEPH L. PICOGNA

To order additional copies, please contact us.
BookSurge, LLC
www.booksurge.com
1-866-308-6235
orders@booksurge.com

CRISIS OF LEADERSHIP IN PUBLIC EDUCATION

2006

"Man is a creature whose substance is faith. What his faith is, he is."

Bhagavad Gita, Hindu scripture

CONTENT

ACKNOWLEDGMENTS

"The farther you reach back in time, the further shall you see into the future."

Mark Twain

I spent zero some time thinking of an inspiration for this book because of my admiration for my wife, Marie Picogna, *a teacher, who taught a thousand children and who loved every child as her own.* While she is certainly multi-talented and accomplished, it is her many years of service as an elementary school teacher in a broken down building in Mount Laurel, New Jersey, that I wish to call to the attention of the reader. She and tens of thousands like her work in increasingly difficult circumstances in buildings that in many cases are so unfit that special [lower] environmental standards had to be developed in order to permit their continued use. For my wife, achieving tenure meant only some protection from a Board of Education that could and would turn hostile at any time with new members seeking election in order to launch a vendetta against some hardworking faculty members they believed had slighted their child. Tenure was never a license to slow down, "retire on the job" as some wags refer to the concept, probably folks who never accepted the challenge of being responsible for children. Rather, when she achieved tenure, in several teaching assignments, it seemed to be a challenge to be even more effective to justify the faith placed in her ability and commitment to excellence. Fortunately she never needed protection from building or district level administrators, working first for really decent and talented people who appreciated her value and later for people who were at least smart enough to know that her husband and her union would make their life absolutely miserable if they trod on the prerogatives that she had earned through many years of outstanding work.

Marie is retired now but I still think of the countless nights she spent making sure everything was just perfect for the next day, the weekends spent endeavoring to make sure no child failed to receive the benefit of the doubt on assignments, and the endless hours worrying that a child had little or no support at home to face the adventure of life. I watched her feeling miserable worrying about parents who brought a first hand emotion of hostility to every encounter and the in-house and outhouse experts who elicited little praise and fewer helpful suggestions. As a non-complaining veteran with an outstanding track record, she often was assigned the "problem" children year after year although she was compensated at the same level as the very poorest performing of her peers. Through it all she persevered, through a sense of duty and a realization that often she was the only one available to serve a particular child. There is something almost magical in watching someone so committed that she would risk life and limb to venture forward on the ice in February, when she had hundreds of leave days at her disposal in the final months of her active service. Finally, I watched a system gone mad wear down her spirits and it was left to me to urge her to stop, pass the torch and begin enjoying a very well deserved pension.

I cannot imagine where we would be without the selflessness of my wife and the thousands like her, for they are teachers, the building blocks of our society and culture.

"Here's To All The Heroes Whose Faith In Children, In Public Education And In Me Was Much Appreciated. It Was The Time Of My Life. To Quote Winston Churchill, "Never Have So Many Owed So Much To So Few'."

PREDICATE

No one knows for sure when the system broke down, just that it doesn't work any longer. Joseph Picogna is one of the people who knew how to get things done, had the courage to take on the establishment, and the skill to protect himself as he worked in the interest of those least able to help themselves. His record of innovation, particularly as to cost efficiencies, is and may remain unsurpassed in the annals of public school administration in New Jersey. He was held in the deepest respect by those working in the public interest and with trepidation by those feeding at the public trough. It was always much smarter to be with him than against him and his professional training and academic preparation was so superior that he operated as if he were in a league all his own. Dr. Picogna retired after over three decades of service yet his contributions shall linger to impact on many generations to come. His dedication, commitment to excellence and selfless demeanor shall be remembered by all who made his acquaintance and untold thousands have a much better experience preparing for life in the public schools because of his dedication.

Carl I. Johnson Ed. D.
Retired Superintendent of Schools

FOREWORD

I had been on the Board of Education for a number of years when we had the good fortune to encounter Joseph Picogna. Delran was in sad shape when I and a few others decided to run for the Board, for whom I would eventually serve as President. The administration was in shambles, the facilities were crumbling, our books were twenty years old in some cases, and the district was actually bankrupt, owing more in fines than it could muster in cash. We had had a progression of business administrators passing through without achieving tenure and things did not begin to turn around until we hired a new Superintendent, Bernard Shapiro. Dr. Shapiro introduced us to Dr. Picogna, who had been serving in Cherry Hill. We learned that the Board there had first issued a non-renewal notice to Dr. Picogna after he had brought complaints against the Superintendent, who then had him fired abruptly. No Board of Education wishes to risk hiring someone who has been fired but we faced two unique circumstances, we needed a quality individual and, after one interview, it was apparent that Dr. Picogna could be that person, so the match was made. I recall that he began working without pay weeks before the appointment became effective and it was soon obvious that we had made the right choice. It was also very apparent that the educators in Cherry Hill would have a tough time surviving the wrongful firing action brought by Dr. Picogna. He and I spoke constantly as he identified one remarkable circumstance after another. I was employed at the time as a Finance Director for the Consolidated Rail Corporation and engaged in what was to become a very well received continuous improvement process evolution. It was quite refreshing to be involved with that experience at work and seeing the same thing happening in our school district. We rewarded Dr. Picogna with early tenure, something extraordinarily rare in the business, in the hopes that he would stay with us for a while. Fortunately he continued his commitment to our community and the ten years he was paired with a new Superintendent, Dr. Carl Johnson may have been the best run any district in the region has ever experienced.

This book tells that story and a lot more, it explains what potential existed in the 1970's, how that potential was exhausted and further, the tremendous cost of resources that was expended in the demise of the dream of truly effective public schools. As a bonus, it offers a really terrific section entitled, "Tool Box for Bureaucrats," which is a compendium of useful strategies for those responsible for operations management in the public domain.

Ronald Napoli
Former President
Delran Board of Education

PREFACE

"In time of war, the laws are silent"

Cicero, a Senator of Rome

"Their demands are insatiable". This quote was breathed by an exasperated member of a board of education bargaining committee some years ago, during a truly difficult negotiation session. The board member, was, as they like to say, a "volunteer" donating his time "for the children", dealing with paid professionals from an extremely powerful teacher "association" that certainly convinced me a long time ago that it truly was a union. The board member was a veteran of such encounters and brought to the table his experiences in the private sector, where the worm had turned against employees some time ago. He complained that the NJEA was not a "mature" union, given their demands, perhaps but they did not have to be; had targeted him in the recent election because he was not a teacher and therefore a member of their union; and had no interest in sharing the burden of coping with rising costs and dwindling tax resources. I told him the story of a meeting held many years ago involving the Philadelphia Federation of Teachers and the President of the Board of Education, Richardson Dilworth, a distinguished attorney, well respected former Mayor, and candidate for the Office for Governor of the Commonwealth. Mr. Dilworth was always a particular favorite of mine, a true public servant, one who had assumed a difficult task in an attempt to provide one more service to the city he loved. Dilworth had built quite a reputation as a conciliator, settling contracts with even the difficult municipal unions but here he was over his head and his repertoire of tactics failed him miserably. The climax of the long evening came when the old gentleman struggled to stand on a table surrounded by a shouting crowd of teachers. When they finally quieted for a moment, he reminded them that all of the financial records had been made available to their representatives and that there was a severe shortage of funds. "I am afraid it comes down to jobs or raises", he said, and then made a fatal error by asking, "Tell me are you interested in keeping jobs or getting the money." "The MONEY, the MONEY, the MONEY," they screamed, with pandemonium breaking out and the defeated Mr. Dilworth almost falling from his precarious perch.

You see the teachers knew the district would give in, back in Philadelphia and in my more current example, for the parents would not let the children stay home, the seniors had to graduate and move on with their lives, the states require a certain minimum number of days so no salary is lost, and the unions are controlled by tenured and very senior personnel who are all but exempt from layoffs. "It is a stacked deck, then, I guess" said my exasperated board member. It is and it isn't, I replied. The teachers earned this power for they have had to deal with some of the most selfish and self-serving individuals ever involved in labor relations, boards of education. Regardless of the circumstances, their political power is enormous although sometimes unused when non-personnel issues are at stake, their fellow members are allowed to dominate the boards of education throughout New Jersey, and their salary and benefits often exceed 80% of the budgets of typical districts enrolling children from grades kindergarten through 12th. Staff raises are automatic or rather because they happen to be at least recently alive on September 1 of each year and all you get from contract negotiations is temporary relief from the threat of having your community torn apart by a work stoppage.

It did not used to be that way. How we got to this point, what we must do to reverse this trend and the consequences if we do not is what this book is about. It took me thirty-five years to live through this adventure and over a year to write about it. Unfortunately, parents and children no longer have the luxury of very much time if these trends are to be reversed. History is written for most, from the "outside", for the most part, to prevent a distortion of the truth. However, while an "inside" view may be subject to personal coloring, there is no better mode to portray the context of important transactions, to know how things appeared to the actual actors, to convey the action and passion, as they really occurred. This was not intended to be a memoir but a tale of what became a crusade involving well meaning people caught up in a situation that became increasingly untenable, indeed almost macabre for the participants. One of my literary heroes, Shelby Foote, who died as this was being written, was known to be a great proponent of narrative history. As a key presenter on Ken Burns classic public broadcasting production of the Civil War, he said of narrative history: "Narrative history is the kind that comes closest to the truth. Getting to the truth should always be your goal". Here then is a narrative of my life work, as I remember it...

Joseph Louis Picogna
Cherry Hill, New Jersey

INTRODUCTION

"I claim not to have controlled events, but confess plainly that events have controlled me."

Abraham Lincoln

I guess it is safe to say that President Lyndon Johnson shall always be remembered for the Vietnam War and the thunderous protests that eventually drove him from office. It is unfortunate that many of his domestic initiatives, sometimes grouped under his "Great Society" programs, have not been given adequate recognition. President Johnson was responsible for rekindling the civil rights and anti-poverty programs of President Harry Truman. During his administration the Elementary and Secondary Education Act was written, adopted, and most importantly, funded, some would say to an exorbitant extent. This singular piece of legislation is still in place today, albeit with countless amendments. Contemporary educators face the "No Child Left Behind" provisions, I guess with the same trepidation and frustration that their predecessors exhibited with ESEA. It is ironic that a program I always thought was quite important and relatively easy to administer was condemned as too restrictive and cumbersome. I wonder what the current crowd of educators would give to get back to what are now regarded as the "halcyon" days of ESEA.

Mr. Johnson's initiative did result in a torrent of funds being applied to the problems facing the public schools, particularly for children facing an often grueling uphill battle in the inner-city. Head Start and all the support programs available under Title I undoubtedly had a very positive effect on the target population. However, it was a bill from the Democratic Party, my life-long party, and as such, it was structured to serve a wide variety of constituencies and spawned its own bureaucracy. Title I funds were granted to states, who immediately created parallel bureaucracies and thence to local districts, who immediately did the same thing. About the time I joined the New Jersey Department of Education in 1972, every state had a separate empire for each of these programs, and many districts had mirror organizations. The newly created bureaucrats even started their own organization, Federal Program Administrators. Schools had teachers and administrators for regular programs, mostly funded with local tax dollars, and federal programs, provided under Title I and II of ESEA, and sometimes even Title III, to say nothing of the burgeoning special education fiefdoms that were sprouting.

While a great deal of money did flow to the classroom, there was a "cut" for "admin" purposes at each level, federal, state and local, with a corresponding bureaucracy in place in each jurisdiction. Soon, there were a plethora of separate little kingdoms in the school districts, especially the urban areas, in which Title I programs were run in a different and most often not complementary manner. Children were pulled out of regular classrooms to take remedial instruction, while their classmates pounded away with new material. Teachers were assigned as "basic skills" instructors and became such a unique entity that different rules governing their seniority had to be developed. Over time, it became popular to place weaker teachers in these roles as they were facing far fewer children and each day they were not responsible for a given class, at the elementary level, from September through June. I cannot begin to recount how many principals did not even bother to evaluate these staff or ensure that their work was integrated into some sort of plan, as this responsibility was assigned to the Title I Coordinator. It is ironic to note that this diversion of assets really did not bother anyone as the evaluation process was worthless and few, if any, strategic plans existed, at least of a sort to comport with commonly accepted standards of organization development.

One of the most intriguing political aspects of Title I was the parent involvement requirement. Now this seems to make sense, even if you do not read the statute, which again appears to have been written with the welfare of children in mind. However, it did not take long for some Title I parents to realize that this provision could be a bonanza and the parent advisory groups soon were winging their way hither and yon to "observe" successful programs and "disseminate" the components back to their communities. Thus was seen the birth of the buzz words and the dollars flowed as more and more junkets were completed. It was interesting that warm weather locations had the best remedial programs.

There were parallel programs for libraries, the so-called gifted and talented students, and special education, of which much more shall be written here, but I think the reader begins to see that the potential for waste, abuse, and in some cases fraud, was prevalent. Each state also got its reward, or perhaps its cash incentive to cooperate, with Title V. This was my favorite, as it provided copious funds with little or no controls to enhance the capacity of state education agencies in the areas of administration, research, and evaluation. Just imagine: no enforcement, a lot of funds, and no impact data expected, truly a gold mine! Title V used to pay my salary when I was holding the position of Coordinator of Research for the New Jersey Department of Education. When a state income tax initiative failed in the mid 1970's, the Department of Education was ordered closed as no state budget had been adopted. I recall that about a dozen or so of us were left on the job, because, according to the official rationale, we had absolutely nothing to do with the operation of the public schools! What did we do? Well naturally, we spent all of our time arguing with the Feds over the issue of whether the Title V money should be cut-off to New Jersey because there was no guarantee that our agency would reopen in the near future. What a way to make a living.

Thus did we spend our modern birthright for education funding in this country. At this time, school districts were growing rapidly, the Civil Rights movement began its focus on better educational opportunities for children in urban areas, and costs were beginning to rise significantly as teacher unions began winning quite justifiable increases in salary, benefits, and security. I am struck with what might have happened had at least one dynamic leader emerged in a key role. When the Country was forming, e.g., the drafting and adoption of the Constitution, everything was not only new, it had no precedent, much as in 1965. In 1787 the Nation was blessed to have Alexander Hamilton in place at just the right time to build our institutional framework. Ron Chernow, in his *Alexander Hamilton*, described this dynamic leader as a thinker and a doer, a system builder who could devise interrelated policies, and build things that made sense, worked well and endured. Unfortunately, no one near Hamilton in ability was available during the formative years of modern education policy making. In fact, I cannot recall being mightily impressed with a single USOE Commissioner, except for someone who was actually in an acting role, Alfred Pierce, whom we shall revisit in the chapter entitled, "FEDS."

Thus, schools were left with a great deal of extra money, which was unfortunately compartmentalized severely, given little control over allocation, and were required to conduct no meaningful evaluation of the impact of the funds. They were however, submerged with meaningless reports and endless audits, few of which anyone ever admitted to have actually read. We saw the beginning of a trend in which these competing entities would one day force everything to come to a halt. Some say the School Reform Act adopted in 2004 in New Jersey did represent Armageddon for public education. But, I take a much broader view. True, the narrow construction of funds utilization could not have been really helpful. I once asked a quite exasperated federal official how tight the audit trail had to be on supplies and materials bought with title funds. His response became a classic in our organizational folklore, "I want to be able to see the money leave a radioactive trail from Washington into student crayon boxes!". Now the educators shall exclaim, "This proves our point!". In fairness to the federal official, no one trusted anyone at the state or local levels to accomplish anything, primarily because no one was ever truly held accountable.

In October 2004, as the layout of this book was being completed, I saw an article written by Andrew Cassel in the Business Section of the Philadelphia Inquirer. Cassel presented an analysis of how the economy could present a slow growth trend without a corresponding increase in jobs. The key ingredient, of course, is productivity, simply put, the ability to do more with less. At the time the economy was growing at four percent annually but with fewer workers than such a rate used to require. You may argue that educators were taught not to be productive because of the environment in which they worked. They at least have been permitted to operate with impunity without ever being concerned with such concepts as accountability and productivity. Indeed, the concept of productivity is an anathema to educators. Consider in my latter years I was never able to convince any superintendent or board of education to conduct a staffing study, under the proviso that there were ample funds if only intelligent choices were effected. I cannot really blame anyone for not adopting this recommendation, which would have made a great deal of sense to my MBA students. You see, in the public schools, there is a competency issue just in getting the job done in a professional manner. No superintendent in New Jersey, and many other jurisdictions with which I am familiar, is required to have taken let alone passed even a single course in management! Also, the superintendent must face reappointment every three to five years and the teacher unions have quite a bit to say in whether or not a reappointment takes place. When you add in the rather significant factor that many members of boards of education are teachers or immediate family members of teachers, well you begin to see why cutting teaching jobs, a natural outcome of a staffing study in this environment, is a forbidden topic. Productivity shall never be a viable concept unless this trend is broken and then there shall be ample funds to get done what needs to be done. For now, those who espouse the need to employ rules of accountability and cost effectiveness become the target of the hubris that drives the educational machine. I recall an episode of the once popular *West Wing* TV series in which a Republic Congressional aide is getting the better of a Democratic Presidential aide in a debate over education funding. In the scenario, the DEMS wanted to specify the manner in which the funds are to be used and the Republican aide fires a broadside in which she explains: "Your boss works for the teachers' union!". Remember the venue which SEN Hilary Clinton chose to announce her candidacy? It was extremely friendly ground, the offices of the National Education Association.

We are about to embark on a journey to describe how this happened, how those who bucked the system were blunted, how, after almost 40 years, the legacy of the great Society funding for schools has been dissipated, and the tremendous challenges that now confront our children because this opportunity was wasted. At stake is the legacy of future development for our children. How bad is the problem? Well, on October 14, 2004, ACT issued a press release dealing with the "crisis" of poor preparation for college by high school graduates. ACT claimed that only 22 percent of the 1.2 million high school grads who took the ACT Assessment in 2004 achieved scores that would deem them ready for college in the "basics": English, math and science! The system is broken, perhaps shattered beyond redemption, unless significant changes are made and soon. Much as Abe Lincoln confessed, in the quote leading off this section, even the best among us have fallen victim to the unprecedented power of a system designed to be just good enough.

THE EARLY YEARS

"In the midst of winter, I finally learned that there was within me an invincible summer."

Albert Camus

"IT'S OK MOM, REALLY!"

I can still recall walking up Broad Street in South Philadelphia, it is September 1970, and I meet my mother walking to the subway and tell her these words. She worked as a tailor until almost her eightieth birthday, before the cancer became too difficult, doing all she could to help her family. She was a woman who missed very little, especially when it touched those dear to her. Just over a month earlier I had consummated almost a year of whirlwind romance and married a terrific woman. We were living in South Jersey in our first apartment and I had just begun my career as an Instructor with the Graduate School at Temple University, the same institution that had awarded me my bachelor and first master degree, and which had also provided me with a fellowship to begin studies for my doctorate. Life was wonderful and then an inevitable cloud formed, in this case, the worsening Vietnam War. Had I had not been faced with a very traumatic situation I guess I would have been touched by the irony of the situation. You see, I had volunteered to be an officer of the US Marine Corps and then the US Army [the Navy being well over booked and insisting that officer recruits begin life with an enlisted experience]. I had been accepted for a commission in both cases before a spot on my lung caused the Marine Corps to offer their regrets. It was then I turned to the US Army, who would grant me a commission, and some perfunctory military training while I finished my first graduate degree, and, then off to wherever, as a second lieutenant! The fates turned out to be very kind indeed, because, while driving my dad's ten year old

Chevy, an inebriated police officer driving what was then affectatiously known as a "meat wagon" ran into me ending that career plan.

Unfortunately, the Army then decided that it would welcome me as a draftee, which happened some time after that terrible automobile accident had damaged my back, which pains me to this day. I can still also remember the scene at the induction center. It was 1968 and a lot of folks were desperate to develop some strategy including a quickie marriage before that loophole was closed, to avoid being taken. I saw a number of my high school classmates for the first time in four years and most seemed to have a scheme to beat the draft. There was the "Italian" doctor that many were sure would never induct a "Paisano", the one who stood on tip toes, almost hopping, to plead his case that his height made him ineligible, and, there was the one guy I remember as being just this side of a psychopath in high school who proudly boasted of his particular remedy: he had slept for many nights with wet cigars under his armpits having been assured this would disrupt his body chemistry. All were inducted and unfortunately most died. Hopefully those who survived learned something from the experience that breathed a little life into moribund brain cells. Looking at the products of the various high schools that day, I recall thinking at the time what a leadership challenge such recruits would pose for any officer. The spot on the lung that turned out to be nothing and the auto accident ended any dream of military service for me at that time. We all went for drinks after the end of the induction rituals and no one could believe I had actually sought entrance to the service, they not being invested in their formative years either by an over-abundance of creativity and or a knack for taking advantage of opportunities.

Two years later, I was on top of the world when the draft board decided maybe the Army could still use me as a private. The back was never to heal, indeed it took me almost 11 years of rehab before I was able to take advantage of a commission opportunity as a Naval Reserve Officer, which would become a wonderful career opportunity before the back and a number of other ailments forced my early retirement. In 1970 the draft board said they were desperate to fill their quota and I would have to have my entire situation reviewed. We subsequently found out that someone who worked with my mother called to complain his child had been killed in the war and I was alive and stateside and how could that be. On reflection it was my first experience with those who felt entitled to something and resented those who didn't and who earned their way every day. That same degenerative sprit may be our greatest threat as we move further into the 21st Century. Well, the docs still said "NO" but I was called for a hearing anyway and went down, heard them reluctantly pronounce my continued incapacity but that "...I would be watched" and told I was free to go, "...for the present."

I had lived with this nonsense for many months and was determined to face this no more and I did what has always served me well, I confronted these purveyors of nonsense and told them their attitude was an insult to everyone who had ever volunteered for service, that their predisposition to turn those deemed qualified for officer status into a draft quota was absurd and, always my best touch, somebody ought to expose them and it may as well be me. I never heard from those folks again and never thought of them until 1996, when standing by my bride in the sunlight of San Diego and listening to the embarrassing platitudes that accompany the retirement of a long serving officer, I was clutching my distinguished service medal.

But in 1970, it was my mom who learned of this first, naturally exclaiming that she had known all along something was amiss, and, one of her favorite remedies, urging a celebration with my wife, the woman she always called her "daughter".

BEGINNINGS

We become what we have experienced and being forced to work from age 14 was a sobering experience. Everyone worked, a lesson learned by those who lived through the depression and World War II. This was the age of the iceman, with his giant tongs; the local grocer who hauled vegetables door to door; the bleach man with his two wheel cart; and, of course, the antique bread truck and the milkman, with his old horse and wagon. The horse was a great favorite of mine because he knew exactly where to stop on the street. Dad had two jobs, with Mom always adding

Saturday overtime in her sweatshop of a men's clothier and I worked for a tile setter. Emilio Miraldo was his name, a remarkable man who spoke little English and had a terrible time getting established with large builders, indeed, even getting product from suppliers when he tried to begin again on his own. His resourcefulness was amazing. He contacted cousins in Italy and had them ship him the tile, he advertised his services outside church every Sunday, and he hired me for after school and Saturday in the winter and every day during the summer. Soon we were doing bathrooms through South Philly, especially in my grandmother's neighborhood of Seventh and Carpenter Street, where a fellow named Rizzo was making his reputation as a police officer and who always took time to speak to a kid who was working instead of loafing. Eventually we began replacing crumbling brick house fronts with gleaming Italian marble as South Philadelphians began turning their small row houses into a bit of the "Old Country". Mr. Miraldo never learned English that well, faced discrimination from many sources but worked hard, provided well for his family as the children were sent to college and professional schools, and gave me my first ride in a Cadillac. He was focused on his values, committed to excellence, and kept focused on fulfilling his vision. He also told me not to mention having worked at age 14 when I had to get working papers for my next job, at age 16. As for Frank Rizzo, the future police commissioner and mayor became a fearsome sight charging into a crowd, astride his motorcycle, wielding the largest baton I have ever seen.

The next job was a real corker, usher at a movie house, for the regal sum of eighty cents an hour, although I was given a dollar an hour whenever I volunteered to climb a rickety ladder to change the letters on a large marquee, 25 feet in the air and seventy-five feet across. Try that on a windy night! The Saturday matinees were just ghastly and, because the manager knew I needed the job and he found me reliable, I was forced to close whenever I worked. That meant leaving at eleven or later and then heading home to any unfinished school work. What was bad enough became worse when his nephew arrived and was paid well and seldom seen. That meant the other two ushers worked alone; for me, it was Tuesday, Friday and Saturday nights and an afternoon shift on Saturday and Sunday. They even made us pay for our uniforms. I am only just now getting to watch the reruns of shows such as the *Combat* TV series, which aired from 1962 through 1967, which everyone spoke of daily at school.

What was salient for me in this job was not only the lesson that blood shall prevail over you every time and boy did we need a union. My parents were always active in their respective unions, my father for the International Brotherhood [no, that's not PC today] of Electrical Engineers and my mom, for the International Ladies Garment Workers [remember their TV ad, "Look for the Label"]. I guess this kind of flowed naturally given their support of FDR and especially Eleanor Roosevelt and a lifetime of blue collar employment. My dad worked at Westinghouse, where they once went on strike just to have the end date of the contract moved to nice weather months to make the inevitable picketing more comfortable. The plant was located in Lester, Pennsylvania, and the area now looks like an extension of the Philadelphia Airport, the company having moved the plant to a place named Ponchatoula, Louisiana, where there was no union. At Lester, they made boiler containment vessels for power plants and US Navy ships, which was very profitable for the parent organization and the workers naturally demanded what they viewed as their share of the pie. One of the strikes lasted nine months and entire families in our area were just wiped out if the breadwinner happened to be employed at Westinghouse. We survived because my father always had two jobs and when a strike occurred he moved to fulltime status at the second job. Nevertheless, we would not have been afloat without his union.

My mother, on the other hand, worked as a volunteer for the garment workers' union. This was a real sweat shop industry with horrid conditions behind the "fronts" of well appointed show rooms where wealthy men would be fitted for outrageously expensive clothes, each costing enough to keep a family going for quite awhile. It was intriguing to see these prices being paid, knowing we lived first with a window box for a refrigerator and then actually an ice box, yes, you had to place a block of ice in the top section to keep the contents cool. The work force was composed almost entirely of second generation children of Italian immigrants as well as the decedents of eastern European Jews lucky enough to have escaped from the Nazis. They made next to nothing and the union was their only salvation. I remember meeting the business agent, who lived very comfortably but no one minded because he delivered, a rudimentary health plan here and there and even an occasional 25 cents per hour raise! Everyone was grateful for work, the late 1940's and much of the 1950's were not exactly a worker paradise, but the union grew, just as in their theme song, because of recruiters like my mom. I often went with her to hand out information booklets and sign up new members, and, she never got a dime for this, just the satisfaction that it was the right thing to do. I believe my dad received a fifteen hundred dollar death benefit when she died, which was exactly fifteen hundred more than had there been no union and twice the benefit granted by Social Security. I never forget the feeling of protection even that rather lame organization was able to provide for its members.

Given the example of my parents, is it any surprise that I became concerned about issues of social justice and adopted among my heroes, people like Abraham Lincoln, Teddy Roosevelt, Franklin Delano Roosevelt, and Harry Truman? My readings of FDR led me to Leland Olds, a famed mathematician who devoted his life to battling social injustice. He worked for the US Government as a labor research analyst during the Great War but soon discovered that to effect change he had to become actively involved so he joined the American Federation of Labor as a researcher. It was in this capacity, while observing the sometimes brutal suppression of strikes against the railroad workers and coal miners in Pennsylvania, when Mr. Olds was shot in the leg. He then joined the Federated Reporter as an editor, authoring over 1800 articles stressing the importance of decent wages and working conditions for employees and the role of unions in protecting the rights of its constituents, while advocating the right of industry to a fair profit; and, championed the importance of labor, thus represented, to the business of business in America. He became a New Dealer and found his true calling, rising to the post of Chairperson of the Federal Power Commission, bringing cheap electricity to millions of US citizens, until he was politically decapitated by Lyndon Johnson in 1949, apparently at the behest of big Texas oil. People like Mr. Olds were instrumental to the American labor movement; they fought to bring dignity and sufficiency of wage to the working person. I wonder what reaction pioneering progressives such as Mr. Olds, would have today, in seeing a GM prostrate before the burden of its collective bargaining agreements, states nearly bankrupt before the billions of dollars of pension obligations that are now unfunded and local communities forced to increase property taxes beyond their ability to pay to fund their public schools.

INTO THE WORK FORCE

I percolated along in this job until my senior year in high school when I was hired by Strawbridge and Clothier as a "stock boy". Three young men hired from over 300 applicants and who were paid the princely sum of $1.28 an hour. I remember the interviewer telling me my test scores indicated I should be going to college and the persistence of her asking if I was planning to go. I realized she would not hire someone going to college for such a job and my response was to ask if promising never to go to college was a requirement of working for this company. "Certainly Not" was the reply and when I did go off to college they liked me so much they let me come down nights and weekends after classes, more evenings at home missed. Actually I should have asked for more money because I was a very marketable commodity, the non-college young men began to be drafted for the Army. All eventually left for the Army but me and they were scared to death because of Old Ernie, who had told them tales of the Korean War and his days in combat. Some years later, blessed with the power of being a senior military officer, I checked and found out Old Ernie was a baker and spent his time in Fort Leavenworth, Kansas, let's just say in a less than active role. Nevertheless, his tales of terror scared the stuffing out of everyone. He claimed that he liked me but warned me to slow down and stop telling people I was grateful for the job. I thought being there was terrific and seeing the staff behind the scenes was a great sideshow. Some of them would eyeball merchandise that would mysteriously turn up with damage, which lowered the price well below the existing employee discount. Others complained about the "Cheap Quakers", who actually paid very competitive wages. You see, the union preached that the employees were being short-changed and this irresponsible behavior filtered down through the organization. It made the supervisors surly and distrustful and they tried to appear to be more productive by assigning people to work above grade, while holding their hourly rate in check, which only exacerbated the ill will among the rank and file. This is how I came to find myself driving a fork truck at 18 years of age, as I was deemed reliable as well as a non-complainer.

They had an elevator in the stock building that dropped below street level, and, unbeknownst to me, then moved across the street to the main store and ascended. I thought I was going to hell, in a giant elevator sized for truck trailers, and never enjoyed seeing sunlight so much when my ordeal was over. Contrary to popular belief at the time, I was not so scared that I dropped a load of china down the shaft, that was a separate and equally regrettable incident, which could have been avoided had I been trained for the task, e.g., that the darn thing turned on the rear wheel. In retrospect, this would have been impossible because the supervisor would have had to acknowledge using me at a higher pay grade or one of my ill-tempered colleagues would have had to take the trouble to give me some advice. I met Peter Strawbridge once. I had stayed late to stock the shelves before one of their big sales, you know the deal, they lower a few prices and raise many more, when Mr. P. came along and took the trouble to inquire after me, e.g., my status, my impressions of working for him, and, took great pains to wish me well in school and to consider a career at Strawbridge's after graduation from college. He was a great person, whom I encountered many years later at a black-tie charity fund raiser that he chaired annually, at which he was extremely gracious as to pretend to remember me. He deserved more from his supervisors and surely deserved a more mature approach from the union leadership and most certainly from the rank and file.

In any event, this job kept me off the streets, gave me some money to help my parents, and was not as bad as some. Years later I would have a senior chief gunner mate in my unit, who had grown up in Philadelphia about the same time as I did. Know what his first job was? Packing manure into junction boxes in the winter to keep gas valves from freezing! Still, those late nights combined with 5:30 AM departures for school kept my drowsy. You see it was a Catholic High School and I had been identified as an altar boy from grade school so I ended up being drafted after all, for all of the crummy jobs the priests needed done, like leaving home in the dark to walk those 14 blocks to school for 6:00 AM Mass! I sure hope they at least remembered to bless me, probably they did for I surely feel blessed with my life, although they taught me very little that was to be of value in college, a precursor of things to come.

FORMATIVE EXPERIENCES

Temple University was to be a marvelous experience for me, coming from a section of the city where you were lucky to enjoy one or two outings a year, in our case the annual trip to Yankee Stadium to see Mickey Mantle, the "Mick" as we came to know him. There were few excursions to the seashore, with the real excitement early on being the five minute update of the progress of Disneyland being built, narrated by Uncle Walt Disney himself, at the conclusion of each Sunday night "Wonderful World of Disney" program. So here was a concrete campus that had more trees than my entire neighborhood and students who talked of Europe, Asia, and safaris, automobiles, the Hamptons, and private boarding schools. There was no such thing as pre-college experiences, e.g., enrolling early in a summer class or two or going to their orientation "camp", for people like me. We arrived on the first day as freshmen did not participate in varsity drills in those days and I can still recall the one orientation session, in which we were told two of every three students would be gone in a year [I guess Europe and a car really could not help that much after all!], and that everyone was on their own. I looked to my left and my right, saw two blonde-haired, well dressed, seemingly confident students and knew I was in trouble.

I met my "advisor" for the first and last time that day, a chain smoking professor of humanities who grumbled about his department being disbanded so he was stuck talking to "kids" who would not make it past the first semester. He told me my high school had a reputation for teaching 19th century material and he was automatically starting me again in French I, for my own good, because he did not trust that the priests had taught me anything. Actually, he was close to very right and it did work out to my advantage because I knew I had to scramble for everything and there was neither time nor money for any setbacks. In this situation, which became too much of a pressure cooker for some, the experience of years of work stood me well as anyone on their own at work from age fourteen had to develop some self-reliance. My advisor had just confirmed something I truly believed, that I had not gotten much of an education in high school, even though I was enrolled in the honors courses. However, I did end up being the only one of 26 fellow pledge class candidates who graduated, ever, and I had only eight semesters to get the job done.

I soon learned how right my cranky old adviser had been about my education. In my neighborhood, the Church was supreme so when the pastor exclaimed about the evils of the public schools [which really had some great programs for hard working students], parents listened hard. The best example I may give of this is from a film called the "Magdalene Sisters", which is based on a true story and as far as I can see fairly faithfully represents the actual events. It is the story of a small village in Ireland in the 20th century in which any young women showing even a propensity for "flirtatious behavior" would be whisked away to a convent named for Mary Magdalene, a "sinner" who had to "...spend her entire life repenting", as a nun explains to a recent arrival. The Church was still propagating the lie of Mary Magdalene being a prostitute in those days. The reality of this convent is that it was a slave labor camp in which the young ladies were condemned to spend many years laboring in the laundry that generated a great deal of cash to benefit the nuns. On a few occasions a child escaped to tell the story to her parents. She was inevitably delivered back into bondage by her parents, because that was the order of the Church. At least I was permitted to go home at night and was not overly abused physically, but, I think you get the idea.

Most of the students in my grade school knew something was wrong, mainly because things there always seemed tense and unstable. I can recall my father being called to school in kindergarten by the nun. When he asked what was wrong as I was a quiet [overly so he always thought] child who had begun his housekeeping career at age six to support his working parents, the nun exclaimed, "I have been beating him but he still insists on using his left hand." My father stated that they had noticed marks on me and then excused me and I heard some loud language. The beatings stopped but the "punishment" for my father's intervention was to stand at a barrel in place of a desk for weeks. Many of the other 56 [Yes, 56!] students in that kindergarten were similarly humiliated or punished, especially if they complained of their treatment to their parents.

There were only two children the same age in the neighborhood, my whole life there as a matter of fact, and my best friend who lived across the street was lost to me as a result of this Catholic School. We happened to be at the general practice doctor, pediatricians were unknown in such a poor neighborhood, at the same time and Ritchie, as he was called, cried, just a bit, when he was given a needle. There were two nuns there for free-bee medical care, including Ritchie's first grade teacher, and she pummeled him for his behavior right in front of his mother. Old Dr. Melchiore, a marvelous man who deserves to have his biography written, apologized and asked the nuns to leave but the damage was done. This nun followed Ritchie over two other grade levels appearing almost daily to tell tales about him we knew were not true. Can you imagine the stress she caused that youngster, whose parents ultimately had to remove him from school? These are the salient memories of that period of my life, along with never being in school with less than 52 children and spending nine years learning by rote, "drill and mental", they called it. I doubt that any of these nuns had even been to high school and there was the added attraction of being in a building that was so poorly maintained that you sat with your coat on in the cold and there was the sudden thrill of a classroom ceiling coming down from time to time. The best part was that parents who could not afford refrigerators paid tuition for this experience!

On reflection, the worst part was a combination of the discrimination, the closed mindedness, and outright meanness. I lived near the Southern Home for Orphan Boys, as grim looking an institution as I have ever seen. The children were kept confined to the grounds and were taken to the public school. They were allowed visitors and while the pool was never operative, they had a small ball field and people my own age. You had to steer clear of the older boys because life had failed them and they all had a chip on their shoulder but those my age were grateful for the company, especially since I was an outsider, albeit one with very limited horizons. I remember asking a nun if the children there might be allowed to attend our school, since it would give me someone to walk to school with and play with afterwards. She was so shocked that she appeared apoplectic, yelling at me to not be ridiculous since these children could not have been raised properly. Thank God people no longer had to wear distinguishing marks such as Scarlet A's. Makes me think of the Nazis whenever I recall the incident. Is it any surprise that as children, our ambition was limited to growing up, earning 10k a year, living in Levittown in a pre-fab home and working on the line for US Steel?

I do not think this phenomenon has changed much. My wife, Marie Picogna a straight "A" student enrolled in strictly honors classes in a private girl's school, speaks of her fear of retribution when she kicked a soccer ball that hit a nun who should not have been walking across the field. The nun's habit was knocked off and so she was "humiliated", thus requiring an apology from my wife. I can recall the first year we were married, one of her cousins lived in Ridley, which had a great public school system, with a high school science program being sponsored by Lehigh University. When I congratulated this cousin on having such a great public school system available to her, she reacted with horror at the thought that her pastor would allow her to send her children to a "godless" school. Whatever happened to the separation of church and state? Anyway, come November of that year when young so-and-so had been enrolled in kindergarten for almost three months, my wife gets a call from her cousin who is concerned that the kindergarten nun sent home a note criticizing her son for not responding frequently in class. On questioning her cousin, my wife was able to learn that the kindergarten held *96 students*, with one nun lecturing and another patrolling with a yardstick to keep order, in Ridley Township! You see you never know how well off you are as my kindergarten held almost 50% fewer students. We shall return to this topic later, as the problem has reappeared several times during my career, including the current fad of Charter Schools in New Jersey, in many cases, being less than desirable venues for children, according to what I have seen.

High School was more of the same but the priests were from several different orders and seemed almost cosmopolitan really, in comparison to the diocesan priests and nuns I had experienced. In high school the average class size ranged from 48 to 56 but, they had an honors section, which was limited to 30, which almost seemed to be a fair return for the tuition being charged. This tuition was the primary reason I had to maintain my employment for the tile setter and the movie house. The biggest problem I saw in high school is that the faculty, both priest and lay teachers, knew very little beyond what was in the next chapter of the textbooks, except for Latin, of course, which some could speak but could not teach very well because pedagogy was obviously a waste of time. We did not have in-service days for faculty training; we had retreats for prayer and pushed forward as quickly as possible in order to close school by the beginning of June. They also had no sense of humor as I learned one day after almost being slapped when I jokingly asked when the school was going to start offering vocational classes. The angry priest stated that Bishop Neumann high school had no time for the lazy young men who would enroll in such courses. Here I grew up thinking that plumbers were first among the chosen.

There was the frigid walk to school at zero dark thirty to be an altar boy. There was the constant raffle mentality that kept us going door to door begging for funds for the school, and heaven forbid if you missed quota, and the regimentation, but, I still have few regrets because the time spent was not the sentence to which I had been condemned in grade school, it was an opportunity, although limited, to get to college, an obstacle to overcome. It also gave me life-long friends such as Ronald Ianoale, who continues to this day as an important part of my life. It was also in high school that I came to admire a few classmates who stood their ground when the absurdity became overwhelming. I recall one in particular, Adrian DiLuzio, a great student, a fine athlete, and someone with the capacity for leadership. Anyone not a member of the football team or the band [they were already there] was expected to attend the Sunday football games, and help with refreshment and raffle sales. Adrian was an extraordinary soccer player, who had qualified for an adult team, which played on Sundays. Since he was not able to be present he was "assessed" the value of what he should have been contributing. Adrian stood his ground and I hope he is alive and well today. You see, the curse of my class was that so many were lost to the Vietnam war, a few to gang battles, some more to jail and so on.

This was a sad ending to a basically non-descript experience. There was little social life, the few dances were strictly regimented with the sexes encouraged to stay apart. Work filled my off-hours and aside from the near riots that broke out from time to time, there was little to look forward to. An exception was all of the "combined" classes we had scheduled. To save money on staff, we took some subjects twice a week in our small groups, with "independent study" two other days [read "study hall"], and then a lot of classes were brought together for the "dissertation" section, sometimes close to a hundred students gathered in one lecture hall, or worse, yet, in one section of the auditorium with another teacher yelling at another such large section in still another section of the adutorium. The lay teachers were most often stuck with these horrible groups and Fridays often featured somebody getting punched out, often one of the teachers who had lost his cool. There was the scenario in which one of the priests got sick and we had no one there for most of the year. Since we were an honors group we were expected to muck along by ourselves. This is how I learned algebra, to the extent that I learned any algebra. Or, the time when a priest beat the heck out of a lay teacher who was caught talking during a retreat. I can see the vision of the young man being dragged away exclaiming "I am a teacher!" There was also the priest who told us "Better you should visit a whore-house than get married for sex". It seemed like great advice but he was replaced after a fashion. Athletes and honors students did not take gym so I was spared that no-man's land, but, the cafeteria was always a mob scene, sometimes violent, and nothing can compare with 3500 students changing classes simultaneously in a small building. On the day that President John F. Kennedy was assassinated, there had been a stairwell riot and several of us were pushed down the steps. No nurses were employed so the athletic trainer, who was a biology teacher, examined those of us who had tumbled down the stairs and already exhibited swelling joints and determined whether we had to get to the ER of the local hospital, which we resisted because it was a charge our parents would have to bear. That is how it came to pass that several of us were sent out for treatment, which involved contacting our parents, and heard the news about the tragic events in

Dallas. Now having a Catholic President had been a real big deal, so much so that there were weekly reminders during the 1960 campaign to get Kennedy elected, because it was "God's Will". It was taken as an act of heresy when we returned to announce that the attack in Dallas had occurred and that Mr. Kennedy was dead. The place went into mourning for the rest of the year. I never understood what they expected from this Catholic President? Did they believe the Congress would permit untoward religious influences benefiting one sect to occur? To show you the extent to which they tried to maintain a halo effect over the man, when I was a senior I wrote a paper in which I related that it was Oliver Wendell Holmes, Jr. a brevet major of volunteers for the Grand Army of the Republic, who, in watching the victory parade over May 23rd and 24th, 1865, said something to the effect that he was so struck by the significance of the events that he realized that it was up to each citizen to determine what he might do for his country not what his country might do him. Sound familiar? Well, not even the presentation of the source material from Shelby Foote was enough to convince the instructor that I was not, indeed, besmirching the reputation of this great man, the Catholic President. I wonder how the teacher reacted when he learned of Marilyn Monroe and the others. This school is now closed, a victim of high tuition and low enrollment. Perhaps people just wised up and realized their money could be better spent on their children.

FIRST TO COLLEGE

Well, it was off to college, Temple University, which became my home away from home for the next eight years. No, it did not take me eight years to get the A.B. degree, it took me that long to earn three of my four degrees. The campus became the major focus of my professional life for the next three plus decades. It was my second home because we could not afford room and board and the football scholarship was just tuition, not even books, which my friends at Strawbridge's took care of. Like so many of my freshmen [fresh-persons?] colleagues reporting for the half-hour orientation, which was really a threat to succeed or else, the focus of my entire family was on my career as an undergraduate student. It was not as if I had to succeed in order to support the extended family, it was just that it was a measure of pride to everyone; aunts, uncles, grandparent [my maternal grandmother lived to 106], and cousins, in the family group that was clustered within a few blocks in South Philadelphia. No one could contribute any money but there was lots of encouragement. Temple University remains a special place for me and each year at graduation there are still a number of families that gather to witness the graduation of their first member, always a sign of hope for a better future, no matter how long the road.

The real deficit to my high school experience was, despite the diploma, which was my entry to the promised land, Temple University, they did not teach us very much of a contemporary nature. We were prepared to compete as if people from our neighborhood were limited by a caste system. As an example, the high school honors biology and physics classes were based totally on memorization, with exams being 400 multiple choice questions to be completed in a 40 minute period, with the grade of "A" being set at 94/100. However, getting that "A", was worth very little when you had never heard of DNA. I often wondered if this was one of the reasons why they made it so hard to get a completed application for anything but a Catholic college. I had the brainstorm of applying directly to Temple and had the university demand my transcript from the reluctant secondary school administration. In most places this chore would have been handled by a guidance department but there was no such thing for us. My wife had to ask her father to appeal directly to the Archbishop in order for her records to be released for her to be accepted at Penn and Temple. It was fortunate he had fixed a lot of teeth for them. In any event, I dreamed of Central High and instead went to a factory. The public schools had their problems but West Philadelphia High School had a national reputation for quality for its science programs and places like Central and Girls' High were just superb. A few years hence great leaders such as Mark Shedd and Matt Constanza were to come along and begin building something special, a trend Paul Vallas is attempting to replicate today. Matt served as Mark's deputy and followed him as Superintendent of Schools and later moved to another challenging assignment as Superintendent of Schools in Haddonfield New Jersey. He is still a friend and the kind of person I wish we could install in school systems across the country.

It was thus armed that I approached my college life. In those days there were day and evening students and those were usually separated by full and part-time status. So it was all early classes, football practice, some nights at work and then home on the subway system to study. That worked pretty well and the first semester seemed to sail by, except for the day we were sent to West Virginia to play their freshmen and spent the entire day upside down. The speed, size, athleticism and meanness of those truly gifted athletes outclassed us all and I recalled the words of Bill Cosby, who had left school a short time before, and was appearing as a comedian at area bars, where most of his material focused on his football experiences. "First and 37, it was always first and 37 yards to go. The other team would kick off and it would be first and 37." And so it was, in fact it got so bad I was tempted to turn around and block for the other team, figuring it would be a lot safer.

OPPORTUNITY KNOCKS

The end of the first semester brought me an opportunity that would change my life. Another player told me there was one job available as part-time help in the Admissions Office, for student-athletes, yes, we could earn side money in those days, and I waited in a huge line to apply and was picked! The office was run like a taught ship by Nancy Quadenfeld, the Big "N" as we called her, and she had a number of young female clerks who answered the phones and a couple of student athletes to run errands. Now Nancy was the sister of our head athletic trainer Ted Quadenfeld, who would go on to a terrific career in sports medicine. I always thought his influence helped open the door for me, especially as I owed him for helping me overcome the results of a separated shoulder suffered in high school, which was left untreated as the high school could not waste resources on such minor matters. I still have almost no range of motion with that arm.

I learned something from this job early on that it was fairly easy in a rank and file job to perform well by just avoiding the pitfalls to which most others succumbed. I arrived on time, was polite, always helpful, stayed without asking for extra pay, and always resisted the flirtatious aspect of so many young men and women working side by side. Nancy was a great hire for Temple, she was smart, dedicated, and completely intolerant of anyone who did not bring their "A" Game to the job everyday. I remember one day when she caught the student-athlete portion of her staff taking time for a recreational swim. The pool was located in the basement of the admin building, and she waited patiently while they held their breath underwater and finally used a rescue hook to drag the ring leader to the surface. I was hysterical with laughter, as I was there taking a class, and quickly learned that mirth at the wrong times was not very well received by most people. This was also the day when a PE teacher we absolutely detested decided to pick me for mouth to mouth resuscitation instruction. After that experience with her I almost lost my interest in getting certified as a life guard. Wilma was her name and I used to laugh every time I saw the Flintstones!

I learned another important lesson on this job, how jealously causes some people to protect their turf when they even suppose someone was a threat. Let's call him "Marc" and he was a self-appointed foreperson for the student workers in admissions. He was not paid more than the rest of us, but, by ingratiating himself with the leadership, he was able to do less because he began giving out assignments. I actually did not see all that much of him because he tended to hang out with the big name athletes, who had somewhat "invisible jobs" and they all liked to drink beer. I did start getting some feedback from the clerical staff that "Marc" did not appreciate the attention I was getting from the administration. Eventually he was to learn a couple of lessons himself. My sunny Neapolitan half often concealed my other half, which was a Sicilian heritage. Also, if you are going to try and stab somebody in the back by bad mouthing him to your superiors, you had better make sure your superiors are in the same league as those of your target.

In any event, this opportunity brought me numerous benefits, I had a job between classes and whatever hours I wished to work on the weekend, now two paychecks as I was still at Strawbridge's, and $65.00 a week total to help at home. I often think I had more discretionary income in those days. The biggest break of all was going to work for John Rhodes, the Vice President for Administration, and his two very special assistants, Dorothy Seagers and Marie Cooney. The Registrar, Libby Landis was another one of the incredible ladies who made the university work so well. Overworked, underpaid, but certainly very much appreciated, she ran a terrific shop and required little supervision and very little outside assistance. The director of admissions, who seemed like a nice old chap but not terribly enthusiastic, also worked for Mr. Rhodes. With semester registration coming up, someone was needed to honcho all of the temps that managed the traffic going through the registration process. I got the nod and the great learning experience of my life was now underway.

In those days, registering for classes was a true test of a person's ability to withstand pain. Imagine tens of thousands of people lined up the night before, for blocks outside our Mitten Hall. You needed a card from the deck for each class in order to register and those who were near the beginning of the line got theirs and those who were not, did not, it was that simple. Miss Seagers ran the show on the floor while Miss Cooney kept the office going. At one time recently, there were over 165 so-called professional staff members in the "presidency" at Temple University. In my time, Millard Gladfelter was the President and his "presidency" consisted of a secretary. That was it. The Treasurer and VP for Finance was a truly amazing gentleman named Sterling Atkinson, who not only served as chief finance officer and the corporate secretary, but taught several advanced accounting classes as well. The VP for Academic Affairs was Dr. Paul Anderson, who went on to become a famous President as Dr. Gladfelter's successor, and, who also taught an occasional class. The only other administrator was John Rhodes, and he ran everything else: facilities, insurance, benefits, payroll, HR, food service, dorms, cleaning, maintenance, registration, records, you name it, it was here and for me it was the greatest lesson possible in operations management. John Rhodes was not only supremely proficient at what he did, he loved the task and the environment so much he gave of himself voluntarily and he became the finest, perhaps the best of the few true teachers, whom I have encountered.

Dorothy had briefed me on the task at hand in advance and I met my crew the day registration began. By noon, two of them were gone, goldbricks supreme who quickly came to the attention of the ever watchful Miss Seagers. Dot explained the best part of the job to me early on, getting to register BEFORE anybody else arrived, because we had to be available to work the entire day, every day for a week. When I showed her my proposed roster, she picked this teacher and that, and I learned not all pigs are created equal. The job did not pay much for the crew, but those who stayed sensed that it was a great opportunity, to score well with classes, to meet a lot of coeds as they were called then and get noticed for one of the rare job openings. Registration was indeed an ordeal, but we more than survived, we never had to line up a day or so early, sleep on the sidewalk, or freeze when the winter semester rolled around. We were still poor, from not very fancy backgrounds, but we were now on the inside, we had the power. This was another great lesson, that power was held when someone could influence others and it did not necessarily flow automatically when someone came from money. It was mostly the rich kids freezing their derriere on the sidewalk.

Here I was, right on the inside and those staff who ended that day with me stayed together the entire four years and several moved into regular student jobs during that time and one might get the grand prize, and she or he could end up replacing me during my last semester as an undergraduate. The key to this was the motivational ability of Miss Seagers. She seemed to touch everyone she met and people warmed to her immediately and probably would have gladly worked for her even without all of the fringe benefits. Marie Cooney was the same way and between the two of them, they really ran things during the period of the greatest growth and maturation of the university. They are long gone, unfortunately, but still remembered. After their passing the Board of Trustees paid them an incredible honor, a building was named for each. Imagine having university facilities named for women who began their careers as secretaries and were never paid anything near their value. Their work ethic, commitment to excellence and dedication to their organization were without peer and I still miss their influence and presence. There was one other benefit of taking this job, I met my future wife, albeit from a distance and very briefly. One of the crew told me he had caught a terrific looking blonde trying to maneuver her way into the great hall. I told him to escort her to the end of the line but to see if he could get her number. He never got close to the phone number and I have been trying to live this down ever since, but we are getting ahead of the story.

FIRST BIG BREAK

After my first registration experience, Dorothy told me that John Rhodes had decided to take on a student assistant and he wanted me. This was a true blessing as I could now afford to leave Strawbridge and Clothier, spend all of my time at the university, and learn from the masters, Misses Seagers and Cooney and Mr. Rhodes. Years later the Navy would credit me, with achievement and meritorious service medals, for "advances" to their processes in logistics and it was really the material of John Rhodes, and his philosophies, that I was espousing.

It took some time to get things sorted out because the Big N was still expecting a fair share of my time and Dot started giving me more and more hours. There were all kinds of lessons to be learned and many were handled directly by Mr. Rhodes. I shall never forget his very succinct protocol for using me to carry messages to some of the "heavies" around the university. This is a lesson that many liaison staff fail to learn with quite negative consequences for their organizations. Basically, a great deal of tact and patience was needed, finding a slim balance between empathizing with the position the target might be in as a consequence of the message received and making sure there was no question about your loyalties. Mr. Rhodes emphasized that having someone who was effective in this role eliminated direct reliance on written communication and enabled the follow-up note of "mutual understanding" to be much softer, a true collegial relationship. I must have been Ok at the task because it became a lot of what I had to do, and, it got me on the inside of all of the operations. Soon department chairs were asking me about their staff; secretaries were asking for the inside scoop; and even the food service people had me sampling menus, in the hopes that I would recommend their suggestions to Mr. "R", as he was known. Even though my faculty association with the university ended in 1996, I still receive the occasional phone call from someone there, asking how "things used to work" during these days.

This job also provided the entertainment portion of my college days. My wife, who was the daughter of a Society Hill dentist, and did not work during those years, often recalls the day Charlton Heston came to town, or the performance of Sammy Davis Jr., or other epic events. Since

I worked all of the time, I missed those but had some great moments of my own. For example, I frequently got chased out of Barton Hall, where in the basement some scientists from Asia were working on projects that no one was allowed to see. Invariably, Mr. R would have a message for them but they rigorously enforced their no trespass rule and refused to speak English, I even tried Italian once to get through. The rumor was they were breeding attack pigs for the military but I can neither confirm nor deny. I finally got their attention when they had some problems with the heat and cooling and their food service orders ran amuck, my first lessons in how networking could pay off!

Another favorite story involved the sacred sword. You see our founder, Russell Conwell, who was a really neat person who dedicated his latter years to building college programs for the poor, was an officer of dubious fame during the Civil War. During the horrible battle of Shiloh Church, called Pittsburg Landing in the North, it seems that Mr. Conwell got caught up in the spirit of the initial retreat and abandoned his sword, a huge implement of war, especially in comparison to the Navy ceremonial sword I was to be awarded many years later. His servant, young Johnny Ring, could not bear the thought of the sword being lost and dashed back across a bridge, retrieved the sword, but was mortally wounded [you did not really expect a different outcome did you?]. Young Mr. Ring was celebrated in Temple lore for all time, with a statue dedicated to him in his "grotto", actually grass hiding a retaining wall that kept a small hill from collapsing on the dining level of the Faculty Club. The sword itself was preserved as the most sacred of relics, in a specially made redwood case in a position of honor in the Office of the President. We had a fine baseball team in those days and there was a great player by the name of Mick, who would later have a brief career in the farm system of the Cincinnati Reds. He could not run worth a darn but could hit line drives consistently. He had a campus job that was a bit less glamorous than mine, he was on the ground crew and picked up paper with a stick and a nail exposed at one end. Mickey also liked his beer, which helped explain why he was so slow afoot, and probably led him on this greatest of adventures. One day I was sent to Dr. Gladfelter to have some invoices signed and neither the President nor his secretary was present. The door was unlocked, which was unusual, until I saw Old Mickey come swarming out, brandishing

THE sword. I checked the office, found the stick and nail in place of the sword in the shrine and then looked out the window and saw Mickey using the relic to pick up papers. Chasing after him and getting the sword back resembled a reverse jail break and the building custodian was henceforth to tell me that the sword just did not look right to him any more. Mickey and I never were friends, we were just too dissimilar but he was part of the group and the lesson here was sticking together even at some risk, which he appreciated greatly. I used this experience many times in working with my senior enlisted as a Naval Officer.

My best recollection of a good time, at least to this point in my undergrad work career, occurred at the annual ceremony commemorating Dr. and Mrs. Conwell, who were both buried in a small alcove in a nook of a building right at Broad Street and Montgomery Avenue. Far above street level, on the sixth floor of this building, was a large classroom now being used as a storage and assembly area for catalogue mailings. People would call the Office of Admissions, one of the clerks would answer the phone, and after a few moments place a code right above the return address on the envelope, hopefully effecting an appropriate match between request and catalogue. They were very proud of this system and also proud of the efficiency inherent in using one size envelope for every catalogue. The envelopes were compiled hourly and carried to the sixth floor assembly area. In the summer there were no classes during the day in this facility and it got to be quite raucous. I had spent some time on this crew, stuffing envelopes, until we got the bright idea of turning the large area into our own private basketball court. We used two trash cans with bottoms out for goals and chalk to mark the lanes, on a very nice scale. We then moved into a small anteroom that had been originally an office for a teacher and set up the catalogue assembly in that area. The finishing touch was inviting the several other departmental student athlete crews to participate. You see they got to play for a while by stuffing catalogues for us. We got the court the remainder of the day and had our work done, which is why the guys had time to go swimming during their shift! This turned into a real Tom Sawyer operation and we had a tough time scheduling all of the teams that were interested. The games got very intense as there were some really fine athletes involved, and noisy. Just before I left to join Mr. R. the lift operator in the building got tired of the noise and threatened to expose the entire operation and some enterprising participants spent the better part of a day plotting to sabotage his elevator by cutting the cables, unsuccessfully, thank goodness.

On the day in question, the entire administration, some of the trustees and the usual crowd of ROTC candidates and the band were all jammed together on the sidewalk, I standing a discreet distance away in proper aide mode, when a basketball burst through the window six floors above and, along with shards of glass, began bouncing on the graves far below. That ended the gym experience but how could a Charlton Heston show top that?

LEARNING HOW TO SCORE

There is a line in the movie "Goodfellas", one of my favorites, when the Henry Hill character, speaking in his youth, describes his initial experience with "wise guys" as learning how to score every day. In a similar fashion, I was learning incredible lessons every day. Mr. R. had me running errands in every facet of operations mgmt for the university, which was growing at a record setting pace, but he always took the time to explain everything to me. He even explained that the administration was able to manage the expansion so well because they solicited inputs from a large constituency but kept decision making close to the vest. They also used their reputation for excellence to dominate some very strong personalities on the board of trustees, because they were well prepared, their analyses were comprehensive yet understandable, and usually beyond argument. This was excellent advice, especially as I got to see it in action everyday and the philosophies of Mr. Rhodes were to serve me very well in my future career. For example, this was the exact strategy I always employed in dealing with my boards of education over the years.

I participated in the development and formation of the university budget, almost a year long initiative, involving a number of very difficult personalities, including: the faculty, who never could agree with anything, except the need for more research grants and less student contact time;

the administration, who at that time at least, worked tirelessly in support of the teaching process; the administrative support personnel, who were constantly being pushed to accomplish more in the service arena with fewer and fewer resources; the students, who were basically given little credit; and, the trustees, who all seemed to follow a political agenda determined by their masters, i.e., those responsible for their appointment. We compiled a mountain of data, involving mostly wish lists from the various constituent groups, looked at what was needed to keep the doors open, the bills paid, and to stay ahead of the debt service, as we were building facilities at a prodigious rate. In the final analysis, we maintained the status quo with a few improvements tied to the goals of the Big Four: Gladfelter, Anderson, Atkinson and Rhodes. I also had staff roles in the day to day admin tasks of the entire place: the ordering of food, the scheduling of staff, the ordering of material and supplies, the main roster of classes, the recruitment of students, their admission, the processing of their records, and some really huge evolutions such as the semester graduation ceremonies. The latter were incredible, with two per year, each quite distinct because of size and thus location. We did the January affair on campus, in what was called the Baptist Temple, a huge church like building located at Broad and Berks Sts, right across from an old cemetery that became the private parking for the head honchos. This was a special spot for me as it held the Chapel of the Four Chaplains, four Navy officers in WWII who offered their life jackets to younger, wounded, enlisted sailors, in an effort to provide these young men with a chance at a life. In saving these lives, they had offered their own and the chapel itself, to me, was a wonderful reminder of their sacrifice, their sense of duty and obligation, and a place where all faiths came together, something that would play a strong role in my beliefs forever.

It was the spring ceremony, set in Convention Hall, which held my eternal interest. It was just magnificent, from the flowers, to the speakers, to the joy of the graduates. I noticed my first time there that you got closer to the stage as you got more advanced degrees and I really wanted to be up front with those doctoral candidates. It was also terrific to watch Dorothy and Marie at work here. They were always enthusiastic, so great was there admiration for all things Temple, but they really sparkled at graduation for it was the fulfillment of their professional lives. I have never since seen anything like that sort of enthusiasm. While I have attended numerous graduation ceremonies and have seen many faculty and administrators offer congratulations, I have not seen anyone like Dorothy and Marie who had invested so much of themselves into assuring the success of others. It was contagious; especially when Dorothy would take me aside, each time, and stress the importance of being there, but as a graduate! These two women were among the finest human beings I have ever met, and, while it has been decades since they played such a major role in my life, I still miss them. Temple University gave me everything I have, and Miss Seagers and Miss Cooney [they would not tolerate Ms.], permitted me to profit by the experience.

ON MY WAY

The BIG FOUR were complete gentlemen and were truly remarkable: incredibly selfless, hard working, determined to serve, and absolutely patrician in their upbringing and orientation. They spoke formally, lived on the main line, vacationed in Cape May, attended Episcopalian churches, and, had an incredibly strong commitment to excellence. This was truly the first time I had encountered people who placed others above themselves and in this case, the others were the thousands of students they felt had been entrusted to their care. I had always been led to believe that college would be a very impersonal experience, and I guess it was for most people and my four heroes were unable, despite their best efforts, to cause the vast majority of employees to share their service orientation. Also, and this was a salient point for me at the time and became a guiding principle my entire career, they regarded the positions they held to be a privilege. Once people in authority adopt this position, the rest becomes easy, that is, they devote themselves entirely to the benefit of others, which should be the essence of service, when one works on the public dole.

I would be remiss if I did not add, from a purely personal perspective, how deeply I was influenced by these people. Aside from my parents, I was close only to my uncle, Paul. A war hero, he was a very proud man who missed several chances to marry and have his own children because he was the primary bread-winner for his mother and sisters.

He had returned from service in the China Burma India Theater, to rise to the position of senior production foreman for a factory, the same place that would eventually employ two of my uncles and my father, but not me, they always promised themselves. From an early age, Paul Picogna had worked entirely with a focus on serving his family. Even as a senior enlisted man in the army, he had applied for a commission, which would have been his had not his company commander, a captain from Georgia, decided that "eyetalians" were really the enemy and thus could not possibly become officers for the US Army. Later my uncle was to be highly decorated for his role in stopping the Japanese advance at the crucial battle of Imphal. I have the letter accompanying the medals in which the theater commander, Lord Louis Mountbatten, Royal Navy, accedes to my uncle's request that his red neck captain be required to present the decorations.

Like me, he worked from a very early age, at first in the family business in Italy and later in the mines of West Virginia. The family business was providing blasting services, usually via dynamite, for the construction industry, particularly roads in the years after the Tripolitanian war with the Ottoman Empire but prior to WWI. The family got caught up in one of the great labor movements in this country and was part of what Uncle Paul used to refer to as second generation Molly Maguires, after the Irish-American mine workers who had protested brutal working and living conditions in the Pennsylvania coal fields a half century or more earlier. The mining combines in West Virginia came to be faced with a similar revolt from the indigenous work force; people kept in abject poverty, paid in script, redeemable only at a company store, which charged usurious prices, living in company owned ramshackle housing and subject to hideous diseases, most notoriously, black lung. When this work force rebelled, the solution seemed to be to replace them via the importation of immigrant European workers, who were treated almost like the indentured servants of the revolutionary era. Because of the special skills of the members of my father's family, they were actively recruited, had their passage paid, and, while they were subject to the dangers inherent in mining, they were the blasting supervisors, and thus lived a much better life, including superior housing. Eventually even the Italian immigrants wised up and balked at this treatment and their reward was to be replaced, in turn, by Afro-Americans brought primarily from Alabama. From a labor perspective it is fairly easy to see the master plan that was being employed by ownership, which was fairly certain that native West Virginians, "Dago" immigrants and Deep South Afro Americans would be at each other's throat rather than a threat to management. They underestimated the ability and commitment of someone named John L. Lewis, who brought these diverse groups together to form the United Mine Workers of America, the only major union with the power to strike during the Second World War. My uncle never tired of telling me stories of this great labor struggle and the perilous early decades. The town where this little drama unfolded was known as Keystone, West Virginia; and, in 1976, a young, now "Dr." Joseph Picogna, was a keystone speaker at the annual Council of Chief State School Officers meeting held at a new resort located in Pipestem, West Virginia. When I learned that Keystone and its cross border twin misery town of Bluefield, Kentucky were proximate, I prevailed on the conference organizers to get me there. Soon I walked the grimy streets where my grandfather and uncles had labored and my father had played, visited the house in which my dad was born, saw the initials "PP" where my long dead uncle had told me he had carved them, and then re-entered the limo for the ride back. I hope he was somehow able to sense that his only nephew, the one he said he counted on to lift the family to the next level, had traveled in style to pay homage to the home of his forbearers.

My uncle was so kind to me that I was always determined to please him. With my father always working two jobs, it was my uncle who took me to museums, taught me the historical significance of our urban landscape, and never missed a graduation or an awards ceremony. It was he who provided a subsidy to my earnings to enable me to get a car before my senior year of college and I can still remember seeing his quiet pride at graduation. He told me he had done his best and was passing the torch to me. We lost him just before our wedding but he had come to know my future wife, of whom he approved greatly.

I have related this story, to demonstrate the kind of feelings I had for Dorothy Seagers and John Rhodes. They were so much more than employers; they were counselors, cheerleaders, helped me set goals, shaped my life vision and were always there. It was like a family at work, this small group for whom the university was a labor of love. I think even my mother was a bit jealous to see Dorothy fussing over me at graduation.

ON THE JOB TRAINING

As our communications, computer networks improved and the length of my service increased, I was given assignments of much more substance. Now instead of carrying messages, I was sent to negotiate a compromise, to audit the implementation of a new policy, to verify the need for a substantial policy, to explain the decision of the university administration. There were days when I had to come dressed with a suit as I was attending a VIP function or standing by to research an unexpected question at a meeting of the trustees. In fact, Mr. R. must have gotten tired seeing me in those few jackets because I got another raise as my responsibilities increased and soon a real prize, an extra job. Now in addition to working all day between classes, I became responsible for the university switch-board, serving from 5 PM to 11 PM, every weeknight and Saturday afternoons after my morning shift for Mr. R. I could say farewell to Strawbridge's, and with Temple becoming a state university during my sophomore year, the tuition dropped to $150 a semester, so it was adieu to football. This became my routine for two years and it was a grand experience in every respect. One interesting sidelight about the switchboard job: the chief operator was named Angie and for the life of me I cannot remember the last name of this fine woman. During the day the place was a madhouse but quite manageable at night, in fact, once I learned to disable the incoming call buzzer and came to depend on the blinking lights instead, I had myself a paid study hall, and, I could call the reference section of the library if I needed something related to class assignments! Angie told me that Dorothy had assured her I was trustworthy, dependable and needed the money, talk about pressure... She also told me that over the years several of my predecessors had come to grief for two major offenses. They had used the big board as a conduit for calls made all over the planet for their friends, who had only to make a local call to connect first to the campus switchboard; and, they allowed a constant stream of visitors to crawl on the catwalk behind the switchboard to spy on the girls' dorm, where the blinds were often raised. Sure enough after only a week on the job I began getting "cross connection" phone requests from friends and visits from frat brothers interested in the young ladies. There was just no possibility of ever disappointing Dorothy Seagers.

Talk abut OJT: I worked with the contractors to develop construction schedules to meet Mr. Rhodes' requirements. He taught me the rudiments of privatization and sent me to observe the critical elements of work associated with our gigantic food service operation, in preparation for subcontracting the work. I represented Mr. Rhodes on a committee working to upgrade our security force from rent a cops to employees, who would eventually bring a much higher level of professionalism to the position, including attending the Pennsylvania State Police Academy. Their performance over the years is one of the key reasons that the campus is seen as such an attractive venue today.

I got to work on schedules, from food service to shift workers and wrote draft policies from codes of conduct to parking rules, which was always a big deal with parking at such a premium. Even I, later on when I was able to afford an inexpensive vehicle and started driving to and from work, as I was leaving around 11:00 PM, was assigned a parking space in area number 2, as close to parking lot heaven as a peon could get. This was really being "on the inside". I recall being almost embarrassed to be seen pulling into that lot, with thousands of students and faculty walking by, as, I assumed I would be somehow damned for smacking of privilege. To this day I still have an aversion to privilege and have never permitted myself to be assigned a reserved parking space.

I also had the honor of working at several faculty receptions and the annual faculty ball, as a member of the organizing committee, and then as an aide to Mr. Rhodes during the festivities. The annual ball was a big deal, held in February, and it seemed the entire campus was transformed. There was a parking service, caterers galore, and lots of champagne. I can remember years later the thrill of attending my first ball as a faculty member and showing my wife the portrait of the late Mr. Rhodes, which hung in a place of honor. A very bittersweet experience, indeed. By the way, since I retired from teaching at the university, they still ask me for money but no longer invite us to the Ball.

There was a rough patch, although it did not last very long. Mr. Rhodes briefly had an assistant; I never knew who established the position. He was a tall, distinguished looking man, and former member of the faculty, whose self-professed ambition was to be a dean of a business school somewhere, an ambition that I believe was eventually fulfilled, and with some distinction. When he came to us I recall that he had not reached the rank of professor so serving as an assistant to Mr. R. must have been seen as a substitute qualifier for his intended big jump. I sensed that this man was immediately in a tight spot, for he was neither cordial to the ladies, Miss Seagers and Miss Cooney, nor civil to me, which was not what I had come to expect in this office but which kind of fit with what I had experienced in life earlier. He used to have me follow him around, taking notes. I remember when we visited his former classroom, and he told me he had taught classes in what was a space being converted to still another computer room. It was obvious that he was speaking not of a fond recollection but of something he had outgrown or overcome. As I was writing this, I recalled a day many years later when I had taken my daughter, Maria Walsh, my son, Michael Picogna, and some of their friends to a NCAA Lacrosse Championship series game at Temple and, after lunch, showed her the giant lecture hall where I had taught most of the few undergraduate courses of my career. My daughter saw the thrill I felt in standing there, indeed, that room and the bridge of the USS Oliver Hazard Perry, where I earned my ship driver's credentials for the Navy, are two of the fondest memories of my life. I recall that things really started downhill when he started giving orders to Dorothy and Marie. I must admit I felt some perverse pleasure in one day informing him that Marie Cooney's sister, Eileen, was the senior assistant to the dean of the business school, where he ultimately hoped to land. Talk about a guy about to pass a terra cotta pipe!

I recall that we had begun a huge project, collecting preliminary data related to the update of the university master plan, the goal of which was to connect the main and allied health science campuses by buying all of the property on Broad Street in Philadelphia, for a distance of some twelve blocks, a very ambitious undertaking indeed. Our new colleague was given the task of having a great deal of data crunched and guess who got to spend hours clunking away at a Freiden calculator, checking numbers that had been generated by computer analysis. Now the Freiden was already an antique, although I would find the accountants in the New Jersey Department of Education still using the devices some years later, due to the reputation for reliability of the machine. There they still had clerks who used the same machines as at the university, with the purpose of checking expense vouchers and the like. It was a real paper and pencil operation; I recall they wore little cuffs over the sleeves of their white shirts to keep the lead from the pencils from darkening the material and, shades, which reduced the glare from the lamps as they starred straight down at their work all day long. Made me swear never to pursue accounting!

I was told to do all of the work and so I sat and entered data. The machine had twelve rows and twelve columns for data entry and you cranked the handle and pushed the CALC button and the springs unleashed a torrent of energy to reveal the answer in a small box on top of the unit. It took me forever and I remember skinning my fingers above the nails as they slipped between the keys, so furiously was I required to be computing. Now it was a real gunslinger mentality that led some of the faculty to prize their speed in using this old piece of junk calculator. My superior was fast, as he used to demonstrate when he would berate me for being slow, as he checked my work, which in itself was a recheck of the computer, which was a recheck of the various departmental inputs. The problem was he was also careless, probably because he was yelling at me, only this time Miss Seagers was standing in the doorway, and saw his behavior, although he never apologized. I never saw him after that day but the project work certainly got a great deal easier. Perhaps it was just his time to move. I cannot imagine a college student getting a better lesson as a work example. We did not have internships then but these experiences certainly qualified as the finest example of them I have ever seen.

When I think of Mr. Rhodes, the rest of the admin hierarchy, and Dot and the Cooney sisters, I am still amazed at how well they treated people, probably because they had been born to much higher social rank while I was just the offspring of immigrants, and, before I met these folks, I had always been treated as if I were redundant. I am afraid that there are still a lot of college students who feel that way and just think of the kind of whirlwind existence the younger students experience. If we had more effective leadership, especially at the K-12 level, the students would be treated as precious commodities, for after all, the best lesson I learned from John Rhodes was that the students were the reason the entire establishment existed. As we shall see, that notion was difficult to come by in the public school establishment in New Jersey and seems to have disappeared completely when a Governor named Christine Todd Whitman came to power. More on this in a few chapters.

ACADEMICS AND SOCIABILITY

Of course there were classes, one hundred and thirty-eight credit hours of them, many more than required for the degree, as Mr. Rhodes was more concerned with my getting an education, not just fulfilling graduation requirements. I do not think the experiences were much different from what any undergraduate student must endure. The science and math classes were a disaster, as none of the graduate assistants spoke English. There are few things as unnerving as being in chem lab being told to "look in the drawer for the lubber tubing" or hearing the command, "see the yarrow frame through the corrault tubing ['yellow flame through cobalt tubing', one of our fellows would translate]. There was the fabulous redhead who taught history, one of my favorites as she loved to sit on the edge of the desk with those great legs. Still cannot believe I got a "B" once from her. Actually history was a bastion for a great many athletes, especially those on the basketball team. This was the age of the great coach, Harry Litwak, and he labored for years in the dumpiest of gyms, known as South Hall. Many of the students would gather there when the team was on the road to hear the closed circuit broadcast of the games and I always had a friend call me at the switchboard and sometimes actually listen in for a while. It was one of the latter times, when they were playing Davidson, whose coach, Lefty Drisell, who created the impression of being a "good ole boy", and whose team had only recently integrated. Davidson had their only Afro-American player on the court, when one of our finest players and a great human being, Clarence Brookings, who was himself Afro-American, fouled the Davison player and we all heard a fan sitting right near the radio broadcaster exclaim, " Hey ref, don't let that 'blankty-blank' foul our 'colored boy'! Racism was all but unknown among us on campus; we were struggling to get by and lived among our neighbors in North Philadelphia. We walked around at night, indeed, I had to walk to a deserted subway station at 11:00 PM, wait for a train, travel a few blocks and repeat the ritual to catch the local to go home. We mixed freely with the neighborhood youths when we went to nearby Blue Horizon to watch the boxing matches on Saturday night, the only night I did not work. We went to the Uptown Theater to attend programs by a popular disc jockey named Georgie Woods, who died in June of 2005 after a long life of activism. Mr. Woods played a lot of MOTOWN, which everybody seemed to love and from time to time he would halt his broadcast, for an hour or more, and bring his listeners up to date as to what was happening in the civil rights movement, especially in southern cities such as Montgomery, Alabama, where Dr. King and Dr. Abernathy were engaged heavily in the cause of freedom. I cannot recall any white student, at least from my circles, who looked at these issues from a racial standpoint. Everybody was welcomed to the fraternity parties and people of all races walked blocks from the local precinct back to campus whenever the police decided to raid a party and scoop everybody up for a ride to the station house. It was a different time.

Places like Philadelphia had been one of the Queen Cities spearheading the civil rights movement. North Philadelphia was the place that organizers had begun targeting votes to help minorities in the South ultimately to enjoy what we all take for granted, the right to vote, attend school, etc. Yet here it was, 1967 and we were listening to this. Anyway, that team was close to us for a variety of reasons and they were to win the NIT. We found out about their propensity for history classes right after they won the championship as several players disappeared immediately, with one said to have accumulated only 28 credits over seven semesters, with most of them in history. I was proud that my non-entity little fraternity dumped our advisor, who was one of the people we felt was responsible for this outrage. In his place we chose one of the neatest people I have ever met, Stanley Herbert Ignatius Turner [he warned us never to use his initials for any purposes whatsoever]. Dr. Turner had a background in sociology and psychology and a huge work resume, including service as a "street" consultant for the municipal police.

He may have used the same tests year after year but we really loved the excitement of his classes. He had fun with the subject matter, he related all the salient points via his personal experience stories and we all had a good time. I especially loved his "Man from the Coast" adventures. These were the stories of a huge man who, wearing only a turban and, brandishing a samurai sword, would swoop out and yell "I am the man from the coast" and then disappear among the alleys of the city. Turner was called in as the consultant because everyone thought the guy was nuts, but, as Stanley pointed out, he was not so crazy as to ever pull this stunt nude in the winter! I was to model my own teaching style after these experiences some years later. We also profited from his practical advice as a fraternity adviser. For example he was the one who suggested we hide in the old coal bin in the basement any time the cops came and come they did. Some of the parties got so rowdy that the madam of a house of ill-repute next door used to call the police to complain about us! All good things sadly end and so did that particular frat house. The block had to be demolished for a new law complex [more lawyers now there is a terrific idea!] and we just happened to schedule the farewell party the day Governor Milton Shapp was dedicating the new college of education building right across this small street, known ironically as Park Avenue. I usually worked between classes everyday and never took off except when I was in extremis with an assignment and had to get in some library time but that day was to be a poignant experience so I asked off for an hour. I did not get to participate in the revelries because the police were there before me. I am not sure whether it was the people on the roof who were alternately shouting at the Governor and pouring beer on those below, or the bottles of beer crashing through windows, or the three Greek letters from the foyer that floated down the steps, or the neighborhood people who started to strip the now condemned buildings for the fittings, but something ticked off the police and campus security and the whole area was cordoned off. I hope everyone remembered the advice about the coal bin. After that there was not only no frat house, there was no fraternity as social probation was deemed an effective remedy. Animal House revisited! I guess we got off lucky as this was Philadelphia, where the police were known for their skills in aerial bombardment, having burned down several blocks during the Wilson Goode administration.

TIME TO GO

Finally senior year arrived and with it, my preparations not only to transition to the next phase of my academic experience and hopefully a related work situation, I thought it was also time to begin prepping someone to replace me. I was the first in the position of student assistant to Mr. Rhodes, and he seemed more concerned with my becoming "burned out" than in grooming someone else. He called me in one day, told me how aides in the military were rotated and said he wanted candidates for the switchboard job and some "runners" for Dot and Marie during the day, all part-time. I must have looked surprised and he said that my job had evolved as my skills and our relationship had matured and he was not going to replace me either in total or with one person. He said he doubted he would find anyone that desperate, and then added, with a grin, or that capable. I doubt that I ever felt so close to anyone again. We then began discussing options and he felt I needed a job that would allow me to get to classes easily, thus no overnight travel or late hours were essential and a living wage would be nice also. Teaching at the secondary level seemed to fit the bill but I was not trained as an educator, actually never have been, but that was not to be an issue. Not to worry as Temple had a program called the Intern Teaching Program for College Graduates that recruited individuals with outstanding liberal arts and science backgrounds, placed them as teachers in the city schools, supervised the heck out of them during the day and allowed them to earn a master of science degree in selected fields, my area of interest, psychometrics, among them. The tuition was quite expensive, with a lot of special fees and extra credits, but I somehow received a grant and used my employee discount, as Mr. R. asked me to give him a few hours each weekend during the academic year. I was set, there was an orientation for a couple of weeks and then my first real vacation at the Wildwoods, where I worked as a substitute life-guard, incidentally with my future brother-in-law, who was a medic with the beach patrol, and had a second chance encounter with my future wife. But first, graduation! It was great, with the whole family present, and my female cousins gave me roses. The university made a big deal out of giving out empty red folders, embossed with the school crest. Your diploma came in the mail after they determined that all grades were in fact submitted and recorded and no fees were owed. You simply picked up the empty red folder as you turned in the cap and gown. I found Dorothy and Marie waiting for me with Dot holding a red binder, which she handed me with a kiss. Of course, inside was my diploma, with a great letter from the two of them. You see, that is how it worked when you were on the inside.

PROVING GROUND

"Youth is not a time of life but a state of mind, a predominance of courage over timidity, of the appetite for adventure over the love of ease"

Samuel Ullman

GETTING READY

I needed a job, but not just any job. It was amazing what opportunities became available via my benefactors at the university. On reflection, pursuing any of these careers, even starting from rock bottom as a newly minted college graduate may have resulted in the same level of success, or I may have just languished as a member of the herd, progressing to some level of middle manager, only to be bounced at the worst possible time later in my life, as such jobs began disappearing by the tens of thousands by the late 1980's. One thing was for sure, all the opportunities sure beat the heck out of assembly line work, however noble a concept that remains.

My thing was to be as heavily invested in academics as possible, with an ultimate goal of a doctorate with a specialty as a research psychologist. I seemed to be capable in the foundation skills necessary to pursue such a career and the question was how to get there. The answer to the riddle had already been formulated, some type of job that would enhance the career perspective while allowing time to cram as much academic work into as short as possible a time span.

Temple University at the time was invested with one of the most comprehensive graduate programs of any major school in the nation, indeed, its programming compared favorably in scope with most of the well known and much more expensive schools. My solution involved two programs. The first was the academic portion and the best alternative was the Master of Science program with a specialty in educational psychology. That offered an even richer spectrum of didactic work in psychology, particularly, group dynamics, organizational development and design, and personality studies, along with a strong program in psychometrics, which was an essential springboard to the next level. The second, and equally essential program, was to provide a teaching job, but a very special one, and Temple again provided the answer via its Intern Teaching Program for College Graduates. This was a highly competitive program available to high achieving liberal arts graduates in the social and physical sciences, who had been accepted to advanced degree programs. The positions involved placement only in selected high schools and required a six week summer practicum, which was very intense, and several hours of interaction with a university teaching associate during the work week. The benefits were many: you were employed in a special category program, that is, by nature of your placement you were identified as "select", which means well supported by the university and supposedly equipped with a quick intellect, and you drew a very competitive salary right out of the box, while having, at least in a comparative sense, more time than most to pursue the MS degree. As it turned out, the studies were so challenging that any time was precious. Best of all, you completed all of this in two years, and if you were compulsive like me, any extra courses you could squeeze in, at the doctoral level, would not only help with admittance for the next degree program but count toward that degree. At the time the master degree required 36 graduate credits and the doctorate, at least sixty-eight more, not counting any of the language classes for the foreign language requirements and special residency work, then the thesis prep and eventually, the dissertation. Makes you wonder what we are missing as consumers with so many of our educational leaders these days shopping for doctorates via mail order programs! Makes me wonder how I managed to have that much energy, even in my youth.

The magic day for announcing acceptances came and there was my name on the list. I had been confident, not many people had the university president and two vice-presidents listed as references and Dorothy was on the phone with the graduate school dean letting her expectations be known. Still, it was a relief. While the rest of the incoming class I was to meet probably had options, and the money to pay for them, it took me all of five minutes to hand-deliver the pre-completed acceptance form to the graduate school. I was all set!

I soon met my classmates at the orientation day, about three weeks later, just enough time for me to get one of those three week, eight hour a day "specials" in for my first three graduate credits. The group was all-white, dressed terrifically, from really impressive schools, and extraordinarily bright. I was not quite so out of place as the first day of my undergrad experience, but this one had graduated in seven semesters, this one had spent junior year in Europe, and that one and the other were magna cum laude. No one else was from Temple University. There was a tradition in those days of 'broadening", e.g., it was highly unusual for someone to attend graduate school at the same institution in which they had received their undergraduate degree, even at a place such as Temple, which offered what seemed like an unlimited number of different degree experiences. There were a few questions and a few more looks when we introduced ourselves and I decided then and there to make my statement academically. Throughout the next two degree experiences, all grades of "A" save for two "B's" were recorded, of which we shall see more later. The grade point average became my bonafides; after all, I could not let down my impressive reference list.

CONTENTED SUMMER

We had a six week practicum experience ahead of us. It was quite busy but I was now making $4800 a year. In retrospect, that $65 dollars a week I was taking down from all of my undergrad jobs did not seem all that bad after all. For six weeks we were to spend mornings in orientation classes, afternoons teaching in various summer schools throughout the region, and four nights of three hours and 48 minutes duration taking classes. The mornings were fun, the afternoons a bit scary, and the evenings, well, everyone has their thing and mine turned out to be becoming all wrapped up in each and every course. The classes were so challenging that there was very little social interaction, a bit surprising since everyone was single and approximately the same age.

My practicum experience was extraordinary as it set very high standards and expectations that stayed with me my entire career. My mentor was a fine gentleman named Norm Hader. He served as the head of the English department at Cherry Hill High School, a relatively new, and quite enormous facility, housing over three thousand five hundred students in grades nine through twelve. I believe that the first graduating classes would number 950 young people! Imagine the tremendous learning opportunities here: there was Mr. Hader himself, a terrific person, well educated and running a prized program; there were the summer school students, more there for enrichment than recidivism, and were they tremendously bright; there was the administration performing logistical miracles in bringing so many pieces together so harmoniously; and, finally, there were superb people cutting their teeth in this fantastic environment, people who would play major roles in shaping my career many years later. People such as John McKeon, Bernie Shapiro and Joan Katz, among others, were already establishing a reputation for excellence in this community that demanded nothing less.

To me, Cherry Hill was a phenomenon. I had been there once as a child but it was not the kind of place that people from my neighborhood would visit, often, if at all. There was this terrific new concept, an enclosed mall, I believe the first large such edifice anywhere outside of Milan, Italy, which was a lot nicer when I saw it thirty years later! There were these stretches of roads along the several large highways that traversed the township, with groupings of stores. They had these terrific communities, which were referred to as "subdivisions", with large single tract houses in beautiful groupings just off the highways, but largely hidden from them. They were all named, had their own little park sections, and even their own little league teams! The houses were magnificent; you almost expected to see Ward and June Cleaver or even Ozzie and Harriett on the expansive lawns. Only one parent worked, no one seemed concerned about money and the moms, almost all wearing skirts and sweaters, presided over beautiful children, who were expected to do well in school and grew up to live their own, white collar, middle class lives or even better. This was a far cry from my neighborhood in which not only was there no separate upstairs room to which children could be banished for a time out, very often there was no upstairs to begin with.

The capstone, indeed the focus of their lives, was the large well appointed elementary school located in most of these communities. The children walked to school and came home for lunch. They then moved to one of three "junior" schools, grades seven and eight, where they gradually experienced a metamorphosis, changing classes and having more content centered classes. Finally, entrance to one of the two magnificent high schools, with modern science labs, large lecture halls with hi-tech outfitting, even little theaters that supported drama programs, and incredible learning opportunities. At one time, the children could pick from over two dozen one semester biology courses and even more chemistry programs. The programming was so sophisticated that the two high schools were on a very short list considered prime recruiting sources for such prestigious universities as Duke, Virginia and Princeton, a fact I was to learn many years later when my own children attended these same schools. The staff, for many decades, was without peer and the taxpayers provided resources worthy of such talent. Take Mr. Hader's English Department for example. To stress the importance of writing, composition work was deemed essential. To provide an environment to achieve this goal, which most towns stopped short of doing, the department staff taught two classes, spending the rest of their work day working with individual students to amplify the skills of each young person. They created "writing labs" years before the concept was categorized as such and decades before computers facilitated the task. Over all these decades, the schools still were the primary attraction for this town.

In Cherry Hill then, public education was the keystone of community existence. The residents enjoyed a school system with a hard won reputation for excellence, which was reiterated year after year. The schools attracted many professionally employed couples, and this caused real estate values to soar, which attracted the businesses that provided an outstanding ratable base. The schools provided community venues for recreation, worship and civic gatherings. Finally, the schools provided a sense of pride for all who shared some sense of belonging, the parents, staff and students, and even the taxpayers without children. It was the beginning of something special for me.

This special yet exhausting experience was to continue for six grueling weeks. The classroom practicum was intriguing and I could see why a career as a teacher in this district was being pursued by so many and thus the process became so competitive. They were expected to be the most brilliant, but, more importantly, when the district selected what they believed to be the very best, they supported them with instructional resources, capable, hard working administrators and a corps of specialists to help with everything from lessons to special needs students.

With most of August available for R and R, I was more than ready for some fun. I did linger a bit in Cherry Hill to attend the summer school graduation ceremony. This event was held annually for students who had missed the June exercises, because of a failed class, illness, some family tragedy etc. The summer school principal had purchased an enormous sheet cake and there were decorations praising the work of the students. What made this special for me was the manner in which the students were treated. It was not a replica of the sometimes overwhelming festivities they had missed and no one pretended it was. The ceremony focused on the spirit of those who overcame some burden to complete their studies and the students were commended for their dedication and hard work. All in all, most impressive! I thought that may have been a unique experience, at least from the perspective of the staff and it turned out I was right. Cherry Hill was and remains a very special place; it was always "home" for me and it just felt right.

I had never been able truly to enjoy our close proximity to the seashore, as family finances did not permit vacations per se and then work occupied me fully. This year as different! I had a chance to visit with friends, take a job as a replacement life guard and live the good life, as seen from the perspective of a 21 year old. I also had time to prepare for my own classes, which would include a full time graduate course load, as well as my pending teaching assignments. As the last one in, I was left with the few choices for my work experience. I had two years in which to complete the master of science degree and it was resolved that I would spend some time in the Philadelphia Public School system before rotating to a suburban district. This arrangement would permit me the greatest exposure to the business I hoped to manage some day, provide me with the job that was so essential to surviving this next rung on the ladder, and keep me from competing with the others, who were certainly capable of more advanced graduate study, although none would enter a doctorate program, but who, for the time being, were to concentrate on a career as a classroom teacher. As it turned out, the career plan was very challenging but doable and if it seemed as though I was in a hurry, I was. Aside from over two and one half decades of university teaching, these two years were the only public school classroom experiences I would encounter, which resulted in my long tenure as a central office administrator.

ON THE JOB

My first stop was at Overbrook High School, a large public school in the Philadelphia system. It was just the sort of place that the Catholic School parents spent a small fortune to spare their children from in the big city, and, those parents could not have been more wrong. Overbrook was very large, and it was "public", which meant that in its neighborhood it was primarily Afro-American. It was already famous as the place where the great Wilt Chamberlain had spent his high school career. Wilt was followed by several other notable players who eventually became professionals and I mention that not only because Wilt was very important to me, his presence there and the championships he had wrought had contributed to a very special school spirit, something I saw reflected in every aspect of the building. The Philly high schools were mostly in old, antiquated buildings. I found them to be anything but decrepit, however old they might be. The very special Joe Clark, was followed by the superb Richardson Dilworth, who had given way to James H. J. Tate, known as "his honor", three very fine mayors, who were unfortunately allocating scarce financial resource to cope with additional students arriving and, unfortunately, quite an array of special needs that dominated financing, even with the advent of federal funding. The result of this was that buildings such as Overbrook really had to fend for themselves as far as keeping the walls up and the ceilings from caving in. One building, Abraham Lincoln, was built with a great deal of wood and yet was to continue in use some twenty years longer.

45

I really enjoyed the experience although I approached the assignment and even the location with some trepidation. The school needed people to teach foreign language, especially French, and I was tapped. Now I had had a number of classes in this subject, and spoke Italian, which was both a help as well as a hindrance, but never expected to be actually assigned to five classes of 25 to 30 students each and be responsible for their welfare and some expectation of learning the subject matter. Complicating the problem was the fact that there was no such thing as a language lab in schools such as this and the teacher was responsible for all of the spoken skills, accents, etc. I gathered some language tapes and got permission to audit a few Temple School of Education grad classes in foreign language methodology. I think what saved me was my summer experience as a life guard. You see, this was the beginning of the great summer migration of French Canadians to the Wildwoods and few of the young ladies spoke English, which gave me a leg up on dates, so to speak, as well as practicum speaking experiences.

I would be remiss if I glossed over how impressed I was with this school, e.g., the staff, students and parents. Sure, any large organization had its weaknesses and this was no exception. I remember being introduced to an older female staff member who was quite pleasant, even courtly, in her manner. When the first warning bell for the next period rang one day, I still recall her smiling face and still recall that she said something to the effect that she now had to go upstairs and teach those "so and so's". I was really put off and there was a share of other equally weak people. The rap on these schools was that the staff came here only because they could not work elsewhere. I am sure that phrase could apply to many school districts in many locations, but it was a gross exaggeration given my experiences with the Philadelphia Public Schools. There were many fine giving teachers at Overbrook, and, as opposed to what I would find later on in my career, they did not demand stipends for every spare moment they spent with students. They seized on whatever they could to get parents involved and keep students interested, basketball being an example. It was the first time I saw a feeder program, e.g., teachers organizing basketball programs in lower grades even though they knew few of the youngsters would grow up to be stars. They kept the children in the game and the results were very impressive. I was to see the same spirit years later, when as a faculty member at Temple, I walked into Camden High School and met a remarkable educator, Mrs. Rioletta Cream, then serving as a principal and who would enjoy a tremendous career, serving eventually as a county freeholder.

The next assignment would be a far different experience and a much more disappointing one at that, service in a parochial school in Northeast Philadelphia. Once again, it was my French, or their perception of my French teaching ability that led to the assignment, Vive Les Habitants de Québec! I found this institution to be a mixed grill. There was a terrific staff, at least in spirit. The lay teachers seemed dedicated and many had strong academic backgrounds and although they were completely devoid of didactic training, it was just assumed that in a parochial school methodology was an unnecessary encumbrance. It turns out, so was curriculum content, enrichment opportunities for all students, continuous assessment and feedback and certainly encouragement. It turned out a great deal had not changed since my high school days, drill and mental and memorization of vast quantities of information were thought to equate with strong laboratory experiences and a language lab would have been an extremely futuristic notion. Many of the lay teachers simply did not have the content knowledge required to properly prepare the students to be their very best. It was an age old selection ritual being repeated: the students were extremely bright, had attentive parents who had spent handsome sums seeing that they were prepared and never hesitated shelling out even more sheckles for tutors and the like. Also, the academic standards were not worthy of the name.

The priests, and there were many, from several different orders, were an interesting lot. Many were personable, although there were language barriers and again they were from differing communities and there was this over-riding sense of a sort of silent competition among them, which was why the diocese wisely assigned one order among them to administer the school. Of course, that also meant the other groups were immediately relegated to second class status and had little access to the plum jobs. Since these other orders had their own high schools to administer, makes you wonder if they sent very many first team teaching priests to the schools that were not "theirs".

The biggest deficit was in the area of pupil personnel services, guidance, counseling and special subjects. I can still recall a "discussion" on "sex education". The students were brought in to a large room with a great deal of solemnity, the purpose of which was to view stylized torsos of human anatomy, that were more sterile than Michelangelo's sketch known as "Universal Man". Most of the discussion centered on warnings that no talking, snickering or other "objectionable" behaviors would be tolerated. Then a pointer was applied to "show the plumbing", which was followed by a dualistic diatribe on the evils of premarital sex and the inappropriateness of sex in marriage for other than procreation. There was no mention of sex as a virtue, especially within the bounds of expressing love for another, which from my personal perspective, would exist within the bounds of marriage. Also, there was no Q&A, etc. I guess in addition to the medieval aspects of the whole thing, the most disturbing feature was all of the negatives and threats rather than the virtues, especially when that expression of love might occur at an appropriate time in the lives of these young people. Later on the lay teachers were dragooned into this evolution and some were good, within the bounds of protecting their jobs, while others were awful, a reflection of how poorly they seemed to perform in the classroom. For example, I remember one, rather popular member of the staff holding an impromptu session on how unclean certain portions of the female anatomy might be?!

None of this sat well with me and I found that even trying to increase the professionalism of these ancillary services by offering to help was seen as a threat and I became persona non gratia. The problem became exacerbated when I was selected by the lay teachers to be their union rep, people who were desperate to have a voice in their professional state of being but were afraid to speak for themselves. I can recall speaking out at a union meeting, pointing out the need to work for fair treatment, equal participation in the business of serving the children, putting off the cloak of serfdom. While I was well received, the clerical network spread the word of my "traitorous behavior" and the phone was ringing as I returned home, some of the finer, friendlier and worldlier priests urging caution as I was now a target. The principal, a really despicable individual who could have been the role model for a movie on Vatican political intrigue, called me in to speak of his disappointment with my behavior and expressed doubt that I would be invited back. I tossed him copies of my excellent evaluations, told him I would be glad to review any aspect of my performance for which there was a measurable deficit and reminded him that I was there for the experience and almost out the door as my master of science degree was only a few credits away. I recall reading how history records that many medieval popes were possessed of such a parochial orientation that they almost destroyed all vestiges of western civilization. Some of these guys would have fit right in.

One of the finest aspects of this period of my life was my newly assigned mentor, Mr. Pasquale Contini. Packy, as he asked everyone to call him, had retired from the Philadelphia Public Schools, where he had won every award connected with the teaching of foreign language, and he worked in a bunch of different foreign languages. He was the most senior person in terms of rank in the system, in this curriculum area, and was afforded many honors for serving with distinction. He loved the public schools, saw every child as both a challenge as well as an opportunity and taught hundreds of teachers to go beyond themselves. He had also retired from the School of Education at Temple University after years of terrific work in foreign language curriculum and pedagogy. He was one of my early heroes in the business and the reason I never requested reassignment from the Catholic school. His weekly visits were extremely welcome and in addition to teaching me so many valuable lessons, he kept me focused on the children and not the awful dynamics that characterized the environment. I never would have completed that contract without his support.

There was one other, and quite tremendous, benefit for me, our out of work relationship. Mr. Contini lived in center city and it was only a short hop from South Philadelphia by subway to his apartment and we spent many Saturday mornings together with him giving me Italian lessons. Like all great educators, he prized the opportunity to work with anyone interested in learning and took all of my dialectical expressions and made me fluent in the language of my ancestors. Packy is long gone now but his career was a testimony to the art and science that were required for someone to be effective in a classroom. He represented everything that was missing in that Catholic school.

CHASING THE NEXT DEGREE

While all this was going on, there was a Master of Science degree to secure, some 36 credits of graduate work. I had taken the newly constituted Graduate Requisite Exam, and done well; in fact I used my burgeoning skills in statistical analysis to look at the success prediction data and was well satisfied. Still, one had to sit in the classes, do the work, complete the study group assignments and complete the exams successfully. There was also a comprehensive exam and a thesis, something that were firsts for me.

Education as always extremely important to me, I guess for two reasons. First, my parents, indeed most of even my extended family, had very little; and two, it was obviously my ticket "out", my best bet to become something more than my neighborhood and socio-economic status would have predicted. Fortunately, I was enrolled at Temple University and no one shall ever be able to convince me to change my mind. I had just loved my undergraduate classes and was really looking forward to the "bigger" leagues; I guess "high minors" would be the appropriate baseball jargon. There was overlap between faculty designated as either undergrad or graduate, at least in those days, which I guess is one of the reasons that the preferred model was to advance to another college for subsequent degrees. I was actually very much interested in seeing the difference between the styles of those I had encountered in the bachelor degree program and my current endeavors. I was certainly not disappointed, indeed, I would say impressed was the best descriptor. Overall, I would say it was a question of style, something I tried to emulate in my own teaching. Even people I had studied with before, while, they were always engaging, had a much more relaxed style, while pushing tremendous amounts of information at the students. Toward the end of this program, I asked Dr. Emil Soucar, a professor whom I had been with in several undergrad and grad classes, and who would become a colleague and friend, about my perceptions. He knew of my own career plans and, as always, spent copious time with a young, eager student, opining freely about his own experiences. Emil pointed out something that the students themselves often forget, they come with a great foundation and have survived a very competitive selection process, therefore, it was appropriate to assume they possessed great capacity for digesting information and analyzing data. Second, the cost of the classes almost guaranteed that few would waste an opportunity and come unprepared and, third, the structure of the classes themselves. Throughout my entire graduate school experience, I went to classes once or twice a week for three hours plus, for sixteen weeks. You just could not keep people in a tense environment for so much time and such an environment would have been counterproductive to maximizing learning. As a student would one day write of me, "He made the classes equivalent to half a Broadway play, with exciting anecdotes, varied activities, meaningful assignments, and several changes of pace." While I was very proud of this endorsement, in truth, I learned this sense of style from people like Emil Soucar, Andy Bean, Joe DuCette, Larry Furst and his spouse, the incomparable Dr. Norma Furst. Norma was the first and only grad student in the history of the university to complete a master and doctorate degrees with all grades of "A", and her dissertation won the award for the finest of all such theses completed in the class group. While that was impressive enough, her personality, teaching skill, capacity for building interpersonal relationships and sense of panache was overwhelming. Her classes were a real treat, material flowed, laughter ensued, learning was facilitated and everyone not only had a great time, they obviously developed a penchant, indeed a passion, for the subject matter. I never encountered anyone like Dr. Furst until I encountered another great female educator, Catherine Havrilesky, some years later. Norma taught me a great deal, she was a true friend to anyone who demonstrated real interest in not only ACING classes but in becoming knowledgeable and preparing for a career similar to the one she had chosen. Some years later she was appointed a dean of the college of education, recognition of not only of her outstanding achievements but also, her outstanding contributions to the students.

Summer school was especially exciting. The degree program was timed so that it could be completed via two years each of two semesters. Summer school was a luxury and an expensive one but the extra classes would only enhance my vita for the next degree and thus help me fulfill my ultimate goal; besides I was receiving a tremendous break on fees. I took two courses each session, four nights of four plus hours each for six weeks for each session. I kept that schedule until the second session of the summer of 1970, when exhaustion and my pending marriage caused some common sense to begin pervading my thinking. Nevertheless, it was something I have always recommended to my own students. Total immersion in a subject matter, great study groups, which seemed to be enhanced by the warmer weather, and I think, less traditional types of assignments because the schedule was so tight. There was also reading, LOTS of reading and data crunching, which is why I think only the young can prosper at such an endeavor. The grades kept coming, the credits piled ever closer to the required number and all was well. By the beginning of the second year, it was back to Dorothy Seagers and John Rhodes to begin searching for a doctoral program that would help satisfy my ambitions. It was no surprise they there was a duplicate of my student file in their possession that had enabled them to track my progress and they were already ready with recommendations.

TRANSITIONS

With classes under control, my work practicum coming to an end, and a short list of doctorate programs to be researched, it was time to start considering how I would support myself after I had earned the MS degree. Permanent employment in a school system, even a shot at some type of coordinator position was well within the scope of possibilities, but held no excitement for me and seemed to be a dead-end, at least in terms of maximizing the potential of my planned education. I was interested in university teaching with a terminal degree affording me additional possibilities in consulting and business applications. I was also absolutely not interested in staying with something that on some days resembled Fantasyland, or others, Adventureland, but, never, ever, Tomorrowland. My future wife and I were to become life-long patrons of Disneyland but if I wanted to work there I would have moved to Anaheim.

Temple, like most large, research oriented universities, offered fellowships and teaching associate positions. The former provided a small stipend, not very much at all, less then two grand [it was 1970!], and free tuition. The best part of the arrangement was that it provided unlimited time for classes, study and research. I believe they were limited at the time to three years. Think of them as a sort of glorified scholarship. The latter was much more attractive, and of course, extremely competitive. They paid a lot more, well over five grand, required twelve hours of classroom contact time, mostly teaching beginning undergrad classes, and free tuition. You could hold one for only two years, but then you could move into an instructor level position, which was even more competitive. The teaching associate jobs paid more, led to a possible career path, and, because they were so highly sought after, looked great to recruiters from other universities on constant search for a young doctoral program graduate who had already achieved the academic rank of instructor. The problem was landing one of the jobs.

The first consideration was grades, and I had them, with plenty of extra credits to boot. Getting the grades was a multi-faceted consideration for me. You needed top grades to get ahead and how could I, even for reasons beyond mere consideration and politeness, ever disappoint the trio of people whose references had propelled me along this path. It would have been wrong as well as just plain stupid to have performed anywhere near just mediocrity. I finally decided that I had earned a shot and could be competitive on my own for a teaching associate position and approached Dottie Seagers and Marie Cooney to confirm my reasoning. When I got to their office they had everything set; you see the top grades had been expected along with scores in various exams and all the extras. Turned out all I had to do was distinguish myself academically and the graduate school dean had been primed to offer me one of the coveted slots. So I had my next job, work was set!

There was one other piece to the puzzle and that was acceptance to a doctoral program. I was smart enough to figure out I could have a slot almost anywhere, because, being a matriculated doctorate student was a precondition of being appointed as a teaching associate. John Rhodes briefed me on a new program that prepared people as research psychologists, was heavy on psychometrics but with a focus on a clinical field, resulting in the ability to conduct research and/or teach at institutions of higher education. I recall that Mr. R also mentioned federal and state agencies routinely hired such graduates, and in highly desirable positions. Presto, now the next job and the next degree were set. I was on the cusp of beginning a third degree in the same institution, three very different areas with almost completely different faculty experiences. A phone call to the dean by Mr. R, who had already asked that individual to review my records and I was welcomed to the doctoral program as soon as I made my desire of a specialty field known.

ROMANCE

Along the way, I had run into a certain someone again, the great looking blonde who some years before had been caught up trying to sneak into the semester class registration evolution. We had met on the beach, in the company of mutual friends, and she was seeing someone, an older grad student who was already enrolled in medical school. She was just as desirable from a personality and human basis as she was gorgeous so I had to take a shot. I was at the seashore again for a few weeks in my substitute lifeguard job as, in those days, Temple began classes significantly after Labor Day. We ran into one another at one of the August series of weekly lifeguard competitions and seemed to hit it off. The record is a bit fuzzy here but I remember going with someone else who somehow happened to begin talking to my future wife and after a while it was just the two of us. I shudder to think what she may have said about me to the other young lady, whose phone number I happened to find some years later after we were married and I should have used that opportunity to find out how she had managed to single us up that first night. As an aside, it would be years before she confessed to being the same young woman I had had ejected from registration all those years earlier.

We dated the next night and started seeing one another frequently that September and I never heard of the other guy again. We were engaged by December and married he following August, of 1970, and we have been together ever since!

It was and has always been very special and I guess a bit private. There is a relevant aspect to the current story, how my spouse has complemented me my entire career, starting with her incredible support during the chaining days of doctoral classes, residency and of course, the dissertation. It was a three year program and *WE* did it in two, after all, the third year was a freebie so to speak, that it, if you finished early, you got an early start on the much bigger dollars. It was also about this time, as you have read earlier, that I managed to get my draft status straightened out and we started a new life together with me studying and working at the same location, a really wonderful situation that I have never been able to duplicate.

CHARACTERS

I encountered a lot of really terrific people during the years 1970-1972 but chief among them was my adviser, doctoral mentor, and one of life's most interesting characters, Dr. Edmund Amidon, or "Ted" as he insisted being called. He had a unique personality, too complex for even a psychologist to describe in these pages but one characteristic was an outstanding sense of humor. About a year into our relationship, he began suggesting universities that had openings for assistant professors, positions that he thought would be perfect for me. When I tried to get some feedback about his own decision making process at that stage of his career, I asked him what he had done between graduating from the University of Minnesota and starting at Temple University. His answer, "Well, I drove from Minneapolis to Philadelphia." This was his way; by that simple response, he made light of a question he did not wish to answer, primarily because the greatest lesson he ever taught me was to exercise my intellect constantly and finding the answers to questions was just one piece of that puzzle. He was so easy going that some people may have underestimated him but he was pure genius and his ability to relate to people especially his graduate students was remarkable. Over some twenty six years, I patterned my university teaching after his model, along with a lot of Norma Furst thrown in. Not coincidentally, they were not only colleagues but also good friends. It was just amazing how good they were at leading discussions about complex problems and then having the patience to direct the students to find the process that would lead to an answer. I am sure that how hard I may have tried, I always fell short of the impact that Norma and Ted brought to their teaching.

Ted was a character in so many ways. The program to which I had matriculated was relatively new and he was building it as we went along together, eventually succeeding in having every applicable certifying agency accept it at the PhD level. I kept in touch with Ted over the years and he had continued to manipulate this and other programs for which he had assumed responsibility, seeing these degrees as cultural events, that is, he believed the programs had to have value to the world of academics as well as practical applications; they had to be seen as valuable by the students, and there had to be a constituency for its graduates. By all measures, Ted was eminently successful. I guess it is best to describe his efforts as keeping these programs fresh, by constantly cultivating new aspects to them, a kind of organic student garden.

Ted also had strict rules that new students had to somehow ascertain for themselves. He expected everyone to attend the faculty parties [Marie and I never missed a one!], he never permitted anyone to write in ink in his calendar, as he was always canceling or forgetting meetings, and, you had to call him "Ted". Given my upbringing, especially the part whereby I always felt like an interloper among successful people of rank, this was very hard for me. I used to wait until he was looking at me so as to avoid the words "Dr" and "Sir". His solution, he would race around until his back was turned to force the issue. I remember one afternoon two grown men racing around for position until I just started calling him "Ted" and he took me to the faculty club for a drink and we laughed about this for an hour.

The best part of my time with Ted was the dissertation process. Because I was so advanced with my classes, he allowed me to skip the seminars relating to the research agenda that would lead to an approved dissertation topic, as these seminars were given at the end of the second year of classes and I had just finished my first year chronologically, but was well along with the entire cadre of classes overall. The idea was I would collect and analyze data, write the dissertation and prepare for the oral defense, while finishing classes and my residency, taking the proficiency exams in foreign language and the comprehensive program exams, all of which should have occurred before I even started thinking about my dissertation. If this sounds daunting it was, yet at the time, it seemed very reasonable because Ted indicated it was his preference and everyone around him always trusted his judgment, especially when it related to his plans for his students.

As so everything seemed set although there were still some very tough classes, a lot of research, data collection and analyses, and of course, writing the thesis, which consumed enormous amounts of time just getting chapters to the committee members and integrating their suggestions. I cannot imagine anyone in this position being able to describe themselves as "patient" maybe "as a patient", but it was a great life lesson, making strides on an allowable bases.

There was the inevitable fly in the applesauce so to speak and it was the last two of the seven required classes in psychometrics, the dreaded multivariate and discriminate analyses sequence. One professor taught both courses and only one and he saw himself, as he himself described his role, as the "keeper to the keys of the kingdom". In other words, he had no intention of allowing anyone to proceed to a doctoral degree in his specialty unless they proved their "worthiness", his words, by achieving at an acceptable level in his classes.

The person was a bit of a wretch and he is long passed so I have decided to let him remain nameless, trusting that all who survived his tyranny shall never forget the experience. For some years after my graduation and subsequent employment as a faculty member, we would see him, usually alone and seemingly forlorn, at the annual faculty ball, the absolute highpoint of our winter social season. I regretted that he was never able to enjoy the camaraderie of colleagues and students, for it was an experience to savor.

But, I am getting ahead of myself. First, the classes had to be conquered. He greeted us the first night by naming us the "Dirty Dozen", years before the Lee Marvin film of the same name became popular. To him, we happened to be twelve in number and somewhat "unclean' in that we were unproven pretenders to a terminal degree. I thought it was an impressive bunch. Two of us were faculty members at Temple, several held impressive jobs at big local firms, and the remaining students were already employed at other universities and colleges in the area. He also told us his ancestors were Huguenots and therefore were superior to the "ethnic stock" he saw before him in class. He proceeded to make his point by then disparaging everybody as he forced us to introduce ourselves, even though he and everybody else knew all about one another. I shall never forget him telling me, "So you live in Blackwood, New Jersey with the other Italians that cannot read and write."

His favorite saying was: "A graduate student is like an oyster, you have to irritate it to get a pearl". I must have heard this a thousand times during the two semesters, and, he demonstrated the capacity to annoy us extremely. His assignments, when they made sense, were almost catastrophic in complexity, and, let's say there was a certain uniqueness to his grading system. You shall like this: the first data analyses took weeks, although we had only two so imagine the wee hours used to complete the work, and, he FAILED everybody in the class. The reason? He said none of us provided a conclusion to the analyses. Not so, said we, but of course said he. Turns out he would not read anything beyond one page! Now we had twelve of the most advanced students among the 51,000 thousand on roll in the university trying to find typewriters with extra small print to get all his requirements within the allotted single page. One positive aspect was that all twelve had to band together. This was a big deal, that is, a very positive step in a highly charged and competitive atmosphere. We used the BioMed and Stat PACK software programs on a CDC 6000 large, main frame computer to run data analyses that seemed to take forever. I had been warned never to store my data cards decks in the allocated areas of the computer center because of the sabotage that routinely occurred as people used any means to undermine their competitors and secure the top positions for themselves. Therefore, although it took a while, having twelve talented people trusting one another was a real benefit. I guess we all united to defeat a common enemy!

It was also the occasion of my one and only rebellion in all the years of struggling to get ahead. I went to see the PROFESSOR and really blasted him as to his methods, pointing out the talent base, the stakes, and the incredible sacrifice being made by each of the families of the students, who had to complete the sequence successfully, graduate and get that dream job, all mitigated against the treatment we were receiving. He said nothing and for a while I expected some sanction but he was probably smart enough to know that any grievance from me would get high level attention. Actually, I never ever thought of playing that card during this entire time, I was just fed up with games, especially from someone who held this position of great trust, and, who never, ever, taught us anything.

I recall the midterm exam, especially when it was returned. There was a hand written "A" with the accompanying note: "Quit while you are ahead". I did not quit, none of us did, and he gave us all grades of "B'. In those days two "B's" were all you got and no "C's" at all would be tolerated at this level so the second semester promised to be real interesting. In any event the second semester was uneventful except for one glaring exception. He had kept repeating his famous slogan, "A graduate student is like an oyster, you have to irritate it to get a pearl", and one night literally shouted it to a female student he had tread on with less than acceptable behavior. She rose, mustered as much dignity as she could under the circumstances and responded: "Honey, how would you like a whole blankety-blank necklace!" and stormed from the room, never to be seen again, except at graduation, which always made me wonder what she told the dean to have this class waived. I could not help but roar out loud and it was a sort of catharsis for the rest of us. From then on, the rest of us just did the work and basically ignored the dynamics and I was rewarded with an "A". Another great lesson, this time is how not to behave toward students.

One last corollary relating to our friend. I was teaching the following fall semester and, as it turned out, right next door to Ted and on the other side was the lab used by my erstwhile stat teacher. Ted and I were walking to lunch one day when I was beckoned by my former professor who bestowed on me what he latter described as the highest form of praise that he gave to graduate students: "You were not very bright but you were persistent". Some faint praise, indeed. I wish I could relate the reactions of Dr. Amidon, which were more clever than crude, but still a bit testy. Good old Ted always knew what to say and which buttons to push.

NEXT STEPS

All that was left was to finish the dissertation, get sign-offs from the committee and prepare for the oral defense, which was before a second committee but open to anyone on the graduate faculty. Getting the paper ready for submission was quite a task. It had to be done on 100 lb test paper, thick enough to wrap fish in without any leakage, and it cost a fortune. The paper had to be procured in a special shade of light beige, for University Microfilming. There could be no corrections, that is, if you made a mistake the page had to be retyped. Yes, typed, these were the days of the typewriter and hand calculator. While we had main frame time available to us as doctoral students, day to day work was done by hand. I can still recall that each multi-factor analysis of variance took me two hours to complete. Ironically, I just realized that I am at the same desk writing these words as when I completed the dissertation, some thirty four years ago! Obviously, I needed help with the paper, the final draft at least, and I turned to Carmella Iodice, actually the only other person of Italian extraction I had met at the university. Carmella worked with Eileen Cooney, Marie's sister, both as assistants to the Dean of the School of Business and Management, Dr. Seymour Wolfbein, a cool guy who would one day appoint me to his faculty. I can still recall Carmella calling me to say: "you do not really mean to say so and so do you? Wouldn't so and so be better?"; to which I would meekly and smartly say: "Yes, M'am." And so it was finished, I guess there was one last minute change regarding the psychological aspects of "selection" and "placement" from some of the personality inventories I was using but Ted pronounced to everyone that there were no problems with the study and the oral defense was scheduled.

There was a legendary story around the university regarding failed dissertation defenses, all of which were repeated from generation to generation, getting people used to the idea of being super prepared and super cool, [yeh, right!]. One guy had someone do the data analyses, which is OK but you had to be able to explain everything that was done and of course, the first question dealt with explaining the data analyses. Supposedly, a flop sweat of Richard Nixon proportions ensued and after ten minutes of uncomfortable silence, the candidate was excused until he could come before the panel better prepared. The second case involved someone who was so nervous that he began to shake and asked to be excused returning a bit later with the toupee he had forgotten earlier. After lighting several cigarettes on the wrong end, he too was asked to return another day.

One side bar about dissertation defenses. A professor and good friend, Andy Bean told me a story that turned out to be perfect advice for the dissertation candidate. He told me that someone would surely ask me to tell a bit about myself and that I should seize on that opening and move right from a short vita to the study and, with luck, I could be half-way through the dissertation defense before anyone was the wiser. As it turned out, everyone was very satisfied with the study although someone I thought was a friend questioned my use of a word, a quick check of the old Funk and Wagnall and darn if I was not right. That was it, although it was formal, it was friendly and an enjoyable two hours, consisting mostly of complimentary comments. Now Norma Furst had been given a birthday cake at her dissertation defense and the committee was so impressed with the package that it waived all interest in even discussing the thesis. That story was also legendary and I was grateful to get out as easily as I could, knowing that no one could top Norma. I left the celebration at the club rather hurriedly, and, as always, retreated immediately to my bride to share the good news. Ted had called ahead and by the time I got home there were banners, guests and food, a most welcome and fitting ending to an eventful two years. My mother had ordered a desk plaque with "Dr. Joseph Picogna" inscribed and it was embarrassing so it was never displayed, but, after three degrees in eight years I guess she too was entitled to be a bit ostentatious. I enjoyed being called "professor" over the years of teaching but "Dr" was always a bit much to me, especially after I got to the level of the local school districts as an administrator and found they all fell over themselves to waive their degrees before everyone, particularly the mail-order people.

Another long period of my professional life had been completed and I had been blessed by having people like Dorothy Seagers, John Rhodes, Edmund Amidon and Norma Furst to guide me. They became my first pantheon of heroes. To this day I still call on their teachings when faced with decisions.

RETROSPECTIVE

On reflection, I can see some merit in the "keeper of the keys" mentality although fairness and decency should not be casualties of academic rigor. There must be standards and they must be set high, otherwise, the degree would be worthless and people would not have much confidence in the ability of those who had earned a doctorate, something like visiting a graduate of a combination aluminum storm door company slash medical school, to be treated for a hernia. Ted and Norma taught people a great deal and did it with style. They were the antithesis of what I had experienced in my public and parochial school teaching, where, although many fine people were engaged, the organizational culture had become riveted in mediocrity.

I must admit that some years later teaching a bunch of students that I knew were taking the deadly duo as the two stat classes were sometimes called, I could not resist saying just once, "A graduate student is like an oyster, you have to irritate it to get a pearl". There was almost a mutiny as people began whispering about the mistake they may have made in registering for my class. It was a great lesson for me in not making bad jokes, at least not until I had built a reputation for fairness and quality and that took a number of years. I found out that when that time came, people began to trust you had their best interests in mind, tended to overlook your peccadilloes and soon began referring to me as "colorful". But, that was well into the future. For now, there was a need to decide on which opportunity to accept and my loving spouse was not all that thrilled with the prospect of moving to university towns, some in the middle of nowhere, some in very attractive west coast locations. I still recall that an offer from Morehead State University in South Dakota drew a particularly cool reception. She was an East Coast woman, wanted to be near family and the seashore. As usual, her counsel proved not only to be valuable but also prophetic.

THE GLORY YEARS

"Trenton Makes The World Takes".

Gateway Sign Lower Trenton Bridge

OPPORTUNITY KNOCKS

For me, the period 1970-72, was one of great fulfillment. I had used the classic tool of advancement for people of lower socio-economic classes, education, to make my mark. I guess this was especially important for my family but I had made sure that I would not be relegated to the assembly line but could make my way via intellectual pursuits. Now I had to put that vita to work and build a new career. I was already employed as a university instructor and that gave me the possibility of staying put and waiting for a tenure track job as an assistant professor to open up, along with the attending research potential. The consulting and a private practice would normally come about much later in one's career. A challenge presented itself in that while the area was noted for many fine colleges and universities, I needed a comprehensive graduate program to ply my specialty. Temple University, of course, was the number one candidate but not normally for one of its own graduates; Rutgers University offered many complementary programs for me at both their Newark and New Brunswick campuses but the commute from where we wanted to live to these areas was impossible. That left a choice between another area entirely or the University of Pennsylvania, with its famed Wharton School. This prestigious institution had a primary focus on finance with other areas such as organization development relegated to, and I use this term not at all in a prejudicial sense, secondary status. U of P also wanted people from other Ivy Leagues Schools or some place with the prestige of a Stanford or Duke. It would be many years before I had an opportunity to work at the University of Pennsylvania.

With the oral defense coming up a real opportunity presented itself, the big break of my professional career, so to speak, in that it got me started on the path that led to this book. A friend from my early Temple faculty days, Dan Bevilacqua, had joined the New Jersey Department of Education. We shall read more about my relationship with Dan below and in the chapter entitled, "The Face of Governance", where he is portrayed as one of the brightest lights I encountered in all these years. He was a student in the same Master of Science program that I had graduated from and it was a real treat for me to be able to work with him. Dan had been recruited to work in the Bureau of Emergency Preparedness Education in the state capital, Trenton, a city that was unknown to me but would soon become my second home. The quote that begins this chapter was the very first thing about the city I was to see, driving to my interview, crossing what we used to call the free bridge and there it was, a reference to the great manufacturing days of Roebling Steel and other giant corporations.

OLD FRIENDS

Dan had noticed an opening in the Bureau of Teacher Certification and Academic Credentials, one that required someone with my credentials and paid the amazing salary of $13,500 a year! This was more than any academic opportunity was likely to offer for some time, and, I could continue part-time at Temple when needed, a perfect scenario. I gulped hard, got my papers together and wrote, actually begged, for an interview. Now it turns out the state education agency employed some thirteen hundred people in those days, a few senior people, some well paid specialists such as I hoped to be, and most of all, people who were accountants, credentials examiners, testing experts, and an assortment of curriculum developers, hearing officers, lobbyists, lawyers, and special and vocational educators. There was also a network of twenty one county offices of education, run more like middle age fiefdoms, mostly under the control of the individual county freeholder boards, and, the entire system of colleges and universities that prepared teachers in every area, along with the pre-professional preparation programs for physicians, dentists, lawyers, and other similarly licensed trades.

This last function was under the auspices of the Bureau of Teacher Certification and Academic Credentials, where my job opportunity resided. This bureau was under the directorship of Ward Sinclair, a knowledgeable and friendly individual who was much admired throughout the professional community. I had met Ward at a conference down south a couple of years earlier while working as an instructor at Temple and so it turned out I knew two people in my prospective new home. It was also obvious that Danny had greased the skids and they were really looking to recruit me based on his recommendation and their paper review of my credentials. The Bureau employed a lot of people, mainly in the third category described above. The job I was seeking was new and part of a master plan to upgrade the middle manager ranks of the organization. The great flood of federal funding via the Elementary and Secondary Education Act of 1965 and its successor amended iterations had provided a lot of positions in the support areas, curriculum, testing, accounting etc., and now it was deemed necessary to move into areas such as organizational dynamics, training, program and staff development, and research. The department was competing with universities and private research labs for the available talent and they were just as happy to have me as I was to be with them. It seemed like a great fit and my timing was perfect, just being in the right place at the right time.

Ward had several top assistants, including Chuck Rutledge and Fred Price, just superb people, and there was an office manager, Sadie Sumfest, who had seemingly been employed there all of her considerable lifetime. They all made me feel welcome and I was able to start just as soon as some class coverage could be arranged at Temple University, a place that I would never really leave. I was going to an exciting venue with exciting work and great people, who immediately made me feel part of the family, a sort of old friend. While the departmental protocol for formal situations required the use of the title "Dr", and Ward and Chuck as well as I had doctorates, I continuously asked people to just refer to me by my first name, a concept that a lot of the support people would have some trouble with. Just before I had left Temple, the departmental secretary presented me with a beat up old ceramic frog. As I was thanking her for the "gift", she interrupted and said I was too polite to inquire as to the nature of the gift and so she told me: the frog was a symbol for all newly minted doctorates, to remind them not to get too puffed up over their accomplishments. It still sits on my office shelf, next to my cherished crystal OWL, which was one of my retirement gifts on exiting university service some 26 years later. I was to use this method for many years not always successfully, in fact, many of my students and staff in the coming years would react the same way I had with Ted Amidon, but, for the most part, I think it helped put people at ease. If people insisted on being formal with me I just asked them to use "Mr.". I do recall some days on campus when I would be talking to a colleague, who would address me as "Joe" until a student happened by and then they would quickly switch to "Dr" or "Professor". Whatever floats your boat, I guess. At the Department, many people insisted on being addressed by their titles, and, you never saw, or I should say, heard, anything like the plethora of titles used in school districts, even among those whose credentials were, let's say, less than inspiring. It was "Dr" this and "Principal" that, as if no one had been given a first name! At the Educational Testing Service, which was proximate to the agency and a prime vendor for our efforts, everyone was called "Mr." or "Ms", etc not "Dr", in deference to the founder, who had no doctorate. I continued to exercise this preference in Cherry Hill, in deference to my hero, John McKeon, who did not have a doctorate degree, and, because I still believed that a title use put people off, and, most people who come to central office in school districts are usually not happy in the first place. Mr. McKeon's replacement, Philip Esbrandt, insisted on being referred to as "Dr", and, had the temerity to tell me my failure to use my title was a slight against his use of the title [not unusual thinking for "school people"] and he actually told me he was going to verify my degree because I did not refer to myself as he did. I would have enjoyed asking him if he intended to publish my list of credentials alongside his, but, I am getting ahead of myself again. There were many years of happiness and excitement to come before this trauma.

NEW AQUAINTANCES

The bureau was so large that it occupied a unique site, a separate office building, known as the "Franklin Street Complex", as it was simply too large to be housed in the main headquarters complex, which was known as the "Marble Palace". This latter facility, which was subsequently closed when it was found to be imbedded with friable asbestos, was located on State Street, part of the state capitol complex, which housed: the State House, offices of Governor Thomas Cahill, my ultimate boss, and his retinue, the Assembly and Senate Buildings, the Historic Prussian Barracks, scene of the climax of General Washington's Christmas attack in the first year of the Revolutionary War, and the State Museum and State Library, both, I was to learn, under the auspices of the Department of Education. Contiguous to this was the Judiciary Complex, and the various departments of state, e.g., State, Labor, Agriculture and Community Affairs, the very seat of power. Imagine how awe struck I was when I first visited this complex of great buildings, a week after my first and only interview, to be "in processed". I had yet to visit Washington DC or New York so this was really something special, especially since my appointment had passed quickly through the endorsement process: Assistant Commissioner for Field Services, Mr. John Rosser, the Commissioner of Education, Dr. Carl Marlberger, and the New Jersey State Board of Education, chaired by the truly magnificent Mrs. Ruth Mancuso.

We were situated a few miles away in our own environment, with two tenant offices, Dan's shop, Emergency Preparedness Education and the Federal Office of Surplus Property. Emergency Preparedness Education was headed by Leon Colavita, another future friend, and Dan, who had taken the spot formerly occupied by Walter Colander, a famous area basketball player who had taken the job as Director of Child Nutrition Services. Wally was also a terrific and very capable person; are you getting the picture? These were superb people and this was just a great experience! Leon was also a famous athlete in the region, as was Fred Price, for that matter, and both would play key roles in our championship fast pitch softball teams over the years. Leon himself actually got a hit off the famous King and His Court touring softball extravaganza. He and Dan would, in turn, be promoted to positions of greater responsibility.

Emergency Preparedness Education was the successor to the "duck and cover" days of the Cold War only they provided instructional materials, training and onsite support in all areas of student and staff awareness and HAZMAT controls, a sort of 1970's version of Homeland Security. One year, before everyone moved on, the Feds declared the curriculum to be obsolescent and told all state education staff they supported in these units to stand down. I recall because it was about the time the Franklin Street Complex closed and Emergency Preparedness Education moved to temporary quarters, in anticipation of being mothballed. The staff members, Leon and Dan, were immediately selected for promotion to state education agency funded positions but were in the quandary of having to fulfill a contract, which required them to do nothing and be able to document their inactivity! Only a veteran of the bureaucracy wars can fully comprehend this lunacy. But, they had a month or two to kill and after a week of transition report writing, taking stock and preparing materials for return, there was literally nothing to do. Their temporary office space was a very small, abandoned two story house with a lavatory at the top of the stairs, just a slight turn to the right. They invented a great game to pass the time, a Frisbee toss with the winner declared on achieving twenty one points. There were circles on the floor leading to the wash room, and points were awarded for getting closest to the toilet. Of course, landing in the toilet on a fly was an automatic win, twenty-one points. There is one other antidote about this unit that I recall fondly. There was another staff member, a secretary named Kay Rick, a great colleague and a really wonderful person, who also happened to be hard of hearing, which she denied vehemently. Fred Price used to open the door and mouth the words "Good Morning Kay" without actually speaking and I must admit it was hard not to laugh. Ward even told me to ask Fred to stop and he did, after a fashion, but every time the story resurfaced, we did all laugh out loud. Now one day Danny was out on the road in a rattrap state car and got stuck. I happened to be doing a desk audit with Kay at the time, as a favor to Leon, when the phone rang. It was pouring, I recall because it was actually hard to hear with the rain and wind pounding on the windows. The phone rang and I could hear someone speaking very loudly on the other end and it sounded like Dan. Kay immediately drowned out the other voice and repeated several times, in her always loud voice, "Mr. Bevilacqua is not in today". I could have sworn I heard Dan saying "Kay it's me, Dan" and it turned out I was right. The thought of Danny walking a distance in the rain and putting his last few coins into a pay phone and getting what in effect was a wrong number still brings a smile to my face. They sort of got even with me. Years later when I began working in Howell I had to deal with a mini crisis, a tiny radioactive chip left behind from a HAZMAT training session given by, you guessed it, Emergency Preparedness Education!

Fred Price was a very busy individual, yet still found time to be courteous, offer help, and, on occasion, plan and deliver a great prank. Fred was the central focus of all the professional preparation programs in the state. As an assistant director, he headed the staff that provided all of the technical assistance to the plethora of institutions that prepared licensed specialists, mostly teachers and administrators. He was truly gifted in bringing people along with him as he encouraged and led these highly independent entitles to improve their efforts, meet new state mandates and perform with a purpose. He was tireless in his efforts to raise the standards of preparation for people who would ultimately be licensed to care for children. He was noted for long hours and making himself personally available to anyone with a question, anyone who was reluctant to set aside personal considerations in favor of a greater good, and especially, to anyone requesting assistance in order to do a better job. Fred also had a terrific knack of keeping everyone loose with his sense of humor. His office was next to one of the few lavatories in our entire building, a thin walled, closet like structure that seemed almost transparent to sound. Many people using the facility would run the water full blast to mask other sounds that would easily emanate from the water closet. A couple of the more senior folks paid frequent visits to the lavatory, as I do today, and Fred would keep a weekly tally on a wall chart, and soon there was an office pool, for amusement purposes only, predicting the "weekly victor". He was also a key player, one of several actually, in a little office drama that would provide a number of amusing anecdotes over my first few months. In close proximity to Fred's office there was a person who was employed as an examiner, who spent a great deal of time on the phone explaining requirements to candidates for certain administrative licenses. The field was complex and therefore the work was time consuming, almost completely phone based. Now this individual was prone to what was referred to by the rest of the staff as "nervous excitement", not exactly a clinical description but I think you get a sense of the problem, which was compounded by the fact that the other half of this little romance was still working in the office, and if anything, exhibited even more of the same "symptoms". I recall my very first day in the office and a terrific woman named Carmella Giovanini, who would be with me for some time, was showing me around and finally took me to the office I would be using. Ms X as I shall call her, entered the office immediately after Carmella and I did, shut the door, and demanded to know why she had not gotten to meet the "new young man". There was only a small window and it was a four story drop so Carmella and I were trapped but, as she so often did during our years together, Carmella took control, and, with difficulty, ushered Ms X out. Now our two lovers ended their affair on less than pleasant terms and one never knew when there might be a confrontation. Ms X had an old automobile, covered with stickers, "re-peel bananas" was my favorite, and she had taken to scribbling hate slogans directed toward her ex, on the few empty spots on the car's exterior. Ms X also had a penchant for dropping in on her ex when he was heavily engaged on the phone and invariably began with a "How Could YOU?!" that quickly extended into a full fledged diatribe. Fred came into play on each occasion by stopping what he was doing and calming the troubled seas. "Anything to get the job done" was Fred's motto, and if I happened to be with him on these occasions, which were frequent, he had to deal with my laughter creating an even greater distraction. He would get even with me, though. I had been given one of those new fangled containers with a magnetic ring around the top, which always kept a paper clip at the ready. Well, the mechanism did not work as intended after certain parties would interlace all of the clips so that they came out as a sort of chain.

Fred was so successful with what he did that his programs in the field had little trouble getting ready for the comprehensive inspections of teams of experts that were assembled by the Bureau's associate director, Dr. Rutledge. Chuck was a former Marine, with combat experience in the Korean War. He was friendly, committed to excellence and extremely well organized, perfectly suited to the always touchy job of bringing really talented people into a foreign environment and convincing both sides to work toward a common goal of program improvement. He had a knack of putting people at ease, from the exit conferences to the copious reports, which spared feelings while staying on point. Like Fred, Chuck was very gracious with me, inviting me in to look at his operation from the inside, which was to make my job much easier. Both Fred and Chuck took the position with their program directors that the monitoring visits should be a time of renewal and a chance to celebrate successes, but only if they worked the programs everyday. This was a lesson that would guide my efforts throughout the remainder of my career.

It seemed as though everyone had a sense of humor, which helped a great deal as the pace was really beginning to pick up. The Commissioner of Education, Carl Marlburger, was beginning a series of moves that would combine a very strong existing staff with a number of specialists, including myself, who were to develop the finest productivity improvement programs I have ever witnessed, a capacity that would be offered to local districts via a series of carrots that placed the onus of success on the state education agency. Carl Marlburger, as we shall see, led from the front.

FIRST STEPS: EARLY TASKS

Ward had a third assistant, a fairly new employee named Robert Boose, someone who was obviously talented, politically astute and a person who would become a very close friend. Bob had an outstanding background in management and his primary assignment was to manage the daily operations of dozens of examiners who conducted paper reviews of tens of thousands of candidates for professional licenses every year. It was a huge undertaking, complicated immensely but the fact that the staff was extremely experienced, and set in their ways, and almost devoid of any technology. In fact, they tended to eschew what little modern resource systems that were available. The icing on the cake was the fact that several had political ties that had gotten them their positions a few decades before and were even more entrenched than their remaining colleagues. It was a great lesson illustrating the false premise that experience is worthless if it means using the same incorrect strategies over and over again.

Bob was just the person for the job. He had recently completed his doctoral residency and was working on his dissertation, at Temple University, no less, so we had a lot on common and I know we would become great friends when he asked for my help with his study, and, requested that I take a first look at his operation, my first chance to show my stuff!

As I stated earlier, I was part of the Marlburger revolution in the agency. Carl had spent his early years building a strong curriculum unit, coupled with regulatory experts who knew the rules and who had been trained to help people meet the requirements rather than being threatened with sanction when they fell short. There was a whole host of accountants, lawyers, hearing officers, and conflict resolution specialists. He then moved into areas such as testing, special, remedial and vocational education, and, launched the very first investigations of programs to meet the needs of students exhibiting characteristics of the very gifted and talented. Now it was his intention to move into program and staff development and he had hired a few people with skills such as research psychologists, to get this new initiative moving. These efforts were to be combinations of the quantitative and qualitative, that is, the goal was to set high standards of relevant expectations, measure the impact of the resource investment, package the success stories and disseminate the results to other jurisdictions demonstrating the capacity to adopt our work. Unbeknownst to me during my first weeks, Dr. Marlburger had decided to begin with the backbone of the agency: the regulatory functions, hence my placement in one of the most bureaucratic, and my first tasks, which were intended as tests of my capacity to move on to projects of greater complexity and hence, more importance.

Bob Boose and I were then turned loose on my first big assignment: examining, researching, coaxing and training people to perform better. There was some sort of incredible backlog in the issuance of needed credentials, over three thousand packages awaiting disposition. I recall my own brother in law, who is a cardiologist, contacting me to inquire why someone they wanted to bring on as a partner had been waiting six months for a "pre-professional" certification when he had already graduated from Harvard Medical School and completed a residency and fellowship at the University of Pennsylvania!

There were plenty of people to do the work, which would be facilitated greatly if only the rather antiquated computer system would ever be used. This was really my first experience with the Mr. Inside and Mr. Outside paradigm that was to characterize some of my finest work periods, those in keeping with terrific sidekicks. Bob dealt with the politics, and very effectively, bringing some sense of order to a system and managed to convince almost everybody concerned that they were better off, at least, safer, playing ball with him. Meanwhile I was hard at work on the inside, managing the project. Bob even managed to convince the Commissioner to bring civil service charges against the one employee who was completely intractable, "pour encourager les autres", as Napoleon used to say. It worked, the others were much more receptive, at least on the surface, when they saw a major complainer, who was a thorn in their side, get the axe. This was Bob Boose at his best, he had complete trust in my assessments about what needed to be done and he had great credibility with his superiors at the divisional level, John Rosser, and an extraordinary person named Catherine Havrilesky, who, in turn, was completely trusted by Carl Marlburger. Bob was very strong, had a comprehensive professional background to establish his bona fides, and he was not afraid to make decisions, although he was also a great negotiator. We were in a hurry, Dr. Marlberger had a comprehensive agenda and, Mrs. Havrilesky knew that the civil servants had not seen anything like Boose and me and that their first tendency would be to try and wait us out.

In little over a month we had an approved remedial plan that focused strictly on building capacity for enhanced productivity. We worked through the bureaucratic maze of new titles that provided a few more bucks for examiner-operators, those who would agree to be trained in the computer systems available to retrieve candidate records, and, issue, electronically and directly to the county office, certificates, that is, the licenses people needed to ply their trade. Pretty neat for 1972, eh? We also released a whole lot of candidate application money to the state treasurer much earlier as the documents were now moving very quickly and the applicant checks could be cashed much sooner. The remaining examiners now submitted to our training program, perhaps not all that eagerly, because they saw the need to qualify for the new position titles as they were to be the only jobs available to them in the very near future. It was at this juncture that we had to confront the redoubtable Sadie Sumfest.

Sadie ran the examiners, or perhaps it would be more correct to say she had the title but seemed to spend all of her time backstopping her staff by retracing all of their work; and, she spent a lot of time doing it. Sadie was famous for returning after dinner to tackle the backlog, which by now had become obvious to me, was HER backlog, and the building entry records showed that she regularly worked Saturdays and sometimes a few hours on Sundays. Tangling with this legend was a bit of a risk, you had to be right, show results immediately, and be gentle in the process. She had been with the agency forever and it was obvious she tolerated both Bob and me, the look on her face clearly indicated she had seen people like us come and go but she was very wrong, there had never been anyone like us there before, especially after we had formed our Mr. Inside and Mr. Outside relationship. It was a bit challenging working with her, the office filled with a dozen or more plaques awarded for never taking leave over entire years. Of course it was also filled with hundreds of packages of license applications, packages she just would not trust to her veteran staff, you see, the Sadie was *the* backlog and she was *the* legend.

I convinced Bob that we could make this work because I thought Sadie was intelligent, you could discuss things with her, and, she had a great sense of humor. For example, you remember Ms. X and her lover-boy? Well, one day Bob and I were going to lunch and approached the central elevator core via one of the four corridors that branched off at every floor. From another came Ms. X, from the third, lover-boy appeared and there immediately ensued a melee. Ms. X began pummeling lover-boy, who was trapped against the closed elevator doors. Bob interspersed himself between the combatants, who were swinging wildly with most of the blows falling on Bob, whose tie was now eschew and his glasses knocked off. I remember him yelling "Help me you SOB" but I was laughing so hard I thought I would have a stroke. At this propitious moment, Ms. Sumfest arrived via the fourth corridor and said: "Good Morning Mr. Boose, I see you have become aware of our personnel problem", whereby I burst out laughing all over again.

Bob was given the responsibility of dealing with this now out of control situation and I suggested that the issue could be our entrée with

Sadie. My idea was to convince her that her job required her to interact with people at a higher level, to serve as a mentor and as a resource person, even to very veteran staff. Bob asked for a complete protocol for pulling this off and he liked what he saw, began selling the notion to Sadie and got her occupied with working through the problem of Ms X and lover-boy. While she was thus engaged, we were to turn loose the examiners without having every package reviewed by Ms. Sumfest. Simultaneously, we started transitioning everything we could to the new computer data base management system. Sadie was thus presented with a fait accompli; we had shown that the staff could handle almost anything, including items in areas for which no precedent existed. We also had shown that we needed her to be the locus of control for continued change, to work with external assets who, over the coming years, would continue to automate these processes. To her credit, she accepted what Bob presented as an inevitable, albeit rather attractive situation, and the project was a great success.

Most people would not trust a budding career to such an educated hunch but Bob knew the path to success was lined with calculated risks; it was to become *his* trademark and part of *his* legend. He continuously pushed for excellence, never accepting anything less, never worrying about the consequences of offending the power elite, although most often his terrific negotiating skills and sense of the politic worked wonders in getting our programs implemented. As for me, I had used my training to begin functioning in the capacity for which I would henceforth be known, as a management consultant, working to develop systems and staff to increase productivity. It was at this time that people in the agency began referring to us as the twins and were deemed ready to take the show on the road, at least throughout the remainder of the division of field services: facilities design and management, pupil transportation, technology, child nutrition programs, organizational communications, performance evaluation, grants management, surplus property, and, of course, emergency preparedness education.

GETTING RECOGNIZED: A PROMOTION

All of six months had passed since I had joined the agency and I had been over to the Marble Palace just a few times, mostly in the company of Bob, as he sold still another one of our program improvement ideas. The Bureau was located organizationally in the Division of Field Services, John Rosser, assistant commissioner and Catherine Havrilesky as his deputy. Jack had a wide ranging experience base, having served as an assistant superintendent in the Willingboro school system, when it was something to behold, and, he had served as an administrator at one of the new intermediate units that were being established, educational improvement centers they were called, regional centers that provided all sorts of assistance, with individual classroom teachers as the targets. He was forward thinking with a great sense of humor and built a powerhouse from an abandoned store front beginning. His ability to keep the staff loose was to see us through some very difficult times over the coming years.

Jack could be very informal with people he trusted, even employees, and, he went way out of his way to make me feel comfortable, from our very first substantive meeting. His idea was to take the same strategies of organizational development and productivity improvement, bureau by bureau throughout Field Services. Catherine, or Katie as she was known to her multitude of friends and admirers, would be in charge, and, Dr. Marlberger stopped by to express his best wishes for success and his intention of moving the program beyond Field Services. Thus, after six months, I had a promotion, I was now known as "Coordinator of Research", new responsibilities and I was now housed in the Marble Palace, my home for the next ten years.

Katie Havrilesky is a superb human being, one of the most intelligent, articulate and honest people I know. It would take a chapter just to relate her accomplishments and professional preparation that led her to the position of Jack Rosser's Deputy. Her career in state government was marked by constant success and, she was the highest ranking woman in the entire establishment. The "movement" for equality and diversity could not have had a finer flag bearer.

Katie took me around to all of the bureau chiefs to discuss our plans and provide me with a first hand look at what I would be dealing with. It was amazing how many people seemed to be distrustful of any improvement initiative. I am sure it was a combination of several factors: some of the really veteran chiefs saw their bureaus as fiefdoms and were willing to wait us out; others detested Katie because she was a woman, and a very senior staff member, and me along with her; and a couple were probably just afraid as this was clearly a new age and one they were not equipped to understand let alone cope with. In fact, they were probably peed off and scared all at once.

A couple of years with Ted Amidon had taught me an awful lot about behavioral psychology and it was amazing seeing those lessons in a real life situation. After only a few of sessions with Katie it was plain what a remarkable human being and superb professional she was, and, how fortunate I was to have her as my superior. She was not only knowledgeable, her ability to interact and articulate difficult concepts was terrific, and, she was a supportive and friendly person. Those people who attempted to tune her out, even though she was their chief, were wasting a remarkable resource, someone who tended to the positive with whomever she worked; looked to raise the capacity of people by building on their strengths rather than attack them for their weaknesses. And yet, there were those who saw her as a threat because of her gender and her ability.

There were also a bunch of stars, people I already knew. Fred Price had assumed control of Teacher Certification as Ward had accepted a job with the Feds, Region II of the US Office of Education, which included New Jersey and immediately gave me an entry into the world of federal education programs. Chuck Rutledge had moved to Monmouth College and Leon was running his own shop as was Wally Colander, who was now the food bureau chief. Danny was on his way to Grants Management and Educational Technology picked up a new director, Joseph DeStefano, someone really cast in Katie's mold, so there were all these development platforms with top achievers as leaders, people ready to embark on a program of productivity improvement. The plan of attack was simple, begin with the strong situations, field testing templates, training and moving ahead, while building readiness in their slower sisters, preparing to move ahead with or without their reluctant leadership. A number of fortuitous retirements occurred along the way.

Gradually we got things rolling and it became a very happy and productive time. Jack Rosser was pleased, and being a very generous person, made sure the Commissioner knew of our progress, which I doubt would have escaped Dr. Marlberger's keen eye in any event. Carl trusted Jack; he was his appointee and soon asked Jack to begin looking at other aspects of the State Education Agency. This was a very pleasant occurrence for Jack as he seemed to be the restless type, always looking for new worlds to conquer, one of many fine lessons he taught me. Jack was not part of the old boys club of senior administrators; he had not served as a county superintendent or been an active politician, although he, like Bob Boose, had a keen political sense. While the other assistant commissioners may not have been active participants, Jack had Carl's backing. With Katie to run Field Services and give direction and legitimacy to me, we started to broaden our efforts and Bob Boose, who had taken on a great deal of the day to day operations of the huge licensing and certification bureau, was able to rejoin me. As an example, consider the Bureau of Non-Public Education. This was a well staffed unit that provided equipment and some funding to non-public, mostly parochial, schools. It was an age of confusion in programming assistance for these schools, the politicians deferred to the mostly Catholic school population while the courts delimited the parameters of the assistance that could be provided, a real push and pull that continues today, although in a much more subdued manner. The real complicating factor was the ever changing case law that created decisions that generated new rules that led to changes in policy. The leadership of this unit had close ties to the Catholic school community, which probably had led to their appointment and my sense, perhaps unfairly, was that they were hoping to migrate to a plum position with that community when their agency days were over. With a program that could be declared unconstitutional at any time that may have been the only smart course of action. One fine day we got word the courts had ruled against the program provision whereby instructional equipment had been given outright to the non-publics, as they were known. The Department of Education was therefore ordered to retrieve all this equipment "forthwith". Non-Public School Education had just been moved to Field Services, a sure sign they were viewed as needing the kind of jump start that only Jack could provide and the kind of supervision that only Katie could give and so now we were stuck with this huge challenge. Jack sold the Commissioner on our answer, have everything inventoried against whatever records were available and then have the material collected and sent to regional locations where its eventual disposition was to be decided. We still had the Bureau of Federal Surplus Property attached to us for just such contingencies, as this was the medieval age of government, a bureaucrat for every season and reason.

Bob and I were hard at work on the remedial education area and thought we might be spared this effort but that turned out to be wishful thinking. The first problem was the fact that the records were not complete, not by a long shot. I advanced an idea of calling every recipient school and asking them to list the equipment they had received as we had to ascertain *its condition,* which would allow staff to complete a viable record and while engaged on the phone, provide directions for the collections that were to take place. I should have kept my mouth shut as Bob and I were now given the responsibility for the project. The director of Non-Public Education at the time was not only a very decent guy, who has unfortunately passed, but he was very methodical, some might say "slow". I can still remember him speaking to a huge throng of clerks who had been gathered from all over the agency and were sitting in our largest conference room with a bank of rented phones ready for service. He was supposed to give them directions and get them started. Instead he had already spent twenty minutes recalling the philosophy of non-pubic school aid when we got Jack to drag him out of there while yelling at us to get the "…dam thing done."

Now our colleagues had sent us the weakest people they had and we immediately realized we needed simple directions, quick training and an even quicker start as we had a very short time period provided by the courts. Bob was great in this role; he spent a few minutes telling them exactly what they had to do, why it was important and how grateful the Commissioner would be once the job was done successfully. At the same time, I was writing the protocol for how the whole thing would go down; from calls to forms to equipment shipment and disposal while Bob charmed the clerks and we were off and running. Some of the school personnel that were called were very difficult to deal with and Bob and I took our share of abuse on the phones, as both of us wanted to be seen as sharing the burdens of the clerks. I recall getting one nun on the line, asking her the condition of the equipment, only to be told "Young man, this is a *Catholic school* everything is kept in perfect condition here." Well, I had risked eternal damnation but we finished, and on time and the clerks seemed to feel some satisfaction, one telling me it was the first time the agency had trusted her with anything important. The climax of the day was a visit from Dr. Marlberger, class act that he was, taking time from his schedule to thank everyone. A few from that group moved to positions of greater responsibility and I like to think that day with us may have inspired them.

Thus the twins were reunited and we were to make our way across the agency and beyond.

HIGHER AND LOWER EDUCATION

At this time there were two agencies in New Jersey dedicated to public education, Higher Education, which had been created as a separate entity only a few years before, and us, plain old ordinary education, the K-12 people as we were known. Higher Education had a chancellor, Ralph Dungan, a very talented and complex person who achieved great things and was to perform a very vital personal service for me. There were great staff members in the higher education establishment, including someone named Burt Masia, who turned out to be one of the most courageous people I was ever to meet, and a future Commissioner of Education, Leo Klagholtz.

I never saw anything "official" regarding the split into two agencies but as with all large organizations with veteran staffs, there were plenty of legends. The most popular revolved around the concept of status, the colleges always tended to be elitist and there were many among them trying to upgrade their status to multi-purpose colleges and ultimately universities. There was also the State University, Rutgers, a fine institution, where status was *everything*. They thought this would best be accomplished, particularly given the somewhat "flexible' parameters to be used in the university definition, by having their own advocacy group, an interesting concept given the never ending monitoring role assigned to the "lower education" agency. Many of the staff of Higher Education assumed a rather snobbish profile, one of my colleagues likened working with them to the trials of a local police department trying to manage a complementary role with the FBI.

Another persisting rumor for the creation of the department, which was patently untrue given the timelines involved, was that the democrats needed someplace to stash one of their own temporarily, the Chancellor, Ralph Dungan. Even those who did not know the true history of this relatively new agency would know the tremendous capacity of Dr. Dungan after only a few moments in his presence. True, he had a background in politics, more likely, political science, and, he was a former US Ambassador to Chile, during a time of extreme strife in that country. Ralph was the first and only ambassador I have ever met and if he was the standard, then they are very special people indeed. He was extremely intelligent, had a huge capacity for productive work, and attracted others of quality to work for him. I found him to be extremely cooperative and on a few occasions when he asked for my assistance with one of his special projects, extremely easy to work for. He seemed to know everything that was going on, had an uncanny ability to make people believe in what he thought was the best course of action, and chatted amicably with staff at all levels. It was about this time that my mother-in-law died suddenly while vacationing in Acapulco. Her passing was bad enough but then a new nightmare surfaced in that each Mexican jurisdiction seemed to want a fee for processing the body for return to the United States. The money was bad enough but the prospect of not getting her returned, especially in time for an open casket viewing, was devastating. Jack Rosser learned of the situation and advised me to go se the Chancellor. It was amazing that he made time to sit and empathize with me. I was merely looking for someone in our State Department to speak with but he calmly said, "...leave it to me" and everything was resolved within a day! I think you can see why Ralph Dungan was a leader without peer, part of that magic time in Trenton in the early 1970's.

Bert Masia and Leo Klagholtz were two of Dr. Dungan's senior aides with whom I worked the most. Bert worked tirelessly on designing and maintaining academic standards for the colleges and universities under the auspices of the department. He was particularly vigilant lest anyone seek to promote their school by adopting a course of study that purported to lead to an advanced degree without the necessary academic rigor. Obviously this was a difficult position to be placed in, but Bert was more than up to the challenge although there were others who were more inclined to place a blind eye to the telescope, so to speak. I recall that he was instrumental in defining the difficulties associated with the new "life experience for credit" programs that began to spring up to grant doctorate degrees and stood his ground when an influential member of another agency was exposed for "earning" his degree under circumstances that appeared to be somewhat spurious. Bert left the agency sometime after this event and I am sorry to say I lost touch with him. Leo was another outstanding individual and a strong contributor to the fulfillment of the Chancellor's agenda. Leo was to return as the Commissioner of Education, of plain old ordinary education, many years later. In truth, I had no contact with him at that time, only high hopes, which were never fulfilled, I assume because of the zero defect mentality that seemed to permeate state government at the time. It was a shame because I thought Leo could have been a worthy successor to Carl Marlberger and Fred Burke, the true stars that I was privileged to serve.

The snob factor in higher education was not only hardly amusing; I think it worked to everyone's disadvantage. Now, I never had enough experience with a sufficient cross section of that agency to consider my opinions to be based on an adequate sample, but there seemed to be few distinguished personages. That was easily contrasted with our agency in which, at least during the Marlberger, and Burke administrations, there were real superstars through the agency, people with national reputations for excellence. I recall quite fondly Dr. Dan Ringleheim, the ultimate guru of special education. Dan could have worked anywhere, indeed, he moved to the US Office of Education during a period in which our leadership faltered. At the time New Jersey sent its special needs children to placements as far away as Texas. Dan was talented enough to author position papers that stipulated standards of service and care, tough enough to fight bias that was often, I am ashamed to say, quite daunting, persuasive enough to get legislation passed and committed enough to see the resource base for these precious children developed thoroughly. I never saw anyone among his successors, including a few friends, who were in the same universe with as strong an academic background, as strong a commitment to excellence and as strong a personality to drive home a point.

Drs. Gordon Ascher and Steve Koffler built what I considered to be the strongest program of psychometric evaluation ever seen in any state education agency. Their efforts resulted in standards that were fair, had a broad constituency and were used widely. Without them there would have been no statewide testing capacity, which in its early days was a model for state agencies across the country. Their strong foundation enabled another noted professional, Dr. Carl Johnson, as their successor, to build an impressive testing program and then guide its continued development through some very difficult periods in which political masters began to dominate the agency. Gordon unfortunately passed on, Steve moved to a sterling position at the Educational Testing Service and Carl was scooped up for a quite substantive local district job as soon as he made known his interest in leaving. Dr. Irving Peterson morphed the Bureau of Facility Planning Services from a graveyard of mechanical drawing specialists turned bureaucrats into a true resource based entity that built more than a thousand new schools at a time when our infrastructure was crumbling and tens of thousand of children went un-housed by ancient, ill equipped schools. I could devote an entire book to the stars and their successes and to their weaker descendants and their pitfalls, but, the key lesson learned was the quality of leadership. People like Dan, Gordon, Steve, Carl and Irv, and many, many more like them were not only talented and committed child advocates; they flourished because of the strong leadership directing the agency, people who provided the resources, and more importantly, the freedom to make things happen. When that leadership came a cropper, then the good people disappeared or became submerged in the new world of finding fault, scapegoating their own errors and passing the buck for their own shortsightedness. Stars do not work in such a climate, at least not as long as they can help it. Perhaps it was fortunate that the Department of Higher Education disappeared after only a short tenure, to be replaced by a rather toothless "commission". It may have evolved in the same manner as the state education agency and that would have been a sad thing indeed.

MUST ERASE BLACKBOARD IN SIXTY SECONDS

Every time I receive another tome from the New Jersey State Education Agency or one of their famous after the fact rule changes that include dire consequences, I cannot help thinking of what has been lost from the halcyon days of this agency, the 1970's and the very early 1980's, when improvement was the goal and providing assistance, resources, and encouragement were the means to achieve this ambitious yet challenging agenda. One of the most complex and far sighted initiatives was called the Performance Evaluation Project {PEP}, housed in the Bureau of Teacher Certification, honchoed by Bob Boose, which means it was well designed, staffed perfectly and run with panache. The purpose of the project was to identify valid and reliable indicators of performance, then train staff in the concepts and measure the incidence of occurrence. The project was ultimately to fail, due to political considerations. Many of the constituent professional unions thought or at least stated the project was a 'front' for an attempt to tie the outcomes to student achievement, which was a ridiculous, yet quite effective rumor. Over the years the unions were quick to support accountability but always with the innuendo that each new such program was, in reality, a cloaked attempt to measure teacher performance in terms of student growth. Now any psychometrician worthy of the name knows there are far too many confounding variables to establish a linear relationship between test scores and teacher performance. From time to time teachers would ask me for advice in dealing with a pedantic principal who, at the annual evaluation conference, would point to test scores and ask the teacher what he or she intended to do to raise them. I always suggested two strategies: first, "Ask me again after you sort out all those without parental support, those who speak little or no English, and those who do not even have a place to study"; or, "Beats the hell out of me, what do you suggest , and by the way, how about providing some demonstration lessons". These work every time! Well, this project may have been still born, and it was one of the major grievances the unions raised against the reappointment of Carl Marlberger, but it was one of the best conceived and well managed programs I have ever seen. Years later, as a management consultant working for Temple University, I was involved with several efforts with fabulous private sector companies seeking to identify key behaviors for staff in different titles, training them in those behaviors and PAYING them more when they consistently displayed these valued competencies. The public domain simply did not have that kind of patience. They had more five year improvement plans than the infamous "giant leap forward" pronouncements of the Mao era in China. Their management plans had the shelf life of cottage cheese and the guiding principle of total quality management, tiny little improvements being effected constantly by the rank and file, simply was not in the works. In the public domain, the rank and file sits back and takes potshots at each attempt at improvement and then uses its political clout when things look too good. The PEP program was generating very interesting and promising results, had involved numerous task forces of experienced teachers and administrators and seemed to be perking along, despite some of the eccentricities of the participants. For example, I was asked to pitch in with some of the measurement aspects of several of the task forces, including the Art Teachers, all of whom seemed nice, although extremely condescending, and well over sixty. I recall our first gathering, after they had been briefed and the group dynamic of generating variables had begun. One woman raised her hand, even though I told them to just speak up, and she said we really only needed one variable: must erase blackboard within sixty seconds. When I asked why, she said: "Young man [I got that a lot in those days] everyone knows you can't have your back turned on those animals for more than a minute", and, the rest of them all agreed!

Another one of our major initiatives at the time involved the considerable programming of the Bureau of Adult and Continuing Education. A new director was named shortly after I moved to the Marble Palace and Katie immediately sensed we now had leadership to make things happen. His name was Tom Serydarian and he was well educated, experienced, and, a hard worker. Tom was the perfect choice for a key job at just the right time. Katie was a person deeply committed to the promotion of diversity and equality of opportunity, and Adult and Continuing Education was a perfect pallet for her efforts. It was a huge operation, providing vocational and avocational programming in virtually every community in the state and it offered study and licensing opportunities for many who would otherwise have been disenfranchised. The staff helped people become citizens, acquire their GED or regular high school diploma, and sponsored a broad array of programming in an area known as English as a second language. Serydarian and Katie were a formidable combination, testing, rethinking, probing and encouraging staff at both the state and local levels to go beyond themselves everyday in support of their clients. This was the first and truly one of the few times that I have witnessed a large bureaucracy devote itself to serving people, who mostly had no political power, with a strong customer service agenda. Of all the incredible achievements that may be ascribed to Catherine Havrilesky, this is perhaps her greatest legacy, and one that goes unmarked as the shifting sands of politics erase the achievements of those who no longer hold such power. Nevertheless, it was my extreme honor to play a part in this extraordinary effort.

One of our greatest challenges took place in West New York, New Jersey, a one square mile community that was famous, or perhaps infamous, as the site of the Aaron Burr - Alexander Hamilton duel. I thought it was a very attractive place to live, and the view, right across the Hudson from Manhattan was just extraordinary. This community had a large population of Cuban refugees, who differed significantly from the common perception of people in such circumstances, in that many of them were superbly educated, having served as attorneys and physicians in Cuba. None were able to ply their trade in the Untied States until they acquired the pre-professional certification and were able to pass the required licensing exams, which of course meant their English proficiency had to be increased significantly.

Since a case {a very weak one} could be made that I had taught foreign language, and passed doctoral level foreign language competency exams, and was trained as a research psychologist, it became my project. The study itself was the subject of many papers, including my first postdoctoral monographs and it was viewed as a rousing success. I published a chapter in a major anthology on ESL and was even invited to speak at a symposium hosted by the University of Wisconsin. I remember being on TV at zero dark thirty, just before the pork belly futures report, but, it was very exciting and I have not seen the like since Katie's departure from the state education agency. Tom and I would work on a number of similar projects over the next few years, and, the effort was continued by his very able successor, Barry Semple, another bureau chief cut in the Havrilesky mold.

MOTORCYCLES AND MORE

Along with all of the work, and it was fun, productive and challenging, there was a lot of R and R. We had dinner together, along with spouses as frequently as possible, played softball together, hit the road for conventions, speaking assignments and orientation sessions in local school districts, as many of our programs and procedures were now ready for dissemination. Bob Boose had acquired a new home, on State Street proximate to the State Capital complex, and many of the gatherings took place there. You could stand and discuss key issues such as funding formulas based on improvement initiatives with state senators and commissioners and occasionally even officials such as a deputy state treasurer. Make no mistake, these were politicians and obviously concerned with reelection and advancement but in these sessions they acted without guile, without rancor, and without agendas, except the welfare of children. I recall, quite fondly, Senator Joe Merlino, a powerful, highly intelligent, and hard working elected official. Senator Merlino had a lot on his plate but was always interested, courteous, and asked penetrating questions. You knew you could count on his support when one of your brainstorms deserved that support, and, he had a sense of humor. Wally Colander, still serving as child nutrition chief, had purchased a motorcycle and all we heard about was the joys of riding as a "knight of the road". He also parked the darn thing by the back door of the main building when he was called to a meeting, sometimes blocking the Commissioner's parking space. One day we got Leon Colavita to take Wally to lunch, preparatory to their attending a bureau chief meeting with Jack Rosser. While the boys were enjoying themselves, Bob Boose and I hijacked the motorcycle and brought it into the building via the ground floor, straight to the elevator bank. Low and behold, we stopped on the first floor only to greet Senator Merlino, arriving for a meeting, who greeted us as warmly as ever, while squeezing past the bike to enter the elevator. He chatted amicably as always on the way to the fifth floor never mentioning the bike, even when he helped us remove the vehicle and we placed it in Jack's office, where it promptly leaked oil all over the rug, just in time for Wally's arrival for the meeting.

On another occasion, Wally's staff closed down a program in Newark and took possession of some really attractive wooden office furniture, much nicer than our standard issue steel grey WWII surplus desks, which he never let us forget. This went on for sometime until Jack got annoyed and had Leon take Wally to lunch, AGAIN. Three of us rented a truck, disassembled and loaded the furniture, and transported it across town to Jack's office, where it was ready for display when Wally returned. The best part of this was that none of us helped him get it back to his office. These were harmless pranks, sure enough, but just the kind of thing that built camaraderie and lessened the grating competition and turf protection that characterizes so many bureaucracies and, I cannot possibly conceive of the state education agency of the last ten years enjoying themselves or building such effective teams.

RESEARCH PLANNING EVALUATION AND WHATEVER

There are always serpents in a Garden of Eden and ours was no exception. There were rumors that the reappointment of our beloved Carl Marlberger, the person who created the chance for good people to take chances and achieve great things, was in trouble. The assistant commissioner for research, planning, and evaluation, a unit we had hardly touched, mostly because we hardly knew it existed, left, leaving a vacancy, the depths of which we hardly plumbed. Jack Rosser was asked to step into the void and that meant Katie, Bob and I now had expanded duties. In New Jersey, and all other states with which I am familiar, there is an administrative code, a comprehensive description of operating rules that complement the enabling statutes, that is, they give meaning to the stated intention of the legislatures. Our department of education had quite extensive code references, an entire title, except for R, P and E, as it was known, which read "RESERVED" for every page of every unit in the division, most of which were amorphous. It was no wonder, while the division was the home of some very talented people, the place was being run like a think tank except that there were no investors or grantors to have to satisfy with actual production. I think Jack may have become enthralled with the notion of hanging around with some of the truly talented people who visited from DC or other agencies and universities, but Katie, while always courteous and supportive, was much more realistic that this was a ship without a port or perhaps even a rudder.

Perhaps because they were smarter than most or perhaps they were educated with a better technical background or perhaps because nothing was expected of them and they had a lot of time on their hands, or I guess most realistically, because they were better politicians than everyone else, a lot of these folks were quite arrogant. Working with them became a headache as they volunteered nothing, aspired to little in support of the operational units, and they accepted no responsibility for anything. They were real sweethearts! I can see why Dr. Marlberger held off having us work for them. They stored data in shoeboxes, although they called it a "management information network". They smoked pipes almost exclusively, seemed to take pride in the fact that were universally distrusted as well as disliked by many; and, even wore a sort of uniform, black turtlenecks with grey slacks. More than half had beards and all spoke in doublespeak so it was like dealing with the Smith Brothers turned Gestapo agents.

Katie was never deterred and if she ever became frustrated by trying to capture Jell-O in her hand, that is, getting a straight answer or commitment, it never became apparent. After all, she had Bob Boose and me to turn loose, which she did. Boose was just as smart, way more political, universally liked and totally loyal to Katie. I too had earned her trust and had a better technical background than most of them so we were able to discern their capacity, identify the roadblocks to improvement, and begin to design some activities that might actually profit the schools. They had their hands in everything but got involved with next to nothing. For example, their so called MIS was responsible for the entire d/p capacity for the agency, which meant they scheduled a few batch jobs with the main frame computer located in the Department of the Treasury, that is, when they could get any machine time at all. As one wag put it, when we complained that we could not get anything done, "...there were too many piglets for the teats available". RPE staff seemed to be satisfied with this. It reminded me of some of our county offices, in areas in which public schools were in serious need of help, and yet some county superintendents consistently refused any staff. You see, if they had no resources, no one could expect them to accomplish anything. This gives you an idea of my initial experiences with RPE. Consider the case of state aid, a function you might think was crucial to the agency. Well, everybody did claim it was crucial yet there was next to no computer capacity to run simulations and no staff, *zero*, for the program. The agency, for years, had a very capable person who actually worked for the state teachers' union. He carried around these key data in *HIS* briefcase and whenever we had to work in this area, it meant getting together with him at night, after he completed work at his full time job.

We had a very strong curriculum and instruction division led by Dr. William Shine, a hardworking genius, committed to serving children by improving the quality of their instructional experience, and a former Marine Officer, who could not be cowered by any political threat. He also seemed to respect Catherine Havrilesky, whereas some other senior people resented her gender and perhaps the openness of her style, that is, she built constituencies and invited people to come along with her rather than staying aloof, or, the model that came to characterize the agency after our departure, threatening people into compliance. Dr. Shine had developed tremendous capacity in his division and was always very supportive of me, inviting my participation in his affairs and recommendations for change. He also commanded a great deal of loyalty from his people and had terrific deputies in William Brooks and Donald Beineman. Don in particular became one of my favorites, building a tremendously successful secondary education unit that achieved great things, in spite of having to deal with schools quick to make excuses why this or that would not possibly work in their situations. He would continue on in various positions of authority for many years, finally becoming county superintendent of schools for Camden County, New Jersey, one of the most challenging assignments in public education at the time, and he handled that as well as he did everything else he touched.

RPE controlled a lot of money in grants, Bill Shine had a large well trained staff ready, able, and most importantly, willing to put the resources to good use. We were all set to move on this when fortune struck us a mortal blow, we lost Carl Marlberger.

FORTUNES OF WAR

Dr. Marlberger was denied another term as Commissioner of Education by a very narrow vote, one vote in the state senate if memory serves me well. He was everything to us, at least those who were his appointees and had come into personal contact with this knowledgeable, articulate and charming man. We were numb when we learned of the news; there was a certain emptiness that bordered on despair. People had moved cross country to join his team, moving families and household goods, etc and now there was no certainty of even work being available. Those who were the most relaxed with the news were the staff that had put nothing at risk, those that had tolerated rather than joining Carl's movement toward progress. Carl was just magnificent, hiding his disappointment, refusing to blame the constituent groups that had blackmailed the senators into submission and trying to assure everyone that life would go on, just not with him or his programs. I still recall the scene of his farewell party, a huge crowd turned out for a night that focused on celebrating his achievements and his promise and to deliver a token of our gratitude, a new automobile!

The agency was now faced with a tremendous vacuum. We had two internal candidates who would have made excellent commissioners, Jack Rosser and Bill Shine. However, it soon became known that the governor's office was seeking external candidates, via a national search. Jack took a position as the Deputy Director of the School Boards Association, which became a spring board to a commissionership in the state of Maine and Bill was welcomed as the superintendent of schools in one of the finest systems anywhere, the Cherry Hill Board of Education. We were left with an interim, Mr. Edward Kilpatrick, a fine gentleman who had served for many years as the assistant commissioner for finance. I remember being called into his office along with Katie. I barely knew the man and was curious as to whether we were to be given our notices but just the contrary. Fast Eddie as he was known, because of his deliberate style, turned out to be quite articulate. He informed us he intended to serve as a commissioner rather than act like one, he told Katie he was counting on her especially to run the agency and he asked me to complete a number of special projects. There was another person in the agency to whom Mr. Kilpatrick assigned special trust, Bernie Steinfeldt, a veteran and quite capable person, who I came to trust completely as a friend and colleague. Bernie may have been the most unsung senior staff member in the history of the agency and served Carl, Ed Kilpatrick and Fred Burke with loyalty and tremendous capacity. I spent a lot of quality time in the company of these four people during the "interim" phase of my state education agency experience. Mr. Kilpatrick is owed a great deal of credit, not only for his years of service in the finance section but also for the posture he adopted during this "acting" period of our agency. While he did not feel justified, understandably, in beginning major new initiatives, he did not shirk from the awesome responsibility of dealing with the myriad of constituencies while acting, always, on behalf of the children. He realized that he was not Carl Marlberger so he did not possess the charisma needed to bring people along to work well beyond the safe operational limits they had set for themselves. In addition, Jack Rosser was gone, although Katie was there and taking on more and more responsibility. Bill Shine was another huge loss, a highly successful assistant commissioner in a key area, outstanding prior service as a county superintendent and as the director of the Bureau of Controversies and Disputes; he was irreplaceable, at least in the short term. We went from long term capacity improvement to chasing after a lot of ghosts: the vocational employee who spent his days selling used cars; the curriculum consultant who always seemed to be between airport offices and never quite reachable; the evaluation chief who was really working on his beach house most days; his assistant who seemed to spend as much time on active duty as a reserve officer than he did in Trenton; the various constituent groups all seeking to fill the perceived vacuum with their own agendas, e.g., the attempt to tremendously increase the number of student classification categories in special education, which would have increased tremendously the number of children sent out from regular classrooms; the physical education people who insisted that no less than 250 minutes of supervised exercise a week was acceptable, etc. Fast Eddie held the line and held it well and both Mrs. Havrilesky and Mr. Steinfeldt became the stars in this production.

The leadership of the vocational division also changed, never to be effectively replaced in my opinion, and that huge, well funded potential instrument of effective change began its irreversible decline, which years later would involve indictments, criminal trials and jail sentences, scandals that also involved staff of RPE, which also had to be reined in after years of little meaningful supervision.

All of this was soon to change because help was on the way, in the person of Fred G. Burke, or Rhode Island Red as Bernie had taken to calling him.

RHODE ISLAND RED

Fred Burke filled a room with his presence. He was a large man, but had a much larger intellect and a certain humility that approached self-deprecation. He was trained as a political scientist, had served as a faculty member at Syracuse University, and had been widely successful in Rhode Island, as chief state school officer, hence the nickname. He was every bit as impressive as Carl Marlberger and was also very successful; he put New Jersey schools on the national map, and all for the better, in my opinion. If we could not have Carl, we could not have done better than Fred.

Dr. Burke was many things, often simultaneously. I never saw him lose his temper, even when he had grounds to do so. When he was frustrated or disappointed, he still retained the capacity to listen and he never, ever, failed to apologize when he felt the error was his, or when he could take responsibility for the failure of a staff member. He was so dynamic and his mind worked so quickly that he often forget why he headed to a particular meeting so we started having someone trusted go along to keep track of his many thoughts and to remind him of the proximate agenda. I do not know if he played chess, but he was always many moves ahead of all the rest of us.

To me Fred was first and foremost a teacher. He had a very inspiring way about him, for example, he must have told me a hundred times, "You are a good person to work through a problem with". That was his way of offering praise along with a lesson, the team was always stronger even if it contained weak members so don't forget to bring everybody along with you. He restored old cars, which he spoke of frequently, and the lesson there was patience. He often told Bob Boose not to forget that most of the people he would be working with were not nearly as smart as Bob and that was a lesson we all could profit from. He was also constantly developing people to move on and out, into assignments of greater responsibility, which most of us feared somewhat but mostly dreaded because we would lose our close contact with Fred. His was the Golden Age of public education in New Jersey, and especially for the state education agency. Fred became a leading member of the National Council of Chief State School Officers, and, his agency won copious awards, many directed at yours truly. It was a terrific time!

It was as a political scientist that he utilized all of the tremendous skills. Fred had reached out and brought new groups into play, for one, the Puerto Rican Congress, which ended up with an impressive capacity as community advocates during my association with the group. The Congress took the opportunities offered and ran with them, naturally being impatient to make an impact and make up for "lost time". The federal bureaucracy did not work that expeditiously and there were pushes and pulls also with groups like the Catholic school establishment, which claimed a portion of every dollar directed at services. I was tasked with funding and problem solving and there were inevitable clashes. The Congress was viewed as too important professionally and politically not to support. Anyone else may have cut corners but Fred was building a strong foundation for future achievement not the usual temporary support for a passing fad. I did not learn until many years later that while I was working to make them legit and keep the effort going, some in the Puerto Rican Congress, those who had worked with my predecessors wanted me fired, for seeking some competition on the grants disbursement. As a matter of fact, I understand that the EIC's were placing the same pressure on Fred. I recall that he used to question me as to what requirements that we had to fulfill that were at risk. Upon my response, he would begin sketching intermediate steps, always forcing me to fill in the gaps. The question: "...if you go here instead of there, can you get to where you need to be?" was used frequently. He was training me to broaden my horizons, getting the job done, and keeping all of the constituent groups in the game. You cannot possibly appreciate the full impact of this description of Fred's awesome capacity unless you had experienced some of his successors in New Jersey, or, his peers in other states. I would also like to take this opportunity to state again that not once, in our time together, did Fred Burke attempt to influence me to compromise our commitments to the Feds and to ourselves. I would say that one of the most tangible accomplishments of my career is that I never was cited for an audit discrepancy or recommendation in my entire career. The template and motivation for this incredible run began during my formative years with Fred. I also do not blame the Congress, as, from all reports, my predecessors used them as a constituency rather than as a resource and they thought I was changing the rules, and, as most people tended to do in the public domain, it was easier, they thought to demonize me. It was a shame because some of their staff, such as Estella McDonald could manage development programs as well as anyone. Thus then the fruits of an appeasement policy, which is the most common characteristic I see in school districts today. Not the sort of environment in which someone like me could be either happy or productive.

Fred's creativity was just as spectacular. He would set aside time in his busy schedule to listen to anybody with a promising idea: using puppets for instructional purposes; early grade exposure to sex education via age appropriate multi-media; expanding the role of school nutrition programs to enable the poor and near poor to enjoy balanced and nutritious meals; and, one of my favorite, a targeted approach for the multitude of grants and resources that were available to schools, but only through the state education agency. His greatest achievement in my opinion was his successful fusion of these resources into a focused, powerful tool for change and it meant breaking down a huge bureaucracy in his own agency, one that had grown complacent and stagnant over the years. Fred was interested in services for children not jobs programs for staff, an attitude that seems ever more refreshing with each passing year.

CAPT'N KATIE AT THE HELM

Fred Burke prized diversity, and was outspoken about our need to be representative so he sent us to go and find talented staff for every area, people of all races, religious beliefs and genders. He quickly realized that he had one gem already available to him, Catherine Havrilesky. Fred had a bunch of weekend retreats, even before he took over officially, and hired some really great people to serve as group facilitators, strategic planning partners and implementation consultants. I recall that Katie was a bit apprehensive at first but soon proved to be a dominant player, simply because she was so bright, flexible and realistic. She was soon appointed as the permanent head of the field services division, was asked to continue her work in building an agenda for the RPE division, and, was a key advisor in ALL areas. During her tenure, everything and everyone she touched was so much the better and she accomplished all this with a sense of panache and a great deal of humor, all the while sharing Fred's propensity to credit staff for successes, and mitigating setbacks. Catherine shared many positive characteristics with the new commissioner; they worked closely and informally with key staff; were absolutely supportive of those making an effort and could even tolerate the few key people who continued to feather their own nest, even at the expense of agency progress in furthering their service base.

Well, it was back to work at RPE and it was then that I met Steve Blaustein, who, along with Carol Hearn many years later, was to be my one of my closest friends ever at work. Steve was working as a per diem consultant for the assessment people and it was obvious that he was bright and capable and, as we would shortly ascertain, he was loyal and hard-working also. Steve began working with me as Bob Boose had moved on to assignments of great responsibility for Fred. Bob was really on his way: county superintendent; state school for the deaf chief; Director of the New Jersey School Boards Association, for whom he provided their golden age; state commissioner in Maine; and, college president. I gloried in each new achievement for my friend although I missed him greatly.

Steve became my partner, he used to say "sidekick", stayed with RPE as an assistant to the new assistant commissioner Gary Geppert when he arrived some time later, rejoined me when I was "dual-hatted" to run the program development operation and serve as chief of staff for the new deputy commissioner, and was appointed as a director in his own right when I left the agency.

I am sure that some of the old hands in field services never had to work as hard in keeping pace with Katie, her sense of building capacity for leadership and problem solving was unlike any other I have ever seen, and no one could count on coming to work to face a business as usual approach. She achieved great things in all areas while preparing some units that were regulatory in nature to eventually spin off, thus freeing the agency to concentrate on program and staff development, as well as its traditional roles in controversy and dispute resolution and finance. As a consequence of her efforts, pupil transportation was made ready to move to the state transportation department, child nutrition, as she recast it, to the department of agriculture, and, facility planning services to several regulatory and planning groups.

It was with RPE that she had her greatest impact. You could just tell the "gents" as we called them, were more than content to wait her out and sit still until "one of their own kind", actual words spoken by a 'gent', arrived as the new sheriff in town. The testing program never really matured until Fred recruited Carl Johnson and Steve Koffler to run it but Katie cast its future and provided a very positive design. The evaluation bureau was always a lost cause but Katie kept them working on meaningful projects and they eventually were to play a legitimate role in the new school approval processes, at least after she got some new blood in there. MIS was better off not discussed, it became a huge headache for me, but we got more and more assistance from other agencies and eventually had some capacity there. It was with the development people that we had the great challenges and the greatest successes.

YOU WANT ME TO DO WHAT?

We had a very large and some would say, aloof, staff that controlled the federally provided funds for New Jersey, funds, which under Title III of the Elementary and Secondary Education Act, as it was then constituted, were designed to promote promising practices in staff and program development throughout public education. On the surface it was an imposing operation with monies being utilized, some would say skimmed, to support the educational improvement centers, which now numbered four, located "strategically" around the state, which meant where they could best serve the needs of teachers, as determined by the politicians. I would eventually take the rather unpopular position that the enabling statutes for these funds seemed to require their being awarded in a competitive basis, without "select allocations" to certain entities, but that is getting ahead of the story. The heart of the program was inviting local school districts, via a very competitive application process, to provide a research and development based initiative, with a goal of productivity enhancement. Everything was to be covered, transitional and transactional leadership, staff competencies, group dynamics, instructional techniques, etc. Every aspect of each project was tested according to commonly accepted validation and reliability standards; indeed, these were the only quantitative based programs I have ever seen on such a scale, during my entire career. The EIC's, as they were known, and which were funded heavily by these programs, also submitted quantitative based data, only theirs never seemed to get past how many teachers came by each month to check out materials etc., you know, the same sort of thing that a library does, but without millions of R and D dollars supporting them.

New Jersey developed a number of programs that passed the very vigorous national evaluation standards and each year, in the spring, the former staff had held a giant, and I mean giant, reception to honor their award winning projects, with speakers, demonstration activities and a terrific banquet.

Everything seemed fine on the surface but people who studied the program always felt the staff could have accomplished more. There were rumors that certain people did very well by the program and the staff involved always acted much more independently than their performance might have indicated, in fact, they were just obnoxious most of the time, refusing to cooperate. People like me were sent to fold their resources into programs supporting strategic initiatives of Fred Burke and they simply blew us off, not a smart thing because we spoke BS just as well as they did, had much stronger academic credentials and professional training in R & D, and were there at the behest of the Commissioner of Education, one of the most astute judges of character I have ever met, and, Fred understood BS a lot better than anyone. It got so bad that whenever you asked them to do something, they just smiled and said "You want me to do what?" It became a humorous mantra for them but in reality it became a professional death warrant because change was in the wind.

I am not quite sure what caused the breach between these staff, which held forth in their own building in the suburbs of Trenton, and the leadership of the agency, a leadership that had become much stronger in recent months with the arrival of one Ralph Lataile, a former colleague of Fred in Rhode Island, who assumed the duties of Deputy Commissioner of Education. Ralph, who came to be known, affectionately, as "Rotten Ralphie", was extraordinarily bright and just as perceptive. It seemed as though Ralph sized up the strengths and weaknesses of the senior staff very quickly. It was no surprise to me that he came to rely on Katie Havrilesky and thus I became acquainted with him, soon undertaking assignments on his behalf. It was about this time that the Title III crowd was removed; some had threatened to resign if they were not granted more power and some were just reassigned. The cover was a revamped ESEA statute that combined Titles II, library, guidance and instructional aid programming; III, program development, and V, augmentation support for the state education agencies, into a new title "IV". I recall being called into Ralph's office, with Fred sitting in, and told that the title three program was a "mess", that something needed to be done with title II and V and that I was the new Title IV coordinator, and by the way, I was expected to also assume the duties of Chief of Staff to the Deputy Commissioner.

Thus I came to pass from working directly for Katie, although her purview was so extensive that I was able to see her often, working on selected projects. I recall one time when we were traveling to Elizabeth, New Jersey, a major city that had fallen on hard times by the 1970's. The district was faced with one of the most challenging foreign language speaking populations I have ever seen, some 36 languages qualifying for ESL aid, and the state sent in a team to make sure there was sufficient capacity before committing a great deal of money, and waiving some rules in the process. For example, they needed a waiver because they were using a custodian along with a regular classroom teacher to try and teach English to students from Russia that spoke a rather unique dialect, and so on. Katie was at her best, leading people to much more sound decisions, providing strategic planning and management assistance and proving herself to be a real asset, not an easy feat in those days. We were on the return trip to Trenton in a piece of junk state car when an elderly man in a big old sedan pulled-up and motioned for Katie to lower her window. She asked me to stop because she was afraid the gentleman might be in need of assistance when he unleashed a stream of vindictive and obscene comments, centering on the fact that we were riding around on his tax dollars. I was appalled but the ever forgiving Catherine Havrilesky simply said, "He may be facing hard times and deserves the benefit of the doubt". I never saw her in a state car again though, which she had asked us to use as it was cheaper on the budget than reimbursing people for mileage. So, we had to drive to the motor pool, stand in line for a rolling bucket of bolts, often getting stuck, without a/c and often with no heat, to save money and be abused! Everyone but Katie forget the incident immediately, as she never took offense, saying it just slowed her down.

TITLE IV AND MORE

Running the ESEA Title IV program was the most exciting thing I ever did professionally. Working directly for Ralph gave me a lot to do, but the work was really integrated as being sent to fix a problem or conduct an organizational analyses often required R & D organizational development expertise. Getting things fixed meant mending fences with the folks in Washington and we set about doing just that, using contacts like Ward Sinclair to establish new contacts, travel down there with hat in hand asking for advice and quickly implementing suggestions so that their field officers could visit New Jersey, view the changed climate and take us off the endangered species list as far as federal funding was concerned.

We managed to do well right off the bat. We began building a staff, and they themselves used to refer to the group as the "retreads' as everyone came from a different program. First on board was Steve Blaustein, just the best friend and colleague anyone could ever have. Steve made sure the staff responsible for the records, finances, etc was just prefect; the last thing we could afford was any shortcoming on audits as investigations of the previous administrators were beginning. Steve was terrific and he ran most of Title V while he was at it! After a bit, Steve added Ted Robak, a tremendous asset, great athlete for our intramural teams and a hard working, reliable, colleague. Sarah Banks, who I would meet again years later as a PhD student at Temple, joined about the same time and ran the logistics side of program development, a tremendous responsibility that was in great hands. Bob Swissler soon joined, charged with directing the combined aspects of the broad-based former title II areas, took control of our new data processing and automation efforts, assumed the role of lobbyist, which he would later reprise for the entire agency, and was part of the troika with me and Steve, making decisions. Bob also did a terrific job as liaison with the Feds. I took care of the R& D projects as well as the top job, and Ron Lesher, a young PhD who had been buried in the agency, came on board to manage the comprehensive data analysis requirements of the very sophisticated validation process. New Jersey, under our watch, led the nation in validated programs and we were feted at national conferences and won all sorts of awards so I think it is safe to say that the gang did their job very well. By this time people like Art Merz were available in the county offices to provide a tremendous resources base for local districts serving as demonstration sites and Carl Johnson had come to Trenton to play a leading role in the assessment program. Carl came to work the first day, we immediately hit it off and I could always count on his support with the data crunching. There were also dozens of new staff; mostly young people who I hope were smart enough to recognize how fortunate they were to be around people like Bob Swissler and Carl Johnson. Of course, Bob Boose was moving to ever increasingly responsible assignment and was quick to support our efforts. The agency also acquired someone from the staff of Governor Brendan Byrne, Arthur Winkler, an attorney who proved to be just superb in every assignments and a close friend. Arthur was always available to "lend a hand", as he put it and his inputs were well ordered, highly insightful, and quite on point. He went from being viewed as a spy to a highly valued colleague who undertook key assignments. Eventually, he came to replace Gary Geppert for a while and eventually moved on to become the executive director of the NJ Meadowlands Sports and Exhibition Complex.

Not only did we set records, we had fun doing it and Fred was always quick to join in. Many of the weekend senior staff meetings were held at his home and he was often late, because he was out kayaking down the viaduct that ran in front of the house or working on one of the many antique cars he was rebuilding and he always encouraged us to enjoy the "lighter side " of things.

I recall that it became a tradition in my bureau to take everyone to the annual national convention where they could get some great inservice training, learn all the nuances in program requirements for the coming year and have fun. They also got a kick out of hearing themselves praised before a national audience! The senior USOE guy, D'Alan Huff became a particularly close friend of mine, stayed with us whenever he came to New Jersey and was always very generous in his praise. We all loved DC and hung out in Georgetown; at a joint called Clyde's. One year somebody got the bright idea to move the convention from Washington to Baltimore. We took an afternoon to visit Fort McHenry. Ron and I were history buffs but it took three cabs to get everyone there. The Fort was at the end of a heavily wooded, undeveloped, and potentially dangerous area but the national park itself was just lovely. It was a warm January afternoon but by 4:00 PM, it was not only dark, the place was closing. I dutifully took out the card I had gotten from the cab driver and called, requesting three cabs, only to learn that without a street number it was impossible to get a cab in Baltimore. The operator kept asking for a street number and I kept saying we were at good old Fort McHenry, that unmistakable national monument, only to be told "No street number, no cab!" I then called the only other cab company listed, got the sister of the first woman on the phone and was then asked to leave the now officially closed aforesaid Fort. We ended up walking miles through some of the worst slums I had seen and I thought the gang would kill me. Talk about cold! Instead, we spent some great time together in the hotel bar, laughing about the day. They were fine people and many of them did quite well with their careers.

I just loved running with that crowd.

POSTDOCTORAL TRAINING

Another benefit of the positions I held with the state education agency was the primo training and licensing opportunities that were available. The leadership, especially Fred and Ralph, knew that people with my responsibilities would get their work done, no matter how many hours were involved, and so they were anxious to broaden the skill base of their key employees. Many of the programs were offered by the federal government and that offered several benefits: the agency profited by having senior people become more capable, while at the same time demonstrating their own talent base to the Feds; and, where could you get that kind of training for free, to say nothing of the copious licensing and certification experiences that were presented to me, of which I was pleased to profit, by the way.

It started when I joined field services in my first position in the certification bureau. The federal government offered licensing programs in personnel administration and labor relations, and I attended every one I could get to. Some were on-site in Washington, over a period of several visits and others were offered in the regional offices in Philadelphia and New York. My next specialty area was in adult and continuing education with a complementary focus on language programming, which led to my West New York project, and its success, by all accounts.

On moving to Katie's service, I enrolled in as many licensing and certification programs, at the postdoctoral level, as I could find in operations management. Food service, transportation, technology, all aspects of facilities [location, layout, distribution systems, work families, lease/purchase], budget, financing, and all aspects of management were other areas of interest. Throughout my entire career, I stayed current with the field of program and staff development, assessment and research, which set me up to run the new Title IV initiative.

I am not sure how many people were proficient in so many areas but the agency routinely employed well educated and highly experienced people throughout its ranks, particularly during the Burke era. That capacity is long gone and its absence is noticeable by the manner in which the agency has operated for years: threaten and damn is their version of shock and awe. The agency no longer attracts people like Dan Ringleheim, that renowned scholar and advocate for special needs children. People came from across the country to learn from this man, and he was always treated with deference by even the most obnoxious federal monitors. We also saw quite a few well educated and capable folks in the local districts, this period predating the fad of mail order doctorates. Most people are quite surprised to learn that you may become licensed as a superintendent today without ever having completed even an undergraduate course in management so the position has evolved to the point of people calling themselves "CEO's" coming from a background of coaches, athletic directors, and principals. In the Burke era, it was like magic: programs and resources being developed, it seemed monthly, and then being disseminated widely, including what were then unique applications for the agency. For example, I had studied parallel compensation programs, where talented people are compensated for their unique knowledge, skills and abilities rather than holding management type titles. When Fred learned of this he set us loose on the Division of Controversies and Disputes, where we had scholars on a civil service salary guide. This experience was to help me immeasurably years later conducting a seminal study in this area for Temple Extension Services on behalf of Rohm and Haas.

I saw the specific value of all I completed in many ways: in getting licenses from the state board of examiners, which was especially tough on agency staff; from the Feds in virtually every area involving labor and R/D; and later on, in the Navy, when I was assigned to complete their post-graduate program in business administration, with a focus on operations management.

TEDIOUS AND EXASPERATING

Even casual observers of the Burke era are aware of the landmark litigation, ABBOTT versus BURKE, which caused a complete upheaval in public education. Young Mr. Abbott was a high school student in Jersey City and was the first plaintiff named in a long, alphabetical listing. There have been reams written about the case and the resulting trauma that resulted but here is a thumb nail sketch: the big cities, which claimed to be losing their ratable base, and therefore having to charge higher and higher rates on remaining tax payers, who were in turn trying to flee the scene, believed, and the courts agreed, that money could "level the playing field" as they began calling it, between the "rich" suburban districts and those students in urban areas. Now, there was no doubt that many urban schools were in disarray, but there was also strong sentiment that a lot of dollars intended to help children were being spent on ancillary areas, including some that saved city hall money and allowed even more people to be placed on the dole. The federal government has, since the inception of the elementary and secondary education act, provided funds for remedial programming, including resources for parent involvement and the various pull-out programs that became popular, e.g., having a child leave the regular classroom to get tutored in a subject while the rest of the class moved on to new material. This work is not intended to either chronicle or provide a definitive evaluation of these efforts but any honest historian must acknowledge the scandals involving use of funds for "parent involvement" that ensued and the tendency of the large districts to establish separate kingdoms for the federal programs, with a mirror bureaucracy to the schools. Many years later in Delran, Dr. Carl Johnson, the same colleague who ran the agency testing program, would show people how it should have been done; integrating resources with a focus on student needs not the bureaucrats. Now, the New Jersey Supreme Court, which lawyers tell me has always had a tendency to "legislate by decision" had deiced that money was the answer, even though not a shred of program evaluation evidence was available to support that conclusion. The powerful Law Center of the State University, Rutgers, had spoken and would get its way, which was usually the case. As an aside, I never met anyone in the agency in those days who disputed our responsibility to help the disadvantaged; it was just that the solution imposed by the court did not seem feasible, and, well, almost thirty years later, 'I told you so' seems appropriate if not gentlemanly.

A lot of people in the agency were first amused and then horrified to see how this was playing out. Directions were flowing from judges, aides to the governor and members of the legislature. The first phase was a real pip, each unit of the agency was asked to define its conceptualization, for its area of responsibility as to what constituted a "thorough and efficient" education for public school children, K-12, with special emphasis on urban areas. The phrase "thorough and efficient" education had been taken from the state constitution to bolster the case that "unbalanced" funding bases violated the constitutionally guaranteed protection of "T and E" as it came to be known, that each student should be able to avail themselves of. We came to call the program "Tedious and Exasperating" for obvious reasons, primarily because some of the agency people were going crazy. For example, the vocational educators, whom I always referred to as the "LEAN-TO U" folks, demanded eight hundred million dollars of funding to provide vocational opportunities for children under "T and E". I recall being sent by Ralph to "deal with those lunatics before they speak to someone" and it was not a pleasant beginning of our deliberations. Fred did manage to get a strong staff group together to work on procedures, resources, etc, and our validated programs were called into play. He also realigned our budget and hired a lot of young, talented folks to work in the county offices to serve as "school program coordinators", and we were tasked to provide them with training models and once again select staff such as Arthur Merz came into play as mentors and role models for these rookies.

This entire effort was to disintegrate with the departure of Fred. The agency under his successor, Saul Cooperman, seemed to be producing positive programming but those of us who had been privileged to be "Fred's people" knew better, that these promising programs were the last trickle of work produced by the master, Dr. Fred G, Burke. When the faucet ran dry the leadership model died and now over thirty years later, the legislature is still screwing around with "evening the playing field" by throwing money at what are now called "special needs districts".

CHIEF STATE SCHOOL OFFCERS

The council of chief state school officers was an organization of the state department secretaries and commissioners of education from every state and territory in the United States. During the Burke era, it was an immensely powerful group, with tremendous impact on federal programs and lobbyists routinely sought out the elite among the council members, for theirs were the ideas that ended up being presented to Congress. They held several full membership meetings each year, which were attended by the Feds, the chiefs, as they were called and one staff member. Fred took me along on a few occasions, and while it was fascinating for me just to listen to the many geniuses among them deliberate challenging issues, Fred was getting me ready for other tasks. There were subgroups among the chiefs, mostly informal, and the best among them picked only the best to attend these meetings and that is where the real power plays were made. Aides were not supposed to attend so Fred made me a presenter, I recall the first time at a hotel located at O'Hare Airport, and once the *agita* from my presence subsided and they started listening, I was "tolerated". It was really something, having people speak about me as if I were not there; with Fred patiently waiting his turn, eventually giving me the signal and off we went. It was on this occasion that I met John Pittinger, Secretary of Education for the Commonwealth of Pennsylvania, a great man and superb leader, whose programs are still benefiting the children of that state, some thirty years later.

Fred wanted me at these meetings, and other staff for subsequent sessions, because he had a plan, as always, to benefit children. His idea was to take the talent from the best run state agencies and created working groups to study and research key issues and develop solutions and programming. Working on these groups took me to North Carolina, Montana, Rhode Island, and Washington D. C. I also had the singular honor of representing him at a chiefs only meeting and got away with it, because Fred had foreseen the need to get them comfortable with someone, me, in the event he would be unavailable and thus New Jersey would not forfeit its participation.

EXPERTISE AND EXPERIENCE FOR SALE: CONSULTING ARE US

I was also selected as a presenter for an all hands conference of the council, which was held in Pipestem, West Virginia, a lovely resort located close to the truly awful mining towns where my paternal ancestors labored to earn enough to bring the entire family from Italy and resettle in Philadelphia. It was a great experience, we still have the crystal bowl that was presented to me in gratitude, and, the organizers took me by Cadillac to Keystone West Virginia to see for myself the very house in which my father was born and raised. I often wondered if Fred had arranged that for me, he was that thoughtful and generous.

I recall our first two trips to Las Vegas, in 1974 and 1975, speaking at conventions, once for the agency and another for Temple and being underwhelmed by the glitz of the famous Las Vegas Strip. I am not a gambler but Caesar's palace was a nice hotel and getting to see people like Frank Sinatra, Carol Burnett and Johnny Carson was kind of neat and people actually showed up at the workshops and most seemed to be listening. It was also the only time I came close to being divorced, or so I think. We were in the company of another couple each trip and after dinner the three of them took their turn at the lowest denomination roulette and craps tables available while I wondered around looking at celebrities. The second year, on the last night, we had attended a banquet and there I was again wondering around, when I decided to 'shoot the dice'. I watched for a bit, grudgingly advanced ten dollars for chips and soon I was winning, had champagne, was talking to a cocktail waitress and having a good time in general, except for getting yelled at for leaving my glass on the felt. Soon Blondie arrived and in typical wifely fashion said: "Don't leave your chips on the table; you are betting against yourself; and, who is she?" As she was picking up the chips, a security person arrived asked her not to bother the patrons whereby she said "I am his wife" and I said "I have never seen this woman before". It took a while to straighten everything out but I paid a severe price for my transgression.

These experiences led to my first assignments as a management consultant. There were the two Charlies: Charles Majowski and Charles Haughey. Charles Majowski had worked for Fred in the Rhode Island Department of Education, in R & D, and was monitoring what we were doing for his work in Rhode Island and North Carolina, both sites involving their state education agencies, along with ties to schools like Brown and UNC and Duke. Charlie and I became fast friends and he used me from time to time for various leadership training experiences with senior staff of his clients. He was very intelligent, quite personable, and easy to get along with, the perfect consultant! He was also very intuitive. He was having trouble one time with a senior staff member in Rhode Island, in the area of decisiveness. There was a cardinal rule among consultants about not letting the target know he or she was the major problem, the solution had to be folded into a pattern of work, most preferably training seminars. In this particular case, Charlie asked me to come to Cranston for a workshop in decision making and described the target. "How bad is it", I asked. "Well", said Charlie, "if he was a jackass equidistant between two bales of hay, he would starve to death." Charlie had a unique ability to convey mental images of problems and he was always on target.

Both of us came to work for the National Institute of Education, courtesy of the second Charley, Charles Haughey, originally of New Jersey. NIE, as it was known, was the premier R & D unit of the federal government at the time and they monitored the progress of much of our development work for USOE and started inviting me to work in support of their R & D teams. At the same time, USOE started using me to disseminate our proven practices to other agencies. Working in DC was always exciting. They expected a lot but treated you very well in turn. Charles Majowski and I were always lodged at the Statler Hilton. One very early spring morning, the two Charlies and I were playing tennis when a fourth asked if he could join us; Senator Lowell Wicker of Connecticut had beautiful ground strokes and a keen interest in public education. At breakfast that day he was remarkably attentive and his comments were unusually pertinent and he thanked us for our contributions and the tennis. It just seems that things do not work that way any longer. The assignment opportunities reached the point where Charles Majowski asked me to join him full time but there was Fred and my classes at Temple and it just did not feel right, even though people like Steve Blaustein and Carl Johnson were reminding me that Fred would leave eventually and the former title three crowd and the EIC people would be back to claim whatever was left, and they were right. Meanwhile, I did accept major assignments for friends, one of whom was Roger Gordon, Deputy Commissioner of the Florida State Department of Education. Working in Tallahassee was a great experience, the agency seemed to employ highly competent people across the board and, since this was a longitudinal study, it was possible to see the impact of my work. Hard to believe things have gotten so difficult when there was so much promise in those days.

There was a federal agency that worked even better than NIE, from a consultant's perspective, and that was Region II of the General Services Administration. There was a gentleman there, the Deputy Regional Commissioner, Thurman Davis, who began as my contact and finished as a dear friend. Mr. Davis was to progress quite quickly through the ranks and rose to the Commissioner of the entire GSA, a position usually reserved for a strong political ally of a president, but, which in this case at least, went to a very fine professional. Thurman may have been the most capable senior level federal government administrator that I was privileged to work with. My second book, Total Quality Leadership: A Training Approach, provides an in-depth description of our adventures together,

Between 1976 and 1996, I completed over sixty major consultancies, most via the Extension Institute of Temple University, the US Navy and Department of Defense. My clients included such notables as: IBM, Rohm and Hass, GE, ITT, Colonial Penn, the US Post Office and the General Services Administration. My second and third books contain descriptions of many of these efforts.

SCANDALS ARE US

Former senator William Proxmire passed away as this was being written. He was best known for his "Golden Fleece" award, "given" to recipients who best represented the rape of the taxpayer. Once, in the late 1970's, one of his staff called, purportedly to gather information relating to the staff running the program development bureau of our agency. I was quite taken aback, primarily because of the scandalous nature of topic and the fact that there was a full fledged investigation of some of those folks under way. While I had no first hand information about the alleged activities of my predecessors, it seemed that everyone wanted to interview me, at least to learn what we were doing now that had been so successful. These events were to dominate the last few years of my service with the agency and they had to be confronted without a key ally, Ralph Lataille followed Katie and Gary Geppert out the door, e.g., they moved to their just rewards, really attractive positions and, as it turned out, Fred was on his way. Gary was an interesting guy, a deep thinker who got things done. He did tend to be absent minded though, and he loved to eat chicken while he was driving around in his state car. The vehicle became legendary, known as the "chicken bone special" to the motor pool gang. Gary was missed immediately and the division never recovered its advocacy role, indeed there was to be a sea change.

THE FEDS

"On my desk I have a motto that says: 'The buck stops here'."

Harry S. Truman

CONTACT

When Ward Sinclair left the NJ Department of Education to join the United States Office of Education, it was a triple play. Ward got a nice promotion, with plenty of travel, which he loved. Only Ward could achieve frequent flier status, which was referred to as being a "Kentucky Colonel" on something called Piedmont Airlines. Our agency got a valuable contact, which was to become especially valuable when we had to prove ourselves beyond a doubt after the very public scandals that were to befall us. Lastly, I was given access to this behemoth of an agency, and all of its component and related parts. Before this my only contact with the federal government had been the draft board, US ARMY officer procurement and paying taxes.

Ward never forgot his New Jersey roots, at least when he was sure that the work being done would not prove to be an embarrassment to him. That meant that people like me always got the benefit of the doubt with regard to program evaluations and grants. Katie Havrilesky was especially creative and had a background in many areas and an active interest in a few more. I recall she would have Bob Boose and me working on something and before it was even done, there she would be, on the phone saying: "Now Ward, Joe and Bob are cooking something up that we really need funds to support and I am counting on you". When Tom Serydarian joined the staff we had still another kindred spirit wiling to invest the time to secure funding for big-time program development activities.

Our relationship with USOE became quite symbiotic. We were learning quite a bit from their formidable staff and, after a while, they began using us for program planning and as resources to other agencies. It all just seemed to flow quite naturally. Today it would take an act of Congress to secure all of the approvals to do anything cross-jurisdictional and I do not see anywhere near the same talent base at either agency.

STOPPAGE

The state education establishment actually closed down completely in 1976, state, county and local districts, because of a dispute in the legislature over passage of the new income tax. Everybody had to clear out their desks and leave, except for ten or so people in the state agency who had been deemed as having no direct impact on the schools. Nice huh? Well, I was one of the chosen few to stay on the payroll and our first task was to hop on the Metroliner train and speed to Washington to argue over something called "maintenance of effort". The Feds gave big bucks to states with the proviso that each would supplement not supplant state and local dollars. Someone down there came up with the big idea that since we were closed and not spending any state or local dollars on public education, we could not possibly meet our maintenance of effort obligations and therefore, this is the best part; we should immediately be denied federal funding. Fred had asked me what I thought and I told him that maintenance of effort was a promise, one that we had never broken, and that denying the funds would cause such and such harm, and that they really had no beef with us until we failed to make effort by the end of the current fiscal year, not the beginning of it. Fred, as always the gentleman, thanked me for my thoughts but said nothing else and began napping as we were on the train by then.

I had torn up my ankle after stepping in a hole while swimming in the ocean and was confined to crutches. Fred Burke was so popular and so important to the national scene, that there was a VIP reception awaiting us at Union Station, vans to take us to USOE, as it was known then, where refreshments were provided. There was even a wheelchair and a staff member waiting to cart me around! Trust me, you would never see anything like this in the present day confrontational environment and it was darn rare back then too.

After juice and donuts I looked around and we had only enough for a pick-up basketball game and they had dozens, including a panel of lawyers, whereas we had nary a one, but, we had Fred and that counted for quite a bit. He rose, greeted everyone with one of his fantastic stories and looked at Alfred Pierce, acting commissioner of USOE and said: "Al, I recall when people like you ran this agency and not the lawyers. I have brought none because I thought this was a program matter and could be resolved by program people, taking a common sense approach." Alfred Pierce wanted to be permanent US Commissioner of Education and it would have been completely understandable if he just turned to the lawyers and set them loose on us, but, he told a story and ended up agreeing with Fred, stopping just long enough to ask the lawyers to leave. He then said "Fred, what did you have in mind". Fred looked at me and said: "Please stand and repeat what you said on the train." I said: "I beg your pardon?" and he said: "You are a college professor; you talk for a living, just take care of this". I did, they bought it and all that was left was to arrange monitoring visits and financial records submission schedules. Since Mr. Pierce's regular job involved my programs, he left everyone else to his staff and invited Fred and me, along with the young woman wheeling me around, to take a VIP tour of the brand new Air and Space Museum, which was not as yet opened officially.

I recall getting home that night about 9:00 PM, my wife asking how this critical day went and saying it basically came down to donuts and juice, champagne and hors d'oeuvres at the museum and cocktails on the train! No one, believe me, no one, but Fred G. Burke could have pulled this off.

NETWORKING

Working with and for the Feds provided me with interesting and profitable connections and thus, great assignments. How about Mickey Mouse? As a child I used to wonder about Walt Disney's Magic Kingdom then being built in some beautiful place called Anaheim, California. It may have been on the far side of the moon as far as I was concerned because in my neighborhood, children had a hard time getting to amusements in Atlantic City let alone Los Angeles! Nevertheless, it was always a dream for me and the Feds helped make it come true.

With the opening of Disneyworld, the stage was set for the fulfillment of Walt Disney's true dream, the experimental prototype community of tomorrow, or EPCOT, as we know it. Mr. Disney envisioned a place where advances in community living could be developed, where children would learn while they were being entertained, where scholars from a number of disciplines would work in pristine conditions. That dream was really never fulfilled, Mr. Disney died well before the official opening, but his brother Roy Disney, accomplished a good piece of the better parts of that dream. If you have been to EPCOT, you have seen the eight foot high squash and other wonders as you have traveled about the attractions. There were young PhD students working with scientists in those areas and those programs had to be validated and presented to the State of Florida in order for credit granting programs to be established. Thanks to the growing network of contacts, I was a part of that and it was an incredible learning experience.

Another project actually took me, and my wife, to Disneyworld, I had made it! The mouse marketers had a brilliant strategy; if they could develop worthwhile programs in areas such as reading, animation and the like, for much younger children whose visit usually centered on the Magic Kingdom; then schools would be less loath to object to the children visiting Disneyworld during the school year. The goal was to develop really great programs and thus have the children receive 'excused absences" for the days of their visits, which I believe averaged four days and three nights in those days. Disney came to the NJ Department of Education and again sought me out. There was considerable resistance by some staff at the visit; a few wore "t" shirts that said: "You don't need Mickey Mouse, you have the NJ Dept of Ed". How could anybody be against the Mouse? It was an issue of alleged discrimination, that we should not be helping to "further the gap" between rich and poor. I recall one activist actually grabbing me and saying "How can someone like you, coming from humble beginnings consent to help them!" I said I was going to Orlando come hell or high water; that perhaps we could have a coupon day if that made her feel better. It was the classic case of criticizing something without offering any alternative. Sound familiar? For these folks, not trying, not doing anything but maintaining the status quo would be preferable to all that was accomplished. The programs went very well, have been attended by goodness knows how many thousands of children and seem to work equally well offsite, in some of those urban settings everyone was so concerned with.

That started a thirty five year love affair with Disney. My wife and I never vacationed without our children as they were growing and so every two or three years we would be there. I can still remember catching up with them in the park after a day of work and there they would be running around with a fist full of E ride tickets. Over the years I have had experiences with Disney University and the Disney Institute, that continue as this is being written and I have sent many of my MBA students there for training. We still experience the wonder of walking down Main Street of the Magic Kingdom. My wife and I also began visiting Disneyland in the early 1980's, as my naval career placed me in San Diego, where we still vacation part of each year. Once a trip, off we go to Anaheim, riding the attractions and just enjoying the children enjoying themselves. Then, there is my wife, enjoying herself as only a teacher of small children can whenever they are among small children. She is there when it opens and never leaves before it closes. I learned many lessons from Disney. The people in charge never lost sight of the goal of customer service, they never relented from the task of creating opportunities for their staff to be successful, never hesitated in providing them with the resources necessary to get the job done, never faltered when it came to establishing training opportunities to renew the creativity circle. I have never seen any reason why we should be willing to accept less from those placed in the privileged position of caring for children.

IN THE NAVY

In the very early 1980's, my work with the agency led to a commission as a reserve officer in the United States Navy. I had been asked to follow up on a project that was of interest to the State Board of Education, the access of military recruiters to high school students. Over the years, I have become more and more cautious about agreeing to provide access to students by anyone. I thought I would choke on my coffee while serving in Cherry Hill and receiving an unannounced visitor who was a rep from what I shall call a "men's magazine" demanding access to young female students over eighteen to be interviewed as prospective models! At the time, I was almost as skeptical about the military recruiters, even though I had volunteered for several officer programs during the Vietnam War. The federal government seemed intent on passing this legislation and our agency wanted to see if we could get a leg up on the process and help form the requirements to something we could live with. The requirement was to be ubiquitous, all districts serving federal funds would have to comply and whatever data was made available to employers and college recruiters would also have to be given to the military recruiters. We were fortunate in that one of the members of the state assembly was a gentleman named Joseph Azzolina. Now, Big Joe was also a Captain in the US Navy Reserve, a highly successful businessperson and one of the most altruistic people regarding young people that I have ever met. His idea was to draft legislation for the New Jersey legislature that would serve as a model, thus satisfying our concerns by helping to shape the federal measure. The result was very successful. It would later seem to be that Assembly person Azzolina was *always* successful when he pursued something. During the course of our deliberations, it was decided to invite military recruiters to visit with the State Board of Education. Four finely turned out young men appeared on the given day and the program went well, for a while. The Army Officer spoke of vocational programs for young enlisted with skills transference after their "hitch" was over. The Navy Officer spoke of the tremendous engineering experiences that would be available and directed his comments toward their career descriptions. The Air Force Officer spoke of the pilot training programs and the incredible life as a civilian aircrew member that would be the ultimate reward. All well and good until the Marine spoke; he kind of cleared his throat and said "We emphasize the killing", and whatever else followed was lost in the cacophony. It turned out that now state senator Azzolina approved of how I had handled myself on that occasion for he arranged for me to visit the main Navy recruiting complex in Iselin, New Jersey. I felt as though I was being interviewed and it turned out I was right. They already knew a great deal about me, thanks to Big Joe, and they were trying to ascertain my knowledge about the service and aptitude for a commission. About a week later I was asked back and informed they would be pleased to recommend me for a commission in a limited duty area, as a campus liaison officer, a post that normally would be reserved for minority applicants. At this stage of my life I was not interested in taking on something that was merely ceremonial. I did not want to seem rude but reminded them I was teaching at Temple only at night and that they had a military science department and, that I would not use my position with the agency to influence anyone at a local school district to give the Navy an advantage. I thought that would do it but they said they were just looking for an avenue to get a promising officer into the service.

A few months later I heard from Big Joe, who said the slot went to a minority after all. I thanked him and we went on working together on a really neat high school program based on a junior naval reserve training core component, with the support of Rutgers, a berth at an old naval station, and a surplus ex sub chaser for a training vessel. I let things go and about six months later I was called and informed that I was the unanimous choice for an "availability", a commission as a logistics specialist, with a real opportunity to serve the operating forces both as a reservist and with extended periods of active duty. I was in!

By April 1996, just a month before I taught my last classes at Temple University, it was over. The Navy did try to bring me back and I accepted a couple more assignments from Temple, but my declining health and the pressure of trying to do all of that and do it well was just too much and I actually felt relief more than disappointment at slowing down. I have my memories and there were more up cycles than down and most people tend to remember only what they enjoyed. My training *required* me to view such experiences with a more critical perspective and it always comes down to the people who you work with and for; those who see themselves progressing by furthering the goals of the organization they serve and those who try to progress by furthering themselves. I had seen too many of the latter.

I really enjoyed being in the Navy. For one reason, they let me work in areas in which I had been trained. This is not an inconsiderable matter as I believe few of us actually get to concentrate on that we which we chose for our life work. Two, they offered me all kinds of training opportunities. The ability to work and train in operations management at the highest levels and with really well known experts was just phenomenal. I returned to my civilian job with far greater insights than I could ever have imagined. Suddenly, after feeding six thousand people around the clock, I now knew a great deal more about meal planning, stock inventories and meal rotation. Keeping over a hundred thousand line items in the pipeline for a ship at sea taught me incredible lessons about logistics, and school districts all over New Jersey had been trained in that model by the late 1990's. Working on the Navy budget, in the billions of dollars, taught me more about finance, accounting and budgeting systems than fifty years of service as a central office administrator could, especially after the pipeline of training sponsored by the New Jersey Department of Education stopped in the 1990's. It was the same in every area, and, I got to go to sea.

The Navy gave me my choice of commissioning ceremonies, from a simple swearing in to something much more substantial the deck of a ship, if I could find one willing to sponsor the event. As it happened, one of our neighbors was the sister of a US Navy Officer, Captain Vern Rossen. I had met the captain on several occasions and when he heard I had been offered a commission, he offered me more than a deck, he offered me an active ship, his, the USS BUTTE, AE 27, an *ammunition ship*, and a ceremony with a great deal of pomp. I recall my wife was not thrilled about the type of vessel, especially when we saw one in the yard that had suffered a fire at sea, but, I could tell she really enjoyed herself. We received a lot of attention; there was a lot of ceremony and, a lot of partying at the luncheon we threw for a number of friends.

The Navy waived for me what they called the "knife and fork" course for direct commission officers, they told me I could teach it, and I met with various unit commanding officers and selected a duty station and began my service. I was soon sent to the postgraduate school for the program in business administration and throughout my career I was able to take advantage of professional development activities, primarily in operations management, but also in the skills one normally expected to find in a naval officer: navigation, communications, weapons, aviation, etc. During my first two years I had two extended at sea opportunities, on the BUTTE, which set me apart from others in my year group, those officers against which I would be measured when it came time for promotion. I was at sea for almost six weeks between leaving the state education agency and starting at Howell, so the Navy was always a tremendous source of extra income; I felt as though I should be paying them at times.

What I really wanted to do was qualify as a surface warfare officer within my staff community; no one had ever done that as a selected reservist and holding forth on the bridge and "driving" the ship became a dream, perhaps an obsession. I saw my chance when I was sent to do a program review and audit of the Navy contracting operation in Newport. I spent my days working on the assignment and at night I wangled some training time in a submarine training facility that I believe I cannot discuss further. The operation I was auditing was in big trouble and it required a lot of follow up. Since the surface warfare school and the war college were both located at Newport, I thought I would drop by and request the "books", a dozen manuals with over six hundred signature sheets covering everything from circuit boards for missile launchers to mooring a ship to a caisson, everything those who run ships for a living had to demonstrate as a skill or knowledge area.

There was a long course with many hours of classroom and practicum experience, with refresher courses, all leading to the examinations for the surface warfare designation. I figured I could teach myself the material if I could get the requirements listing. I went to the school, thinking they might prize my initiative and they looked at me as if I were from outer space. "I do not think a logistics officer is bright enough to complete this course successfully, let alone do it on his own," I was told by the OIC, officer in charge. I was tempted to let it go, after all, this was equivalent to passing the bar exam without ever going to law school, and, I even downplayed some of the problems this command had registered as a consequence of the audit. I did not want to give them an excuse for their mediocre performance rating.

I needed a training platform and a sympathetic CO and I found one in John Brunelli and the USS OH PERRY [FFG 7], which means the seventh ship in a series of guided missile frigates, a real warship! I had wangled this assignment by pulling out all the stops as there was a bunch of more qualified people. In fact, I was to be assigned to the USS PATTERSON, a less capable and frankly almost obsolete, ship but the CO turned out to be a jerk and the USS PERRY came to Philadelphia and fortune smiled again. Incidentally, years later one of my bosses in the pentagon was Vice-Admiral Joseph Metcalf. I worked for him on and off for two years and one day he took me to lunch as a 'thank you' and told me he had noticed that my record was 'exemplary" but noted that I had spent only a day about USS PATTERSON. I told him the story and while the PATTERSON was now razor blades, the offending officer was still around and I heard from the flag officer aides that he happened to run into ADM Joseph Metcalf one day and got an earful. One more on Admiral Metcalf, he had a tremendous sense of humor. He once introduced me as "one of his boys" to the NAVAIR guy, the senior admiral responsible for aviation. ADM Metcalf said: "Joe is from Philadelphia where the police force has more experience in aerial bombardment than your guys", a reference to the tragic loss of life and several city blocks during the administration of Wilson Goode.

Back to the PERRY. I figured it would be a good idea to work on the ship for a while until I built a reputation and would feel better about my special request. There was no active duty counterpart to me, the same thing that had happened on the BUTTE. In this case, the poor lad got terribly sea sick and could not deploy. They asked me to cover so that he could pass through this sea tour without being relieved officially and I was glad to help, especially as it got me to sea when there were no other reserve officers present. One day the ship was conducting OSCAR [sailor overboard] drills. When all the actives had completed their drilling, it was almost dusk and the CO asked me if I wanted to try. Talk about a deodorant moment! I said sure and the planets must have been aligned properly as I maneuvered the ship through a hard-over rudder major circle at full speed so that the bow glided with the wind right up against the dummy, earning the highest score of the day. Captain John Brunelli said I had the eye of a natural seaman and I figured it was the time to make known my request and he said "YES". Having an active duty ship in support meant I had no trouble getting the material and then I spent as much time as possible over 18 months getting everything completed.

The final exam was several hours long. You stood before a reviewing board of officers who fired highly technical questions at you, which you answered without references to notes, doing any required calculations in your head. The Navy may have bought $600 toilet seats but they would not buy any slackening of performance standards. I passed and there were ceremonies with admirals awarding me the pin; it happened so often for publicity purposes that I got tired of smiling. Trade magazines picked up the story and my career was made. No matter where I went after that, the initial response was always, "So you are the one". I do not know of any active duty sailor who did not enjoy and profit from his time with John Brunelli. I tried to highlight some of his magnificent leadership traits and accomplishments in my third book, Command Personality. For my part I was deeply honored to be treated as an active duty officer and twenty years later after illness had hobbled me severely, they came to take me to the twenty year reunion of the wardroom and we visited the PERRY, now covered with rust and never to sail again, but still the best looking ship I have ever seen.

Incidentally, many years later, still proudly wearing the pin and once again at the Pentagon, I was placed in charge of a planning group and guess who was there, on his last tour, the same OIC from Newport who had denied me the books. He ranked me so military etiquette required me to leave the first move to him, although I was tempted to ask him if he were bright enough to be with the group. He waited until we were alone and apologized for his "intemperate" remark those years earlier. Turned out to be a decent guy and proficient in some areas. He also knew I had given them a bit of break on that audit. I can't think of very many senior people I have met in public education since the Burke years that would take responsibility for anything but a rousing success, and then they are usually stealing someone else's thunder.

Another example of extraordinary people I met while in the Navy came on my last Pentagon tour. The admiral commanding my section arranged a VIP tour for my family and along the way they encountered Secretary Cheney, Joint Chiefs Chairperson, General Colin Powell, and DOD Spokesperson, Mr. Pete Williams. Mr. Cheney was very courteous to the family and excused himself, but GEN Powell and Mr. Williams spent a considerable amount of time pointing out key aspects of Eisenhower Hall and they thanked my family for sharing me with the Navy. I had met both of them previously, and am sure they had no recollection of those meetings and that they were simply being thoughtful in the presence of the family of a serving officer. I can also assure you that the nation is much poorer without Colin Powell and Peter Williams in its service. To me, GEN Powell was the Fred Burke equivalent in DOD and you just cannot over-emphasize the importance of that sort of leadership, and he is profiled in my third book.

Another reason why I enjoyed the Navy so much was the opportunity to meet and work with incredibly gifted and dedicated people. I could name hundreds but here are four that became very close friends and colleagues: Earl Johnson, Garrett Gummer, James Garban and Max Baumgartner.

Earl Johnson was already a senior officer when we met in 1982, he was a data processing executive with IBM, and would go on to ever increasing assignments of responsibility in his civilian career. He was serving the Navy at the time as the executive officer of the Naval Regional Contracting Command, located in Philadelphia, which was a huge hub for the Navy: hosting support services such as parts procurement and contracting for the entire service, operating ships, cargo handlers and construction battalions [SEA BEES], air stations, hospitals, Marine Corps units and one of the largest ship repair and construction facilities ever established. The area was a figurative gold mine for young officers such as me. The NRCC, as it was known, provided logistics support and approval authority for the operating forces of the fleet for the entire Eastern seaboard, forces at sea, and deployed overseas, from Keflavik, Iceland to bases in the Persian Gulf, which would come to play a key role in the first Gulf War. Earl seemed to be everyone's favorite, his knowledge base for both his civilian specialty and Navy procurement rules was unprecedented, his demeanor as an officer was viewed as an asset by every command in which he served or commanded, and his ability to shape young officers as top performers was to become legendary. Earl was the product of a Navy family: his brother rose to flag rank as a civil engineering officer and his dad flew at Guadalcanal, with a famous WWII fighter pilot for the Marines, Joe Foss, and became an attorney in later life.

Earl and I seemed to hit it off immediately. His advice was a marvelous resource and he paid attention to everything, in a very low key way. I guess the best lesson I learned from him was to work to increase the capacity of those in your charge to build the productivity of the unit. It was a lesson that shaped my career, especially as a college professor and management consultant as I came to focus on organizational development. It was also the guiding principle of my efforts in running large education establishments for school districts something that seemed to be all too rare in that environment. Earl and I have remained friends to this day; he wrote the preface for my book, Command Personality and I was most honored to serve as the *best man* at his wedding. It is via people like him that the best of the service goes forth to serve the nation.

Edward Garrett Gummer, or 'EGG' as I like to call him was a senior lieutenant when we met, also serving under Earl in the NRCC. My wife always asked me why everything in the Navy was called by a name no one else would recognize. For example, a senior lieutenant would be known as a 'captain' in the other services while a 'captain' in the Navy would be known as a '"colonel' in the other services. Not to digress, but once when she went on base to pick up a set of travel orders for me, she asked why they said I would be assigned to the 'bachelor officer quarters'. I took my shot and said that in the Navy when you were away from home you were officially viewed as a bachelor, but got shot down in flames.

Garrett was and still is a terrific person. He helped me tremendously even though he was finishing a graduate degree at PENN and on his way to law school. My background had caused the Navy to waive all of the lower level certification courses in procurement and logistics except the heavy duty stuff, where you earned licenses and signature authority, was something else indeed and EGG and I took a lot of the course work together. Garrett also went on to a very fine career, commanding some of the largest procurement units in the Navy and being recognized for his efforts with a number of prestigious medals. We served together at contracting centers all over the Mediterranean, were called to service for Grenada and during the UN incursion into Yugoslavia, and were billeted together in Bahrain in the Persian Gulf for Desert Storm. I found Garrett to be one of the finest teachers I have ever met, always striving to lead others to extend themselves. It is almost a shame he was so successful as an attorney because he would have made an excellent superintendent of schools. Perhaps that is part of the problem; we cannot normally attract people like Earl and Garrett to public education.

Captains Jim Garban and Max Baumgartner may be the two finest officers I ever encountered, of any grade, in the armed forces. Jim was a star football player and graduate of the Naval Academy, while Max graduated from USC and like Jim, completed several graduate programs. They are highly intelligent, deeply committed to the values of the service and worked tirelessly to achieve excellence, every day in every way. I met Jim upon reporting for duty at the Fleet Industrial and Support Center in San Diego, the largest of the largest procurement enterprises in DOD, its command structure and responsibility stretching from the gulf shores of Texas, north to Puget Sound, and west to Pearl Harbor, with assorted detachments around the Pacific Rim. The FISC touched on every aspect of the fleet, engineering, medical, aviation, surface and subsurface units, and support services and employed thousands of civilian workers, with hundreds of military officers attached. It was the plum assignment for the logistics community. Jim was the executive officer to Max, who had assumed the command upon detaching from the Aviation Supply Office in Philadelphia, in itself a very large, albeit with a different mission, inventory control point. As the executive officer, Jim had a multifaceted role. He took charge of the daily operations of the entire structure, he assumed responsibility for the professional development of the organization, and was ultimately in the hot seat for the recruitment, employment, advancement and evaluation of thousands of employees. In addition, he was a key player in the executive team of CAPT Baumgartner, which was crucial because he was a kindred soul to Max and because the FISC was undergoing a complete transformation of roles, from a warehouse holding, materials procurement, industrial contracting enterprise to a newly conceived enterprise based on modern methods of customer service, logistics and auditing.

Keeping a huge organization such as the FISC operational while changing its very culture and leading it to a contemporary approach is an enormous chore, one not normally pursued successfully but the FISC had an ace in the hole, Max Baumgartner. Articulate, passionate about his service, knowledgeable, personable, willing to let people explore their limits even if they occasionally fell short and constantly striving to improve the capacity of his staff are the leadership traits I would ascribe to Captain Baumgartner. In addition, he led through the use of referent power, e.g., people in this huge bureaucracy who had spent years working in a system in which control was prized over initiative, came to respect Max because of his knowledge, his very visible successes and because they believed he was worthy of their support. He had held every highly competitive billet as his career progressed, been promoted to each grade at the earliest possible time, and screened early for flag rank. The FISC folks knew they had a proven winner. I think this is tremendously relevant to the context of this book for I have not seen such leadership being exhibited at the highest levels of the education bureaucracy since the days of Fred Burke.

Max had invited me to begin working in San Diego based on our collaborative efforts at ASO and I enjoyed the assignment tremendously. Military command tours are relatively short in the life span of an organization, three years, so many recalcitrant types, especially those intent on holding onto their fiefdoms rather than progressing, try to wait out anyone working as a change agent. This is a real problem in public education where tenure makes progress resemble glacier speed, if any forward movement at all is possible. Despite this limitation, Max developed people beyond their own estimation; he brought many along with him in the pursuit of excellence, recruited many more to join him and was eminently successful. That story alone would require a monograph but I think two examples shall suffice in describing how modern tools of organizational development can shape a bureaucracy and why the absence of such techniques from our education bureaucracy seems so appalling. We conducted a broad based job analysis, as a prelude to a privatization – outsourcing initiative, and we used my three piles theory, or as a grad student once referred to it, the 'hemorrhoids approach'. After comprehensive training, the staff went through an exercise in which they detailed the tasks absolutely essential to the fulfillment of their mission; then they listed that which they were tasked to complete that added nothing to mission fulfillment and finally, those tasks that actually got in the way of completing their assignment. Pile one was normally the least crowded, with pile two getting bigger and, the usual result I am afraid, the pile listing items that got in the way was the most populated, e.g., they spent more time on useless activities than not. In this manner we were able to redefine role assignments, eliminate a lot of unnecessary and actually counterproductive work and remove a lot of counter-indicated bureaucratic levels from the process. As another example we redefined the concept of customer service, which was actually a joke among the fleet units before arrival of Max and Jim. There was a bank of telephone operators who could not really answer any questions because they had no authority to commit the organization to anything and had limited access to the data files in which the client order was being processed, there being some eleven major data bases at the time. Concurrent with a sweeping modernization of the data bases and communication equipment, there was a complete overhaul of the staff, which was at the very bottom in terms of pay and prestige. Following the MICROSOFT model, we made successful service in this new call center essential to career advancement and we developed a career ladder within the call center and instantly raised the pay and prestige by making people accountable as problem solvers and giving them the authority to commit the organization as to materials availability and delivery dates. Max literally took the least and made them the greatest, in terms of his customers and when the customers began singing the praises of the new FISC, all constituents came on board. Again, these are complex tasks requiring commitment, courage and talent but they were successful and are proven. In contrast, I have never, ever, seen a school district in New Jersey conduct even a staffing study to determine the essential elements of work and core competencies that could lead to similar advancements. Instead, the districts are burdened with ever more convoluted seniority rules that seem designed to maintaining the status quo.

Still another reason the Navy was good for me, except for the occasional armed conflict, was the ability to lead and develop some really fine people. When I was assigned to the Keflavik, Iceland, Naval Air Station as the fuels officer, I got to serve with some pretty spectacular enlisted people. I found that paying them even some small amount of attention was enough to bind them to you forever, and some always transferred to stay with me wherever I was assigned subsequently. I started a professional development program and nine of the senior enlisted went on to 'make' chief petty officer and two received commissions. Making 'chief' was a really big deal. You had to not only pass but score extremely well in a very challenging exam that changed every year and making it as a part-time reservist was hardest of all. Even after you passed the exam the Navy might not need very many chiefs in that cycle and you had to start the process all over again the following year. Makes our teacher licensing programs look a bit timid doesn't it? People like Master Chief Larry Garafalo, Senior Chief later Commander Mike Mariakis, senior chiefs Larry Mitchell, Jose Morales, Charles Hewlett just to name a few were the bedrock of the Navy. It is to them that I extended the honor of dedication for my third book. All are retired and some are deceased but they once asked me how they could pay me back. This was after my retirement, when a few of them had assembled the shadow box, a container of various medals, rank insignias, etc that I had been awarded over my career. That was significant enough for me, but when they persisted and since I was becoming more ill by the year, I told them I would need pall bearers and now I have got that covered. Gentlemen, it was a pleasure!

Of course there were ample challenges along the way. Among the most interesting was a project involving Max Baumgartner and two admirals named Davidson and Mitchell, the tale of two flag officers. The job was to combine the two great Philadelphia region logistics centers, the Aviation Supply Office and the Ships Parts Control Center into one giant inventory control point. Admiral Davidson was the commanding officer at ASO, as it was known. He had been the long-term exec under Admiral Eichleberger, a no-nonsense, dam the torpedoes, risk your career to get the job done for the fleet, officer, and I think Davidson was cut from the same cloth. I enjoyed all of our encounters as I was there a lot. I had been assigned there numerous times as a reservist, been called for special periods of active duty to work on various projects for the center and, as a young officer, even served as flag aide years earlier. I also spent a considerable amount of time on board as a civilian consultant. I knew ASO and the people knew me. I had worked on the F-14 project. This was the front line air superiority fighter of the carrier fleet, a remarkable airplane that cost over $45 million each at the time, a plane that weighed in at 83,000 pounds, with incredibly complex systems, all of which had to be maintained by ASO. Admiral Davidson whose new exec CAPT Lonnie Mitchell was also just superb, asked me to come in and lead a team to examine ways of streamlining the procurement and support process for the F-14, which would then be disseminated to the other units, each of whom supported a major aircraft procurement center. We chose the F-14 to start with because it was the hardest aircraft to support and had the most veteran team. I knew these people to be highly capable and frustrated, because they could not use their talents quickly enough, having to sell every idea to layers of bureaucracy and decisions took forever to get and never violated status quo. This was a problem that infected the entire center from time to time. I had worked on the GECAL assumption of Colonial Penn Insurance Company and one of the key components of that model involved placing decision making as low as possible in the organization, particularly in the claims division, where an adjuster had to face a seemingly endless line of sign-offs from higher-ups, who initialed the paperwork while on the phone, thus documenting how important their role was to the process. Certainly not the GE way! We found the same thing at ASO, which had been established during WWII and which always had significant capacity among the worker bees. ASO had grown up with a rather large number of technical assistance units, as their charters indicated, infusing themselves in the bureaucracy and purportedly offering services such as 'expediting" the completion of priority issues. The first thing I did with these very senior civilians with a sprinkling of very senior officers was to explain that once an organization had to establish a role for expeditors, it was signaling that their basic operating systems were flawed. That raised quite a few eyebrows and if my track record, academic credentials and professional vita were not well known to these people, I would have been finished before I had gotten started. A few of the officer types were aware of a job I had done at the DLA procurement center during the run-up to Desert Shield. This was the main procurement center for DOD in areas that were not specific to one service, e.g., food, uniforms, medical supplies, etc., obviously a huge endeavor. I had taught several MBA classes for the senior civilian population on-site at DPSC [Defense Personnel Support Center] and worked on special projects from time to time, involving some of the officers who were now at ASO. With the preparations for Desert Shield going forward, DPSC was faced with the problem of keeping things crawling along at peacetime levels or suspending a lot of rules and getting the job done. I had showed that the rank and file had the talent, capacity and motivation to do the job right and many of the rules requiring endless sign-offs were suspended. Guess how many defects were recorded during the entire Gulf War period? None, yeh, ZERO. We were planning the same model for the F-14 and the preliminary results were also impressive. Davidson suggested we disseminate the model to other units and possibly even to SPCC, which was the most backward, poorest run, procurement and logistics center I had ever seen. It was headed by another two star admiral named Mitchell, who seemed to take an immediate dislike to me, while I had great difficulty looking past the man and respecting his uniform. There is a line in the movie "Other People's Money" in which the Danny DeVito character, who is attempting a LBO of a company whose product has grown obsolete, says: "I bet the last company to make buggy whips made the best buggy whips ever". SPCC built the best buggy whips ever and they fell farther behind the times as the dust settled ever higher on the computer in Mitchell's office, which I recall had the cover on every time I saw it and was too far away to ever be used conveniently.

I kind of thought that this is why Davidson had me work on the so-called interweaving project for Mitchell had been promoted to Chief of the Naval Supply Systems Command, which he had co-located on the SPCC compound, very convenient. He clearly had in mind to dominate the show. I would not say I was to discredit the idea, just provide a strong reorganization plan that demonstrated synergy and preserved the best of ASO. The ASO comptroller at the time of the F-14 project was CAPT Max Baumgartner, who was assigned to head the interweaving project, which became our first opportunity to work together.

I cannot ever recall enjoying an assignment more, at least until Max and I were reunited in San Diego. The job took months, I remember many 11:00 PM departures yet we could not wait to get back at it the next day. We involved large numbers of staff from both ASO and SPCC, using video teleconferencing extensively and you could just tell there was significant support at ASO while almost zip at SPCC. In fact, a few of those officers I had served with previously, confided they would not dare express support for our idea. We also had a mole in place, CAPT Pat Cummings, with whom I had served throughout the Mediterranean, who was a great officer who was highly intelligent and contemporary, and who was a big help to Max and me in reading the enemy camp.

Our big moment in the sun actually came at the end of a very long day in which we made our pitch to what seemed like a couple of hundred people. Lonnie Mitchell was just terrific, allowing Admiral Davidson to pick his spots. Finally as we seemed to have beaten down every nonsensical objection, Admiral Mitchell turned on Max and was obviously using rank to win an argument. CAPT Baumgartner, who is one of the smartest people I know, calmly addressed every issue raised and then turned to me and asked me to address the Admiral's concerns. It was brilliant. While I was in uniform, it was the civilian with the rep talking and I really wanted a piece of this guy, respectfully of course. Turned out the problem would take care of itself some time later when Admiral Mitchell resigned unexpectedly. Eventually another strong leader was to assume this position, Rear Admiral Lippert, who had followed Davidson at ASO, another great officer with whom I enjoyed working. Lesson learned: you just cannot recover from poor leadership and the problem is particularly acute in the public domain.

There are lessons in all of this for public education. One, the problem of leadership is a direct connect to the capacity of the superintendents in place. Two, how about allowing all of these terrific teachers more latitude and overcoming the prohibition of their union of paying top performers differentially, instead of the present model in which everyone recently alive gets the same percent raise on September 1 of each year. If we could recast the civilian bureaucracy of the Navy in an effective fashion, the public schools should be a snap. There are districts that have taken the steps to put real CEO types in charge that are working on this very issue as this is being written. Talk about a good idea to disseminate! Unfortunately, there are few Baumgartners and Davidsons to be found anywhere on the public dole.

In any event, by the spring of 1996, I retired from the Navy in April, in a wonderful ceremony hosted by Max in San Diego, after my last tour; and, completed my service to Temple University the following month, whose faculty also went out of their way to honor my work there. I continued to handle civilian consulting assignments for the Navy and for Temple, but, it was time to go and I still enjoy the memories.

There is a line from the movie, "From Here to Eternity" where the Montgomery Clift character is speaking to the Donna Reed character about his life in the Army, and he says: "Just because you love something it doesn't mean it has to love you back." I have really pleasant memories of the service, my time with Fred Burke, as well as my time teaching at Temple, but I have no desire to go back and repeat those experiences. The Navy moved on as did Temple and the state education agency, for that is what organizations must do. It is left to the analysts to assess to what ends.

CHALLENGES

The people I met, served, and became friends with were indeed an impressive lot. Those relationships served me well throughout the period of both my agency service as well as my career in the Navy. With the agency, there were the inevitable repercussions as people were replaced, power shifted, and honors were being bestowed on the new sheriffs in town. It is rather amusing in retrospect, because Catherine achieved marvelous things without any concern for personal honors, and expected as much from those who served her.

Now the people we replaced had their own constituencies in Washington and as many bureaucrats do, they went underground awaiting for the predictable shift in the power base. Locally, those folks who remained were always chirping away and eventually did rise again in positions of authority, I guess during the administration of Governor Tom Kean. I recall that period as the beginning of the great politicization of the department of education, although I have no idea whether such action had been ordained by Mr. Kean, who is still held in high regard by most citizens familiar with his administration. This surely was the time of the resurgence of several staff formerly associated with the EIC's, although, as we shall see below, events would soon lead to their demise.

Ralph Lataille taught me to move without fear, especially if the evidence suggested that we were on the correct path. He also warned me that "they" would be waiting to reclaim their thrones, which ended up being a pyrrhic victory as all of the centers eventually lost their preferred status for funding and three closed completely.

My contacts with the Feds also helped dramatically only these were senior officers of the US Navy. I was always fortunate in that I had ample contact with the active duty Navy establishment. My schedule allowed me to accept additional periods of active duty and I was often called to work at very high or at least very visible levels on these occasions. There was a saying that we served the Navy not the naval reserve although there were an awful lot of people who tried to profit by maintaining a truly separate establishment, one that had lost the respect of the active duty community and was to struggle constantly to prove its worth. Naturally, someone with my training and inclination could not support such behavior. I recall my time on board the USS Oliver Hazard Perry. The commanding officer, Commander John Brunelli was just a wonderful teacher and a gentleman. He worked extremely hard for the betterment of the Navy and I think that quality served him extremely well as he was to rise to the rank of Rear Admiral [upper half: two stars] and service as Chief of the Naval Reserve, which was certainly the most productive time of that command. He knew of my interest in earning the surface warfare designation for logistics officers. As we have read, no "selected reservist" serving with the supply corps designation had ever won this prestigious designation. I could not have fought through the bureaucracy that wished to maintain status quo, that is, prevent me from enrolling in the program, without him. He was also just superb when it came to integrating the reserve with the active duty components and achieving a whole that was much stronger than the sum of its parts. When I joined the PERRY ward-room, there was a terrific reserve "coordinator" by the name of Mike Powers, or "Shorty" as he was known. Commander Powers had no agenda other than to serve CDR Brunelli, no ambition except to make the PERRY the finest unit in the fleet. It was amazing how they worked together to make this happen, until, Shorty's term was cut short, so to speak, by still another shift in the political winds. I was already scheduled for departure but got myself relieved even earlier as the people who came after Shorty immediately morphed into two separate establishments, with reserves reporting to reserves and not cooperating with the active duty people unless it furthered some unfathomable goal of the reserves. Naturally, I supported Shorty and used my considerable contacts, or "back door" establishment, to make known who was doing what to whom. Now the Brunelli-Powers combo was a rarity and the active duty community came to expect a lack of cooperation, a diminution of resources. It took quite a while for me to make the rounds and convince people that I was of the Brunelli-Powers mold, and once they recognized my orientation, I was set no matter what challenge came along. For example, there was the time when a former mentor who seemed to have lost his way, asked me to amend a report I had written for an active duty command, at the request of the active duty admiral in charge, who incidentally had anticipated my findings. Now the fly in the ointment was this reserve officer who attempted to interfere with the process. He was honest enough to tell me that a report that was so critical might impact on his ability to secure a much needed period of prolonged active duty. When he hinted that he might influence my fitness report if I did not acquiesce, I went to the admiral who supported me and when I got heat from the reserve establishment, I filed charges against the errant officer, knowing I had the full support of the DC crowd. Unfortunately those on the wrong side of me in this issue tended to keep score and reverse their "losses". You just need to keep a stronger constituency than what they could manage and that is why the Feds served me so well during these two powerful and consuming periods of my life, as we shall see in even more graphic detail as we read on.

FRIENDSHIPS

Charles Haughey became a close friend and an active colleague. In addition to my work for NIE, we were able to convince his federal agency to support his presence in our agency for a year. I could devote a chapter to Catherine Havrilesky and Charles Haughey, they were great individuals and together they were down-right magnificent. Their work in teaming within the agency and with constituent groups has never been documented but there has never been an effort like it since and few approaching its success. We had validated programs galore but the work of Katie and Charlie got those projects disseminated within strict adoption rules and the success stories spread, all the while the EIC's were still counting teachers who came in through the front door. Charles, Charlie Majowski and I were in demand, especially by the USOE Division of State Educational Assistance Programs. The work that we were doing was affecting legislation on a *national* level and it seemed as though a "thank you" letter arrived weekly. Catherine and I were also having quite a bit of success with grants, mostly from the Feds, and primarily in the area of alternative educational programming. These projects were so successful that many resulted in published papers. It was heady stuff! Katie, Charlie and those they touched were just cooking for the sake of children and no one seemed to give a hoot about the politics, e.g., whose ox was getting gored.

USOE brought me into contact with a number of remarkable people, none more so than D'Alan Huff. Mr. Huff was a combat veteran of the second world war, having served as a young officer on the staff of General George Patton and was assigned to guard former SS troops after the conflict, so he had gained quite a perspective on life.

D'Alan impressed me for a variety of reasons but perhaps most of all that he took his duties at USOE as seriously as an officer would care for their troops in a combat situation. He was knowledgeable, helpful, but, most of all, fastidious about his responsibilities. Of course it did not help that he was coming to us on the heels of an alleged scandal. Once again, Fred Burke was magnificent, at the opening conference he welcomed the "assistance and intervention" of our USOE "guests". He introduced his "new team", told them he believed they would soon have as much confidence in me as he did and asked them to "spare neither their efforts nor our feelings" in making recommendations. Fred went on to state that he was confident that ours would eventually become the highest rated such program in the nation, given the assistance and close cooperation of USOE. In this instant he set a goal for us, invited their help, while making them part of the needed solution. The staff was worried, Steve Blaustein smoked so many cigarettes he resembled a chimney, because we were all new and these were, after all, the "Feds". I asked each area chief to do what I had been advised in my dissertation defense: start talking about themselves especially why they were selected to work on this program and then slide right into a description of what we had found, what we were doing differently, and what, with their help, we hoped to achieve. It worked like a charm especially when the first periodic reports had to be presented, and then they met Katie. I had no concerns about Ms. Havrilesky as her quite evident commitment to excellence, her charming demeanor and twin abilities to listen well and assimilate even quicker were legendary. I was concerned because the USOE team, aside from one female member who disappeared almost immediately with the library science staff, were men, almost all of whom were WWII veterans who had retired from the US Army and then continued their voyage on the dole, except for D'Alan who completed his military service and then accumulated quite an academic and professional vita to claim his current position. My fears were wasted as they all immediately hit it off, so well that I gave our exhausted staff a break, excused them for the rest of the day, and stood by myself and watched Katie go to work. Soon there was newsprint all over the walls with plans, schedules and expectations. This continued for the full week and before they left, we were told that if we accomplished what we had set out for ourselves, that ours would indeed become a model for program development that they would disseminate across the nation.

It took some time but that is exactly what happened, our agency came to develop more validated programs, in more subject areas than any other, a record that still stands as that level of R&D programming is long gone. We had people in from all over and each year at the national conference, many of our staff members were featured on panels, work shop leaders, etc, which tended to cut down on our time at the Smithsonian Institute.

There was the one conference in which D'Alan did more than just recognize New Jersey as the best of the best in this area. On this occasion, and thank God I was in the audience, he gave a speech about "…a man who had dedicated himself to excellence and to service". He went on for a while, named me before the entire assemblage, and asked me to stand. It was quite a moment for all of us and he certainly gave me quite a code of standards to maintain.

D'Alan, and his immediate superior, Alpheus White, spent a great deal of time with us and their onsite comments, exit conferences, and follow up reports were amazingly helpful. I never did learn the full extent of the supposed transgressions of my predecessors although there was a lot of questionable baggage to clean up, particularly among the EIC's. D'Alan always stood by me and he had confidence in Fred, who was supportive and responsive. I cannot recall a single instance in which Fred asked me to bend a rule, even when the recipient might have made a highly effective constituent.

NEW PERSPECTIVE

A good friend, Gus Ruh, replaced Ralph, and my duties changed, as Gus anticipated Fred's departure and began focusing on the county offices. Gus was to replace Fred for a while as Acting Commissioner and he reunited me with another former colleague, John Flynn. In this capacity I was assigned to provide support to the twenty one county superintendents, people in tough spots who had to enforce the ever burgeoning rules and regs being promulgated by the legislature while attempting to provide tangible support to local districts. I often found myself taking a hit on behalf of the agency so that the county superintendent could publicly, in front of his/her local superintendent, castigate the various new bulletins further constricting the flexibility of the local districts. Gus was a long serving and very accomplished county superintendent, indeed, he seemed to have created the role, and Jack was a dear old friend and colleague of ours, as committed to Gus as Ralph had been to Fred. We did whatever it took to keep the county superintendents happy as they worked their constituents and thus provided a larger constituency for Gus. I even had one call me to ask if I could change the apportionment of seats to a regional board of education because "someone had been promised a seat". Fortunately the county superintendent died before this became another hot button issue but I think you get the idea what was occupying my days at this time.

STAR WITNESS

D'Alan was also there after I had left the agency when several different sources brought pressure to bear to investigate the workings of some of the old title three crowd; most particularly the granting of monies to projects that supposedly did not earn the funds via competitive bids, which included the EIC's in large measure. When Gus' tenure as acting commissioner was over, he was replaced by Saul Cooperman, whom I never got to know really well. I had my eye on the deputy superintendent of schools in Howell Township, a large and still growing, well run school district, serving students and parents with high expectations. I was on active duty when Dr. Cooperman took office. Saul was noted for being a supporter of the EIC's and reportedly depended heavily on Thomas Hammill, the director of the EIC Northwest and someone for whom I had found nothing commendable in my dealings, either with him or his center. Since I was being told that Cooperman did not have a good reputation, indeed, I was even receiving warnings from people who had encountered him as a Naval Reserve Officer, it seemed even more prudent to take advantage of my reputation and move on. When I returned from active duty, Dr. Cooperman asked to see me and stated that Mr. Hammill, of all people, had completed a review of my operation and there would be changes, with the EIC's playing a larger role and that my position was to be eliminated. I thanked him for seeing me, told him I was hooked up and we discussed a roll-over date for me to complete outstanding projects in which he really expressed no interest, granting me permission to complete the work from home. He did thank me when I told him I would be in the office every day until my departure and sent me a very nice note praising the manner in which I had handled myself. Jack Flynn had already left by the time I returned to the agency and so I had time to concentrate on getting all outstanding work finished. It was a few months later that articles started appearing in the Newark Star Ledger authored by Bob Braun, detailing a great more about alleged misuse of federal money than I had ever been aware of. I had always found Mr. Braun's columns on the agency to be instructive and informational. When he interviewed me, I found him to be well-prepared, with no pre-conceived notions and fair. It was interesting that he neither offered nor did I solicit his opinion regarding my performance in re-establishing order and federal confidence in our R&D program.

I had just started in Howell when Bob Braun's articles started appearing and they were quite critical of the entire project development and grants process, with people not taking the trouble to ascertain that he was not talking about me or my team. There was an elderly secretary who made it a point each day of clipping the articles and circulating them around the district, I am told because it was her understanding that one of my tasks was to reorganize her and her boss out of a job. While Howell was committed to a strong program of development, involving a reorganization of resources, there was never an agenda to eliminate anybody, least of all our tattle tale. I recall that the articles appeared every few days for a long time and finally Braun got to me and was extraordinarily generous with his comments, repeatedly pointing out instances when I had stopped this abuse or that, risking my position etc. It turned out to be great press, but a funny thing was happening. As soon as my name did appear and in a very positive context, the secretary stopped circulating the articles. I assumed the task, dumping several containing highly laudatory references to myself, including Bob's summative description of me as a "hero', on her desk, telling her I understood she enjoyed clipping articles and was sure she would enjoy these. I did have the final word here, as we shall see in the next chapter.

Meanwhile in Trenton, all hell was breaking loose. This group and that announced investigations, all sorts of people wanted to interview me and I, obviously, was away from the agency. Fortunately, D'Alan had kept a perfect record and had been working behind the scenes both to alert the powers to be to the problems that existed and my efforts to clean them up. There was testimony in Trenton, which I missed as I was at sea on the USS BUTTE, an ammunition ship that fortunately experienced far fewer fireworks than were occurring in Trenton. One of the best or at least funnier aspects of the first set of hearings was the attempt by several very senior EIC people and some of the old title three crowd to depict themselves as crusaders who had labored intently to correct abuse. Ralph Lataille was later to tell me they would have all pointed the finger at me had not the record been so clear as well as so perfectly maintained by D'Alan. Meanwhile, Bob Braun was writing piece after piece including one in which he inferred that Mr. Hammill may have falsified data regarding non-pubic school participation in the grants application process. Wonder how that worked out for Saul?

Some time later I guess it was decided to let the Feds take the lead and I was asked to appear before the House Committee on Education and Labor, chaired by a remarkable person, Carl Perkins. I was in DC on a special period of active duty working in the Pentagon on the Navy's annual budget request, meeting with investigators for Mr. Perkins, chatting with D'Alan and with Ms. Marge Roukema, another spectacularly bright person, who was a representative from New Jersey and a member of the Committee. I cannot say enough about either Mr. Perkins or Ms. Roukema but perhaps I shall let it rest with a statement to the effect that they made you feel good about the work of Congress. On the appointed day, I changed from uniform to civilian clothes, Ms. Roukema sent a car, which took me to the Rayburn Building and I spent some interesting time with the members, in a hearing room with media, interested parties etc., just like in the movies. They were very generous with their comments toward me, thanked me for my efforts and I had lunch there after we broke and was driven back to the Pentagon. Mr. Perkins was so considerate that he took pains to have delivered that day, a letter to my commanding officer, thanking him for allowing me to testify and stating that I was called "...as an information resource and not as a consequence of any accusation involving his [my] administration of the program or his [my] person". A very generous act by a special person! And that was that, I never spoke of or corresponded with anyone on this issue again and focused instead on my brand new career in a very promising local school district.

DOWN AND DIRTY

" I am an idealist without illusions".

John Fitzgerald Kennedy

FOND REMEMBRANCES

He came to seek me out; there was a hug, and a whispered: "You are a good man to work through a problem with." He was gone, and I never saw him again. The long fight was over and we had lost a menche perhaps even a mitzvah, Fred Burke had left. A new administration, Governor Thomas Kean, widely popular and overwhelmingly elected, needed a prominent Republican not a prominent chief state school officer and I do not think he succeeded in getting either. There was a court fight over the definition of when a term began for the state education chief and then it was decided that the term must coincide with that of the governor and Fred was told his time was up. Governor Kean did succeed in politicizing the agency, for the first but surely not the last time, and Fred was certainly not the only casualty, just the most prominent, perhaps the biggest loss ever.

The times were a changing, even the departmental insider newsletter, *Counteract*, which was published surreptitiously by Carl Johnson and Ron Lesher, as an "anecdote" to the official rag, *Interact*, was no longer eagerly anticipated. Everyone had had fun with *Counteract*, even those, including yours truly, who were objects of the humor but it seemed as though there was no honest fun to be had any longer. Gus had a lot to deal with and some of the EIC people and the remnants of the old title three crowd were rearing their new found political alliances and it was time to go. I am not even sure how much notice Gus received that the new governor had appointed a "Republican" rather than a scholar or even a noted educator to replace Fred but Gus was given a new term in another county as its superintendent as his reward for bearing the burden of the agency transition before the Saul Cooperman administration.

And so the Fred Burke era had come to an end. I am not sure whether his style would have endured in the political climates that were to follow but I would not have bet against his continued success. He simply was the best equipped, the best trained, the best admired, simply the best, and, we never saw his kind again. The worst part was that the children of New Jersey lost him because the political stars were misaligned and few now know his name, some twenty five years later. No one ever took the time to pen a tribute, there were no celebrations or cars given as gifts; the times had changed in just a few years. It was once written that "…the greatest regrets are what might have been". I have never lived my life looking back, ala Satchel Paige, and so I looked forward to the next day, trying not to regret. I miss him all the time and hope others shall remember him as fondly, when they read this section, which is not a tribute but a memorialization of his successes as an educator and as a man. For me, the departure of Fred Burke represented the death of innocence for us all. We had been stung by the politically inspired downfall of Carl Marlberger, and now this, which seemed like a rebuke of all that we attempted. For the agency, the loss of Fred precipitated a crisis in leadership that persists to this day. The time of people who labored with a sense of obligation and duty was now ended. It was the beginning of the time when a sense of entitlement would flourish and, in time, this entitlement mentality would filter down to all levels and infect the school districts.

LOCAL EXPERIENCES

In the fall of 2005, as this chapter was being developed, I conducted a successful search for Terry Kraft and renewed our acquaintance, after twenty years. Fortunately, I found my friend healthy and quite commiserate over my failing condition. We both expressed regret for allowing the years to pass, we both recalled quite fondly all that had been accomplished when we were together, and he told me something that he said should have been stated long ago: "You taught people how to become more productive, to be more focused on improving the lives of children, and then you gave them the freedom to accomplish great things. That is why we supported you so strongly". I am not sure I deserved that praise but I could not have stated the case for inspired leadership any better. I use the term "leadership" collectively here for whatever we achieved was a combination of some terrific teachers, really superb, a few great middle managers, just a terrific chief executive, William Pelaia, and a strong board, cooperative and hard-working board members, including Terry Kraft and Basan Nembrikow, two of the finest I have ever been privileged to serve, for this was the time of Howell Township.

This was a steadily growing community in Monmouth County, New Jersey, traditionally an area dominated by strong school districts featuring the best administrators, high achieving teachers and very supportive and demanding parents. Howell was fast becoming another bed-room community for New York with all kinds of new transit connections bringing a lot of people into town. There were also a number of sub-communities in the township. There was still a strong farm presence, a significant second and third generation "home grown" component, including the mayor who used to remind us at budget time that classes in his day averaged 48 pupils. There was a sect of the Lamaist religion from Tibet and Mongolia who had settled locally after a long trek from oppression in their native lands, and a bunch of locals who made their living from the schools, many of whom of course always knew what was best for "their" town. The parents were very strong, I recall no one from council who ever attempted to advance themselves at the expense of the children, the board of education worked closely with Bill, and there were a lot of volunteers, including the chief of police whose name I wish I recalled. He was just fabulous; appearing at all the events, teasing me that my office was located in a remodeled jail cell from the prior use of our building, working with youth groups and was always a friend of the schools, even though he always asked me if there was not some way to cut taxes, just a bit.

In retrospect, I think the challenges were fewer than someone in my position would normally expect to confront because most people were supportive of the schools. A lot of this had to do with Bill Pelaia, a superbly prepared, veteran educator, who was eager to make his staff more productive, enhance the value of the educational opportunities available to the children in his charge and someone very open to new ideas. It was indeed, very creative of him to recast the position for which I was hired into a functional deputy superintendent of schools, hire a non-school person for the job, and then send me forward to work in every area of the operation. Bill was also working on his doctorate from Fordham, which shows the dedication and strong intellect of this fine administrator, and I came on board just as he was working on his dissertation. The board secretary was Herb Massa and he was someone I truly enjoyed working with, given my background in operations management and his patience, intellect and dedication to excellence.

Howell was blessed with a number of terrific staff and this offered an interesting perspective on the issues of privatization and outsourcing. There were a number of highly educated and successful mgmt types living in town and from time to time I was asked the question about subcontracting. I had learned years before that an organization should be loath to lose people it valued and that was especially true of our staff in the support areas as they were: flexible in their outlook, anxious to improve and never a burden financially. It would be an entirely different experience years later in Delran, when what some observers refer to as the largest and most successful sub-contracting effort ever was launched.

My first impressions were very positive, especially given the obvious talent base available via the teaching staff. There were some excellent principals, including Andy Rinko, and Dave Thompson and others whose names time has dimmed but I can still recall their performing admirably. We had our share of those who time had passed but people like Andy, who already seemed destined to profit by his time with Bill Pelaia and move to his own district as superintendent, made the unit very strong. The district was also amply served by a very strong special education network, headed by Hugh McCullough and there were various and sundry, and very fine, support staff people including supervisors of instruction, reading and media specialists and chiefs of busing, maintenance, food service, curriculum and personnel. There was also a lot of tension on the board of education, even though everyone treated me very cordially and seemed supportive.

That support may have waned a bit during the two weeks or so that articles began appearing in the Newark Star Ledger regarding alleged scandals in the NJDOE in program development, which people knew had been my area of responsibility. As was related earlier, there was one secretary in particular who seemed to take great joy in circulating these articles, until those mentioning me in a highly praise worthy manner began appearing. I did have the last laugh here, though. The old girl enjoyed taking what we called a "nooner" in the Navy, collapsing on a chaise lounge at lunchtime in the back yard, which was adjacent to a large vacant field. Now our custodians were always collecting empty wine and beer bottles from the woods at the end of the vacant lot, which were stored for pick-up in a recycling container. We had an in-house newsletter in those days and one issue mysteriously appeared with the old girl on the cover, snoring away in her chair, surrounded by empty beer and wine bottles! I shall neither confirm nor deny any other knowledge of this event.

At the first election for members of the board immediately following my appointment, there was a change in the membership of the board of education; different leadership and perhaps a different culture; although the change remained invisible to me, at least in terms of the support I was receiving. Terry Kraft assumed the presidency; Basan Nembrikow took on a larger role and people like Ellen Baines Johnson came on board. As I have stated, I had no reason to root for anyone; however, I spent the majority of my time with the "new" group and they were as effective a group as I have ever seen. They accomplished this in spite of some serious chipping from those who sought the same offices and that dynamic was to be a burden that the district had to overcome, and I think we did, thanks to the incredible professionalism of Dr. William Pelaia and a terrific staff. I just cannot overemphasize how capable were the teachers and support staff of this district.

CALM SEAS AFTER A STORM

It would not be accurate to say the storm of that first election ever subsided. At times there was so much rancor that it never even seemed that we could get the minutes approved, there was so much debate over who had supposedly said what. The district had hired a court reporter who worked late afternoon into early evening, mostly transcribing minutes, which had to be verbatim, even though only the actual votes were the only viable record that had to be maintained. The evening meetings went on forever and I guess we got by because they argued with each other, or at least some of them tried to embarrass the majority, but Bill and I seemed to be left above the fray and had our recommendations approved. After all, the staff was trying its best to serve their children and I think accomplishing its goal.

I can recall the first computer lab being setup in time for summer school, which I had volunteered to serve as "principal". They were Franklin machines, which the staff immediately put to good use. It was such a nurturing environment: the curriculum development process proceeded in each area and on a consistent basis, the evaluation of student achievement and goals satisfaction were both sophisticated processes and there never seemed to be questions or challenges about such work, just a desire to always improve. I can still recall Bill's calm demeanor, explaining each new initiative and always bringing the staff along with him, through some of the best group dynamics work I have ever seen in a school district. I recall only one labor issue, a one or two day work stoppage over a contract issue. Even this episode was tempered by levity. One of the principals called to say that there had been a water main break on the first day of the stoppage and that no buses could get through. "I have a perfect building, he said, no students and no staff." The other fun moment for me involved the picket lines. I set up a contest for best sign and we all had fun, saw the matter settled quickly and amiably and moved on without skipping a beat. That was a tribute to the work of Terry and Bill. It was also a very social group, often gathering on Friday evenings with spouses to share gossip, chat about forthcoming challenges and just relax. Perhaps time has dulled my memory but I have no recollection of any staff member that I wished was employed elsewhere. They were that dedicated and while I found any number of hardworking very dedicated teachers wherever I was engaged, the teachers of Howell, as a group, stand tallest. Perhaps it was just the times but the people were special and the district leadership created a very positive work environment, despite some of the penny ante antics of a few. We never had an occasion when an improvement strategy would be suggested and that would precipitate a visit from a union leader. It was a total school community, with everyone rooting for everyone else. For example, Terry's wife, Barbara, was a terrific kindergarten teacher and yet you would never have known she was the spouse of a board of education president. She seemed to work all the harder to spare us the burden of being accused of favoritism, even when she became the target for a few who were seeking board seats themselves.

APPALLED, AGHAST AND ALARMED

Terry and Basan especially were magnificent, fulfilling a leadership role while dealing with the "crazies" and being responsible to the normal element in all towns that does not care about the welfare of children in the public schools. They were patient, hard working and inherently bright and child centered. They had to keep the district moving ahead through arguments, stall tactics and some personal attacks. The meetings were held in the municipal chambers on Wednesday nights, and some people began calling the sessions "the best show in town", with one of my secretaries dubbing the proceedings, "the Wednesday night fights". Every week there would be a debate over the minutes and other mundane issues, this after several work sessions in which Bill always presented a strong agenda along with very persuasive arguments and Terry had invested a huge chunk of time and effort in bringing everybody up to speed. We moved quickly so if you missed a little, you missed a lot. The public meeting should have been a time to celebrate the tireless efforts of the staff and the achievements of the children instead of the constant wrangling. Yet there were people who seemed to feed off this discontent. There was a regular, a widely unkept woman, who appeared every week to announce that she was "appalled, aghast and alarmed" and proceeded to launch a tirade, perhaps harangue is a better word because I do not think she ever expected a substantive response. If she heard a rumor that some child had lice, she wanted free medical treatment for her children and her house fumigated. If some children got newer books, then her children required a complete set of brand new materials and so on. It was almost humorous seeing everyone else mouth the words "appalled, aghast and alarmed" as she started to speak. Makes you wonder if we do not need licensing before people can become parents. Then there was the night the board decided to honor me with early tenure. I understand this is a very unique tribute, one that I have enjoyed in all the districts in which I was employed. There was a crowd and people usually come out when they feel strongly and usually negatively. A couple of people had spread rumors that everyone was being granted tenure and that some of us were being granted fantastic salary increases. We got through some routine business and after the break I decided to hang back while Terry explained the basis for their proposed action. He did a terrific job while I pretended to be one of the crowd and actually egged on a few people and resumed my seat, to applause, only after the vote was taken. The district leaders were tremendous people who were not afraid to take heat for doing what they thought was the right thing. That sort of behavior characterized my experiences with the majority of members of this board.

While the board dynamics could have been improved, the district itself was moving along at a very promising pace.

MOVE FORWARD AND DRAG THE PAST ALONG

One of the major accomplishments of this time period was a functional reorganization of the district. The goal was to move resources from administration, especially where such resource expenditure had resulted in a somewhat redundant service base and divert more resources toward the incredible teaching staff, and thus the children. Having people like Bill Pelaia and Terry Kraft out front for this endeavor, highly supportive, aware and intelligent individuals, was instrumental to our success.

The district really had a superabundance of administrative staff, not unusual for school districts either then or now but really unnecessary with an involved, aware board of education, a very capable chief school administrator and just wonderful teaching and support staffs. There were directors of curriculum and personnel on board, who were very traditional and hierarchical in their approach, and several supervisors of instruction, who had enormous content knowledge but were entrenched and saw themselves in the chain of command rather than at the service of the teachers. It took a while to convince everyone that excellent teaching was our goal and that only those who produced such results or assisted others to get there were necessary. I have always believed that a school district should have as few people as possible not directly engaged in the teaching of children. This was the heuristic that guided our work in program development in Trenton and in Howell, I got to see the payoffs immediately. Losing people is no easy task, especially people who have been in place for a while. There is both a human as well as political element to consider and deal with. Everyone was made aware of the transition in philosophy, the expectations of service to teachers being paramount and a scope of work relating to those goals had to be developed and implemented. In the meantime, searching for other positions, both within and external to the district, counseling the staff and trying to restructure their perception of their responsibilities and building a new skill base was very time consuming. Some of the folks actually made things easier: they demonstrated neither the aptitude nor the inclination to join with us and displayed what I refer to as a "malicious compliance", a sort of sub-rosa sabotage approach. These positions were eliminated and the dollars reassigned to student computer labs, curriculum materials, and staff development. Eventually I held the curriculum and personnel assignments directly within the purview of my office. The schools were given additional assistant principals, that is, people with strong content knowledge were reassigned where they could provide some administrative cognizance while supporting the improvement of instruction. Even adding these jobs resulted in a net saving because of the reallocation of staff, and, these dollars were redirected to the classroom. The result was just marvelous, decision making was pushed down in the organization and people began accepting direct responsibility for what was happening in the classroom. Again, we had a great bunch of people and all that remained was increasing their role and thus their share as stakeholders.

TEACHERS ARE US

The signe quo non of this program improvement initiative was the heavy involvement of the teaching staff in the planning, development and execution of new curriculum and instruction efforts. My first step was to remove the administrator as the automatic chair of each of the numerous committees that Bill kept running, everything from planning inservice to new curriculum development and the testing of new analytical models and tools to teaching techniques. I have never seen such a comprehensive program as Bill put in place, with the strong support of people like Terry and Basan. Now, people earned the chair for these committees and it was not long before a very strong TEACHER came forward to claim these positions, and, I must say, with almost no bitching from the administrators. Most of the latter were terrific in their own right and saw this as an opportunity to spread the work load, take a position as a colleague rather than an overseer and, most importantly, earn a leadership position because of their contribution rather than a title. It was the perfect example of the strength of a referent power base model functioning smoothly. The work progressed at an unexpectedly fast pace, in fact we often had to slow everyone down to catch their breath, do some field testing and regroup. Another important aspect of this was to move all of this committee work to after school and pay the teachers for their time, with the chairs getting more hours given the preparation and extra effort they expended. Everyone agreed that the children profited by eliminating a major cause of teacher absenteeism from the classroom, something I believe that seriously impedes the progress of children everywhere. The next phase was to involve parents and who better than our teacher-innovators to make this happen.

Howell was just superb, a place to stay, enjoy, and grow; however, it was a long commute, we were not going to uproot the family and events were to provide even more exciting opportunities. It was tough to say goodbye especially after I was offered financial assistance to relocate and the round of farewell parties and gifts was remarkable. It was a truly humbling and enjoyable experience. Catherine Havrilesky, Fred Burke, Terry Kraft, I had worked with some incredible people and the best, and the worst, were yet to come.

GREATEST DISAPPOINTMENT

"These are the times that try men's souls!"

Thomas Paine

CAMELOT

One day at Howell I got a phone call from Don Beineman who told me that Cherry Hill needed an assistant superintendent, someone who had a strong background in operations management and program development. He told me that the incumbent was a trained engineer who had been most capable but was retiring on the very day he vested his second pension. Don said the district wanted to upgrade the position even more and he thought I would be perfect. I loved Howell, was treated extremely well and was tenured and well positioned. Nevertheless, it took me all of five minutes to dispatch a letter of application. The process seemed to go very quickly yet was extremely comprehensive. I was vetted in a variety of ways, had interviews with the superintendent and then a subcommittee of the BOE, visited with some of the senior staff and then they came in force to examine every aspect of my operation in Howell. There were interviews with parents, staff and some of the BOE, a few of whom refused to participate, telling me they would not accept a resignation. Normally, when you let people know you are leaving, or worse, hoping to, they can turn on you in a New York minute. Here it was just the opposite. Terry told everyone that Cherry Hill had always been my dream and that they should cooperate fully. Finally, members of the two boards met and Bill, Terry and Basan carried the day. I do not think Terry realized that the walls between my office and Bill's were very thin and I arrived just in time to hear him say: " I hope you realize that you are getting a superbly prepared and accomplished executive who is not yet forty years old. He shall be missed here." There was a subsequent meeting with the full board at Cherry Hill and they hired me on the spot. Talk about class: there was a reception to announce my appointment, press coverage, the works. It was even more than I imagined.

The superintendent of schools was a gentleman by the name of John McKeon. Mr. McKeon could have been a success in anything and had been in many areas, having served as a naval officer in WWII and as an executive with the family business. Jack, as he was known, loved children and sacrificed income and probably a lot of nights and weekends at home for the stress of running one of the most prestigious school districts in the country. In his spare time, he volunteered as a board member for the Friends School in Moorestown, NJ., again one of the finest private schools anywhere. Cherry Hill was still an entity with extremely bright students, interested and cooperative parents, and a superb staff.

I started immediately and recall my wife telling me she had never seen me so immersed in anything other than our children. Jack took me around the community, showing me the well kept houses, telling me the extent to which the parents supported their children and recanted some of the truly exceptional academic and athletic achievements that had come to be regarded as the norm. Jack also explained to me that the district needed to maintain a continuous improvement cycle in every aspect of its operations, particularly in the classroom. This meant that every dollar had to be saved wherever possible in order to maximize the learning potential of the students. In this regard, the district depended heavily on curriculum and instruction and the staff who worked in those areas. Indeed, the parents, children, incredible board of education, super-strong curriculum support, a bunch of terrific teachers and principals and people like Bill Shine and Jack McKeon, all added up to an unbeatable combination. While the pieces were all in place, and had been for some time, Bill and Jack became the enablers, the people with vision who had the courage to lead. It would not be too many more years before everyone learned that without such leadership capacity even all the proper pieces could not be brought together into something productive.

Cherry Hill then was a very successful operation and had been for some time, especially during the period of Bill Shine's superintendency, followed by the rather remarkable years of John McKeon. Bill was a legend during his time in the district and a board member, who would later become president of that body, Roberta Richterman, told me he was the model against which she measured all others and I think the district got even stronger leadership, given the challenges presented at the time, during the McKeon years. There is no question that Bill was not only dynamic, he was viewed by some as slightly eccentric. Knowing him as well as I did, that was just in a broad array of leadership traits that he presented to different audiences as situations were encountered. I remember that Bill displayed his usual courtesy in calling me my first day on the job, to tell me that I would be perfect in the role, especially as I could expand the position much farther than it had even been envisioned. That was Bill Shine as his best, an incredibly generous and knowledgeable individual, always motivating "his" people, even when he was several hundred miles away, working in another state! Bill also told me that he felt Jack was the best person for the superintendency and that I would both enjoy and complement his skills. That was some day: most of the board called, the president, Steve Barbell dropped in and I got a lot of time with Jack; it does not get any better, especially for someone who had waited all these years to "come home".

Mr. McKeon had spent his entire professional career as an educator in Cherry Hill as a teacher and principal under Bob Holl, another noted chief executive and then as an assistant superintendent during the Shine years. I had no idea that he was contemplating retirement at the time he hired me, and, that his greatest priority at the time was filling my position with someone "capable" as he used to say in his always understated manner. Ordinarily, someone, especially someone coming from such an attractive situation such as myself, should never consider a senior job in a district where the leadership shall change. I must say, with all candor, that I knew there might be difficulties ahead when I learned of Jack's planned retirement, but, after spending even a short period of my career under his tutelage, I would have come willingly even with the prospect of shoal waters ahead. Jack McKeon is a fine human being, served with distinction during a period of transition that presented great challenges in Cherry Hill, and always stood by me, one of "his people".

A SECOND REVOLUTION

Jack McKeon was absolutely the best all-around professional educator I ever encountered, and I knew a bunch of them. Ironically, another great performer, Carl Johnson, had been a science teacher in Moorestown N. J. and had taught Jack's children and to this day tells me how much he had gleaned from the experience of knowing and interacting with Jack in those days.

The staff in Cherry Hill never fully appreciated how well he protected their independence and professional integrity as parent after parent attempted to bypass these safeguards and exert undue pressure and even retribution against staff they felt had failed to fulfill their expectations. It was interesting to observe how he calmly dealt simultaneously with strengthening the capacity of a teacher or principal whose performance may have been lacking while at the same time, fending off demands for the demise of the same individual. I recall the parent who actually had her child classified by a psychologist in order to facilitate her demand that the youngster be allowed to attend one of the schools on the "better" side of town. As always, Jack calmly worked through such challenges, building staff capacity as he went. I guess having been a combat commander provided him with a certain strength of character unknown in most of us. Moreover, his calm demeanor in all circumstances resulted in the rest of us never really feeling any pressure, just the joy of employment in an extraordinary situation. The senior staff meetings were indeed something special. It was an impressive group, especially as Jack had assumed the burden of the weaknesses of each at the same time broadcasting their strengths while always crediting others for each success. Person after person brought him problems and he patiently probed them for solutions simultaneously solving the problem while building the capacity of the staff to act on their own when facing a similar situation in the future. For those who refused to grow in productivity, for those who refused to assume responsibility commiserate with their rank and compensation, he made adjustments, moving better people into key roles. The majority of the central office staff responded extremely well to this leadership style. People began doing a lot extra. I had started the practice of opening the office on Saturday mornings, providing an opportunity for the department heads, principals, rank and file etc. to meet with me in a relaxed manner, with coffee and donuts always available. People started gathering and soon others were doing the same thing and the positive reaction from the parents and board members at seeing staff cars present at the admin center on a Saturday reaped great benefits for the district. People did extra for Jack because they felt they owed it to such a leader, one who never let them down, who shared their burden and assumed their frustrations. His was a perfect model of referent power: he influenced others because they saw traits in him that they imagined as the best of themselves. I never saw an attempt to punish or coerce anyone; his reputation and title were enough to provide him with legitimate power and he employed reward power also but never intentionally, it was just that so many people took pleasure in pleasing him and receiving that positive reinforcement.

Jack also manifested another naval officer tradition to very good advantage, the heuristic of working with those you find in place when you assume command, giving each a fresh opportunity to prove themselves. I recall one day in the office being visited by a young student from High School East who asked to take my picture for the yearbook. I told him it was unusual in my experience for someone in my position to be invited to participate in this experience and he told me that the yearbook was to present the entire school community, recognizing those who had contributed to the success of the student body. In retrospect, the only time this privilege was ever extended to me was during my time with Jack in Cherry Hill. In any event, when he finished with the photo, he asked me where the building was with the "failed principals". I had no idea what he was speaking of and on further questioning, he said "… you know, where they put those people who used to run the schools." Subsequently, I found out that a number of the central office specialists had formerly served as principals apparently, where Jack was unable to raise their performance to his standard, he labored to find a spot where they would be able to contribute. Now many districts, too many in fact, hide inferior people, mainly to avoid tenure cases accompanied by collective bargaining troubles. I am not referring to that at all by this example. Mr. McKeon would never hesitate to pull the trigger where necessary; he just had the capacity to ascertain the strengths of a person, the fortitude to fight the bureaucracy to make a place for them and the foresight to rebuild his organization when necessary.

Jack believed in placing as many resources as possible in the service of the children, and, he always measured the impact of his investments, particularly in areas such as administration and support staff. We operated as a bare bones administration and were proud of it. I recall a principal coming forward to complain that his office needed decorating and Jack's response was a classic: "You should be out in the schools during the day and who cares what the walls look like when you are handling paper work at night". There is an awful lot of symbolism in that statement.

Jack believed in full disclosure to the public and we invited people into our discussion groups, something that I enjoyed tremendously. It was kind of neat, spending an evening in mostly pleasant surroundings, speaking to parents about the problems surrounding the maintenance of the high standards the community had come to expect. They understood that labor and materials for repair work had grown more costly. They understood that attracting superior teachers required competitive salaries and benefits, and thus higher taxes. Mostly, they trusted Mr. McKeon, not because so many had come under his direct spell, but, because they were intelligent enough and involved enough to see the results. The public wanted to help and they were very satisfied. As usual, he was right on target. I found people asking us to upgrade this or that for our staff or just being generous with their thanks. I particularly enjoyed my time with the Zone PTA, a rep from each of the twenty or so buildings plus a few officers, who got together in our small admin structure from time to time. These ladies were magnificent. They were smart, active, true child advocates and once they had reason to trust you, it was a joy to be among them. They also baked me cakes and that has always been a cherished memory. Whenever I needed to get something under way, after Jack and the BOE endorsed the idea, I would turn to the "Zone". I made a few phone calls, which in turn were repeated via a chain and soon there were two thousand moms working to get support for a new initiative. I recall one such effort involving a reallocation of funds, e.g., getting voter approval to spend funds for a new library at HS West, dollars that could have been used for tax relief. To me, this was a no "brainer", the high school in question was an older building, one in which we invested a good deal of money during my tenure, and there was a phenomenal staff, headed by my all time favorite principal, Dr. Joan

Katz. Joan was one of a slew of superb educators who "grew up" under Jack's tenure in Cherry Hill, maturing into positions of leadership. She was more than just admired; I can state without reservation that she was beloved. Everyone wanted to be Joan, or, they wanted her to find favor with them, or they were grateful just to receive one of the dazzling smiles she displayed whenever something terrific occurred for her students. The trick was to make sure the rest of the community knew what a bargain they had in Joan and that giving her and her senior librarian, Denise Wiltsee, another of my all-time favorite people, any resources was indeed a great investment. I believed people like Joan and Denise, along with Hal Melleby, Reds Jordan, Dennis Davidow, Barbara Banks and the rest of the great West team, took a dollar in taxes and turned it into ten dollars of benefit for the children. Joan and Denise were more than just effective, they were downright charming and we used the zone PTA to create a road show so that the entire town could sample the magic of these two people. The referendum was my first in that assignment and I was extremely proud to announce, before a hugely joyous crowd, that there would be a new library at West, for the question had been overwhelmingly approved. Joan and Denise and the rest of the staff were so excited; it obviously never occurred to them that they had just given themselves a tremendous increase in workload; all they could see was the great new opportunity for the children in their charge. I do not ever recall being defeated at the polls in Cherry Hill, at least the electorate never let me down, and neither did the staff either, despite the pressures that would be placed on them in the near future.

Jack's model was evident; he built a true community based support system around strong parental participation, defusing tax payer angst via the positive support of the active constituents and always building staff capacity. I think that his greatest achievement was perhaps intangible, the concept of value. People saw worth in what we were doing: every dollar possible used in direct support of children; strong teaching and comprehensive support for the teaching process; and a very visible, yet small, senior staff. For many years one of my hobbies has been writing restaurant reviews for fine dining venues, for a variety of rating services. After all the commentary and scoring for food, décor and service, the main consideration remains value. People will pay more to maintain a standard if they see value in the service or commodity being provided. Cherry Hill parents paid a slew of taxes, had huge expectations, and we had to use those circumstances to further the expansion of services for the children.

Jack's ace in the hole was the tremendous teaching and supervisory staff. The teachers were veterans, having worked in the district, on average, for many years, primarily because you had to be crazy to ever leave for anything less than a significant promotion. They had been selected because they were the cream of each recruiting class, often winning jobs against hundreds of other applicants. They had also been nourished professionally, given tremendous resources, capable building administrators, and I think most importantly, people like Jack McKeon honored them for what they accomplished on a daily basis. The district also made an investment in a group of the finest people I have ever been privileged to call colleagues, the department chairpersons and curriculum supervisors, to depict their collective functional responsibilities. The department chairs were working supervisors, e.g., they taught classes and provided hands-on training. Pick one, in any subject field, and they were an ace. I could publish the list of chairs from this time period and write a chapter just devoted to their accomplishments. There was Harry Zakarian, the science chair from High School West. I came to admire him very quickly, his entire demeanor was directed toward providing an excellent experience for his students. He was absolutely perfect in the role, his classes were terrific and he purposely rotated his teaching among all ability groups, and was equally fantastic with each. The rest of the department could not possibly find a better demonstration model for their own didactic preparation. As a department chair, Harry was like a lion in demanding resources for his programs. He was very intense in his commitment to excellence and quite meticulous in planning for every contingency, from funding shortfalls to the assignment of staff to situations in which their skills would be maximized and whatever weaknesses they possessed, mitigated, usually with Harry's able assistance. I have never seen anything before or since to compare with these remarkable people.

These folks were one of the first casualties of Jack's retirement, as they were soon swept aside in favor of more administrators, some office bound sycophants, hired by a less talented "leader". I am not sure the parents ever knew what their children were missing, people do not miss what they failed to realize was worthy, but the district was never the same. This is the tragedy of the all too familiar tendency of new people to broadcast their own supposed value by changing things, frequently not for the better. This occurrence seems to be ubiquitous whenever weaker people replace very capable persons as chief school administrator, change for change sake and form over substance. The children lose whenever this happens yet we, as parents, tolerate this behavior, because we are disenfranchised. The best part of this is that you may be sure that the boards of education are trumpeting the "achievements" of their new selectee.

In 1985 in Cherry Hill, the curriculum specialists were also special people. As an example, I would like to mention Dr. Barbara Solly, a very talented and charming educator, who was everyone's favorite in this role. Barbara knew a lot about children, about teaching, and about her specialty areas yet she worked like a demon to constantly improve. If a program was running at night or a weekend in one of her areas, she would be there. If someone asked for her assistance, they were sure to get it. It is hard not to contrast her incredible work ethic with my last years in Delran, where, it often seemed, you had to pay some teachers to even answer the phone.

Above all of this talent was John McKeon, forcing people, especially his principals, to expand their horizons, work smarter, and take risks by being creative and flexible. Jack was much like Robert E. Lee, known for his willingness to delegate, his uncanny ability to place the best possible person in the correct job, and his incredible foresight.

One of the major lessons Jack taught me involved dismantling a school district, something that had to be done, given the declining enrollment; something that few stakeholders would admit to needing. All the while this painful evolution was progressing we needed to maintain standards that actually ended up being strengthened as the expectations and demands of constituents were expanding. He achieved this goal in a brilliant fashion and sad to say, there was little notice of his accomplishment for two reasons: he was incredibly modest, deflecting whatever praise was available to others, and two, because he was retiring and the board of education was already planning to find their next great leader.

ABOUT FACE

Jack's retirement was a shock to me. You just do not accept a job like this, freely adopting the role of being the "point" person for a lot of touchy issues, only to find your mentor and confidant leaving. However, in retrospect, I would not have traded my time with him, especially after he took pains to inform me that he was comfortable leaving the district because he had successfully filled a very key job before his departure, mine.

I recall his working just as hard until his very last day, although with all of the propaganda about the new superintendent, he told me he felt like "...a half eaten sandwich". You have to experience this to understand the poignancy but the best of the best was gone. Fred Burke, Ralph Lataille, Bill Pelaia, and Jack McKeon: incredible people who wanted talented staff around them, who built capacity by developing people. I had little idea at the time how incredibly lucky I had been in working for these giants and how rare an occurrence in the business they were.

The board of education that greeted me was still in place at Jack's departure, although there was some transition and a lot more to come. They were admirable people and even the subsequent events have done little to change my very positive impressions of people like Faith Jerome, David Molotsky, Mary Ann Raphaely, Jim Marino, Eleanor Stoffman, and others, including one of the most unsung public servants of all time, Dr. Steve Barbell, one of my all time heroes. Although my time with Steve was relatively brief, over the span of three and a half decades of service, his service to Cherry Hill, in so many key civic roles, sets him apart. I regret deeply that my community has done little to acknowledge his service. I still enjoy being in his presence, he is still my dentist and he is superb at that also.

Steve was mainly responsible for the strong work ethic, heavy community involvement, and smooth operations of the board of education. These characteristics were always present, despite the fact that the members were all highly intelligent, had individual constituencies and interests and often pursued different agendas. The fact that they accomplished all they did, in a seamless manner, is a tribute to their dedication to the children above all other considerations. These people worked hard and I enjoyed my time with them. There were committee meetings, rolled into work sessions the following week, and the regular monthly meeting, which always seemed more like a celebration of some pretty neat accomplishments of the children and teachers and some pretty impressive staff work. The meetings were always well attended by the public, but in Jack's day, there were few staff. He expected that he, I and a few others would handle questions and issues that might arise. Later on, these meetings would turn dramatically, into a heavily confrontational environment and a circus like atmosphere with rows and rows of administrators trying to placate a public that had always been activist but now seemed skeptical. It looked like the wrong technique for my town and there seemed to be a lot of out of place people muddying the waters.

As Jack's departure drew near, the board of education began laying the ground work for finding a successor. In what to me seemed to be an incredibly short-sighted decision at the time, and which was to be prophetically accurate, they decided to "go cheap" on an advertised starting salary for the new superintendent, in the hope of truncating the salary demands of all other ranks in the districts. This was telling for me as it represented a sea change in the district where I had wanted to be my entire career and I have lost count of how many talented school executives called to confirm what they had read before reluctantly deciding not to apply. It was the kind of thing that could not happen with Jack in charge but this was the first evolution to proceed without Jack's involvement.

STORMY SEAS

"You are a nefarious character, one whose behavior was criminal in nature".
Thus did Philip Esbrandt come to judgment before the Superior Court of the State

of New Jersey {findings of the superior court}. Of course, the members of the board expressed disappointment with the decision, trying their best to calm the outraged cries of their constituents, who had finally learned the truth concerning my abrupt departure. The fact that the court assessed Esbrandt a punitive fine of $50,000, which the board agreed to assume, only exacerbated the community angst. Thus began a long period of further decline as they tried to stay about business as usual, while dealing, with what came to be known during the Clinton era as a "distracted" administration.

That is the way it ended but the beginning was not too smooth either. I recall our first meeting. I was working late and Philip Esbrandt had come for an interview. Now I knew nothing about the candidates, which is as it should have been. I was only aware of the classic people who declined the opportunity because of the advertised salary, which ironically, ended up being bumped up for Dr. Esbrandt. Now I knew this person not at all, yet his first question to me was, "How do I handle the question of the strikes in my current district?" I could only advise that the truth had always been the best course for me, and recommended that he offer a detailed explanation of the key events, should the issue arise. With that he abruptly left and my only contact with him before he assumed his duties many months later was indirectly by phone or note, dealing with ordering a precise automobile model and having it ready for his arrival [it was not available exactly as desired], and paying him for days he spent consulting with the district before he actually arrived. I recall that when he decided that he had little choice of survival save for ruining my career that he told me that my working for days and days without pay prior to my own arrival was an "embarrassment" to him, although it had occurred years earlier.

Thus it began; however, my loyalties were to the district and this was the superintendent so I followed what I knew, offering all of my expertise and all my loyalty. I had to threaten sanctions for staff members who kept bringing me "horror" stories, rumors really about the man's character and performance, as provided by insiders at the former district. Just the kind of crap that people love to spread, witness my initial experience in Howell. I also spent a considerable time trying to calm my peers who were getting worried at the abrupt change in style. Ironically, many of these people were among the first to act disloyally when it became obvious the board was going to back Esbrandt. I came to feel as though I was living through the "Caine Mutiny" storyline.

All around us, things seemed to be not just changing but collapsing, in terms of accepted strategies of organizational development. Terrific people were leaving, folks like Walt Belfield, the incredible social sciences department head at HS West. Others who were ready for advancement began to look elsewhere. I shall never get over the loss to my home town when Dr. Hal Melleby left to begin his meteoric rise as perhaps the finest current example of excellence as a chief school administrator. Change for the sake of change and form over substance, with successes attributed to the superintendent, were the new heuristic. You could not very well behave this way and have someone around who knew anything about organizational development and measurement so I was told, bluntly, to stick only to my specified areas, by "Dr." Esbrandt, as he wanted me to call him. This was a completely new experience, one that I would see only once more, thankfully. I still chuckle when he arrived to tell me that he was "investigating" my doctorate, because, I had the staff continue to answer my telephone as "Joseph Picogna's Office", the office I had always wanted and which was destined shortly to be ripped from me. Instead we had committees after committees, none with any power and fired part-time retired teachers who filled jobs such as the district testing program only to replace them with fulltime, higher priced people, who established offices to manage the same tasks, but who owed their loyalty to Dr. Esbrandt. It was later to come to light that, although I never considered applying for the superintendency, that Esbrandt became aware that many had encouraged me to do so and came to see me as a potential rival.

Nevertheless, I had my job, was secure in my performance and would never abandon my oath. You see the corporate secretary in a district is the locus of control for financial oversight. Dr. Esbrandt's downfall is rooted in this concept and the examples, while numerous, are best left to the serious reader who can easily examine the court records. Someone in my position simply cannot ignore such issues for she/he is the accountable financial party, and faces serious sanctions for permitting questionable financial practices. I had to maintain this posture even when confronted by a superintendent who told me, and this is taken from the findings of the court, "I am going to get you and there is nothing you can do about it. Think about this over Christmas" {findings of the superior court}. How is that working out for you, Phil?

FIGHTING BACK

"Joe Picogna may be the best business manager/board secretary this district or any other district could ever have and herein lies the problem. Dr. Picogna was good, and his took his responsibilities seriously. He was not a rubber stamp, he would not yield to pressure and this is where the problem developed with Dr. Esbrandt" {findings of the superior court}.

It was Philip Esbrandt's great misfortune to attempt the destruction of someone who was so uniquely prepared, who, not only knew how to care for himself, but had never shied from his responsibilities. The key to dealing with people whose arrogance is exceeded only by their ignorance, and a lot of school people fit this description, is to get them before the real courts, not the commissioner of education or some administrative law judge. Cherry Hill spent a fortune trying to keep their superintendent from facing the music, at least on center stage. It was obvious that they had weighed what it might cost them for their actions and they spent a year and a half trying to force a subordinate jurisdiction to handle the matter, thus the basis of how they valued their settlement offers. I guess the cost to the district and the children never entered their calculations. Yet, here they were before the court for big-boys and watching them turn pasty faced and then folding like a collapsible boat was indeed priceless. Never, ever, have I heard of any finding so devastating to the actions of a chief school executive, a person who had been so protected for years. In fact it is a shame that there was no video of the trial for it would have been made quite a lesson for aspiring superintendents, especially those enrolled in the mail order programs.

There is no way that I could ever recommend such an experience to anyone, it is simply too devastating on self and family. When you are dismissed publicly you begin wondering why the world seems to be progressing so normally without you. Fortunately, and this drove my adversaries crazy, I had Temple and the Navy, so my income perked along and my consulting practice, thanks to Temple's extension institute, really took off. Thus, they were unable to drive me into bankruptcy and force a meager, silent settlement. I also had two superb lawyers, Joseph Audino and John J. [Jim] Finnegan III, dedicated men who know the law and supported their clients magnificently. The truth would have been buried had it not been for these two incredible gentlemen.

MISPLACED LOYALTY

Faith Jerome was a terrific board member in Cherry Hill and someone I liked a great deal personally, particularly because she was so child centered. She tended to be quite vociferous about youth soccer in the community, a strong program that consumed a great deal of resources, some would say proportionally too high. Faith was another of the key actors in building bridges for public schools, people that I admired greatly as their efforts were often indefatigable. Faith also blindly followed the advice of the superintendent of schools, Philip Esbrandt, and voted for my dismissal, "reluctantly" as she stated. Years later under cross examination she told the truth and could relate no reason for the breach of contract that terminated my employment. Her testimony still followed the party line but provided no help to the defense. Bobbi Richterman also told the truth during her deposition, and you could see, under questioning, how she came to a realization that she had erred, as she was forced to answer each question, each answer raising more questions about the actions of the superintendent.

David Molotsky was another favorite of mine in Cherry Hill. He followed some super-stars in the position of president and unfortunately for him was stuck with Esbrandt as superintendent. David was well meaning, hard working and committed to children. He also believed the nonsense that he had an obligation to support the superintendent he had hired over my proven performance record and he paid the price. You really have to read the court transcript to get a sense of the awful combination of ignorance and arrogance running amuck. The judge, in determining that my contract was breached illegally, had Esbrandt stand before him while punitive damages were assessed. To this Mr. Molotsky could only say that he was disappointed. Humiliated may have been a better descriptor but he made his choice and forced the district to reap the whirlwind.

Eleanor Stoffman was much like Molotsky, i.e., the same positive characteristics. While I would welcome an opportunity to spend time with Faith or David, I am afraid that even as a gentleman, the best I could muster for Eleanor would be to turn my back on her. She testified at the trial, and I guess you had to be there to appreciate it, but she attempted to turn every comment I had ever uttered, every joke I had spoken, into something worthy of being fired. The memory of her arguing with the judge is still priceless and is recalled fondly to me by those who were there on my behalf. They had no case, could not possibly justify their actions, had only the public purse to fund their endless appeals but between Esbrandt and Stoffman as witnesses they were dead ducks, or, as an experienced trial lawyer stated, the case, had it been a boxing match, would have been called early.

LESSONS LEARNED

Since these events I have grown accustomed to board members supporting "their" choice, even if he or she is driving the ship of state into an iceberg. I am not sure what choice they really have. If the absence of effective leadership is a major problem for the public school establishment, then this failure or perhaps inability of boards of education to take effective action against chief executives is the major symptom of that problem.

Sometimes it is just the luck of the draw. For example, I was able to spend some time in the company of Dr. Mort Sherman, who succeeded Esbrandt. He seemed extremely capable, was very professional in his approach, and, as a parent and taxpayer in Cherry Hill, I was most satisfied with his vision. He certainly began the process of recovery until a very attractive assignment led to his departure. Had Mort followed John McKeon, had Mort been able to work the tremendous capacity, culture and enthusiasm that was Jack's heritage, then I am sure the district would have profited handsomely. You see mine was the rare experience as Fred Burke, Bill Pelaia, John McKeon, and later Carl Johnson, were intrepid leaders, working without guile, maximizing the talent base of their staff without fear that their own reputation would be lessened. These were people who inspired others naturally, for whom people were pleased, indeed felt obligated, to deliver their best. They were perfect partners for me but, unfortunately for children everywhere, they are few in number.

I am not sure that I shall ever understand or forgive those staff and professional service providers who jumped ship, after, as you can find in the court record, raising some of the very same questions. Fortunately, they were called to account for their actions {see the findings of the superior court}. There was one person worthy of note, Steve Tuchin, who had worked for me only briefly as transportation coordinator. They called him in, and I had no idea what they expected him to say, but the told the truth and left them shaking their heads. His job was later eliminated and I cannot only hope that he went on to a position commiserate with his outstanding abilities. *I mention this to demonstrate how incredibly nasty may be this business of educating children.*

THE PICOGNA AMENDMENT

"This event was not one within the range of human experience and I so find that without question. It was something that far transcends anything that any person of a reasonable mind could ever experience, anticipate, or should face. To be vindicated by the court has to help but that is not going to blunt everything that went before. He is a sincere, dedicated, hard-working person. Dr. Picogna had a very heavy responsibility. He was truly the guardian of the funds. He knows what his responsibilities are under the law and he is not going to yield to pressure from anybody, to intimidation or threats. I am satisfied that Dr. Esbrandt acted with malice, with a complete disregard for the rights of the plaintiff with an intention to injure and destroy him. I am finding a judgment of liability against Dr. Esbrandt, which will serve as a purpose of punishment, and certainly I think it will prevent him from similar conduct in the future. Hopefully, it will send a message to others who would be tempted to act as he did in connection with this case" {findings of the superior court}.

Thus, my time in my dream job had come to an abrupt end. It was traumatic, in fact devastating, and the financial compensation does not help with much more than the bills. The concept of vindication is helpful but interesting as it is blunted by the denials of responsibility by those already adjudged liable, and, ever since, a lot of superintendents around the state have been regarding me with some weird combination of awe, fear and disdain. I recall hearing from Katie Havrilesky in the midst of this. "You are still my hero", she said, and that was rationale enough to keep going.

Years later a new administrative code for financial operations was adopted by the legislature. It acknowledges the unique responsibilities of the chief financial officer and provides the protection that any negative action against such a person by a board of education or a superintendent is subject to review by the commissioner of education. It has become known, among my colleagues, as the "Picogna Amendment", thus my legacy to the profession.

By this time, I was snug in what would become my home for many years, the Delran public schools, a place once ignored by most with talent, but, which, under Carl Johnson would rise to greatness. Cherry Hill was no longer Cherry Hill and may never again reach that level of greatness, which is a terrible legacy for Esbrandt but again, they made their choice. As the judge said, "...you have fired the wrong Dr" {findings of the superior court}.

GREATEST TRIUMPH

"Most of us enjoy preaching and I have got such a bully pulpit!"

Theodore Roosevelt

SECOND CHANCE

One day during my sojourn from public education, I received a phone call from my dear friend Joan Katz. Joan and a number of other former colleagues from the district kept in contact and kept an eye on certain district officials as my children were still in the system. I owe them more than can be repaid, for their loyalty and stand-up behavior. Joan was calling to tell me of a vacancy, in Delran, New Jersey of all places, for a central office administrator. I was at first reluctant as Delran had had a terrible reputation throughout my career but I did not wish to seem ungrateful and I had a significant pension stake sitting out there that either should be resumed or terminated. On the one hand I was still damaged goods as the trial would not occur for another two years. On the other, the consulting work from Temple had really taken off, there was a lot of active duty time for the Navy, and I really enjoyed teaching my university classes during the day, for a change. What clinched my decision to move ahead was Joan's revelation that the Delran superintendent was Bernie Shapiro, a legendary principal in Cherry Hill who had moved on in the same capacity at Haddon Township, another community known for its excellence in public schools. Bernie had really been the one who had built Cherry Hill East High School, still one of the premier institutions anywhere. He had managed over 3500 students quite successfully, having one graduating class of almost 1000 students! Perhaps "managed" is not the correct word as there were highly sophisticated programs in copious areas for students of every ability level [think: bright, brighter, brightest] and interest. I know that if anything could ever be made of Delran, Bernie would be the one to get the ball rolling.

Delran had had, I believe, four business administrators in the last five to seven years and the place was bankrupt. When I assumed my duties we had $27,000 in the bank and owed $49,000 in fines to the State for various transgressions and accounting violations, the budget was not balanced, as was required by law, and even the then county school business administrator could do little with the mess. We would, of course, ultimately become the wealthiest district in the region, in terms of available cash, in a town with only moderate resources and little inclination to spend. Getting there would require tremendous effort from a lot of remarkable people but for now, just getting by was the watchword for everyone except Bernie, who was already scheming to implement his "world class school district" strategy.

The admin "offices" were atrocious, we used to call it the "million dollar" building because there were $500,000 in potential fines for code violations and not even $500,000 in repairs would have remedied the defects. There was only one office available, a small conference room with plastic, with mostly broken chairs, no potable water, only a sludge like substance that emanated form faucets, that resembled that which had gushed forth into sinks in that movie, "The Money Pit", and worst of all, an un-vented toilet in a small closet that opened directly into a cramped room that housed six people and one antique "computer" with enough cables, as one staff member so eloquently stated, as to guarantee that anyone working there would become sterile. There was another toilet, in the basement, set on skids to keep it above the water that constantly lined the floor of what was the "district storage facility". The only access was up a long flight of narrow *wooden* steps in a *wooden* stairwell, affectionately known as "fire trap mountain". I recall it used to get so hot in the summer that the paper for our sometimes working small copier would wrinkle before it could be used. I mention this in some detail as these conditions turned out to be symbolic for everything I found there, a total emphasis on sports, which had been blasted in an article published by a nationally distributed magazine, little support from the community, zero computers for instruction or operations management, decrepit school buildings and some text books that were over twenty years old. The science books were over twenty five years old and we used to joke that they may be missing some of the planets! The place had such a lousy reputation that I had trouble getting some professional service vendors to even consider servicing us. Some consented even though, as one said, "This may be too much for even you to pull off". At my first meeting, I recall several parents criticizing something they perceived would cost money and one said, [this may have been their anthem]: "This is Delran, we don't want nothing fancy, our kids do not need it, they ain't going to Harvard". I guess this is what hurt most, the prevalent attitude that good enough, and the accepted standard for that was way too low, was just fine but they would accept anything, as long as it cost nothing. Years later when another superintendent, George Sharp, devised what I thought was one of the finest building programs I had ever seen, from the perspective of very strong instructional programming in a number of areas, one citizen summed up the attitude of those in attendance by saying: "...this is not for us. My daughter graduated from high school fifteen years ago and got a wonderful job in a bakery, and that was good enough for her".

This was the situation into which I walked. It was time to get the pension building again, it looked like a great challenge and Bernie was just the kind of visionary that could tackle this seemingly impossible task.

OPPORTUNITIES

The district had several outstanding attributes, however, some truly gifted teachers, a number of capable and quite dedicated support staff, Bernie, a knowledgeable, caring and highly proficient administrator, and the ace in the hole, the incomparable Ronald Napoli, president of the board of education and one of the smartest and perhaps most prescient people I know.

Ron Napoli is a truly gifted person and, although few are aware of his achievements, he is the person most responsible for setting the conditions for what came to be known as the "Golden Age" for Delran. I took an immediate liking to him. He was remarkably selfless, which always allowed him to take the high road, had a keen political sense that was to guide my actions for years, was very hard working, and, he commanded respect. It is no secret that the unions spoke despairingly of him from time to time, especially during negotiations, because they feared him, particularly his ability to sense what people wanted for heir children, and his commitment to excellence and inner strength. It was he who enunciated the most courageous comment I ever heard in receiving contract renewal demands one year: "It is not that we do not have the money. We do not think you are worth the money. Prove to us that you shall deliver that level of value to the children." There is simply no way that you would find even a half dozen other board members, anywhere, willing to take such a risk. Indeed, after his departure, I sat shaking my head as his successors always looked for ways to support the burgeoning program of labor peace. It seemed to become a major escape tactic for some who followed him many years later to try and explain their latest fiascos somehow on the "contentious" board members who had come before??!?

Ron had joined the board when it had become obvious that the entire enterprise was doomed to bankruptcy and continued failure. Every building had serious problems as maintenance had been simply cancelled. Roofs leaked, heat systems did not work, indeed there were two entire schools in which all the classroom unit ventilators had been disconnected! Fields were overgrown and district vehicles barely ran: there were several trucks in which the floor had rusted out and you were treated to the sight of roadway speeding by as the vehicle moved. Perhaps worst of all was the staff, especially in the support areas. It was incredible watching custodians spread wax over a dirty floor, telling the single hard-pressed and overwhelmed "supervisor" what he could do with himself, laughing that their union and the town politicos were there to "protect" them. The trick of the status quo crowd was to blame the supervisor for failing to evaluate his staff and "bring cases" against them while all the while undermining the supervisor and eventually replacing him. When I was hired these same people "cautioned" me that they were expecting a strong evaluation system. Well, they got it, and some sixteen were fired and stayed fired after all of the grievances were heard; and, the rest were dismissed as a consequence of a highly successful program of privatization. The district saw an immediate saving of a quarter of a million dollars in payroll and the systems were never maintained better. Sure, I had the skills and the intestinal fortitude to make this happen, but, without Ron Napoli, there would have been no enabler to cause this to happen. You should have seen him, operating on an intellectual plane far above everyone else, yet able to articulate highly cogent arguments that all could comprehend, all the while calmly addressing each issue. There was the time that we privatized transportation. The system was a disaster, the buses were in decrepit shape, the network had not been managed properly and the costs were astronomical for the services rendered. I recall that the board proposal would have enabled the staff to have saved their jobs if they gave up one percentage point of their raise, which they of course refused, preferring instead to frighten the parents into believing that "circus freaks" would be hired by a contractor, thus endangering their children. Indeed, the argument got so heated that the spouse of one driver leapt over the BOE table to try and unplug the mike, only to be faced down by other members of the board while Mr. Napoli calmly pushed forward. The proposal carried, thanks to Ron's competence and influence base and the children were never safer, having professionally trained and closely supervised drivers caring for them. One of the best attributes of this entire system was the right of refusal for any contractor personnel in any area, so tight were the specification packages and contract documents. This eliminated the eighteen month struggles to remove incompetent people, who all the while had to be allowed to remain in close contact with the children. I do not know how you put a price on such courage, but, thanks to Ron, the taxpayer also saved a bundle in the process.

This was a community that obviously spent little or nothing on its public schools and if it had not been for Ron Napoli, the district may have been the first in the region to simply collapse. He was quite simply the best person at the right time, perhaps the only person, who could have put the brakes to all of the insanity and ineptitude and begin again, using his tremendous persona and professional skills to build a new infrastructure, indeed a new culture, while maintaining daily operations

Ron was joined on the board of education by several other dedicated new members, among whom I recall very fondly: Bob Sheeran, Bob Mull, and Harry Gautileus. Both "Bobs" had strong backgrounds in business and operations management, Harry was the principal of George

Washington HS in Philadelphia, one of the largest and best run in the area, and all had strong personal ties to the district and were committed to inaugurating a program of excellence for the children. A few years later another of the great all-time members came on board, Chuck Perritt. This quiet, unassuming person worked tirelessly in support of children. He assumed the toughest, most thankless jobs year after year, such as the negotiations chair, and set a tremendous example of self-sacrifice that, unfortunately, not many followed, at least after the departure of Ron Napoli. Chuck has a very sharp sense of humor. It was he who once commented, "If you see a teacher, they are being paid". Chuck is among the few for whom a thank you and a plaque were just not sufficient but such stars are normally so actualized that they take pleasure in a sense of accomplishment.

Ron's first accomplishment was to get Bernie on board, a person who would make gold out of dirt if it would benefit children. Bernie, who was a master tactician, began formulating strategic plans while strengthening day to day operations. Most importantly, be brought a sense of panache and vision to a place that had become pessimistic, that seemed to have lost hope and a sense of future. I knew he could become frustrated while waiting for others to become turned on to his initiatives but he always portrayed a highly enthusiastic demeanor to the public. Bernie also began recruiting highly talented people, building on the best that he found and improving those who could be saved. He relied on his instincts and took a chance on what he knew about me and Ron Napoli took a similar risk. They never expressed any reservations, only great promise. They were anxious for me to continue with my teaching and I still had vacation time for my consulting, all of which contributed to make me stronger in my operations mgmt role in the district, a win–win situation if ever there was one.

In the first year of Carl Johnson's remarkable tenure as superintendent of schools, these people would seek to reward me by again offering early tenure, that singular honor that threads its way through my career. Soon after, the courts had spoken, my achievements were being broadcast throughout the state and people I had not heard from since the end of my days in Cherry Hill wanted me for other assignments and began wondering how I could stay in "something small" like Delran. Well, they never got what we were about, it was glorious and it never, ever occurred to me to leave while Carl and Ron were working their magic.

NEW BEGINNINGS

There was a secretary in one of the schools, an older woman, a veteran of many years service, but with more than sufficient talent to have been successful in the private sector. She was one of many fine professionals whom I encountered in my career on the dole who gave up quite a bit, including salary, recognition and some self-respect, for the pension, benefits and days off that were offered at the time. Nevertheless, she never forgot the time that she described as "having really worked for a living" in the private sector. She used to tell me that the teachers should be forced to take a sabbatical every five years, during which, over a period of six months, they should have to *really work* for a living. This was my introduction to Delran.

There was indeed a very strong entitlement mentality, one that would resurface and grew even stronger some years later. People were just not used to trying to go beyond themselves, and, a few others, just a few, really, looked as though they had no business being around children. They were so mean spirited that they were depressing. There were a number of really fantastic teachers and I recall one in particular because she was both superb in the classroom and was also the union president, Mrs. Marge Guessman. Marge taught first grade and everybody seemed to want their child in her class, she was that good, so good in fact, that she was the number one target of the moms, you know who you are, those who would politic each year with the principals as to why their child just "had to be" with Mrs. G. Since there was never any concern with Marge's performance, she had incredible props with the entire school community and we knew that whatever she supported for her constituents was to benefit the group, not herself. I had truly enjoyed working with Pi Siriani in a similar capacity at Howell, and Marge and Harry Zakarian from Cherry Hill made a triumvirate of great performers who were quite capable union chiefs.

The principals were also terrific, especially Jim Duda, Mike Galucci, Rose Prestopino and, later on, John Fricke. Jimmy was Mike's assistant in the high school and I always teased him that he was a better principal than he was as an assistant. Actually he was terrific supporting Mike, he was just much that more incredible in the top job, as an advocate for children, program manager, staff developer, and parent "soother". Mike was one of the best in the business; treating every day as if it was a virtuoso performance and he delivered. Everybody admired him for his strong work ethic and sense of style. The district was extremely lucky to land John Fricke, another proven performer when Mike retired. Bruce Smith was much like Jim, a steady and reliable assistant principal but when his turn came at the top job, he made a very challenging elementary school into a model learning environment and Rose matched him stride for stride in her parallel assignment. I have always measured the worth of a colleague by my inclination to have them serve my own children. I would have had no hesitancy at all as far as this bunch was concerned, especially during the Johnson years. Just a few years later Linda Gringeri would join the district and provide terrific service in a variety of administrative positions.

Sue Veratti, Sue, Szychofvski, Donna Hammer, Doreen Lawrence, and Rosemary Smith were among the finest school secretaries I have ever encountered. Thousands of children directly benefited by their caring attitudes, their wise disposition of every grievance and their ability to reduce each enormous crisis in the life of a child to something bearable. There are just not enough words to properly convey my admiration. Finally, the "special education ladies", under the very able leadership of Dr. Alan Elstein, the very professional psychologists, social workers and learning disabilities consultants served our special needs children with great success. I was privileged to work with three different groups during my era and each was just terrific. Things were really looking up for Delran, indeed, they had at last acquired competent leadership in Bernie, who suddenly decided to seek early retirement and accept another position. My first inclination was "here we go again" but things were to get even better. The Johnson years were about to begin.

GOLDEN AGE

"There is no justice unless it sails in the heart of its Captain". These words were taken from the findings of their Lordships of the Admiralty, in the matter of the Lieutenant William Bligh and the mutiny abroad HMS Bounty. Bill Pelaia, John McKeon, Bernie Shapiro, and Carl Johnson all shared many positive leadership characteristics, two of which, were extremely rare. They were very competent and they acted always with an incredible sense of justice and caring. They were the 'heart" of their operation, head and shoulders above those who talked a blue streak, mostly about themselves, and were satisfied with survival year to year, in the increasingly complex role of a chief school administrator.

I would like to illustrate the comprehensive nature of Carl's influence and remarkable run by mentioning two names: Alan Elstein and Strauss-Esmay. Alan came to us via New York and immediately took charge of the Child Study team and the entire realm of pupil personnel services. He was the best I have ever seen in this role, knowledgeable, caring and patient. We became friends as well as colleagues and Alan always attributed whatever success for which he was recognized to the leadership of Carl Johnson. For someone to be effective in Alan's job, they had to know someone had their back, that their snap decisions on behalf of children, even if parents became upset, and ran, as they inevitably do, to complain to the board of education. Many superintendents tend to 'take things under advisement" and then "give up" the staff member, at least to the proximate audience, to calm the complainant, at least temporarily. That is the way it is in the world of form over substance. This is the biggest criticism of Delran before this era, everybody was promised everything and then when it came to collect, the bankrupt philosophy led to a bankrupt district. Carl Johnson always built capacity for the long haul, his sense of strategic management and his planning skills to get us there were remarkable. His low key demeanor was the icing on the cake for us but, unfortunately, it meant that many of his achievements went unnoticed, particularly in an arena in which people tend to triumph their supposed successes on a routine basis.

Judy Esmay was an old friend of mine, having served as a consultant to the hearing officers in the state education agency in my time and she ran the premier policy development service with her husband, Bob Strauss. Delran had no policies, at least few that were actually written down and even fewer that made sense. It would take a half chapter to accurately describe how bad things were but suffice to say, Carl immediately began moving to rectify them. I had to beg Judy to speak to Bob to even get them to consider being our professional services vendor in this area, a relationship that would mature over sixteen years, yielding many advances that were adopted by districts everywhere. Bob had several reservations. I remember him telling me that Delran always wanted something for nothing, never followed through and quite often could not get something correct. This was true but then he met Carl and the deal was set. We were the first district to make our policies and regulations available on an electronic basis, with centralized control over modifications. At the very least we solved the problem of people not only never opening their manuals let alone updating them. Not to put too fine a point on this but, few, if any, of the very fine professional service vendors mentioned in the "Tool Box" section would have bothered seeking our business had it not been for the achievements and advances of the Carl Johnson era.

Carl was unique in another way; he was actually recruited for the position. With Bernie leaving, Ron wanted the best available and he brought the rest of the board along by having them interact with Carl in comprehensive discussions about public education, our challenges, his capacity for meeting them and his plans for doing so. I recall he was originally concerned about the reputation of the district but Bernie and I told him there were some great people in Delran, in every category. Bernie showed him some of the foundation work that had been accomplished and I was able to illustrate our already strong financial position and he was 'in". The onsite visits to Carl's district sealed the deal and he could have stayed a hundred years if he wished.

The plethora of great people also extended to the business office. Maureen Bartlett, Pat Tracy, and Judy Napoli were caring and capable people, but, who were underpaid and underutilized. Doris Christy stayed on to become Carl's administrative assistant and became another cornerstone of our remarkable run. I was not surprised at how terrific these incredible ladies were; that was obvious at our first meeting. What surprised me was the enthusiasm, creativity and commitment to excellence they displayed, so quickly and so continuously, once they were given a chance to strut their stuff. They very quickly gained my confidence and were encouraged to work under only the most general of supervision. With so many people working on advancements, we quickly earned a reputation for excellence. They never, ever, had an audit exception or deficiency finding during our years together. I used to tell them of some very fine organizational development models, such as Johnsonville Foods, which I used for my MBA classes at Temple. The staff was especially interested in the role that worker groups developing advances in quality had achieved; concepts that could never have been addressed with the principals and teachers. I was to enjoy working with many of the support staff in professional development workshops. They were the bottom of the Totem pole, the poorest paid, the least respected, and yet, the most valuable.

There is a name missing from that list, because she deserves a Marquee all to herself, the incomparable Carol Hearn, the one person Carl referred to as the "only indispensable person" in our operation. Carol was on board when I arrived and she was chomping at the bit for someone to give her a free hand. Her achievements are described in some detail in the "Tool Box" section but suffice to say, although she was never recognized properly in her home district, she achieved fame for her work throughout the state, as people from districts in every county came to learn from the master. Isn't it ironic that the person with the greatest reputation for excellence in the state from our district was not a principal or a supervisor or a teacher, but a support services staff member? Only under someone like Carl Johnson could the remarkable talents of these stalwarts be unleashed to the benefit of children and the taxpayer. It is frustrating to contemplate that with hundreds of school districts just in New Jersey the incredible potential of these people remains unfulfilled simply because the leadership is not up to the task. It is also equally frustrating to think how few people get it right, the way Ron Napoli did with Carl Johnson, despite all of the pomp and circumstance that accompanies the anointing of each new superintendent as the greatest thing since sliced bread.

KICKIN' BUTT

Once we got going, Carl was able to institute his plan for keeping taxes low; we had the lowest school tax rate among our comparison group for many years, which, incidentally, was another area in which the municipal government foundered badly against us in comparison. Our outsourcing and privatization programs exceeded theirs significantly in tax savings and quality; while they joined county co-ops, and paid the inevitable admin fees, we started our own groups and did much better. For example, our South Jersey Natural Gas Consortium, with me as the non-paid executive director bought gas from the same vendor as the township, but, at a significantly lower price. It often seemed as the more we advanced, the more they attacked us. We were the wealthiest district located in a community not only far from wealthy but also not very interested in supporting public education. The strategy worked so well that for over a decade we averaged a million dollars in earnings or cost savings to be applied to tax relief, a program that was so successful that Dr. John Rocco, chief of the Assembly Education Committee, introduced special legislation to allow our district to profit from this performance in the calculation of annual budget spending limitations, which were actually revenue top-stops. The provision became known popularly as the "Delran Amendment".

Another attribute of our efforts was seen in two other areas: one, the incredible investment in capital improvements, especially technology, which came from having another million or so dollars available via a continued paradigm of cost efficiencies. The second was also very tangible, having the ability to attract the very finest staff available to fill vacancies. At a time when most districts were hard pressed to hire beginning people, who came at the lowest step of the guide, Delran was able to have its pick of the very finest teaching talent available, people who came at a considerable premium but who paid great dividends for the children placed in their charge. The district built an incredible science department in this fashion, something that became impossible just a few years after Carl's departure.

I must say that we accomplished a lot without much support. The budgets were passing because the tax impact was minimal, i.e., the board was in the enviable position of having enough tax surplus to consider a tax holiday for one year, thanks to our cash horde, and then there was Carl. He seemed to be all over, spending 130 nights on average each year on district business and he was admired by his colleagues, held in the highest esteem by the state folks and admired by the citizens. The PTA members were very supportive and appreciative but for the most part people accepted what we gave their children with the extra dollars that we generated but I felt the parents would be equally satisfied with less as long as taxes were kept as low as possible. Even the PTA had their moments. I recall a debate over several years about not taking a stand regarding spending referenda, something about such positions violating their charter. In particular, I recall the paver incident. When we were planning the new intermediate school we had the idea of asking the contractors to subsidize the placement of bricks leading to the entrance, bricks on which the names of the first classes of the children would be inscribed as a memento. The cost was very low, just the cost of the lettering. You might have thought we had insulted the Pope from some of the flack we caught, especially from one woman, who, about six months later, was overheard exclaiming about her Disney vacation and, you guessed it, the couple of hundred bucks she had spent on a brick that she might never even see installed. Go figure! Unfortunately, in a very few years after Carl's departure, the district went from first to worst as they say in the NFL; five years of deficit spending to cover spiraling labor costs, the labor peace phenomena, had literally bankrupted the operation.

THE CHARGE OF THE CHEESE CAKES

We were really on a roll in those days and it seemed as though we never had to say "No" to anyone with all of the cash, and perhaps more importantly, few staff gave us any reason to say "No", there was such a sense of team under the auspices of Dr. Johnson. Carl had a master plan for the improvement of instruction, involving building improvements, lab upgrades, new text series, the best possible teachers, and, computers and a strategic management plan to make it happen. We kept generating cash and he spent it wisely. All of a sudden, there were computers for principals and teachers, hundreds for student use, networked and available at every grade level, and administration machines, for the child study team, school secretaries and central office. Transportation records and schedules, attendance, grade reporting and a slew of others all became automated, with all applications designed to complement and connect to one another as another thing we were able to afford were the finest professional service vendors in each area, which meant a firm called TekConnect for technology. File sharing, word processing, email, a web page, automated payroll and absence requests with electronic signatures came into play, saving us time and money, and began to be adopted by districts throughout the state.

We unbundled gas purchasing; developed outsourcing in all support areas, developed strategies such as minimum premium programs with dual levels of insurability to keep health plan costs down and on and on. Each innovation saved cash, which ended up being spilt between benefits for the children and tax savings that got our budgets passed. We also rebuilt everything and built a new grades 3-5 school and added wings to the other buildings so that we achieved four campuses, K-2, 3-5, 6-8 and 9-12 with parents becoming stake holders in each facility and real payoffs in programming improvements with the student numbers available via the non-redundant building grade structure. When we built the Intermediate School, grades 3-5, we timed the construction so that it coincided with the expiration of retiring debt so there was almost no increase in taxes. To eliminate any increase in taxes for the building, we chipped in $750,000 in cost efficiency savings to make up the difference and add a lot of extras to the school. Then there were the roofs, which we replaced in every school. Before I got there the district had adopted an eighteen year plan to replace the high school roof, which would have cost $950,000 before the eighteen year financing costs were added. By the time I got there it was a twenty year plan because two years had expired and they still had not been able to arrange financing, that is how decrepit their financial management systems and reputation were. Well, we got ourselves a bridge loan, did the entire job in one summer, saved all the interest costs and paid the entire thing off in six months, which is exactly how we built the new child study team and admin building, again, without a referendum and without a cent being added to the tax levy. From there we completed something really spiffy in the same manner, resurfacing all of the parking lots, an ocean of macadam, something school districts just do not ever have the funds to accomplish. Of course people began to take such extraordinary performance for granted, especially after Ron Napoli left the board and that would normally really grate on the staff responsible for such successes, only in this case, we were doing it for Carl and Carl had convinced everyone the extra work benefited the children. Just one of those little intangibles

Speaking of the board of education, there were terrific people around in those days. My dear friend Morris Burton, with over twenty five years of service; Jean Gandy and Sandy DeSimone, lovely people who were teachers and thus understood the challenges staff faced daily in the classroom; Brian Sherin, a remarkable gentleman who served with distinction for several years. There were Joan McHugh, Ken Mitchner and James Hatzold, who were hard working and very supportive; likewise, Lynn Jeney, another person with a strong business background who gave freely of his time for the benefit of children, even after his own had graduated. Then there were two of my all time favorites, Mary Genca and Karen Davis, great moms who raised a bunch of kids, worked night and day and never, ever, were afraid of doing the right thing for children; they were an absolute dream duo. Sandy DeSimone and Lynn Jeney followed Ron as president and even their most severe critics had to admire how hard they worked, how selfless they were, and they provided the district with years of stable leadership.

The board seemed to take on the demeanor that Carl displayed and while there were honest differences, they were always worked out in order to represent a consensus as an opinion. The board met a lot, went to workshops and dinners together and even attended the annual fall workshop offered by the school boards association that was held in Atlantic City. During this time, our people were rally something, actually attending workshops and seminars, exchanging ideas with peers and in general having a great time while expanding their capacity as board members. Carl was always in the center of this effort, especially as he was so well known and admired, and he made sure we got together with spouses once a year at the convention for an evening social. I was proud to be associated with this group as the board members in general had a reputation for outright gluttony when it came to this particular evolution. People who had trouble spending a nickel on children fed freely at the public trough in Atlantic City. I used to watch them argue over how they were going to get to the free cocktail partiers, then rush to the dinner the public was paying for and then hurry over to one of the dessert and cordial parties later on, sometimes having to squeeze in a free big band dance party. Poor dears must have been tuckered. Our group always had a great time and acted in conscious recognition of their status in the public domain. It was at one of those dessert socials that Carl and I encountered the epitome of culture shock. We were standing in one corner looking out at a sea of tables piled high with cakes, pies, ice cream, every possible confectionary. People were not taking just slices, they were taking the entire cake or pie back to their tables, trying to balance drinks in the other hand. Unbeknownst to us, they had set up an ice cream bar behind us and then made an announcement that sundaes were available at these bars located around the ballroom. We looked around to see the ice cream sundaes being made and then turned in horror to see the people galloping to get there first, with us in the way, still carrying the cakes and pies. Carl called it the "charge of the cheese cakes" and we laughed ourselves silly at the gluttony.

FLYING CIRCUS

I only saw Carl become angry on a few occasions and even then he maintained his demeanor. The reason for his infrequent ire was normally an out of control staff member who seemed to have been relieved of duty in almost every job category but had earned tenure years before our arrival. She was noted for acting on her own agenda regardless of how it interfered with the goals and objectives of the district and she was always out of step with what needed to be done for the common good. There was simply no end to her pattern of intransigence. We had trouble getting staff to work with her, indeed she could not be trusted with anything of importance and deadlines, quality control and other basic accouterments of organizational discipline were unknown attributes. One of the school secretaries gave us an egg timer, a kind of neat thing shaped like an hour glass with three minutes worth of salt inside. Carl developed the habit of flipping over the device when our friend visited and then he would sit patiently, not speaking, until the salt ran out, whence he would leave and not return until she departed. Apparently that was enough for him to make sure she still had nothing important to say and then it was back to business.

To others, he was a master listener, a devoted colleague, a cheer leader when necessary and an honest broker always. Carl could always be counted on to do the right thing whatever sacrifice had to be made and this integrity furnished him with an outstanding reputation among his peers, constituents and those in Trenton at the state education agency to whom we reported. Delran always was granted the benefit of the doubt because of the reputation we built; at least they did in those days. He encouraged everyone to try and improve themselves, without risk or assigned blame. The occasional failure was a learning experience and it was truly encouraging to see people with tenure and little incentive to improve giving their all. It was incredible watching the momentum for innovation build and seeing the master template of encouraging people to excel rather than forcing them to conform develop. He created all of this with a bit of a Monty Python approach and I was proud to be part of the team, Mr. Inside to his Mr. Outside.

LOOKING AHEAD

I guess what we ended up achieving was building a culture, that is, we proved that success could be achieved by placing talented people in the right slots and then providing them encouragement, resources and the freedom to exercise creative and self-improvement. As always, this is a function of leadership, perhaps the ability to create such an environment is the only leadership trait that truly matters and in Carl, we had it all. Unfortunately, this is all very rare on the public dole. Carl was always reluctant to accept praise, preferring instead to recognize others, much as did John McKeon; are you sensing something here? I used to remind him of a superintendent in a district that we were both well acquainted with. That superintendent had served for years and the only distinction that we could recall was the fact that he stood by the "employee" entrance every morning at opening, staring at his watch as each person entered, not even bothering to say "Hello". Contrast that with Carl, this warm, eloquent, modest man, who meant so much to so many.

REMINISCING

If I could categorize the wonderful people with whom I was associated during these years, in organizational analysis terms, I would refer to them as "honest brokers for change" agents. These were the people on whom we counted to test the limits of their creativity on a daily basis, to develop solutions to problems in areas for which no precedents existed and to maintain a firm commitment to excellence. And yet, the very folks who were always at the forefront of innovation seemed to hold the most apprehension of the future. While they had confidence that Carl's successor would be capable, I guess they could sense the darkening clouds of funding problems and the mounting presence of the union influence.

I was hopeful that we, as a unit, would not be part of a self-fulfilling prophecy; that is, we would continue to work for success. I am sorry that the heuristic was soon to change, that our work, while still praised loudly, would be considered secondary, a mechanism to keep the wolf from the door, that being the mounting deficit spending. The Golden Age was over.

The "TOOL BOX" section of this book contains a description of the award winning procedures, programs and protocols that were developed during this period of my career. The descriptions give some idea of the techniques used to generate so many millions of dollars in tax savings that were used for tax relief and badly needed improvements. Carl used to say that the children were only entitled to the quality of education the parents were willing to pay for and, that my operation had given them an awful lot more. It was the best of times for me, and, these techniques became the topics of so many training and demonstration efforts we hosted over a decade.

IRREPLACEABLE

Fred Burke, Catherine Havrilesky, John McKeon, and Carl Johnson, my own personal Mount Rushmore. Throw in John Rhodes, Dorothy Seagers, Ron Napoli, Bill Pelaia, Terry Kraft, Steve Barbell and the "Navy Gang" and you can see that I have indeed been blessed by working with giants, a pantheon of stars, people who taught me so much and allowed me to use all my training and talents everyday on the job, a situation that should be a common experience for employees everywhere but one that remains elusive, especially on the public dole. The time for giants had passed and I never again felt that kind of euphoria at work. It seemed as though five minutes after Carl was gone, most people began touting the "new era" that was about to begin and several took exception to my keynote at Carl's retirement dinner. They wanted a thank you and got an overview of his great performance. My calling this period the "Golden Age of Delran" certainly did not help either. I wish I could prognosticate lottery numbers as well as I predicted how this transition would fare.

THE DEATH OF SHAME

"Every person has to test themselves and if they are courageous and perhaps lucky, they find maturity. This is all the reward you may ask for, or are entitled to, the privilege of growing up".

Ward Just

SUCCESSIONS

And so the term of Carl Johnson, what I still refer to as the "Golden Age" of the district, came to an end. However, the transition, while ostensibly smooth, almost took on a type of Napoleonic convulsion, or at least, a sense of déjà vu. You see Carl could not get out as the board was initially unable to attract someone of quality. He worked on for almost a year, this quiet unassuming man, so anxious to be with his darling wife, children and most importantly, his grandchildren, worked on, perhaps out of loyalty but probably much more due to his incredible sense of professionalism.

The district did try to recruit a successor they just were not very successful. There was a marked contrast to the solicitation that yielded Carl Johnson. On that occasion, the board, which had a different culture, met regularly and effectively to get the job done. They went through a planning process, studied the paradigms that often mitigated against success, and developed a list of knowledge, skills and abilities, just the way a real organization would, comprised the data into a job analysis, which then became the template for the ads, selection of candidates to be interviewed and the ultimate selection meetings. Before a final candidate was selected, the top individuals under consideration received onsite visits. These visits were well planned and comprehensive in nature, with very pithy questions being asked to ascertain the capacity of the candidate for leadership, and, they were asked of a number of individuals representing different aspects of the constituency. Thus we see again the value of having someone like Ron Napoli in place, and, the results speak for themselves.

In this case, the board, which still contained a few hold-overs from the evolution described above, was no longer meeting with the same frequency, and perhaps, not the same intensity. I must admit I was a bit dumbstruck when, after Carl explained the process used to recruit him, the sitting board immediately decided to hire the New Jersey School Boards Association. There was some credibility in this choice, i.e., the board bought themselves a public criterion to justify their choice and I think they were only charged something like seven grand for the entire package, an absurdity, e.g., a very low sum but one that seemed to prove the old adage, you often get what you pay for. I had to swallow hard many times watching these people conduct a paper screening for the district. At least some of the board members were careful to prevent the old boy network imbedded with the state constituent groups from stealing the day. They finally got to some level of confidence with a couple of people, one, I believe was not currently employed, and began interviews. There was some angst in reaching a consensus, although the tradition of presenting a united face to the public once a decision had been reached was still the operative culture.

The person chosen to be superintendent was ratified by the full board and the leadership was authorized to make an offer. The district solicitor and the insurance carrier had expressed some surprise that no background check was to be conducted, indeed, such a common place tool, one especially vital where the business involves the welfare of children, but, this was apparently not within the protocol used by NJSBA. When I mentioned that a background check had been suggested and was indeed common place, there was an immediate and quite forcefully negative reaction, against me! I was told that what I was suggesting would be considered "an insult to our consultants". Well, far be it for me to be insulting anyone but, in a preview of how things were changing, all I could do was notify the solicitor and the carrier that the board had been warned there might be a gap in their hiring protocol but that they decided to depend on the rather limited screening processes of the department of education to save the day. The problem with this is that people are fingerprinted for a cursory check only if they are out of work for over a year and all of the people under serious consideration were employed currently and thus would not even be subjected to this rudimentary event. Theoretically, they could have worked thirty years or more without even a cursory check. In any event, this selection fell through when the candidate chose to introduce into the process an attorney who presented a number of demands, which seemed to both frighten and anger the board. There was considerable rancor among the members, with some fairly influential people wanting to move ahead but a majority was not achieved and the process began all over again. Thus did Carl have to soldier on even longer past his planned retirement date.

NEW ORIENTATIONS

The second try turned out to be almost as bankrupt, which serves to illustrate how barren the pickings are these days. The process ground down, a lot more expeditiously now, to two people who were interviewed, one of whom, I am told, impressed nearly everyone as being a complete idiot, one whose major selling point was a plan to drive around town and force the banks to contribute funds to the district!? That left George Sharp and the district was fortunate to have him. George was experienced, having served two districts as superintendent, well educated and knowledgeable. I am also of the opinion that he was a child advocate.

I say the district was fortunate because the only reason George was available was that his commute to his previous assignment had been so onerous that he had been forced to maintain a second residence. He was able to return to his primary abode, still with a commute of just under an hour, got the assignment in a district that had recorded no deficiency of any kind for years, and, was one of the wealthiest districts in the region, not because of the tax revenue or the tax base, but because of the funds being generated each year via cost efficiencies.

Thus, the stars were aligned properly and a district with a tradition of excellence, under the gun to hire someone quickly, attracted a qualified person with a track record of excellence, at a time when such people did not usually move among districts.

The transition was seamless, due to a number of factors. The first was Dr. Johnson, himself. Carl worked hard to promote the new superintendent as to talent and orientation to excellence and made one more tour among the constituent groups highlighting the capacity of his successor to do great things. Another factor was the board of education. As much as they truly admired Carl, they were ecstatic over having hired "their" new superintendent, this one truly theirs, as the board had come into place after Carl's arrival. This had a bit of déjà vu for me and my fears were somewhat realized when, all of a sudden, they started attributing things to George that were really Carl's. This is not a rare occurrence, unfortunately, but in contemporary times, boards of education are ever too anxious to default their oversight and cognizance roles to the chief school administrator, or as NOVA University seems to teach their newly minted doctoral graduates to call themselves, the "CEO's". It would be unfair to call this a complete abrogation of responsibilities; I think it is a combination of many factors: one, the boards are grateful to have someone in which to place their confidence and that forces them to defend their leader to the public and staff whatever the consequences; two, the business has become so complex and so intimidating that I wonder if the public policy role of directors has become too blurred to be comprehensible; three, very often the new chief executive was hired to be the "fronts-person" for the board member personal agendas, in this case the program of labor peace advanced by the superintendent was exactly what they seemed to be looking for. At one time during this period, I was informed that all nine members may have had a conflict of interest of some sort regarding the state teacher union! In addition, there were several members of the board who actually admitted to me that defaulting to the superintendent's judgment was a condition of his acceptance of the position. This tactic may even be inferred from what the lawyers describe as the case law and actual statutes and makes sense from a leadership perspective. It should also be obvious how problematical this may become, both for the welfare of the children as well as the tax payer.

From a positive perspective, the focus, as it should be, was now clearly on the future but, with such an edge that it was clear people were NOW to expect something special, as if that had not been the case for the last ten years! I was tempted to recall the publicly advanced notion of the "world class school district" that been advanced by Carl's predecessor, Bernie Shapiro, a program that made sense, was cost effective, could be measured for its efficacy, but, unfortunately was never funded even though it cost a pittance compared to what was now to occur.

An important attribute that kept things rolling was the same cadre of terrific principals. The high school was in capable hands with John Fricke, a seasoned pro who knew how to concentrate on the important stuff and delegate the small stuff, although sometimes the people to whom the stuff was assigned may not have been up to the task. Linda Gringeri, who was destined for assignments with much more responsibility, was doing a great job at the intermediate grade level building and in the middle school there was still Jim Duda, one of my favorite all-time principals. Jim was the one you wanted, as a parent, to be in charge of your children during the school day. He worked tirelessly on behalf of each child and while some parents thought they knew better, and had success by-passing him, they were really wasting a great opportunity for their child to learn something from Mr. Duda. He, like the others, fought for every resource for their children, and made do with what he received, never complaining about decisions once they were made. He is one of the few people I regretted leaving behind when I retired.

Finally, a great central office support staff was still available along with the incomparable Child Study Team, still headed by Alan Elstein. And, let's not forget, the incoming superintendent had tons of cash, the same renewable money fund that had paid for almost every improvement in the district for over a decade.

On a positive note, the board members kept up what I believe was a great interest in the activities of the district, the fun part of the assignment. They routinely worked well within the crowd and managed the disgruntled, rude and often chaotic criticisms from the public very well, especially Lynn Jeney, the personable and responsive gentleman who had become president of the board. Where I did see a falloff was in interest and attendance at board meetings. It fell off dramatically, sometimes people showed up for roll call or to have their pictures taken and left and many started coming late. On one occasion there were not even enough members present to address a critical and time sensitive resolution for a bond refunding proposal that was to save the taxpayers some two hundred thousand dollars. This occurred even though the item was presented at a regular monthly meeting and the board had been briefed in advance as to the importance of the action. The proposal eventually was adopted but the delay cost another round of fees and the interest rates were not nearly as favorable. This was the only time in my entire career that such a problem had occurred.

There was also an ever increasing attitude toward explaining things away rather than dealing with them, especially when the board and superintendent were directly concerned, as we shall see below.

TRANSITIONS

Thus, did George begin his administration. The preview comments were certainly accurate: George conducted himself as a gentleman, was superbly prepared as an educator, and certainly was knowledgeable about all of the modern requirements of the curriculum and staffing issues. I have no hesitancy ranking him among the top ten superintendents that I knew well during my career. He was certainly a terrific choice for the Delran public schools. A lot did change with the departure of Carl. He seemed to be omnipresent, out all kinds of evenings but always in the right spot. By this I mean he always seemed to be with the right group saying the right things. In addition, Carl is still a legend among the central office types across the state and was well known to both state as well as county education agency personnel. Delran always got the benefit of the doubt because of Carl and that was something that was irreplaceable, especially, as George was much more like me, an office type not given to attending many meetings or especially social events. Carl used to refer to the two of us as "Mr. Inside" and "Mr. Outside", that combination was now dissipated. Even after years of service, the county establishment still did not know George well and whatever we got as a consideration was based on my three decades of service, more exactly, my performance record. George considered himself to be a CEO, which I find to be a common appellation these days among these new age superintendents and we worked on very little together over the years.

There was a significant style difference too between the superintendents. Both gentlemen were graduates of NOVA, the out of residency doctorate program. Carl asked me to review his study, finding my academic, consulting and university teaching experience as a valuable resource. I do not think George ever discussed his thesis with me. While many have found much to criticize in this route to being called "DR", NOVA graduates now dominate the current wave of new superintendents as school districts want people to have doctorate degrees and seem to not care much where or how they are acquired, at least in comparison to the "old days". I have known enough of these folks to state that there is some substance to the program. Carl's thesis was application based, like everything else about him, done well and with a highly useful focus. This notion of usefulness, perhaps practicality is a better word, permeated Carl's career and, as a result, people saw him as down to earth, plain spoken and possessing a great deal of common sense. His addresses to the public were on point, presented in everyman's language and were highly successful. He never went out of his way to force a speaking opportunity at a meeting either. The public responded magnificently and expressed outstanding support for the district. As of this writing, the new regime had passed only two budget referenda in six years, and one of those possessed the tremendous revenue for tax relief left by Carl, and only one other after several failed building improvement referenda, again subsidized by over four million dollars to lower the real impact of the tax levy. One may argue that economics played a major role but the two leaders had a much different economic outlook.

The outright assignment of blame for things that were to go wrong on the past administration, while some might say inevitable, I came to say "over my dead body", was still in the future. I am very confident that, in my absence, the situation may have become more pointed much more quickly. For example, very early on in this administration, the parents became disenthralled with the grade system in the high school. It was not a project that involved me but I was present for all of the work that had been accomplished and had some notion of what had happened. To me the parental complaints were not very well founded. Sure, every system occasionally may present unforeseen and unfavorable circumstances to a particular student situation but the comments of the parents, which were widely welcomed by the board and the superintendent, i.e., they agreed wholeheartedly with the mob that descended on the public meeting, tended to illustrate the fact that they were interested in their children getting the highest grade point averages with as little work as possible. One of them actually said to me their only goal was getting their children into college, no matter how poorly they were prepared, and the rest would take care of itself. The notion of "good enough" being "just right" permeated the atmosphere. In fact, I never, in seventeen years, had a parent approach me demanding that more tax dollars be spent to advance a program of academic excellence. In the proximate case, the program that was now under heavy criticism was developed under Carl's regime, AT THE REQUEST OF THE HIGH SCHOOL ADMINSTRATION AND TEACHERS, who developed the specifics of the plan, which was then explained in detail to the board of education, which then approved the plan, the same board who now displayed selective memory loss. I always thought the new protocol was necessary but a bit lean on achievement demands but Carl knew what would fly and saw this as an improvement and a good first step. Now the teachers were joining the parents and everyone seemed to forget their role, including the parents who had participated in the planning of the program now dismissed as too complex but in actuality was deemed too demanding on the student. There was a trend of such behavior in the district. In the past the parents had demanded and won the right for their children to miss final exams when their grades reached a certain level, forced the district to allow the student to return home after taking one midterm exam during the year, and, my favorite, often insisted that days available beyond 180 be cancelled instead of used for additional instructional time.

The problem of placing blame on previous board members really escalated as the new administration ran into difficulties. As time progressed, the recriminations toward "previous boards" increased. Some six years after Carl, we were still hearing things like "There were members of a previous board that were contentious and damaged the district relationship with the township". It got so bad that I was told by several sources to try and quietly inform people that there was a record that contradicted this position, and, that there might be some personal liability involved for people who felt free to damage the reputation of others in such a cavalier fashion. In truth, while there were certainly members of previous boards who were not afraid to defend the district, it was a matter of record that there was at least the appearance of closer cooperation, the district did far more for the community via the township in those days, and there had been incredibly generous donations of funds and lands to support the initiatives of the township, indeed to even bail them out of problems they had created for themselves.

One final transition is worthy of note and it was to become a major influence on the district over the next few years, my changed role. Under Bernie and Carl, much like under Bill Pelaia and Jack McKeon, I had become used to getting involved, by invitation, in almost everything. This was the model that sort of had developed for my career during my time in the state education agency, under the tutelage of Fred Burke and Ralph Lataille. After all, there were not many other business types with expertise in operations management who had been trained as a research psychologist, trained in organization development, managed over sixty consultancies, and taught at a major university for two decades plus. This came to the forefront in Delran when the district decided to launch a "Baldrige" type initiative. I of course volunteered and just as promptly disappeared from sight in this area. I expected that George, despite what he had heard from Carl about me, had no experience with someone of my breadth so I briefed him on my experience in the area, the invitations to be a reader for the annual award winners at the national level, my data analysis capacity, the graduate courses taught over two and one/half decades in the discipline and the consultancies focused on productivity improvement. I prepared a paper listing the categories of the classic Baldrige evaluation, the measurement tools and other analytical devices and the strategic planning strategies. This material was also shared with the leadership of the board. There were a few miscalculations in this. First, a new superintendent was not about to share the limelight with someone else, especially someone with my track record. Second, the district, naturally enough, was pursuing the public domain version of the template, the one that had been created when the original, with far more comprehensively designed requirements and extensive data analysis models used by the private sector, had fallen off in popularity. Winning that award was well neigh impossible for an organization with a culture such as that which existed in Delran, but, even going through the process was extremely challenging. The new system, for the public domain was watered down to unprecedented levels. In Delran, which I soon learned, there was to be no data collection of substance at all, nothing was put at risk. You could not very well have someone whose life was based on measurement and satisfying challenging goals running around in such a system, the questions would be too embarrassing. Occasionally someone would ask the "why" question and my only response could be that my own assignments had gotten very complex and what time I had available had to be focused on my primary duties. In the final analysis, the district expected the superintendent to be responsible, although not really accountable. Therefore, it was only fitting they keep the focus on their achievements. This is reasonable and in the world of form over substance, absolutely mandatory.

LABOR PEACE

The new administration, and the board was certainly a major player here and this shift in policy was to have far reaching consequences, almost completely invisible to the public. The superintendent called his program "labor peace" and the board, especially the members with conflict of interest issues with the teacher union, which was soon to include near everybody, seemed to almost leap for joy. In truth, having an environment in which employee morale is high, with people working to improve their productivity and constantly working toward excellence is to be valued. The truth is far less appealing. In October of 2005, *BusinessWeek* published an article in which they examined the road to almost ruin for once proud Mercedes Benz. This company had invested far too much in labor peace, with no resulting increase in quality. In fact, when crunch time came, they found the employees more interested in the next contract than in restoring the proud label. The result, the company was saddled with billions of dollars in debt and facing significant layoffs, along with plummeting quality control ratings. In Delran, as we shall see, the potential bill was much more staggering considering the relatively low base on which the mounting deficit was based.

We began seeing the effects of this in every area, and, since most people benefited, mostly only the business office staff, the people who had to deal with the deficit, were concerned. Perhaps what angered these folks even more was the fact that my programs of cost efficiencies far exceeded what they had learned the typical operation had to do to be labeled "successful". When their compensation schedule began to ignore their superlative performance, when they as local taxpayers, saw their own local property tax bills skyrocket, when they as insiders knew where the funds were being spent, then even that terrific group began to grumble. There was no end to the extravagance. When the supervisors of instruction had to be assigned different duties, their compensation and summer hours expanded until they were almost entitled to vacation. Speaking of summer work, when I first started in the district, there was none, by the first "summer of George", it resembled a jobs program. All of a sudden many of the secretaries in bargaining units could no longer cope with the work load during the regular year and overtime became more plentiful; all this while the non-affiliated support staff members were being asked to do much more with no overtime available. The guidance people could not get their work done without extra summer days and their support staff followed them to even higher paydays. The child study team could no longer get their work done during the school year, a trend that, in fairness, began before George, but was now exacerbated, and summer time became a circus of activity, again with attendant increased support staff going on the dole. In fact, the number of secretarial jobs increased even though everybody had computers and many people operated via software packages. For special education as an example, the staff dictated or wrote out reports that were then typed into a software program, the same software program that the "certificated" personnel had access to. Why they could not just enter the data, cut out the middle work and perhaps save time and money was not an issue anyone would consider, that could easily trample on the great rice bowl in the sky. If people needed extra hours during the school year, that was OK, as was overtime. Almost every teacher had a significant extra income by covering classes for their colleagues. This came atop the monies they were paid for chaperoning student activities, performing home instruction duties, etc. Stipends for coaches increased in amount and frequency. One of the music teachers was earning several stipends for activities that seemed to require simultaneous supervision; I never could quite figure that one out at all.

I finally had to approach the superintendent and board president to show that we could not afford this, especially as we had kept the tax rate so low in the previous administration by paying for such things "out of pocket", i.e., out of monies earned for the district by the business office via our extensive program of value engineering, which came to permeate every area of support services. I was told that it was important to "hit home runs" with the union and so that became just the tip of the iceberg. Here again, before the reader judges these words and actions too harshly, please keep in mind that the superintendents work on a three to five year contract and they shall not get renewed in most districts without the support of the teacher union, especially with a teacher dominated board of education. Still, while the policy may be one of survival, it is simply bad business for the customer, the children, and their financial patrons, the tax payers. However, no one really learns about such things until the wheels fall off. How bad can this business become? For the 2005-2006 school year it was reported in the media that the Willingboro Public Schools in New Jersey appeared to be some nine million dollars in debt! This problem is widespread, so much so that it should be considered a ubiquitous trend, and is the tip of an iceberg in which short-term gain, usually measured by labor peace, transcends all strategic planning and management considerations. The legislature, state board of education, various commissioners of education and the courts all deserve a fair share of the blame for this situation.

The effects of this program of labor peace were manifested in every area of operation, areas that also resulted in much greater cost. "if you see a teacher, they are being paid" became a mantra. From dances, to tutoring, to "advising" students and event traveling with them, the stipends mounted. When assistant coaching vacancies existed, the head coach got both stipends. When staff members were injured on the job they still filed for extra compensation for duties unfulfilled as if it were guaranteed. People were allowed to file for stipends connected with extracurricular activities even though the activities were not completed, so dubious were the expectations.

There is surely something to be said for labor peace, it buys superintendents time to build a reputation, builds bridges with the union, and, keeps grievances at a minimum because an unhappy faculty can simply file grievance after grievance and basically halt everything worthwhile in the district. However, following the heuristic, "their demands are insatiable", there has to be a reckoning, one proportionate to the deficit spending. The union never takes a step backwards, after all the people who run things are senior enough to outlast almost any level of layoffs, and, they have a magic weapon, the parents, who are in constant contact with the staff, not the administration and board members; and the teaching staff is accustomed to placing blame elsewhere. The parents also are never supportive of a strike, preferring instead to read statements, often prepared by the union, declaring and decrying all of the money being wasted. In Delran, with raises for collective bargaining members averaging well over five percent, even as late as 2006, the union was quite anxious to simply renew the current contract, and let the district worry about the trauma. They love to cite the "benefits' of resolving contracts quickly, in the interests of "harmony", another euphemism for labor peace. Unfortunately, many districts find themselves in this position, and, I have encountered a few board members who were also teachers who were quite anxious to settle under these terms.

In the case of Mercedes Benz, a decade without strikes, followed by a period of, as yet unknown duration, extreme turmoil, was the result. Perhaps that is the fate of every school district that over expended its budget, creating deficits. For fiscal year 2006, as an example, Delran used over four million dollars of cash and cash credits just to balance the budget and deal with the deficit over the revenue CAP reflected by the state funding restrictions. In contrast, GM and the UAW, two of the great protagonists in history, had spent years battling over labor contracts. GM got labor peace, along with a comparatively terrific deficit, and a bill of thousands of dollars in building overage costs for each of its vehicles, against the costs being registered by their competitors. Things got so bad that there were thousands of workers furloughed at almost full salary, sitting home watching OPRAH, because the contract contained a floor below which workers not needed would still be paid. This helped drive the company to a one billion dollar loss in health benefit costs. Finally, in 2005, with the company facing extinction, the union relented and provided "give-backs" worth millions. There is an old Sicilian dialectical expression, "ASPETA", which translated loosely, means: "do not hold your breath". When it comes to expecting any relief from an onerous contract, "ASPETA", when it comes to teachers working in the public schools. They knew the parents would not tolerate any disruption to their lives and the nine citizens sitting on boards are helpless before the onslaught of threats and recriminations. My advice has come down to this: negotiate a contract that you believe is fair to the staff and taxpayers and children, and then worry about the reductions necessary to fall within ever shrinking state funding guidelines. It has become an old fashioned decimation, after the Roman practice of killing every tenth man in the event of a prospective mutiny. In the public schools, the costs build like a volcano until the taxing limits are exhausted and then there is significant retrenching and the process builds anew.

KEEPING WATCH

The program of internal control in a school district is supposed to be managed by the board secretary but this is hardly a concept that endears that staff member to the superintendent and the board members, even though he or she was acting on behalf of the latter, theoretically. Of course, if the board members and the superintendent were pursuing different interests from the board secretary and there is no other tax payer advocate, and I am speaking of degrees of difference here, there could be conflicts galore. There are several bases for this concept. One, it is just common sense, the school business administrator, who traditionally also fulfills the role of the corporate secretary, works, like the solicitor, for the board of education, acquires tenure, and is the only person available to keep an eye on who may be doing what, from financial, risk management and legal perspectives. The heuristic used to be "there is no such thing as a unit control district when it comes to the board secretary." This phrase referred to the duality of control systems then in place. In the unit control district some superintendents apparently though their word was law, not so when it came to the duties of the positions I filled for many years, as was made painfully aware to Dr. Esbrandt when he was unable to successfully defend himself against my law suit. When tenure was removed from the chief school administrators and they began working on a renewal contract period, all kinds of rotten things started happening, including a formalization of the unit control system. What of keeping an eye on the proverbial chicken coop? Well, you can certainly trust the state education agency to always exert oversight in two key areas: how much damage they shall allow lay persons who become board members to cause, and, two, watching over the money. Thus, a new stratagem was developed, for the second area, the money. The administrative code for business operations was rewritten, this time with a provision that any negative occurrence in the professional life of a school business official was reviewable immediately by the commissioner of education, through her/his delegate, the county superintendent of schools. This came to be known in many circles as the Picogna amendment, referring to my willingness to risk all to expose the events in Cherry Hill and the subsequent action of the courts in condemning my firing.

I know that Carl had told George two things: that he thought I was "the best", a phrase George himself began to utter freely, and that he would be much better off working closely with me, a concept that seemed *foreign* to the new administration, that is both superintendent and the board of education, which was acting as one and that now had changed their perspective in the area of locus of control.

I began learning of precedents that had been violated where the teachers would now benefit: questionable assistance being rendered to maximize leaves, sub-rosa negotiations to increase summer work, to say nothing of items such as behind the scenes contract negotiations that cost big bucks, and even opening up air conditioned schools at tax payer expense during the summer, to provide teachers serving as private tutors with office space to ply their trade. "I have not got time to worry about stepping on someone's toes" was the rejoinder to my complaint that I had been informed that a behind the scenes concession on teacher health benefits would prove "ruinous".

The record of rationales attempting to justify such behaviors was consistent in two areas, the behaviors were always defended and/or justified, and, they were mostly ridiculous explanations, usually quite humorous, unless of course you knew something about organizational development and could foresee the eventual outcomes. Regarding the unapproved use of the schools for private employment, I actually had one board member deny that it would cost significant dollars to turn on the air conditioning, in a multi thousand square foot section of a school! The best or worst of this situation, it was always me who played the heavy, the one who had to raise objections and listen to their rationales. I became the scapegoat, always the one blamed whenever some idea to advance their perquisites was stopped. It is just too ubiquitous and really too much to expect most people to deal with.

All of these items came with a cost: in dollars, in precedents, in lost management initiative, and in exposure, especially the latter. In addition, staff got away with murder. Some of the music teachers refused to lose their after school private lesson income and lobbied successfully against a plan to build in more instructional time during the work day. Another music teacher refused to move from classroom to classroom to ply his trade and established a substandard and illegal instructional space on the stage of a large assembly hall. Now no one in a school district can authorize such an action but this went on for a while, supposedly with the knowledge of a lot of senior people, until a custodian took the initiative to call and report the violation. The custodian knew nothing about the rules for securing state education agency approval for creating instructional settings in non-classroom spaces. However, the custodian knew that the small stage did not have sufficient lighting, had dangerous steps to be traversed for access, via an equipment laden maintenance area, and most importantly, the custodian knew that it seemed dangerous to allow small children to travel unescorted down a maintenance access hallway, officially off-limits to the children, because it was the entry way for outside vendors to access the entire service corps of this large building. Fortunately, our 30k a year custodian took the risk to contact me because it appeared something was not right, no one in authority was doing anything about it, children were at risk, and "it did not used to be like this", in the words of this brave employee.

Another artifact of this was that staff discipline, always a perilous concept, became almost a joke. Sure, several non-tenured teachers were not renewed, including one who built a strong case that there had been no supervision during his few months in the classroom, these folks are traditionally cannon fodder as they are entitled only to an innocuous "reason" for non-renewal. People parked where they wished, especially at the high school where teachers had numbered, assigned spaces and still parked in the visitors' lot behind the admin building, believing it was more convenient. A staff member was caught stealing food from the lunch line, made physical contact with the kitchen manager who attempted to stop him, was reprimanded by the principal, rejected the reprimand, and went merrily on his way, in what we referred to as the "meatball king" episode. Another staff person tried to bill the district for a "commission" for writing musical pieces for the HS band, which had two other and very fine music teachers on its own staff and, best of all, a real effort was expended trying to pay him, until you can guess who said "No Way".

The list goes on and on. Some of the parents began to complain when the teachers in one school began wearing shorts. The staff were quite candid that it was their way of protesting the lack of air conditioning in the school. There was a quick huddle and the board of education first said that there was no dress code and while they deplored the action, there was nothing they could do. When I countered that the attorney had ruled the board had authority over health and welfare issues without reference to the contract, I got the "fish eye", there was another huddle and now they said that one of their spouses worked in another school district and it was Ok to wear shorts there so it must be Ok to do it here. Thank goodness they were not into nudity in the other district as this circling of the wagons, i.e., using occurrences in one district to justify the conduct in another, goes on like a perpetual motion machine. By the way, I checked and the teachers in the other districts were not allowed to wear shorts, which does not mean they paid any more attention to rules and propriety than ours did. There is no way to work with a conscience in my position and not try to intervene in such matters, and, as we say in the Navy, a stern chase is a long one. In this case, never knowing of these things, finding out by chance and then having to deal with them became quite difficult.

Obviously, such a situation soon became untenable. I became quite concerned as there is personal liability for those with knowledge of such events who fail to take action. But what sort of action? The district leadership seemed content with the "you are only guilty if you get caught" approach, and, in their defense, there were plenty of examples of events in surrounding districts in which those leaders were more than content with a laissez faire approach, particularly when it came to upsetting the routine and wishes of the staff.

I began by calling attention to the issues, first, verbally, and then in writing, indeed, as time passed, in language that stressed the urgency of some of the events. Some notices were ignored and some were subjected to tortuous rebuttal with certain individuals, but never the superintendent, expressing frustration directly to me. As events progressed, I began seeking advice from the attorneys for the state association, county superintendent staff, and the district solicitor. We finally settled on a system by which I would share concerns with a few members of the board, and, of course, the superintendent, which detailed the problem, described consequences and suggested remedies. Often these were accompanied by reports submitted by the risk management consultants employed by our insurance carrier. One among these in particular, Joseph Chiaravello, was just magnificent: knowledgeable, courageous and articulate. He had seen it all, had a terrific style in communicating problems to staff, had a plethora of solutions to offer, and, was one of the folks certain people in the district tried to keep out.

Boy oh boy, did we need Mr. Chiaravello and his colleagues, as the entire concept of accountability seemed to be collapsing around us. Consider some of these examples. Theft: money and equipment at times seemed to fly out of some of the buildings. The number of missing pieces of equipment included laptop computers for administrators, which went into one of our elementary schools. I became incredulous and asked what seemed like a very simple question: why was the administrator who kept "misplacing" such pilferable equipment not held accountable for the losses and forced to reimburse the district? Well, I was told, that it is impossible to determine who stole what and given the press of business it was impossible for the person to properly secure her allotted equipment on several occasions and thefts occurred. {THIS IS AN ACTUAL RESPONSE TO MY TANTRUM!}. Quick now, raise your hands if you think this type of behavior would build confidence in our constituents. You see, the taxpayers, including the parents, never find out about such things as they are ignored and tucked away, with the rationalizations that were written in response to my attempts to set things straight.

The fact that there were problems in this building was hardly a surprise. This was the school were the teachers where most vocal about anything they felt inconvenienced them, added any work to their assignments or failed to compensate them for anything EXTRA they felt they were being asked to do. Now my wife was required to show up several nights a year and most schools require elementary teachers to participate in evening activities close to that number. In Delran, where the parents were constantly complaining about no nights for conferences, the teachers convinced the superintendent to use the two nights for what came to be called "the nights of excellence" and "back to school nights", thus exacerbating the problem. This was the school where every teacher wanted an aide, which came to be known euphemistically as "classroom management aides". When the previous superintendent had balked at extending these to all the grade levels, a few of the teachers responded by hosting an information session for the parents, pointing out what desperate straights their children would find themselves because the teachers were overwhelmed with work. Eventually even the teacher members on the board had to back off as people started appearing at the meetings questioning what the teachers were doing all day if everyone needed an aide, to say nothing of all of the stipends for this and that.

That minor victory was in itself a compromise as two thirds of the teachers in the entire school were eventually given these aides, and, if you ask the parents, it was a terrific idea and they probably needed even more help. This was also the school where, during a major construction project, a teacher led tiny children out through a door that had been secured, with very notorious notice, because it emptied directly into the path of bulldozers building a huge extension to the school, an entire wing, along with an enormous new cafeteria. Now, this was the second occurrence of such behavior and, on this date, had a construction supervisor not been present, a giant dozer might have pulverized the children. The administrators thought nothing of it and repeated their normal defense, that the teachers were being terribly inconvenienced. The teacher mouthed off to the construction supervisor, who came to see me and when I complained, the matter ended. Not too many years earlier, under Carl Johnson, two teachers from this building had salary increments withheld for refusing to provide the expected array of activities for the children during their annual field day. Speaking of those days, in which even limited accountability was now long gone, in fact, one of these teachers was ultimately to have his increment restored. I was not surprised at this, only that he failed to demand the cash back with interest.

Since all of the buildings had been made secure to an unprecedented level, the thefts had to be inside jobs. The buildings had been re-keyed, there were TV monitors with electronic locks and swipe cards recording entry data whenever a door was opened. All of this cost a fortune but could not keep the children secure from the demands of the staff who wanted keys to everything, which is exactly what the district had tried to prevent by re-keying all of the buildings periodically. In addition, some of the teachers started taking to propping doors open so as not to have to walk to a door where entry could be monitored. Have you ever heard of such a thing!

As soon as we learned of how the principal was granting access wherever and whenever demanded, it was case closed on stopping the thefts and the band played on as if this behavior was normal or perhaps I should say "reasonable".

The risk management people also were a tremendous resource in battling some long festering problems at the high school and middle school. Several of the shop teachers were CONSISTENTLY negligent in maintaining the power equipment used by the children in a safe condition. One of their favorite ploys, WHICH WAS DISCOVERED DURING INSPECTIONS SEVERAL TIMES, was to disconnect items such as finger guards from saws, on the theory that they were very hard to clean. Needless to say no substantive action was taken against them.

The science labs were another area in which mischief was rampant. There were repeat findings that the labs were not being locked and that children were entering the spaces and vandalizing equipment, turning on gas jets, etc. At least part of the damage to my internal organs occurred from stress during this period, first in the shock that this was happening repeatedly and then when absolutely no disciplinary action was taken. We regularly found auto parts, such as acid batteries, which were the personal property of teachers, stored in our school closets, where children were exposed to the dangers. Private automobiles were being repaired in the auto shop, despite the published regs against this practice, and the rejoinder of the insurance company about coverage issues. According to a report from insurance investigators in response to a law suit, one of the high school teachers failed to move his class to a lab equipped with the necessary safety equipment when conducting an experiment. That evolution resulted in an explosion and a student was burned.

The coup de grace for me was the mercury incident. Because the labs had not been locked, the students apparently stole liquid mercury designed for experiments. Now then, mercury is a hazardous substance. The district had a HAZMAT coordinator, who had consultants and providers on-call. Her role and the protocols had been well publicized and each building sent reps to the regularly scheduled Safety Committee Meetings, at which time the HAZMAT procedures were reviewed. The students spread the mercury around various parts of the building, including the lavatories, on toilet seats etc, places where students would come into contact with the hazardous substance. When the school discovered the problem and started receiving student reports of the material being present in the OPEN where students could become contaminated, the school did not contact me, they did not contact the HAZMAT coordinator; in fact they contacted only a custodian, and had him VACUUM the areas where the material had been spread. At least the custodian had the common sense and the courage to blow the whistle. By now, as a reader, you must be expecting to read that nothing further was done here. Well, you are wrong! While nothing of a disciplinary nature occurred, they all claimed ignorance of everything, the person responsible for ordering the custodian to warm up his vacuum was commended for his role in notifying staff of the potential danger, after my office ordered the notices distributed.

One of the most remarkable moments of this entire period was the admonition to me to keep "those guys" out of the district because it was "their job to find fault". "Those guys" referred to the risk mgmt types. One of the staff, openly expressing the opinion that he was operating on the instructions of the superintendent, did indeed treat the consultants so badly that they stopped attending the safety meetings. Gentleman, my apologies, for you must have been among the few honest brokers involved in this crisis at the time!

Gradually, when the knowledge that a lot of people had joined me in exercising cognizance, things calmed down a bit, there was a record that established who knew what when and what types of warnings were advanced, and, we even began discussing SOME items in advance. However, it was clear that the Golden Age, as measured by all the available criteria, was over.

SPEND CITY

Home work advisors, parent program presenters, and so on; you have to admire the inventiveness that went into each new category of stipends and the bills piled ever higher. We brought more and more volunteers into the district, without fingerprint checks by the way. They found themselves into the classroom as the staff decided they were too busy for the mundane work teachers had shouldered for generations; they were brought onto the playgrounds for recess because no certificated personnel were available, and on and on. One of my all time favorites was the "math prep instructor", a person paid extra to help the students prepare for math exams. I am sorry but I thought this was the job of all of the teachers. There were even reading coaches assigned when the regular classroom teachers had failed to prepare the children to achieve satisfactory test scores in reading.

The consequence of this and the other trends described above was the reallocation of more and more dollars into salaries and benefits. Still, no one in authority dissented from this continued slide into a financial abyss. The board of education, acting well within their authority, and adhering to the wishes of the superintendent, seemed to have no interest in saying

"YES" to any cost saving initiative. Spending freezes were adopted and then immediately violated whenever a "special need" was identified and they were identified all the time. It got so bad I just stopped recommending the practice. Building allocations kept rising until the average per pupil expenditure was significantly above the allowable range. We kept ahead of the game via two factors. First: sleights of hand that were designed to raise the allowable spending thresholds, through spending growth limitations adjustments, which were mainly an exercise in logic, writing skills and using up, very quickly I might add, the considerable benefit of the doubt our reputation for excellence had earned the district. Second: the dollars that we had accumulated over years of cost efficiencies were now being employed just to balance the budget, e.g., using cash to offset the budgetary overage, that is, the dollars used to increase the spending limitations because the cash was being used outside the funding formula. Each year the personnel being bought in this fashion increased in cost just as they progressed up the salary guides and their benefits increased in cost, and at an alarming rate I might add.

It should be noted that the board of education was completely within its right to act in this fashion. In fact, if the taxpayers would tolerate such a notion, they could allocate every dollar into teacher salaries and benefits. When pressed for a rationale as to the mounting deficit spending, the board responded, and I wrote this rationale for them by the way: 'they were determined to maintain the current scope of services as long as possible and remained confident that the state would restore full funding'. While, in retrospect, this seems like a red herring or perhaps a pipe dream, it was a very legitimate stance. As one of the lawyers helping me keep an eye on things once said of the mounting deficits, apparent lack of accountability, and increasing number of board members with union conflicts, "It may be legal, and that shall probably never be tested, and, it may also be one of the biggest rip-offs of the taxpayer." At this time the average per pupil expenditure had grown to over $10,000, almost one thousand dollars beyond the state spending threshold; and, even as a research psychologist, I could find nothing to measure that would indicate that productivity was rising.

LIVING ON DEFICITS

The outcome of all of this was not very positive. New members of the board of education began to ask just what the differential was between what the teachers were getting as raises, and what several members of the board of education might have wanted to continue as the trend for their raises, and the three percent now being given to the non-affiliated, the "benchmarks" for future cost economies. The answer to this question was straight and staggering, FIVE HUNDRED THOUSAND DOLLARS! There were hidden costs like these infused throughout the daily operations of the schools. There were simply no data available, indeed there was no attempt to collect any, which showed any progress had been achieved by any measure, toward providing a higher quality education for the children. I recall walking down Orange Avenue in Coronado, California some years before, a town noted for its public schools, where my wife and I maintain a vacation retreat. There was a sign outside the municipal center announcing a board of education meeting in progress. Having my interest peaked, I strolled within just in time to hear a citizen mildly admonishing the board and its chief executive, for not budgeting enough money in support of the PERFORMANCE BONUS plan for the teachers. I later ascertained that the teachers did more than receive automatic raises because they were recently alive each September, they received additional payments whenever they demonstrated a number of behaviors deemed important, a list derived via the collective bargaining process. The thought would have been enough to cause everyone back home to break out in hives. There was a second significant finding that night, the chief executive <u>was</u> a chief executive. He had a law degree and an MBA in management. The kind of person who would be superintendent of schools in New Jersey was the curriculum guy, and, had often come up through the ranks as an athletic director, assistant principal etc. The biggest surprise was that in California, they were able to attract such highly qualified people on a salary scale that was competitive with my experience on the east coast. Having been a fan of the Philadelphia Phillies baseball team for many years, I was used to hearing the question, "don't we deserve more". I was just not satisfied with receiving less when it came to my chosen profession.

Prior to this period, the district not only maintained extremely low tax rates, which were admired widely throughout the region, we were able to maintain the budget well within the taxing authority, which shrunk annually, granted by the state. In fact, we were informed over several budget years that our cumulative tax savings, that is taxing authority below that which was permitted, was the highest per capita in the entire state. That led to numerous districts being referred to us for training in our operations protocols by various agencies. The synopsis of these cost savings techniques are presented in the *"TOOL BOX"* chapter of this book. No one ever said "thank you!', no one even noticed but you had to smile with remembrance as we came to be known as "spend city".

Thus the district proceeded from one of the lowest school tax rates in the region, from which popular support for the budget and building improvement referenda was widely evident, to a series of stinging budget and building referenda defeats, precipitated by ever burgeoning tax increases with no visible increases in services. Perhaps ironically, this trend proceeded to gain momentum even as the business office was generating record setting sums to offset budget deficits and hold down tax increases. For the 2006 fiscal year, it took over four million dollars of earned cash and cash credits [dollars saved in prior years] to balance the budget by reducing the taxes and chop off some fifteen cents from the prospective tax increase!

We had reached the point described in the old saying: "as long as you can burn the furniture it shall stay warm, but, at some point you run out of furniture." Poor Richard and Ben Franklin would not have been amused.

This unbridled consumption by peripheral participants such as teachers and parents is just not natural to the business of educating children in the public domain. Many believe that this troublesome trend, an offshoot of the widely condemned "entitlement" mentality, is symptomatic of the decline of many situations, including the public schools that were foundation blocks for this country.

WHAT PRICE GLORY

The following memo gives you some idea of the magnitude of the price of continuously spending every available dollar to sweeten the rice bowl for rank and file employees:

Business Office

Memo

Date

From: J.L. Picogna

To: Members, Board of Education

Subj.:   Contract Costs

In response to a question from a member, which I thought would have interest to all: the estimated difference across our payroll accounts of a 3% raise vice the current range of increases for the teachers and other employees represented by collective bargaining agreements is one-half million dollars, assuming staffing is frozen at current levels.

In response to a second question, the estimated CAP overage for the coming budget cycle may be calculated as follows [all approximates]:prior year cash provided for tax relief [and CAP expansion], $2.4 million; residual cash credits from prior years provided for tax relief [and CAP expansion]: $1.3 million; first of five payments for emergency repairs: $315,000; PLUS: any reductions from State Aid; PLUS any reductions in trend of increased student enrollment; PLUS any increases in the current year expense budget. [FYI a five percent increase in CE budget amounts to $1.6 million extra]. Thus, the potential CAP overage is: $5.6 million, assuming no changes in funding formula, plus any reduction in aid and/or income and enrollment trends.

I have also been asked the cost of extra stipends for the teachers for activities, class coverage etc. Excluding summer pay, the amount spent for these hidden costs amounted to $789,000 last year. I must also disagree with several colleagues and some of the members of the BOE who insist such data must be kept confidential. They are in the public domain.

Also, the benefits budget growth trend is approaching almost one million dollars a year since almost no cost controls are ever built into the negotiation process.

It would appear that continuing the previous range of raises, benefits and extras creates some serious questions as to the ability of the district to remain solvent, especially in light of past abuses regarding salary and benefit obligations. This then is the price of years of deficit spending to fund excess labor costs. The district has reached the point whereby essential services to children are to be curtailed in order to support items such as summer work for teachers.

Copy: Superintendent
           Solicitor

Can you even begin to imagine the frustration of trying to fight this trend from the inside, when whatever infrastructure that may exist seems committed to giving away the candy store?

What do the taxpayers get for this incredible investment? Here is a copy of an actual set of "challenge" objectives for a school district, something they are required to submit for approval to their state education agency each year. As you read these, please note, for yourself, the lack of exciting outcomes, the absence of any excitement and the ho-hum attitude regarding whether they are achieved or not. Here is the kicker, they were developed by well meaning people working to the limits of what they might propose, given the control of the teachers union and the

Kool Aid attitude of the parents, and, they were among the best I saw at the time!

XYZ School District

Pupil Performance Objectives

{PLEASE NOTE: WHILE PUBLIC INFORMATION, THE IDENTITY OF THE SCHOOL DISTRICT IS BEING WITH-HELD IN CASE THERE ARE ANY INNOCENTS TO PROTECT}

Lower Elementary Schools

• The incidents of teacher discipline referrals to the principals will be reduced by 10% across all grade levels..

• 75% of the students in grades one and two will demonstrate competent knowledge of the Math curriculum with a score of 75% or above as evaluated by quarterly assessments.

Upper Elementary Schools

• 75% of all students in grades 3, 4, and 5, who will participate in a minimum of two text book investigations units, will score a 2 or 3 (based upon a 3-point rubric scale) on the End-of-Unit Performance Assessment.

• 75% of all students in grades 3, 4 and 5. who will participate in the social studies program; will improve their score by a minimum of 10% from the initial to the final Developmental Spelling Analysis Assessment.

• Students in grade 4, including students in any and all subgroups (i.e., Race, Disability, Limited English Proficient, Economically Disadvantaged, Migrant), will achieve adequate yearly progress (AYP) on the Mathematics portion of the Assessment of Skills and Knowledge (ASK 4). (AYP is defined here as 62% of the students scoring in the proficient or advanced proficient bands of the ASK 4. Students may also achieve the state standard by achieving "safe harbor", defined as reducing by 10% the number of 2005 students scoring in the partially proficient band of the ASK 4).

• Students in grade 4, including students in any and all subgroups

(i.e. Race, Disability, Limited English Proficient, Economically Disadvantaged,
Migrant), will achieve AYP on the Language Arts portion of the Assessment of
Skills and Basic Knowledge (ASK 4). (AYP is here defined as 75% of the students scoring in the proficient or advanced proficient bands of the ASK 4.

Students may also achieve the state standard by achieving "safe harbor", defined as reducing by 10% the number of 2005 students scoring in the partially proficient band of the ASK 4).

Middle Schools

• General education 8 grade students will attain an average of 7 correct responses out of 12 (or an average of 58% correct responses if the number of questions per cluster changes) in the spatial sense and geometry cluster of the GEPA mathematics test.

• Students in grade 8, including students in any and all subgroups (i.e. Race, Disability, Limited English proficient, Economically Disadvantaged, Migrant), will achieve adequate yearly progress (AYP) on the Language Arts portion of the Grade Eight Proficiency Assessment (GEPA). (AYP is here defined as 66% of the students scoring in the proficient or advanced proficient bands of the GEPA. Students may also achieve the state standard by achieving "safe harbor", defined as reducing by 10% the number of 2005 students scoring in the partially proficient band of the GEPA).

High Schools

• The number of teacher referrals to the administration for 9 grade students will be reduced by 10%. {As a result of continued implementation of this project, the number of teacher referrals to the administration for 9th grade students will be reduced by 20% (second year of a two-year goal).}

• As a result of the implementation of Rigor and Relevance Era (including the Bloom Taxonomy of the Cognitive Domain) in a stratified random sample of English classes, academic evaluation will reveal an increasing emphasis on the upper continuum of the domain (application, analysis, synthesis, and evaluation).

Fifty percent (50%) of all teacher-developed student assessments and questioning prompts will reflect these criteria as evidenced by a score of 2 or 3 on a locally developed 3-point rubric scale.

Of course they were approved, and in comparison to the submission of many other districts, they were worthy of a commendation in that "best of the worst" world in which children are forced to labor. There is little impact on their world if the staff manages to accomplish these objectives and who would notice if they did not. But, the objectives cover each grade grouping and many different areas and seem to be dependent on the presence of contemporary well written and illustrated text books. This too is a bit scary because, with over 80% of many public school district budgets consumed by salaries and benefits, there is precious little to spend on technology and other learning resources. Here is something else to consider. For all of the hysteria expressed by the teachers and administrators in preparation, which takes almost a year, for the various periodic monitoring visits by various state officials that take place every five to ten years, the whole thing is mainly a paperwork exercise, with the only districts placed in remediative care being those that everyone knows are just awful, whether in leadership, or staff capacity, or parental involvement or some combination of all three. In fact, the only area in which the performance of school district employees is measured objectively, comprehensively and annually is the financial audit process and those folks, no matter how splendid their performance may be year after year, are not paid on a performance basis. Indeed, the current trend is to pay them far less as to percent increases than the teachers, as they are not normally represented by collective bargaining units.

Notice that there is little consideration for meaningful outcomes and none regarding desired behaviors being displayed by the teachers. However, they are a great deal more creditable with what is routinely accepted on teacher performance improvement plans, or PIP's, as they are known. These statements of anticipated performance improvements are normally not worth the paper they are printed on. I have kept a private log all these years and the following represents one of the most frequently seen PIP objectives I have seen: "Please continue to read NJEA articles".

Now, that is just the sort of promise that would encourage me to fork over thousands of dollars per year in property taxes.

Contrast this nonsense, in which no one is held accountable, no one is responsible for anything meaningful, and nothing of worth is measured, with what happens in the private sector in which even processes are measured as to their efficacy. Consider organizations such as GENERAL ELECTRIC and MOTOROLA, noted for excellence in leadership, manufacturing, customer service and marketing, among other areas, and their Six Sigma programs. This effort requires a close examination of every facet of their operation, including operational processes. The public schools are not even in the same universe and the children suffer and John Q. Taxpayer takes it in the wallet constantly. To illustrate this point further, I have never seen a school district that has ever conducted a staffing study, in other words, they have no idea if they have the right jobs and the right number of jobs on the dole.

One of my most enjoyable assignments for the extension institute at Temple University involved CONRAIL, the Consolidated Rail Corporation. This was a fascinating organization that for years bowed to Congressional pressure to cut costs by doing just that, cutting costs. They dropped tens of thousands of jobs without rhyme or reason and soon they came up almost short in being able to run the trains, a bit embarrassing when that is your business. A great CEO, Donald Levan, started a program entitled, CSI, for "continuous process improvement". This was not just some prophylactic approach to problem solving; it was a complete immersion in productivity enhancement. Everybody became TQL [total quality leadership] conscious and in a hurry. To illustrate, there was no TQL Office because the entire entity operated in this fashion. My future good friend, Ron Napoli was one of the first and primary players in this effort, in his capacity as a finance director. Ron's unit was in collections and it was fascinating. Whenever a train moved to someone else's tracks, the tariffs would change, and the collections people were the focus of the problem. There were estimated error rates of close to 5% and the goal was to reduce the rate to 0.5%, an amazing improvement, one worth millions of dollars in revenue. I used the Johnsonville Foods model to orient people to the new regime and trained, trained, trained people in my own project with ITT Engineered Valves, which became the paradigm for this effort. Well, to make a long story a bit shorter, thanks to Ron and a bunch of great folks like him, the effort was successful. Talk about leadership, Ron had to allow a bunch of his supervisors to become worker bees, depending on the training to convince everyone of the need to work more quickly and more effectively. They did and it was a winner. Two points here are relevant to public education, the first is that I can not even explain any of this to an educator for they have absolutely no background in productivity improvement, and, two, it should be obvious why Ron Napoli was so superior to any of his peers as a board member.

Thus the difference between the real world, in which investors expect results, and the public dole, in which everything goes unmeasured. The price, then, of their feigned "glory" is wasted opportunities for our children and a multi-billion dollar price tag.

AT WHAT COST

What happens when the concept of labor peace causes precious dollars to be fritted away? A lot and all of it negative. When you add to the mix a situation in which a huge labor establishment has been created, with huge payments being expended routinely for "hidden costs", stipends and summer jobs programs, the cost is enormous, particularly to the children, who end up paying for the folly of the adults in charge.

The concept is called "dismantling" and it occurs in two ways.

The first is a natural occurrence when enrollment begins to tumble. One of my fondest recollections is the manner in which John McKeon, the legendary superintendent of schools in Cherry Hill during the 1980's, refocused the energy and resources of the district in an effort to maintain the outstanding quality of instruction that was the trademark of the district, while contracting the capacity of the district to manage only 10,000 children, down from a high of 18,000 only a few years previously. To make matters even more challenging, Cherry Hill had been organized around the concept of neighborhood schools rather than large campus locations, which began to find favor in the 1990's, when resources consolidation due to financial constraints became a major consideration. This forced McKeon to close neighborhood schools, almost an impossible task in many towns and cities. McKeon was nothing short of brilliant, and I believe his reputation for humility, service, intelligence and integrity were the keys, first in getting people to listen and then to join in the effort to remake the district into a smaller more efficient yet still rich in quality entity.

Jack visited the buildings frequently, allocating even more of his precious nights to this campaign. People respected him so well, indeed his very presence was reassuring, a quality I was to find in my other great local superintendent, Carl Johnson. This was Jack's entree into meetings in which parents were naturally concerned and a bit skeptical but they knew they had a leader to manage the crisis, one who had proven again and again that his first priority was always the welfare of their children. And so, schools were closed, programs were consolidated but the quality of instruction never wavered nor did the support of parents. Imagine a superintendent of schools approaching a staff facing huge layoffs and telling them that all he had to offer was more hard work and a chance to share in the sacrifices being faced by the entire school community. I cannot think of this working anywhere else because nowhere else had Jack McKeon.

The second dismantling scenario comes when the teacher compensation and benefits package has been expanded beyond the public purview, which means that the cash reserves of the district were being employed to support these ever expanding labor bills until the funds were exhausted. This dismantling evolution comes silently and quickly and with devastating consequences, particularly given the need for the leadership to try and explain the phenomena, which often costs them the remaining shreds of credibility. Parents are faced with the prospect of "pay to play", which means items like sports and expanded busing are no longer covered by the ever growing BASE property tax bill, and, the diabolical combination of cuts in services accompanied by equally staggering increases in local property taxes builds incredible resentment. Most interestingly to me, the same union members who so greedily gobbled up every crumb that could have been spent more wisely to avert the crisis, now show ZERO loyalty to those who so eagerly feathered their nests and join in the condemnation. The culture collapses and the entire school environment becomes one of mistrust, which can take years to rebuild, if ever, given the staggering deficits inherited. Can this scenario be dealt with, can it be managed? The answer is "YES", provided there is a corresponding growth of very complementary skills: integrity and management acumen.

Here is a template that I have used to convey the painful lessons to those whose lack of foresightedness caused the problem in the first place:

XZY SCHOOL DISTRICT
Business Office

Memo

Date

From: J.L. Picogna

To: BOE President, Superintendent, Solicitor

Subj.:   Budget Planning

Obviously, the piper has to be paid in the forthcoming budget cycle and the projected budget overage, in terms of the revenue CAP, is enormous. You can wipe out a significant amount of the CAP overage by attempting strategies such as limiting collective bargaining group increases to three percent and freezing the next current expense budget at the existing levels. Amazing how just two such acts slices the indebtedness, although the implementation shall certainly not be easy.

One of the consequences of adopting a business as usual strategy, knowing this day was coming, is that the district is forced into dealing with what is really a strategic mgmt problem with only tactical solutions, that is, we may now only focus on the coming year. Here are some ideas:

1. Hold next fiscal year spending at current levels and this means everything possible. To accomplish this, a different look at using grant monies such as the so-called title grants and items such as bilingual monies have to be effected, to insure the monies are serving primary needs here. This would include also special education. With all due respect to our colleagues in that area, who truly deserve all possible praise, you may have noticed how often, over the years, the statement that something is "required" wilts under questioning by me. To accomplish this everything gets reduced to zero and items such as required busing, funds for HVAC etc. get put in and whatever remains is all there is and those dollar amounts drive the remainder of the budget. Now I have never seen a school district pull off something like this, especially during my time here where every attempt at a freeze is prostituted immediately by "exceptions". Just witness how the no field trip policy turned into quite an expenditure of funds, for certain students only, immediately after the edict was promulgated.

2. Whatever remains shall not be nearly enough to run the current scope of programming so the next step would be for the superintendent to solicit approval from the County Superintendent of Schools for certain separate budget referendum questions, that is, additional spending authority resolutions, that would be placed on the forthcoming ballot. You may recall that we have avoided this all these years due to the extra cash we generated via cost efficiencies, which seems only to have raised expectations to unreasonable levels now that the loophole is closed. To quote Sir Winston, "Never have so many ignored so much accomplished by so few." The entitlement mentality among staff and constituents shall not be dissipated even

by a crisis of such dimensions but that is another artifact that must be dealt with.

3. Once we know what may be placed on the ballot for separate voter approvals, then the next step is to eliminate all of the extra work that has sprung up around here over the last few years. It used to be that not even the child study team needed to work over the summer but that is a time that is "gone with the wind". Nevertheless, I believe strongly that the labor peace initiative is largely responsible for the deficit spending so it seems logical that what got us here has to be undone. I am particularly concerned with all the extras that have been built into contracts. I do not believe anyone shall accept "we have a contractual commitment "as a valid excuse because those extras were freely entered into with the full knowledge that this crisis was proximate, thus the specter of deficit spending.

Obviously this is not an easy prescription but when you are talking about the potential of eliminating almost six million dollars out of thirty three million, taking these steps, however, difficult save much of the infrastructure that truly matters. Also, the district would then be back where it was financially some years ago, one of the strongest fiscal positions among all districts in New Jersey. In any event, these are my thoughts for whoever may be interested. We are well past the point where some strategic planning has to begin.

Well, if they were ticked off at receiving this, they mostly hid their angst, I guess because the material presented was not only true but an understatement as to factors such as their role in propagating this impending disaster, and, I very graciously ignored the not trivial matter of how many warnings they had received over the previous years, each time they took another step that inevitably brought the district closer to the edge of disaster. Some months later there was still no sense of urgency as to taking the necessary steps to get ready for the next budget cycle. Even though the solicitor warned that the district should immediately give notice that all of the extra stipends, summer work etc., that the teachers had come to view as part of their work ENTITLEMENT [trust me, you shall never, ever, encounter any group with a stronger entitlement mentality], a decision was made that a business as usual mentality had to be maintained. It was deemed more important to "stay on track", rather than "cause discomfort" to the parents. I guess all this means they did not want to acknowledge a potential problem of this magnitude before they asked voters to approve a $20 million plus building improvement referendum, the third time in two years they had tried to secure voter approval for this measure. Later, someone would ask me why anyone would keep proposing referenda when they were faced with the prospect of laying off huge numbers of staff. In effect, why build more classrooms when there was such a strong chance that the coming surfeit of teachers could very easily leave large numbers of rooms vacant?

In September of 2005, *BusinessWeek* highlighted the resurgence of the Canon Company, of photocopier fame. The article focused on the plant managers, whose role in life was to be sticklers for efficiency and financial prudence. Can you imagine how these school district leaders would fare in such an environment? I am reminded of David Halberstam speaking of the early origins of TQM in Japan: "…tiny little improvements in processes, occurring every day". In the school district, the leadership may have spent several years pursuing a Baldrige improvement paradigm, but, with one important exception, they never measured anything. "Why?" you may ask. Such measurement is the essence of this process, which is sponsored by the Federal government with the express intention of measuring improvements. The district only said that they were not "ready" to implement measurement, a concept that made no sense to a research psychologist and an organization development expert like myself, one who had been invited to participate many times as a reader in the awards process. I know of a secretary who came from a private sector company, one that had a great history of success with continuous process improvement. She was invited to participate in the district process as a new employee and she later confessed to me that she was incredulous as to what she had witnessed, particularly, among the teachers, who had no sense of what was expected, and who were completely uninterested in being involved with accountability. This was bad enough but what made all of this worse was that it was another exercise in form over substance and an expensive one at that. The price of the endless talk about "successes" with this effort are hard to calculate exactly but let's try: they employed a consulting house as facilitators, at 20+ k a year; there were various other speakers from time to time, let's say at another 5k, and, by the time you add in all of the food provided at public expense and the cost of the days off work and the substitute teachers etc., then you are looking at the value of an extra teacher a year and they did this for years.

How strong is the union? It is a ubiquitous force and its members, as a trend, follow its dictates without question. A long serving employee in the "utility" category once came to my attention, because he was more comfortable with my advice, and stated he believed he was entitled to a higher rate of pay because his duties resembled closely those receiving a higher rate of pay. It was a classic case requiring a desk audit, that time honored HR process by which actual work, as it derives over a period of time between job analyses, is measured against that of others and the compensation they receive. To repeat, I laid this all out for him, told him exactly what to do to initiate the evolution and promised my full cooperation in working with the process and reviewing the results. I saw him again in two weeks and asked what progress he had made. I knew I needed him to start the process because: a. the request should come from the employee and b. the superintendent in that district, who was in charge of HR, had glazed over eyes when I tried explaining this to him. I was not surprised to learn that the union rep stated they were not going to sponsor any raise for this employee because the clerks had been promised higher pay. I spoke to that person and the area rep for the union also and explained to both that the employee had a right to ask for the audit but they refused to cooperate. When I next saw the employee, he stated that it would not be in his best interest to pursue the matter. How can anything that works in such a corrupt manner be counted on to deliver the goods in what is supposed to be the rather altruistic business of serving children? The people to whom this book is dedicated are the ones who made the choice to always place the welfare of the children above their own.

LIMITATIONS

Notice that this section is not entitled "SOLUTIONS", because I see few and most of them seem unworkable in today's political environment. Many states have joined with the federal government in seeking solutions to the dual problem of controlling spending and searching for accountability, perhaps the most elusive of any goal ever pursued by any entity. The Feds started the ball rolling with the Elementary and Secondary Education Acts, in the mid 1960's, which were pure entitlement programs, e.g., hugely funded efforts to get massive new programs going in states, and having been a veteran of the national scene almost since the first iteration of ESEA, I can well attest that the dollars were needed everywhere but especially in areas such as Louisiana, Mississippi and Arkansas, where it seemed no one paid any attention to the welfare of children. Despite the concerns reported earlier in these pages surrounding the waste that accompanied these programs, they provided a mightily needed infusion of cash to kick start a moribund system of public education, a system that continually looked to the past while becoming trapped by the future.

The days of entitlement programming are long gone and now we are charged with controlling spending, well after the proverbial fox has emptied the hen house. Some years ago, California created a stir with its proposition 13, and several succeeding similar passed proposals that have seriously damaged the capacity of the state to care for its residents, especially its children. More recently, the Governator led an effort to prohibit children of illegal immigrants from public schools and other social services. This problem is almost immeasurable in terms of financial impact, especially in a jurisdiction such as Los Angeles County, where the tab reached to the level of billions. And yet, as a superintendent of schools of Los Angeles said a few years ago when this effort became popularized, "Am I to condemn tens of thousands of children to the street, because the state pretends they and their parents are not here?" I could not agree more, even as a price fighter. The Governator would be much better advised tackling the state teacher unions, particularly their pension system, which some years ago began making investment decisions to support political positions and is reportedly on the brink of disaster, especially as the employees shall never be asked to make sacrifices to bail out their own fund, and you can take that to the bank!

What then is to be done? The No Child Left Behind program seemed to be well intentioned but came under attack as soon as the NEA detected that their "professional prerogatives" would be impinged to say nothing of the use of the dirty word "accountability". For people whose professional goals normally extend no further than "continue to read NEA journals", just mention measuring anything and they have apoplexy. In any event, the entire effort is being sand-bagged in classrooms all over the country; the parents have been convinced that the testing provisions constitute some terrible evil for their children; and, [this is my favorite] the program is too costly, this from people who just absorb money, people for whom the concept of labor peace knows no financial restraints.

New Jersey is trying a novel approach. During the term of one of the most insipid individuals I have ever come to know, Christine Todd Whitman, the state took a nose dive financially. Reprising strategies from the era of Robert Taft and the republican dominated congresses of the Truman and Eisenhower years, Governor Whitman: began under-funding everything, established controls that would eventually bankrupt many needed services, froze state aid for schools no matter how much their enrollment increased, cut into the state pension funds to hold down tax increases, and, in a really short-sighted maneuver that guaranteed ever increasing property taxes, cut the state income tax. During her administration, the abortive McGreevy tenure, and for the foreseeable future, state aid stayed frozen, a clear violation of the state school funding act. However, clever devils that they are, the governor's annual budget message transcends existing law concerning mandated spending. For example, no mater how many statutes may exist that require replacement of bridges on state roads every so many years, the annual budget message can establish a financial roadblock, at least until the bridges start falling into the rivers and streams. In addition, Ms. Whitman chose to ignore the proposed provisions in the state funding law that waived the necessity for a budget referendum when district budgets were within state imposed growth limitations. Powerful political interests for the municipalities reportedly refused to relinquish control over the schools, as local government bodies took control of budgets after election defeats. Thus, Ms. Whitman was able to pander to still another group, much to the disadvantage of the children, while not offending the state teacher unions. For the six years or so that the frozen aid system has been in place as this was written, the typical K-12 schools district in the state, approximately 2500 students, grew by approximately 600 students on average. With regional per pupil expenditures of over ten grand you can see how the bills start piling up. Indeed, pretty soon you are talking about real money. Since the state aid was frozen, local property taxes had to be raised, by a huge margin, to cover the shortfall. Now, I have no doubt that much that was being spent was unnecessary, nevertheless, as the state was unwilling to come to grips with the political power of the union, leaving the locals to clean up their mess, and, since the districts were limited in the amount of revenue they could raise each year, most people would say enough is enough. However, when the citizens began organizing around the issue of increasing property taxes, their power base rivaled that of the teacher unions and so both entities had to be appeased, once again at the expense of the schools. The state took tenure away from the superintendents. The state allowed teacher unions to run amuck, from education department policies and administrative rulings to ethics commission opinions. The state allowed teacher union members to sit on boards of education not only feathering the nest of their fellows in one district but establishing a system of ever increasing benefits and salaries in neighboring districts, including those that employed the teacher union board members. The state forced districts to cut their emergency operating fund to less than three percent of the operations budget and seized the money for tax relief. The state established, retroactively, spending limitations on administrative costs and then published lists of districts that exceeded standards no one knew existed until six months after the fiscal year began. The state published pronouncements that school districts had ill-served their constituents by permitting teacher unions to enjoy such "lavish" raises, all the while hiding the fact that the state "mediators", in many cases, were responsible for "suggesting" the settlements that were now being condemned. The state made it virtually impossible to keep school districts open during illegal work stoppages, thus pandering to the real strength of the union; they cannot lose money because time lost on work stoppages is made up, i.e., the sacred 180 day school year.

As if all of this were not enough, in 2004, the state announced the "final solution" [where have I heard that one before], one that the politicians were trumpeting for national adoption. They called the measure Senate Bill S1701.

S1701 is a really interesting concept, as has been related earlier. It was adopted three months after the start of the fiscal year and, in the best tradition of New Jersey politics, was made retroactive to the BEGINNING of the fiscal year. Thus, at the end of the first quarter, almost 600 operating districts were given new rules that, among other things: caused them to have already and unknowingly, violated new transfer regs; seized almost all of their operating surplus; and, made use of the remaining free appropriation balances almost impossible. No one is able to answer the question: "What happens if a wall falls down", because the state has all of the funds tied up, in many cases, reallocating them to big cities, which receive a fortune in extra funds even though many seem beyond redemption, but which also provide a vast reservoir of votes. At the same time the folks in Trenton informed the public that S1701 would "guarantee" the severe reduction of teacher salary and benefit increases, while all the time consciously leaving in place all of the factors that made this a barren promise. The full effects of this lunacy have yet to be discerned. I fear my former colleagues who believe they have hit rock bottom may have quite a bit farther to fall. Please remember, the rationale behind S1701, this draconian act, is twofold: the state refuses to fund their own school financial aid formula and has not for over six years; and, two, they blame the locals for "giving away the store", i.e., unfettered increases in labor costs with no evidence of increased capacity being available. While the "locals" ought to be ashamed of themselves, and the model giving them this power should be amended drastically, this situation would not have occurred save for the state. If the state had not allowed teachers to serve on boards of education then they could not have "given away the store". If the state had not issued ethics opinions removing conflict prohibitions under their "doctrine of necessity" then they could not have given away the store. If the state were not afraid of dealing with statewide employee unions then they could have controlled the increases themselves. If the predictions of natural gas and fuel oil for heating doubling during the period following the hurricanes Katrina and Rita crisis prove valid, then the current spending controls are simply not up to dealing with the resulting budget challenges.

As I move toward retirement, the brighter kids are becoming more numerous and need special care to foster the development of their marvelous foundation, there are many more children, especially those with non-English language skills, who need extensive programming to get them at least "even", and, all of the children need a nurturing environment, some to replace that which is not available via their own homes. Still think this system is capable of generating that kind of support?

DEPARTURES

The cumulative effect of all of this on me was a decision to "go over the side" as we say in the Navy. Although I always felt I was paid generously for the profession, someone with my training and experience always gave up a lot of salary to work in the pubic domain. The people, i.e., business administrators mostly, that I encountered who fell into this category made this sacrifice usually for two reasons: the satisfaction of contributing to the welfare of children and the pension and health benefits program. I made up the salary difference and much more by teaching every semester for what seemed like an epoch; using vacation to conduct seminars for the extension institute at Temple University; serving as a naval reserve officer; and, writing several books. While the cash was impressive so was the wear and tear, especially the stress of working for several masters simultaneously, to say nothing of the back-breaking hours. Eventually you get to the point where the value of the pension becomes so high in comparison to your salary that you are working a lot of hours for well less than half pay. I had reached that stage a few years before the ennui of a system gone amuck and the sheer frustration of chasing after almost every transaction to get a fair deal for the district became overwhelming. Thus, I moved to what I hope was a well deserved reward and resumed my interest in the private sector.

As for the district, I predict that the place shall continue to appear to be well managed, at least at long as they are able to retain some of the proven professionals that permeate the support staff ranks. To his credit, George was well prepared for his role, knew what to do, and recruited a great number of creative and high performing new teachers. Also, he had worked hard to concentrate staff focus on test scores and knew, better than anyone, how almost helpless a superintendent is today in the frothing environment of stilted funding, angry taxpayers who seek seats on boards of education and staff more concerned about carrying the wounds of dissatisfaction than in seeing to their duties. Indeed, in this environment, it is almost difficult to imagine many people doing any better.

A less experienced, non-tenured business official is much more likely to tend the books, not get involved with internal control issues and be more "pliable" to the rules. There is a new cadre of board members who are more discerning in their questions and less likely to adopt recommendations without some examination. All in all, I think this to be a healthy situation in terms of checks and balances, probably one that would have been much easier for me, so a positive prognosis is in order, assuming that the financial angst passes quickly. and the slimmed down district moves ahead in a more cost effective manner.

THE FACE OF GOVERNANCE

"Now I Have Become Death, the Destroyer of Worlds"

Bhagavad Gita, Hindu scripture

HOW BAD HAS IT BECOME

How bad indeed? Well, I have worked with a few superb board of education members in each assignment, outstanding people whose only thought was the service of children. They have been undermined to such an extent that they have almost no authority left and little capacity of effecting change. To illustrate, I am presenting a draft of a template I often used to welcome new members to the board of education after the annual elections in New Jersey. Please note that they are expected to be sworn in and immediately start approving bills that they dare not question and endorse personnel appointments over which they have no control:

Business Office

Memo

Date

From: J.L. Picogna

To: Newly Elected Members, Board of Education
Subj.:   Welcome!

Although this may be a bit premature, since I have heard nothing of write-in candidates and I do not expect any of you to get yourself arrested or suffer some disqualifying event before your investiture, please let me extend an unofficial welcome to you, at least as perspective members of the Board of Education. The material that I am presenting is all in the public domain so nothing is being compromised.

The role of board members has been truncated significantly by the Department of Education over the years, until, as many experts believe, the primary remaining functions are to deal with disgruntled parents and conduct negotiations with teacher unions, two areas which the State of New Jersey avoids at all costs, as there are insufficient funds to satisfy either group.

Board members may appoint staff, but only if they are recommended by the Superintendent. They may approve a budget, but only within very severe financial limits that no longer cover even the status quo. They may approve curriculum, but only within the parameters established by DOE, and, they cannot even discuss staff unless the staff member is part of some official item brought before the Board by the Superintendent. In addition, "NO" votes on any financial item require a "substantial reason" and are subject to review and actual modification by the County Superintendent should the item in question fail passage by the necessary majority.

These are among the several reasons why service on a Board of Education has become a very difficult commitment and also why so many communities are finding it hard to attract child advocates to serve. In my time, the majority of members who served here did so with distinction, placing the welfare of the children above all else. Not only is the job getting more difficult, it comes with some personal liability. There is insurance coverage of course, but the carrier provides no protection for damages awarded as a consequence of gross negligence or what they refer to as "bad acts". You shall find that it is far different sitting at the table rather than with the audience. Comments from the floor, while potentially slanderous, are often ignored because the speaker has no real power to cause some official or staff member of the district to suffer any loss. Board members, on the other hand, despite their relative powerlessness, are seen quite differently and are subject to intense scrutiny. I would advise being very circumspect in your dealing with parents and staff. You shall find that anyone who finds fault with you shall undoubtedly attempt to cast you in a very negative light, probably by claiming that you have, at some time, attempted to win special privileges for your children. Your entire history is now open to review so acquiring a thick skin is a very definite asset!

I am told that boards of education are the most sued entity in the public domain in New Jersey, and, after over three decades of central office service, I can see why. In this community during my tenure, many have tried but none have succeeded. We have been blessed with excellent representation over the years by our solicitor, the superintendent works tirelessly to deal with issues before they escalate, and the board members have been both involved heavily yet careful in their behavior and the district has remained unscathed. You should be aware that there is a policy that provides for only the board president and superintendent to serve as the spokespersons for the district.

As new members of the board, you shall be required to attend weekend orientations hosted by New Jersey School Boards Association, who shall report your successful completion of the programs to the Commissioner of Education. Most veteran central office staff and board members seem to agree that this "training" is the only tangible service this organization provides. Please recall that membership in NJSBA is mandated by law, and previous boards have explored the potential of opting out. I am afraid that we are at a point where they have to do something to justify the dues being levied; goodness knows their other services seem to play no critical role, and so the Legislature has given them this mission.

You shall also come under the control of the School Ethics Commission and be required to file the financial disclosure forms. Please call me if you have questions about any of these items. I have been asked about the persistent rumor that the required training sessions shall be increased in number and scope but I have received no official word of any such change.

Soon you shall receive a copy of the reorganization agenda, which shall be your first meeting following the recent election. This agenda contains required appointments and each provider has served the district well for many years. The material pertinent to the annual reorganization of the Board precedes the official action agenda, which shall be similar to that which you see on a monthly basis. Please feel free to contact this office should you have questions on any of the items. You shall also be receiving a copy of the next bill list. You may contact someone in accounts payable should you have a question on any of these items. In addition, the monthly report of the treasurer and board secretary shall be distributed. I am sure that the superintendent shall be providing you with copious material to get you oriented and I suggest that you contact the superintendent with questions about district programming and the proposed budget. During the period between the election and the reorganization meeting, you should direct any questions and concerns here as there is no board of education meeting scheduled during that period. You should forward your contact information, home phone numbers and email address, to this office. In the past the Board has published these data for its constituents. One bit of good news, I have decided to forgo my prerogative of administering a literacy test for this group of perspective new members. Once again, welcome and best wishes for success.

Copy: Superintendent
          Solicitor

It is any wonder that I find it amazing that anyone with a serious personal or professional agenda would seek to serve on a board of education, given the delimitations presented above? Unfortunately, I have seen my share of rotten apples, whose burning desire was either the promotion of their own child or the satisfaction of their own ego.

There was a strong candidate for this section who was a long term member of the state board of education. I was truly surprised to learn that he was deceased because he never appeared to be alive during the 1970's, when he served with less than distinction. You have to have spent most of your life on a desert island not to realize how people get appointed to such lofty positions. However, I met board members such as Ruth Mancuso and David Brandt, among others, who were extremely proficient and quite unselfish in their service, and the children profited. I could never figure out why our current subject even accepted the appointment. He never spoke, indeed, he voted by raising his hand and the staff joked that he was actually a mummy that was wheeled into position before we were permitted to enter their chamber, and then the arm rose to signify acceptance of still another resolution due to some sort of post-mortem electrical stimulation. I did see some life in the old boy during the pre-meeting luncheons of the state board. You did not need to know their calendar to determine when they were meeting. One had only to be able to inhale to experience the delights of the Lobster Newburg and other delicacies the caterers provided at taxpayer expense. He gobbled up just about everything, again while never speaking. I think he was a rich, politically powerful old man who had very little else to do but attend these meetings. Unfortunately, he seemed to add nothing by his presence and the children would have been better served by having an activist as one of their advocates.

I know of several board members who later became employees of the district where they once held governance positions. One, Warren Benedetto, was a terrific board member and an even better superintendent of schools. I am afraid that the positive comments must stop with Warren for many of the rest seemed to be true feeders at the public trough. One in particular was a true sycophant, preaching against this and that while working behind the scenes to feather her own nest, that is, secure premium status for her children. Her efforts paid unexpected dividends when she was given an administrative position with a district some years after her final term on the board, a "sole applicant appointment" as it was described to me. Quite a coincidence if you ask me.

DOING GOOD

A number of people I have encountered were not only participative and child-oriented board members, they expanded their role by working hard with constituent groups and local municipal governing boards to support the best alternatives for children in related areas. Joan McHugh was just terrific in Delran. She prided herself on being known as a "senior citizen" but she catered to no one but the children. I used to tease her by asking what the old woman was up to at any given time. She would respond in two ways, first, by reminding me that I was not that much younger than herself, and, two by launching on a dialogue about her latest effort to rein in more support for the schools. She may have had a few years on her but her child advocacy orientation would have been worthy of a college age activist. She always saw the best in any group, even the town council in Delran, which never impressed me at all. In fact, there was ample evidence to suggest this group almost welcomed the opportunity to scapegoat key issues such as property taxes, onto the backs of the schools, and thus the children, as if the board of education and not the council persons were responsible for the poor decisions that caused the town to be characterized as it became, mostly residential, with relatively low ratable values, with a high percentage of lower income apartment dwellers. Joan was highly intelligent and she realized the facts of life but she never let that reality dissuade her from winning over converts. She was one of the finest board members I have ever been privileged to serve, and, she came to the board known as the "senior citizen".

My dear friend, Morris Burton, was one of the longest serving board members in the history of such office. Nevertheless, his enthusiasm never waned and his behavior mirrored that of Mrs. McHugh. Morris' specialty was going out on the stump, even at his advanced age, and he worked tirelessly to pass building improvement referenda in a town where people spent freely on great cars but were satisfied with mediocrity for their children, as long as mediocrity did not cost much. This gentle giant never became frustrated, always looked forward, and never stopped trying. The fact that a school or at least an athletic complex is not named for this great child advocate is quite unfortunate, in my opinion.

Bob Sheeran and Bob Mull are other examples of pragmatists, willing to fight the good fight, and never stop trying. They were part of the group Ron Napoli brought to the board of education in Delran, the group that led to the golden age of that district. Without people such as these, even the talents of the great Carl Johnson would have been wasted. You had to be there the night these people stood against physical threats to approve the privatization plan that generated both the cash as well as quality service providers that launched what just may be the most exciting time of my career. It was easy for the union types to cast them as "anti employee" because Sheeran, Mull and Napoli stood for quality and fiscal sanity. They were also not afraid to make investments either, once they saw the cost benefit aspect of the proposals. My hat is off to these fine fellows!

I never worked for Joanne Pelly and Peggi Haynes but I was able to watch their performance as board members very closely and for many years. I am pleased to be able to refer to them as friends because they achieved much on behalf of children, and over an extended period of time. They volunteered, actually were begged, to remain on the board of education in Mount Laurel for several terms, long after their own children had passed through the system. They bore the brunt of a massive population explosion in the community, with a corresponding flood of new children and significant increases in property taxes as the state was unable to fund its own school aid formula. They held the line, they maintained quality through lean times, they made several excellent personnel choices such as Art Merz and Rob Wachter, and they rebuilt the physical plant, despite strong taxpayer opposition to building improvement referenda. The latter accomplishment describes the finest achievement, building bridges on behalf of the schools among all possible constituencies. I think it was a spectacular performance, especially since they were always widely admired.

HALF AND HALF

This section is reserved for members of boards of education that I have encountered over the years, some I worked for, others served in districts with which I am familiar or served in some advisory capacity. These folks achieved less than they could because of their union affiliation. Once again the names have been with-held, in part because they offered much that was praiseworthy and they shall know who they are, and, because those in the last group are gone from the scene. The lessons for the reader once again involve vigilance and action. Parents must be vigilant as to those who purport to be "volunteering" to serve their children and also be prepared to take action once someone proves themselves to be a stinker. I was fortunate because I was associated with people, administrators, solicitors, board members, and parents, who would not rest until these harmful presences had been forced to leave. It is simply unacceptable, once a mistake has been made regarding the candidacy of a board member, to simply wait until their term of office expires and then work for their removal. Just think, an entire freshman class of students could pass through high school under the influence of such people!

Let's take a look at the syndrome of people with redeemable qualities who fail ultimately because of their affiliation with the teachers' union. Make no mistake; this is a very difficult position to find oneself as the pressure to conform, the challenge of proclaiming independence, the consequences of forgetting your union membership are very severe indeed.

Having members of the teacher unions serving on a board of education is a ubiquitous situation so get used to it. When they run, they do so with the support of all the teachers in the community. This means there are copious opportunities for teachers to interact with parents to promote the virtues of "their" favorites. The teachers who serve as members of the PTA are in a position to influence the questions for the candidates' night as that evolution is organized and controlled by the PTA's. Best of all, the teachers' union provides mass mailings extolling the teacher candidates and contacts personally each member of the union who lives in town to encourage parents to get out and vote the union slate for the board. Also, in today's society, there is a great deal of movement of people from community to community. Board members are no exception: they are transferred, laid off, get divorced, etc., and move as frequently as any other demographic. When a vacancy occurs, a board may fill the slot in any manner they wish, without even a "by your leave" from the public, thus opening even more seats for the union crowd.

My first two were known as "the twins". They were colleagues and friends, both teachers and I have always counted them as friends of mine, I hope they shall not be offended by this section. First of all, they were quite likable people, terrific moms, strong parents and served their district for many years, often with distinction, first in the PTA's and then on the board of education. They were supportive of their superintendents, when a long-serving chief executive with a distinguished record retired, they worked tirelessly to find an adequate replacement. The next in line was articulate, friendly, and talked all the right moves. He deserved their support until at least some time went by. However, they supported him without question, much to my surprise, and stated publicly that they had an obligation to do as it was a "condition of employment". Their support was even more unrelenting than they had expressed for the previous superintendent. I believe the reason to be that the new superintendent was one that was also committed to a program of labor peace, which seems to be ubiquitous. The twins played their role well, supporting every raise, ignoring every benefit giveaway, opposing any disciplinary effort involving teachers. They were especially active in the creation of board-based "professional development" programs that involved a majority of the staff, and, got them out of the classroom frequently. I would like to say they all lived happily every after but you see, they bankrupted the school district and, for all the money spent, had not a single measure of performance improvement to support their long tenure. They participated, quite legally, in what one attorney called the possibly greatest rip off of the taxpayer he had ever seen. They took an oath, they were supposed to stand for something, but unfortunately, that something often seemed to be their union.

My next example was the board member who fought her way to the top via the PTA. This woman was reasonable, a heavy participant [unfortunately a common trait among those in this section] and mainly supportive, at least of me. She caused problems in three areas: she tried to push [unsuccessfully in my time] to have her children placed with teachers she deemed to be superior, in every grade level and later on in every subject level. She never stopped trying and you would almost have admired her tenacity had it not been focused on the dark side. Two, she tried to build liaisons with the teachers with the full expectation that her kids would be "cared for", with good reason for this is one of the most unfortunate artifacts of the public schools today. Three, she supported the PTA members no matter how ridiculous or costly their demands might have been. I shall call this one "ski mom". The PTA held several annual events that were fun, raised vital funds for the schools, although only for projects they approved, and were often quite worthwhile and educational for the children. One example of these events in our story was the ski sale. I made the mistake, in response to a question in a committee meeting, of revealing how expensive it would be to adhere to all of the demands for district resources for the annual ski sale. They wanted EVERY vehicle and EVERY maintenance person available, on an O/T basis for Friday night and Saturday, and, on a double time basis, for Sunday. It would cost the district six times the expected income for the PTA and so I pointed out it would be cheaper to scale down the event considerably and have the district donate the money to the PTA. Well, you may have thought I attacked the gods! I was immediately dubbed "anti PTA" for my comments. They got their ski sale but on a vastly more economic scale and I do not think anybody noticed as the event seemed to be as successful as ever. I joined the PTA's in the district to have a voice and to let people know they might have to face me in their coffee klatches so they needed to be judicious in their comments.

There was a twin to this person, and their careers on a board of education overlapped. This one exhibited the same three issues for the district as the prior example although she too was active and supportive. Her thing was the music program. The unfortunate state of affairs financially for many years has reduced programs such as music and art to "also-rans", expensive entities that are provided only to the extent they offer class prep opportunities for grade level teachers and little more than a vocal or band experience in high school. I have known many administrators who privately state they would dump the programs because of their cost and relatively low student participation. Of course, the programs are very worthwhile and, as a parent, I would support them even if only a handful of children participated. The money flow does not support this position and the reality is that the programs often have no permanent classroom location and differ from year to year as to their extent of their offerings. Here again, I was attacked for answering a question honestly, e.g., the cost of providing the extra lessons demanded by parents, and the music staff after school, with attendant busing, custodial care etc. I also had to answer a question as to the ever escalating cost of sending the marching band to one of their programs. Now this had become quite an evolution: several buses, at least one truck, and several drivers and maintenance staff, several teachers and a few more as chaperones, all being paid stipends. You can see this was quite a rice bowl for all concerned and their cover was perfect, they had a spokesperson on the board of education who was responding to her power base on the PTA's. I was now dubbed "anti-music" and responded by breaking out in my best Sinatra, singing *"the lady was a tramp"*. The revenue cap was getting tighter and tighter in this place and eventually it came down to math and science vice music, at least all of the extra music and the "basics" won. Shows what happens when you try to bite the hand that feeds you. Of course, some of the music teachers who lost the after school and summer work did not speak to me and that became the icing on the cake.

Our next case was a highly intelligent male who wanted to run things, somewhere, and finally got his chance when he backed into a board of education seat unopposed. He was not exactly supportive of me, or anyone else, but seemed to come closer with me once he had some notion of how things were working and who was on what side of the issues. His wife was active on the PTA and they seemed to operate as a matched set. I am not quite sure why they offended so many people of the establishment but it seemed to be caused by their interest in questioning the status quo. These were intelligent and articulate people, interested enough to have even experimented with different venues of early childhood education for their own family. There was a strong PTA connection but, at least on the surface, there was something short of a complete abrogation to the interests of the PTA. There also seemed to be a connection to the local political establishment but the main issue here was an independence from the common interests of the board, an inclination to rein in the administration, and a strong desire to dominate and run things operationally, as a board member. While he was mostly on the same side of issues as I was, his lone wolf approach resulted in several spokespersons dealing with the public, one unofficial of course, and, provided alternative courses of action to anyone seeking relief from the established rules and policies of the district. The result was a great deal of confusion as to who was in charge, and at least two factions competing for the same power base.

GIVE ME A BREAK

Those who outright were harmful because they sought and unfortunately won office to further their own causes are represented in this section. In this group, I am still undecided if those who unabashedly advanced the cause of their own children at the expense of the others were more of a distraction than those who worked to satisfy personal ambition, whether it was to secure better employment, higher office, or just plain old fashioned fat contracts for themselves at the pubic trough.

Here are just a few examples. Case number one was a real creep. She used to "poll" the community before voting on important issues and even tried to "get the feel" of a particular meeting audience before she would take a position. I remember one evening when raises for some of the non-affiliated secretaries were on the agenda. There was nothing out of the order about the raises but two senior citizens approached their champion before the meeting and demanded she vote "NO". What made this ridiculous was that she was taking a position against a raise for veteran, high performing staff, when she had revealed that she had turned down a job in a neighboring school district because the salary proffered was too low, and THAT salary was much higher than those she was prepared to vote against! Nice to be around people with integrity, isn't it. Well, she had the temerity to approach me before the meeting and stated that because of "pressure" from the audience she would be forced to vote against the raises and that she hoped I would not take it personally. I told her I could understand such a vote if she were opposed to all raises but that coming from a hypocrite, one who displayed multiple choreographic techniques ['ability to dance to several tunes simultaneously': I had to explain it to her also] I could not and this would finish it with us. This woman was heavy baggage on top of everything else. She forced the high school to make a phone available to her son every day right after school so that he might call home after dismissal and review what had happened in every class that day. At the annual school boards convention she grabbed everything that was not locked down and when she got caught, I refused to vouch for her. Pretty stupid behavior for someone who had aspirations of being elected to the office of county freeholder. Eventually she tried to discredit a competitor by attacking through their child and somehow word got out and she decided discretion was the better part of survival and resigned and moved away.

Our next person was another doozy. She had several major faults. She was completely committed to her own advancement and decided that seeking and winning political office was her ticket to riches, i.e., by feeding at the public trough. She was a teacher, actually a basic skills instructor, so she must not have been one of the better teachers, who spent more time off as a consequence of routine worker comp claims than she did in the classroom. Never was anyone so gravely injured so often by carrying books. This gave her ample time to pursue her political career. She was often seen in the company of local political hacks and soon the going joke was that if her benefactor stopped short, well, I am sure you have heard the rest. I remember her telling me that the district needed an objective set of evaluative criteria for the custodial staff that were "not performing to expectations". The truth was the place was filthy and the staff completely out of control. Given what I had heard, I was surprised, because she was union through and through, So was I for that matter, but these people were way over the line and something had to be done. It turns out she had been around long enough to believe no one could do anything and that the custodians, whom she measured as part of her constituency, would continue along their merry way, putting wax right down on top of dirty floors. The answer to this dilemma was two fold. First, privatization took care of the recalcitrant staff, and second, a series of well attended meetings with very pithy issues on the agenda, forced her to take public positions. It was almost comical watching the poor thing almost get hives worrying about betraying her constituency and yet not daring to disappoint the general public. An election defeat ended her tenure.

My next example is, unfortunately all too common also. He was a teacher in another district who had lost his supervisory position and had been "demoted" in his opinion, back to the classroom. This meant he lost a great deal of flexibility in his work day because he now had to be some place all of the time and he was teaching five classes instead of two and now was a member of the rank and file. Parenthetically, let me espouse another generalized finding. Now generalizations are always dangerous but as trends they can be illustrative. In this case, I found, especially among older teachers of my generation, a lot of animosity as to their lot in life among the men primarily. It may only be a measure of the problems in role differentiation between the sexes but the women seemed to be happier as just plain teachers and far less likely to seek what I refer to as false credentials, i.e., calling themselves a coordinator or chairperson just because they were asked to be something extra, than were the men. The women dressed a lot better than the men, across all age groups, and were much more likely to spend some extra time after school helping students, although they were just as aggressive in pursuing any available stipends dangling out there. Even during my long career as a college professor, I would encounter a teacher from time to time, just disgusted with his status in life, determined to make a fresh start, at 40 some years of age plus. These were obviously burned out individuals who all stated they felt trapped by circumstances, i.e., avoiding the draft, needing a job that allowed a lot of time for other things, such as extra income, a willingness to accept less pay and no status for a pension and a great benefit package, etc. They were all men, all angry and mostly disappointed in themselves, and, sorry to say, none of them got very far.

Our proximate case, fit this mold, although he seemed far too lazy and not nearly bright enough to pursue a graduate degree in something substantive. Instead, he milked what he had, tried to parry his seat on a board of education to elected or appointed office with pay and even more benefits, and, danced adroitly between satisfying his union and his constituents. You see, he played to the general citizenry by claiming to be in favor of such slogans as "tough negotiations" and "teacher accountability" all the while working behind the scenes to help satisfy the goals of the local teacher association. Once he was demoted in his own employment situation he did begin to exhibit what I would describe as a knee jerk reaction, chipping at the department heads in our district, trying to restrict the per diem, questioning their days on the road attending workshops etc. Somehow word got back to the union leadership and he actually admitted that he was "warned" to toe the line, or else. Thus he remained an angry and unfulfilled human being, one whose ambitions, orientation, and character seemed totally inappropriate for a position of trust, especially one impacting on the welfare of children.

The next example is a person, who seemed dedicated to children, especially to his own and the schools they attended, to the detriment of everyone else. You could tell when he was ready to go off on something, his soft spoken demeanor would gradually increase in volume and intensity, peeking with now wildly gesticulating hand movements. He had a flair for the dramatic. One of his children was involved in the music program, the marching band, which was his passion in life. The school was small, having less than forty participants in the marching band, and they just could not compete in sound, arrangements, or presentation designs with outfits fielding three hundred musicians To wit, every time a small band would turn during their routine, the sound was lost on spectators, and judges, seated in the opposite stands. The three hundred unit ensemble just kept right on truckin' along, creating magnificent designs on the field, with enough musicians to fill the stadium with music in every direction. This did not deter our determined parent, however. He would make late and very dramatic entrances to board meetings, dragging poor students dressed in their band costumes before the public. You see, it had to be the costumes and thus it was someone's fault. I recall the time he entered with one of the flags used by the "fronts" of the band. I thought he had finally flipped and was going to skewer someone, but, he marched to the front of the meeting hall and raised the flag over his head and slammed it to the floor. Then raising his hand to his lapel in a true Lincolnesque gesture, began to preach how the district let down its students by allowing them to participate in band competitions with such "shabby" equipment. Again, it just could not be the limited number of performers and the quality of play that was responsible for poor performance, there simply had to be fault assigned.

I thought he might have apoplexy when the band in that school voted to disband and concentrate instead on evolutions such as chamber and jazz music competitions, where their numbers were not a hindrance. This seemed to take a lot of steam out of the old fellow but he persevered for a while, threatening to resign whenever he did not get his way. When people began asking him to follow through on his threats and leave, he gave up the ghost and no longer sought office. Another example of a one-horse candidate, who only won a seat because so many other parents would not take the trouble to make this same investment in the future of their children.

How about an entire board gone crazy? The majority were teachers or married to teachers and the rest went along for two reasons, they told me they were tired of swimming upstream and they feared for their children. This group gave, that is right, outside the ongoing negotiation process, a sick leave buy back plan that takes the cake. The teachers used to get $30 a day for each sick day not used at retirement. These rocket scientists, with no data to justify their decision that teachers would retire before they were ready, decided to give them full, per diem value for the sick days, to a *maximum of forty grand*, just for having 20 years in the pension system and resigning, not retiring, which meant they were technically able to be rehired, *an average windfall of $34,000 per teacher!* There was a requirement that twenty teachers take advantage of the plan but when only sixteen opted, the board majority still said "GO", even though their calculations neglected the payroll taxes the public would have to pay for the extra compensation and the fact that some cockamamie tax shelter plan was found to violate numerous federal and state laws. Just another pleasant day in *teacher-land*! I actually now refer to this phenomena as the Sodom and Gomorra approach to school district management.

Our next case for this section was a bright, well-educated man, who seemed to care for children, tried to strike a balance between recruiting and retaining staff with an attractive salary and benefit package, was fair in his dealings with employee and student discipline cases, and routinely made himself available to entertain parental concerns. He was also widely supportive of me. Sounds like a dream candidate for a board of education, doesn't he? Well he was, except for one flaw. He too saw himself as underemployed and he spent an awful lot of time trying to get me to buy products from his company, which were just far too expensive being designed for different applications than our needs. When this failed, I found myself dealing with dozens of other companies that he was brokering to the district. I finally gave up and spoke to the solicitor and the person calmly finished his term and was never heard from again. Seemed like a great waste to me.

Then there is the male-female team that hated everything that was not their idea and everyone who supported the new majority on their board of education. They had held power for a long time until some of their colleagues hit the skids via scandal, excessive spending and effective campaigning. I knew most of the actors very well and still remember the following conundrum. Whatever their faults, the incumbents who lost their seats were, in most cases, far more decent human beings than those they left behind. The newcomers who won seats and formed the next regime were really wonderful people, true child advocates, whose behavior was impeccable and therefore unassailable. That did not stop the loyal opposition from making life miserable for everybody, especially the staff who continued to try and make the place work, which I understand now should have been easier because of the nature of the new majority caste. They fought like dogs and cats over everything, even adopting the minutes became impossible unless the five member majority was present. They could not be satisfied unless everyone catered to their tantrums at the weekly, yes weekly meetings, which thundered on into the night and then early morning. "How thin is thin" became a joke in the area as word spread of our dynamic duo refusing to yield the floor, questioning an engineer for hours over a leaking fuel tank, and causing a several month delay in the repair. They became known as the bitch and the idiot and God knows how much damage they really caused.

These are examples of scenarios being played out every day in school districts across the country.

What to do if you find yourself working with a cipher for a board member? Well, as stated above, you cannot wait for them to expire; you have got to help them self-destruct. I once had a colleague who was a very successful board secretary and served with distinction for many years. He was talented, successful but faced a major difficulty, an absolute witch of a broad member who spared no effort in embarrassing the administration and opposition on the board. I can still visualize her working against a badly needed facility improvement program for the children, apparently for the simple reason that everyone else thought it was a good idea. She made his life a living hell and he complained constantly about her behavior. I really grew tired listening to this week after week, primarily because his only solution was to wait her out. He told me that she would eventually move or grow tired once her children left school. He was right, but, it took 12 years for her to move on. Imagine how distracted he had become by then; to say nothing of the physical wear and tear and the disruption for the district.

You simply cannot allow something like this to continue. The woman who wished to use the schools as a springboard to her political career eventually posted a questionable voucher and was given a choice and left. The woman who spent her life promoting her son eventually tried to harm other children and got caught. The man who wanted to direct lighting contracts to a subsidiary firm was defeated for a second term simply through the expediency of releasing certain public information at key times. To accomplish this you have to know what you are doing. You need to be able to communicate freely with the solicitor in a highly confidential manner, and, you need to be one with the superintendent and have a majority of the board of education with you.

The system is not helpful as there is no equity for someone who works to right a wrong such as this. One slip and you face years of lousy salary increases; a major slip and you might even face tenure charges, regardless if they are warranted or not. The best solution is for the parents to be vigilant as ultimately, they hold the security of the district, and thus the welfare of their own children, in their hands. The parents can defeat a candidate who appeals to certain elements of their community who wish to economize beyond what the education standards can stand

and still remain viable. The parents can defeat the union candidates and the self-serving individuals. The reality is that so few even bother to show up and vote; unfortunately these days many who do vote come solely to insure their property taxes are not increased. The parents have responsibility for their children and yet often refuse to invest the time necessary to screen the people to whom they shall entrust their children. I am a firm believer of a candidate gaining a constituency via a reputation of excellence by long-term service on a PTA, which, to me, is the perfect minor league experience for ultimate service on a board of education. I could not consider supporting someone for a board seat if they had not served this apprenticeship. It is tough to hide motives and weaknesses after years of working side by side with other parents working for the betterment of their schools.

For the dedicated administrator, the struggle is akin to the battle that raged between Mark Felt, now known as Woodward and Bernstein's 'Deep Throat' and Richard Nixon; the eternal struggle between temporary political power and the permanent bureaucracy. Here is where tenure is essential as a shield. It is only a pity that so few chose to use this vital tool as there is simply little equity available in doing so and the potential grief is daunting.

SCREWBALLS

I guess the opposite category for heroes could be called "losers" but my wife objected, thus the name chosen for this section, a pantheon of low achievers, who consumed vast quantities of public resources and contributed very little worthwhile. Here is my favorite all-time screwball, whom we shall refer to as DR. WHAT!?, "Dr" because she insisted on being called by that title and "WHAT!?", well, because that was the reaction of one of her superintendents who always seemed to be incredulous when confronted by her behavior.

She really was the epitome of someone who hides out on the public dole, insisting on interfering with common sense and trying to impose her own idiotic approach to things. More than anyone else, she categorizes the sobriquet, "her ignorance is exceeded only by her arrogance."

DR. WHAT!? was employed for many years in a school district with which I was familiar. In fact, on the day of my very first visit, she was the first person I encountered. She trapped me against my car in the lot of the building for which she was serving as principal. Without even identifying herself formally, she told me that she worked eighty hours a week while naming a colleague who was principal of another school who Dr. WHAT! claimed worked only 40 hours a week. I guess because I had been around and had come to expect most people in this environment to behave this way, I immediately responded, "Thank God the children are fortunate to have [the other colleague] employed here as she can accomplish what you do but in half the time." To her credit, she immediately switched to another topic. I later learned that she always did this because she was interested only in prostilatyzing not listening. She turned to me and asked me to observe her children, who were at recess, particularly how perfectly behaved they were. At this point, and I still cherish the moment, a little rug rat came up to her and said: "Gee, DR WHAT!?, what a big ass you have!" I actually resisted telling this story for a number of years until the depredations of this person had numbed me to my former standards of propriety.

I soon learned that DR. WHAT!? may have been the most disliked employee of the district, perhaps in its history and this place had had a reputation for many years for employing bad people. Their salaries had been at low ebb for a long time, their infrastructure was decrepit, and the leadership unspeakably bad. I was there at the beginning of the naissance of the district but it took years to turn over the staff and this person, due to her tenure protection AND the refusal of two of the three superintendents who led the schools during the time in question obviously had no interest in pursuing what I believe would have been very legitimate reasons to end her employment.

DR. WHAT!? had been a guidance counselor until her colleagues strongly suggested her removal, which, in this never-land existence, turned out to be a promotion! The district solved this problem by moving her to a position as a principal, "where she could do less damage". Thus, her placement in a position where she could influence dozens of teachers and hundreds of students. I recall another occasion when I ran into DR. WHAT!?, who was seeking permission, in the absence of the superintendent, to return to her former building, for a meeting she wanted to attend, but to which she had not been invited. Imagine my amazement to hear that an adult, especially one that was in a position that normally would require trust, needed a note to enter a school. Her former principal was called to request entry for her to the building and even her temporary presence proved to be a disruptive force.

When anyone asked for her version of these events, they came in for a harangue about how less talented people were jealous of "altruistic superstars", as she actually had the temerity to describe herself. Eventually she would pass her probationary period as principal and become tenured, one of the greatest injustices I have witnessed. Remarkably, and please pay attention parents because this happens a lot, a sympathetic superintendent failed to notify the board of education that her probation period was expiring. The board was just furious and insisted on placing a resolution on their next agenda stating that DR. WHAT!? was awarded tenure "with reservations", the only time in over three and one-half decades that I have seen anything like this. Nevertheless, she motored on her merry way. Indeed, by the time these words were written, perhaps only I, with access to the records that had long grown obscure, even recall these incidents.

In any event, the building where DR. WHAT!? presided was demolished but the parents insisted that she not be assigned to another building where small children were involved and the staff was yelling "No Mas". There was a new superintendent who had local ties and he was well acquainted with the character of DR. WHAT!?. In fact, he spent considerable time making sure she was notified whenever a vacancy occurred in the county, at least until a county superintendent of schools asked him to desist from the practice.

Unfortunately a vacancy in the middle school occurred and the new superintendent reluctantly had to follow the advice of the solicitor and placed DR. WHAT!? in that building, on a "temporary" basis. Well, it did turn out to be temporary, because she was so bad in the assignment. She continued her streak of never noticeably contributing to the improvement of instruction. Instead, she angered another staff, spent countless hours worrying about uniformly even shades, and ticked off the parents. The phone calls and letters from the parents were remarkable, still she resisted all attempts at supervision, usually depending on what came to be referred to as the fad of the month club, the New Jersey Association of Supervisors of Curriculum Development, which periodically published "new strategies" that were "guaranteed to work".

I recall her prohibition on certain types of vehicles being used to bring children to the eighth grade prom, an interesting concept in itself. Such divergence of automobiles was thought to be anti-egalitarian, perhaps a noble concept but in the hands of this woman, it only served to anger our constituents even more. When she decided that children at her dances were being inappropriate in their behavior, she failed to deal with the issue, not remarkable given the fact that she could muster little support from the faculty for any initiative. Her solution, hire a person to teach line dances, the only style of dancing that would henceforth be permitted. Aside from the lunacy of the concept, imagine the shock to the parents when the children returned from what should have been a fun night, extremely frustrated with the new "policy". Imagine the surprise the following Monday morning when the superintendent of schools began fielding calls from irate parents about this new policy, of which he knew nothing.

Her behavior became so bizarre that it was impossible for colleagues to even attempt to mitigate its effects. Eventually she had to be removed from the middle school, as both parents and staff were outraged by her mere presence and central administration had become convinced that this woman would never pay attention to any directive with which she did not agree or any that would diminish her authority.

Where to place her, that was the question now that she had worn out her welcome from grades six through twelve. Well, the story has several more twists. It soon happened that the lower level [grades K-2] school needed a principal after its principal retired unexpectedly. I was aghast at the possibility of placing this nincompoop in charge of anything, let alone over 700 tiny children. In addition, the school was staffed by excellent yet veteran teachers, people who had earned a reputation for excellence by years of outstanding work. Also, the staff controlled the surrounding community, a not uncommon event, as the mothers would spare no effort for their children to be placed with selected staff, especially when the second or third sibling came along, who would be expected to fare just as well as the first born, with the same teacher. It is really a sight to see as the year progresses, the opening day luncheon, the endless stream of classroom volunteers, the holiday and birthday gifts for the teachers, the subsequent "luncheons for every occasion", and finally, the really big gift at year's end, when the politicking for the following year placement began in earnest. And so it went, year after year, with a capable, yet respectfully distant principal, caring for paperwork, seeing to supplies, disseminating platitudes, and mainly staying out of everyone's way. Yet, however useless this may sound, it is a scenario that occurs again and again and often represents the best we may hope for, a school with a veteran staff in charge, with a principal ready to act as a resource but most likely, never daring to risk providing leadership, with no one being pushed to increase their productivity. Into this environment strode DR. WHAT!?, someone with a reputation for obstinacy and buffoonery, who placed great store in form over substance, who almost stank with failure. I know that the superintendent had tried to counsel her, on several occasions as related by a friend of a friend of mine. It was incredible to witness her complete denial of the truth. When someone spoke to her of the hostility she had created in the middle school by dogging the staff for uneven window shades while failing to lead her staff in any way whatsoever, she responded by saying they needed discipline and cried. When she was told of the complaints by the parents, which amounted to an outright rebellion as well as repudiation of her very presence, she denied the parents could have ever said such a thing because they really loved her, and she cried. In fact, I never saw anyone who could cry so realistically on cue, she made Loretta Young look like a piker. She would play this "cry on demand" card for years until, completely ineffective, she resorted to a more traditional approach, promising to retire in just "one more year" if left lone, a tactic that earned her many more years on the dole.

Back to our story: she was more than just a disaster, she was an unmitigated disaster and from the first day. This district had instituted a new software program for transportation scheduling and the program had a bug, one that misstated times by a few minutes for each stop. The result was about a twenty minute delay for each of the three transportation tiers, something easily correctible, and the problem was readily apparent that morning. The word went out to the schools to get the children ready early to mitigate the late runs, which would be corrected over-night. I remember the superintendent telling me about cautioning you-know-who about cooperating. He recalled that he just could not believe that even DR. WHAT!? would fail to cooperate. While I truly enjoy being right, that day would have been the exception as the consequences for the children were extreme. I was called by this superintendent sometime later and told that he departed for her building when he learned the buses had not left her school and they were already forty minutes late. He arrived just after a gaggle of irate parents, immediately relieved the principal, and took control of the scene. She had spent more than twenty minutes on a day when speed was essential, forcing the children to line up by height and then alphabetically! Once again, she did it her way, with no compunction as to ruining opening day.

It was during this time that she pulled one of my all time favorite gaffs. She took it upon herself to inform her building parents, again these were little children in grades K through 2, that the kids seemed to get too excited having a Halloween parade on Halloween, therefore, it "would be in everyone's best interest" to hold the Halloween parade some two weeks after Halloween!!!!! The parents thought we were all stupid and whenever anyone asked me about this, I simply said that the woman had taken leave of her senses. This prompted me to write a calendar which I named after DR. WHAT!?. This new calendar moved Independence Day to Christmas, to limit celebrations; moved the Monday holidays to Tuesday, moved Valentine's Day to June whenever it would be warmer with more daylight for lovers, and so on. It was a bit hit and it kept the lunacy of this principal in the public consciousness.

The district really needed the support of this particular school community, they could not pass their budget without the 1200 or so

"YES" votes that were delivered annually by the parents of the children in this school, parents who had begun to feel disenfranchised in what they had come to believe was "their school". When the budget began failing passage, not coincidentally when these parents withdrew their support, then even the moribund personnel system of the public schools had to be tweaked to give the district some relief from the depredations of this woman.

The solution was not uncommon; throw even more money at the problem, with the net result that the taxpayer took another hit, and a huge one indeed. The taxpayers in this particular town were most interesting. They seemed satisfied with good enough, and, their standard of "good enough" would never have flown in my native community of Cherry Hill, where there was a decades old tradition of instructional excellence all across the K-12 curriculum, even during periods of less than excellent leadership. In our story town, people would volunteer the opinion that "our children do not need fancy facilities nor should we spend more than required for the 'basics'." I was told a story by a superintendent there, during one of their many failed building referenda, that he was nearly assaulted by a "well dressed woman with a filthy mouth" who physically arrested his progress to inform him that she did not care whether her children attended school in a tent just as long as her taxes were not increased. I mention this to illustrate the fact that these people were particularly attuned to what was being spent. They refused to support any "extras" in central office having disposed of an assistant superintendent before the mid 1980's, when dollars were actually plentiful. This is an important concept to remember because, the solution for removing DR. WHAT!? from direct contact with children, staff and parents was to create a central office job, this one entitled, "Director of Instruction." Most remarkably, the citizens, who would spend nothing unless mandated, raised nary a peep, because, they were willing to pay the price to get this person away from their children. How big a price? In this average sized suburban town with approximately three thousand students, the presence of this character, with her long tenure and benefits and support, actually added almost one full penny to the tax rate, thus impacting every home in town in a negative fashion.

As you may expect, this move also caused the district some grief. Despite specific orders that she stay away from staff, she proceeded to move beyond her role of procuring "curriculum related" materials and tried to impact directly on the teaching process in the schools. Principals would stop by a classroom and find her mandating certain strategies that often directly contrasted what they had asked the particular teacher to employ in their daily routine. She once again began to lose access to schools as most of the principals filed complaints requesting that she absent herself from their building. She was then assigned the task of arranging workshops for teacher in-service days, on the surface an innocuous job, one certainly within the capacity of any moderately trained person. Well, think again, dear reader. This fell apart when she, without the knowledge of her own superintendent, invited a superintendent from a nearby district to appear as a keynoter for a workshop, promising him over a grand to boot. Now, the two superintendents were not exactly friends, and the invited speaker was known as a "droner", someone who could put anyone to sleep. This invitation was canceled abruptly when the district superintendent learned of her plans and despite a stern lecture about organization communication and chain of command, she did the very same thing, a few months later, inviting the very same guy again without the knowledge of her superintendent.

Since this move did not work out, the next move was to "Director of Special Projects". In this capacity she was expected to care for all of the fill in work: affirmative action coordinator, e-rate reimbursements [federal government subsidy to encourage computer use], federal title program paperwork submissions, and the like. The district was left without any help for a busy superintendent in the area of instruction and curriculum but again, this was viewed as a small price to pay for keeping this person from bungling every assignment. Not to overly encumber the reader with a too long story but this also became a bankrupt notion. Her work in the grants area led the auditor to demand her replacement [she once almost cost the district an entire fiscal year of federal funding], she was so damaging in the affirmative action officer role that the superintendent had to appoint himself "compliance officer" to satisfy an insurance carrier that threatened to reduce the district umbrella policy in part because of the potential damage that could be done by DR. WHAT!?. Her presence on the paperwork end of the grants became so abusive to staff in the business office that one of them threatened to fill a hostile work environment complaint unless DR. WHAT!? was removed from that function. I never heard of this happening before in over thirty years of service.

When I lost track of her she had moved to the position, "Director of Guidance", right back where she began over twenty years before. Once again a principal had to be forced to accommodate her in a school and she was given the assignment of "tracking guidance requirements with the strict understanding that she have no contact with staff". Wonder how that worked out for them. The district, of course, is at fault for not having the courage to embark on a tenured employee dismissal case, especially when the "I promise to retire in another year if you leave me alone" scam got very old. The state is at fault because they have created a dismissal system that is so cumbersome and time consuming that districts tend to avoid invoking its provisions. The parents are at fault for tolerating such a disgrace, after all, this person directly undermined the quality of the programming their children received, and, for over twenty years, she was allowed to gallop merrily along. Ultimately, the tenure system, which has proven so necessary to protect staff from the foibles of boards of education, protected someone who deserved to be dismissed and directly harmed children.

Here is another of my favorites, the spaced-out art teacher. She used to tell people she had tenure and that just about enabled her to do anything she wanted. The district in which she was employed used to move her among their elementary schools because no principal and few of the faculty could take her for more than a year at a time. She literally showed up just barely on time, spent more time playing with the kids than teaching them anything and was a royal pain in the butt. She simply refused to accept any supervision, and for this she should have had charges brought against her, but, her behavior was so common that not even a competent superintendent or an experienced solicitor were confident that they could sufficiently differentiate her performance from that which had become the established norm. She became so obnoxious that she took to calling the food service director at home each workday at 7:30 AM to custom order a salad for her lunch. The salad was a really a cover from what I heard, it was the cheapest thing she could order, although she made sure it came with plenty of extras hence the personal touch of the pre-work phone call. You see, her real meal was gleaned from what she could stuff in her mouth as she performed her activity period as a cafeteria monitor. Watching this performance one day I could see why it was rumored she never had to worry about dinner. She finally got herself in trouble when she spent a full day helping each class write letters for their parents to send to the board of education requesting that she be given time off with pay to visit her sick mother in Florida, in the middle of winter. Well, her mother was not sick and was not in Florida. Our friend wanted some time off and she could not even pretend to be sick and take leave because, in twenty years she had used every day available, ten per year, and had even been docked an average of five more days of sick leave without pay. For the year in question she was already out of sick leave time by February. For her efforts she had an increment withheld, which was promptly restored the following year under pressure by her union! Imagine what a teacher dominated board of education is capable of achieving when they put their minds to it. I can recall this particular board of education being described by a central office secretary as a group of people who regularly lined up to kiss the asses of the teachers.

Our next little example is an assistant principal who never was. No, she existed, in body only, came to work some days and was paid a handsome salary. In all the years I knew her, she showed up for only one meeting of the board of education, and got away with it. She had completed law school but was rumored to be unable to pass the bar exam, hence her continuance on the public dole. She also qualified as a minority employee, as did I, but to the disgust of all of us thus qualified, she did not earn her way, she bullied people barely able to govern and only under the almost nonexistent circumstances of public education. There was actually some behind the scenes discussion to deny this person tenure but in a weak moment, the superintendent sold the notion on the fact that he expected her to leave and become a lawyer so why invite trouble with the "civil rights people"? The district had had three civil rights complaints filed by various disgruntled parents, and, in a predominately white community, these cases were all pursued by the Feds but each was dismissed fairly early in the process so there was enough talent to win the day just not enough guts. My favorite story involving this person involves her refusal to abandon her office in the summer, for all of the few weeks she came to work, and forced the district to invest a fortune in air conditioning for one space. You see the a/c was shut off for this space because the block included two large spaces, a library and faculty lunchroom, which were not only unused in the summer but also cost a fortune to air condition. Why was her refusal to move so egregious? Well, she would have had to move back and forth exactly twelve feet to the next room, which was part of the central office block and thus had a/c all summer. I never saw her name affixed to a single document adding anything to the improvement of instruction for the children, yet she had the temerity to write a two page memorandum expressing outrage because it was suggested she move her derriere next door. She was, however, acceptable to the teachers because she never did anything to disturb their equilibrium.

Another gem was one of our absentee teachers. This person had not only logged almost fifteen years with no leave accumulated, she had actually averaged ten days being docked a year and got away with it. I tried to explain that when someone was out of time, neither seniority nor tenure could save their job but the BOE followed its practice of annually granting a few more days with pay to its routinely over-absent staff and then finally, when the bounds of propriety had been snapped, began docking their pay and still they were out, for days at a time. The case law decisions impacting on this area certainly reflected the influence of the state teacher union, they do prefer "association", but that word carries too much of a professionalism tag to be applied to such a cut-throat entitlement based group. Boards of education were allowed to decide on a case by case basis to provide additional paid sick leave to teaching staff members, thus, they could state with all candor that the merits of a particular case had been considered and that the additional leave was not allowed to be considered precedent setting. Some parents did actually complain, when someone averages twenty days out sick, three personal leave days, and, on average at this time and in this district, some thirteen days for "professional" development and curriculum work, it does not leave much time with someone other than a substitute teacher, whose credentials need not exceed sixty hours of post high school course work, even from a community college, with no requirement for subject matter content or pedagogy. They also could not work in the same assignment for more than twenty days, which I guess was a rule designed to prevent a sub from being in place too long, but, with the extraordinarily generous leave policies in place, the rule that was designed to protect the children actually forced them to move among several teachers. The family and medical leave laws, which many of the states were quick to not only copy but make even more generous to employees, only made the situation worse. You see, there were precedents of teachers taking maternity leave for more than a year, after working almost to the birth of their child, and, in many cases for a year more. In some districts paid health benefits were provided for the duration, in addition to the paid health benefits that were paid to the long-term substitute teachers. Also, all it took was a letter from a doctor and the teacher on maternity leave was able to combine their leave in conjunction with the accumulated sick leave and they were gone a long time and with pay. The newly enacted family and medical leave acts, which were intended to provide child rearing leave for people with no entitlement to maternity leave, of course now added twelve weeks ADDITIONAL leave to the world of our public school teachers! Thus, it became he norm to lose teachers for close to two years on maternity leave, with at least a portion of that time having their health benefits continued at public expense.

Back to our story. Our seldom seen teacher, in this particular year, had been absent for 22 days, being docked for 12, and had also used her three personal leave days. She arrived in my office and approached my assistant with a novel idea. She wanted to join her husband for a trip to Turkey, related to his work, and at least was ethical enough not to request more sick leave. This time she wanted to borrow from her bank of FUTURE personal leave, a total of nine days from the next three years. Now the staff was not only extremely capable and loyal, they maintained extraordinarily high standards of professionalism and had little tolerance for the nonsense that pervaded our contacts with many of the teaching staff. Their response to this little theatrical production was laughter, just plain laughter, continuous and uproarious, until the teacher just got up and left.

Here is another vignette about a teacher's quest for mediocrity that led to advanced station and a very impressive paycheck. She started as a teacher assigned to a distributive education program, which meant she spent her day supervising the work of the students she had placed in work situations and the remainder trying to find placements for the rest. The net result was that people could never find her and they gave up trying. I did have first hand experience with some of the young people enrolled in this work-study program and they were bright, hard working and engaging. However, I was left with the perception that they were so impressive despite the presence of their mentor not because of it. As an aside, how many times do young people of character separate themselves from their peers, rise to do great things, mainly because they need to work, they must achieve more to earn scholarships, etc., and who are simply shuffled off to lesser programs, i.e., programs that are "business" oriented. New Jersey has always been a gross disappointment to me in this area. They provide vocational education in abundance and so there is an ample supply of vital skill people becoming plumbers and electricians while students interested in the many varied career paths related to what we recognize from university business schools are limited to a few courses in idiotic topics such as key boarding and computer literacy, things they already know outside of schools, plus a course or two in accounting, and they are exposed to people like the subject of our little story rather than the stars of the faculty. An example to wit: my daughter, Maria, had a terrific high school career; she ended up being enrolled in both the academic as well as athletic halls of fame. She was one of seven summa cum laude graduates, and, given the fact that she attended a wonderful high school in Cherry Hill New Jersey, got to major in an area, in this case, physical science, in grades seven through twelve!. Of the seven summa cum laude graduates, one, my daughter, became a chemical engineer, one became an attorney, two entered pre-med programs, and THREE went to Wharton to major in business. From my own career of over two and one-half decades teaching for the business school at Temple University, I never ceased to be amazed at the quality of young people entering the field, except from much of New Jersey, where the kids simply were not given enough exposure to the kind of head start programming necessary to have a proper foundation in subjects such as statistics, accounting, and marketing. Again, an incredible waste, due mainly to the fact that places in the classroom need to be found for weak sisters like our "heroine".

Back to our story: the distributive education program went belly-up for lack of federal government funding and it turned out that the district did not dare expose this teacher to a regular classroom, despite the presence of all the certificates [read licenses] that she possessed. She ended up being assigned as a guidance counselor, a really plum position, but proved so incapable in this position that the district had to cave into parental complaints and they moved her once again, can you imagine, to the position of department head, that is, a supervisor of instruction. In this position, she received a hefty raise, taught only two classes a day and in general probably had the time of her life. She taught keyboarding of all things, and quickly became the joke of the district because the students already knew the topic better than she did. Can you imagine condemning students to take this crap, for credit no less, because their department head could not teach much of anything? The district had acquired a new superintendent by then and he wanted the students to experience accounting and several semesters of accounting at that. The department head had a certificate in accounting and the superintendent expected her to teach and so she eventually retired. A splendid pension after a career that certainly never strained her and thus the circle of life for these people goes on.

I actually started laughing out loud as a record of the antics of this panoply of screwballs was being written, until that familiar chill came over me as a realized what waste was involved here, what damage to children was caused here.

There were a couple of central office types that have earned placement in my hall of shame. One in particular hurt because I was fond of the guy and ignored all of the comments about his purported villainy. This person used to urge stronger performers to take decisive action, which often would benefit primarily himself, and then stop short of actually entering the fray himself. He reminded me of the countless individuals who, while never fighting for the Confederacy, were never to admit defeat for the South. They were: "indomitable in peace and invisible in war", according to Confederate General Joseph Johnston.

The circus freaks were certainly not limited to the local scene either. Consider some of the lesser sorts from my days with the New Jersey State Department of Education.

My favorite was one of our all-time obnoxious do-nothing's, who displayed outright hostility to anyone not of his race. He caught on in one of the remedial education programs and quickly pissed off everybody, and made quite a joke of his abilities, or lack thereof, because he never seemed to accomplish anything. He was always nice to me until an assistant commissioner pointed out that he was using me as a sounding board and then taking my analyses to the commissioner as his own. My position was secure so I did not really mind and felt everybody who counted knew who to turn to and run the constant array of projects that dominated the agency in those days. Those were indeed heady times and people like Carl Marlberger and Fred Burke were achieving great heights in building productivity and capacity for improvement in the public schools. The beginning of the end for this joker came, unbeknownest to us at the time, when he enrolled in one of the new experimental doctorate programs, the kind of doctorate programs now most popular, by the way, as residency and severe course requirements have been eliminated and replaced with a correspondence type experience. Some of my friends who worked in the department of higher education at the time still bemoan this period as one in which quality and accountability started their separate paths to oblivion, and a few would come to lose their jobs when they tried to buck the tide here. Our friend completed his doctorate and began the tiresome trend of printing "DOCTOR" in front of his name and "EdD" after and became even more obnoxious, insisting that he be addressed by his degree. It is amazing how many people I have met who act in this manner. You came to feel that he was always primed to stick a thermometer in your mouth when he approached you on any topic. Turns out he had lifted much of his so-called dissertation from other, previously published, sources. I actually got to see the thing, it was hand written in part and the chapters, especially those which were borrowed, did not present a continuous flow of content. It was like reading a treatise on brain surgery, with chapters on overhauling a car engine interspersed. He did manage to secure ever higher levels of employment in the field, however, a testament to how rotten things had become. Some moral to the story you must be saying!

Next we had the guy who sucked continuously on his pipe, and, well, I cannot think of anything else he accomplished except earning a pension at the level of "director". He worked in the evaluation area and he spent his time both sucking on a pipe and collecting huge amounts of data, which he stored in shoe boxes, nothing relevant you understand, but there was a lot of it. This was in the division of research, planning and evaluation and in over ten years with the agency, I never did figure out their place in life in the main. To illustrate: I was once given the assignment of reviewing the entire administrative code of the department in preparation for a rewrite, and, was quite surprised to find that there was no code at all for RPE, as we knew it, the printed pages in the statute books said "reserved", which gave them carte blanche to do what they wished, which most times amounted to very little in those days. Our friend thought of himself as the "go to" guy when information was needed; you just had to tell him the topic and the date range and he gave you something, not really what you were looking for but he was adroit in explaining why it would have to do. This was the beginning of our management information system! There is an interesting side-note to this character. He was a high ranking officer in the reserve forces of the United States and he was always leaving for periods of active duty. It turns out that he was really a volunteer at a local reserve center, which I was able to discern once I was embarked on my career as a naval officer, not quite the glamorous and exotic duty stations he described on his return each time. I let this go as he was basically a decent fellow and it was hilarious to see how others worried that he might accidentally launch an air strike on a major US city when he was away on "duty".

The next guy worked with the first, actually, he succeeded him and he acted so NUTS, it was frightening. He had a long, scraggily beard that made him resemble Rasputin and he acted even crazier. He had had eye glasses made which were upside down, i.e., the nose bridge was turned in the normal plane but the glass lenses, which were quite large, were reversed. It was a shock when I was asked to straighten out this outfit and inherited this guy. He spent hours on the phone each day, claiming alternatively to be with the CIA [do not laugh, there actually was an employee who worked simultaneously for both AGENCIES, if you catch my meaning] and Israeli intelligence. He told me he was still an active officer in the Israeli paratroop corps and was on loan to us and that is why he spent so much time on the phone and disappeared for weeks at a time. He was quick to reimburse the agency for thousands in dollars in long-distance phone calls each month but most were to Amsterdam not Israel. Complicating our life was the fact that he did seem to have some high placed connection in government. My secretary took an immediate dislike to him and said he resembled a pimp, both for his demeanor as well as for his violet colored Cadillac. Well, it turns out he was a pimp and his high placed connection was based on procuring whores nothing at all more substantial. We were rid of him when he was arrested and convicted, and sent away, I doubt to serve in the Israeli army.

The next case involves someone who worked in one of the agency field offices and was brought to Trenton in a minor capacity and being the king of sycophants, soon worked his way into a position where he could do real damage. He had no academic training that we could discern but latched his star to the burgeoning basic skills programs and voila, here we have another director. This one spent his time running around promoting something called the BSIP, which I originally thought was a re-launch of a long dormant railroad. Do not laugh, at this time the state was sponsoring the rebuilding of many 19th century railroads, this time as tourist attractions. BSIP actually referred to the basic skills improvement program and a fortune was being spent on it. What most people did not know was that the state was backing into the funding for particular jurisdictions, particularly the cities, reportedly guaranteeing massive funding to the correct political divisions. Our hero had the job of running around trying to explain the funding formula, which was convoluted to say the least. Many of the great characters of which you read earlier refused to be involved with this nonsense, including, I am proud to say, myself. After a while we noticed that this individual was never around and we often could not find him where he was supposed to be, preaching on the stump trying to convince people that they were being treated fairly at the funding pump. This went on for sometime until Mother Nature intervened, in the form of a hurricane. Our friend had a small house at the beach and he had been spending his time renovating the place all the while being paid on the public dole. We caught him on the news behind the sliding glass doors, trying to keep the water out by stuffing rice into the tracks. The water was already half-way up the door and, on TV, he looked like a giant fish trying to get back into the bowl.

Our next person was working in education only until he could secure his dream job, the position of chief philatelist for the Smithsonian Institute. He was religious to the point of using his beliefs to determine his behavior toward members of the professional staff in school districts. In other words, if he did not like someone's morals, their projects had trouble being evaluated successful as worthy of funding. He also tried to ingratiate himself to those of us he believed shared his enthusiasm for God, not realizing that, while we were strong believers, we actually loathed the manner in which he forgot that little concept of separation of church and state. While we worked behind the scenes to overcome these outrages, it was still obvious that he had to be discredited. Our opportunity came when he was assigned to attend a national convention along with many of "us". When he asked what the "gang" was going to do that night, I told him we were meeting at the Georgetown Theater that night to attend a film that was a historically based drama. We needed something spectacular, something very visible, so we invited a lot of top brass to join us for a light supper at Clyde's, a restaurant right up the block from the Georgetown Theater, which for five years, had shown nothing but the XXX rated film, "Caligula!"

Our next case shall be referred to as the "hyphen". She was a political appointee who had secured her position because she had worked in the mail room of a local campaign office on behalf of a successful gubernatorial candidate. She not only filled a key position in an area in which the state education agency needed a proven professional, she soured everyone with whom she came into contact and certainly diminished the status of every female appointee. She professed to have a doctorate, another mail-order job, but we could never ascertain in exactly what discipline. Her major attribute was that she was almost psychotic in insisting on being referred to as "DR" and heaven forbid the person, especially a member of the secretarial group, who ever neglected to append "DR" in their salutation or refer to her by anything other than her full, i.e., double last name. She once threatened to file a complaint against a male mail room employee, who never having met our subject and interested in only a mail delivery, had the temerity to call out the last name he had read in the address line on the envelope. I was hoping he would pop her in the kisser but cooler heads prevailed and he retreated after uttering an interesting and almost appropriate epithet. This set our person off even more but since everyone present denied having heard the comment. She was left to just simmer. I found it to be particularly entertaining to cover the "DR" and hyphen on her name plate. Her response almost resembled that of CAPT Queeg in the "Caine Mutiny" when he set out to identify the non-existent thief of his strawberries. We finally rid ourselves of this person when her governor published a call for persons to serve on a women's issues task force. We often relieved ourselves of baggage in this manner; in fact, the first great drought in the late 1970's enabled us to dump three people who produced only negative numbers for the agency. Now armed with a mission in life, she tried to ingratiate herself with the few top ranked women in the agency but they had nothing to do with her; it was almost as if they realized their own road would become even more difficult via this association. Thus, she made her way merrily along and survived long enough to vest a pension. Ironically, she became a victim of another administration, one in which political orientation first played a serious road in the staffing policies of the agency. Years later I was to receive an award from a group representing the interests of women's equity and the specific citation was for "supporting" diversity in my teaching. I am sure the subject of this vignette would have pitched a fit to learn that someone like me, rather than someone like her, could be so honored.

How about these two, an assistant superintendent and her curriculum coordinator. They apparently each wrote letters for the other, on their district stationery, proclaiming that they were representing their district, a not for profit entity [that did not pay taxes!] in providing workshops BUT the checks were to be made out to the individual and mailed to their home address. When I called to tell them no dice, they had the temerity to inform me that all the other districts were Ok with this! Wonder how they made out with the IRS!!!

HEROES

"I need a hero!" A catchy tune, especially if seen within the context of the movie, *Shrek 2,* whereby the would-be heroes are constantly striving against over-whelming evil. A stirring concept and certainly our children are worthy of heroic efforts. For all of the so called child advocates it is amazing how few people I encountered who consistently placed the students before themselves. Some professionals simply learn very quickly that there is very little equity in combating the system, indeed even the so-called "teacher of the year" awards seemed to be granted by "turns" in my experience. Indeed, toward the end of my career, a teacher who missed almost the entire year with a worker compensation injury was awarded the title! Thank God the stipend that was formerly paid for this "distinction" had been stopped by the state because of budgetary concerns. Those who go along get along, according to the legend and most people are satisfied with this. This strategy leads to tenure, the ultimate job security, which leads to seniority on professional committees, and, may even lead to the ultimate, the holy grail of pubic education employment, a job with one of the professional associations after retirement. Someone who is a vocal critic of the system, who fights against bureaucratic nonsense, who confronts those who shirk their responsibilities, is highly unlikely to be welcomed by the sycophantic societies that dominate the schools.

We have already met a lot of very solid people that I encountered over the years, including some of the following. What made these folks extra special is what they were willing to risk to maintain their standard of ethical behavior, indeed their self-respect. However, none of them went so far as to commit political suicide, since, figuratively speaking, dead heroes are of very little use to anyone. In this case, working to the limits of the system, and, pushing those limits back a little each day, was more than anyone had a right to expect, especially since such behaviors come with a very heavy price tag.

Catherine Havrilesky is one of my all time favorite people and she was one of the brightest lights of the very best times ever seen in public education in New Jersey. She called 'em like she saw 'em and was one of the very first senior members of the education establishment to recognize that the balance of power, so necessary to moving forward, had begun to swing widely to favor the teachers, thanks to their ruthless wielding of political power. Even members of the New Jersey Education Association told me they admired her intellect, welcomed her creativity and applauded her achievements, while working feverishly to ensure her demise. She was the highest ranking woman in the department of education, one of the highest ranking and most admired in all of state government and should have become commissioner of education. Her subsequent career with the Educational Testing Service added quite a bit to the educational establishment and also served to emphasize again how much the children lost with her departure from the department of education.

Bernard Shapiro lived his entire life dedicating himself to the improvement of society. He and his wife made a conscious decision early in their marriage to live in Willingboro, New Jersey, which, at the time, was billed as a grand social experiment, a community that prized diversity. While at Cherry Hill, he mastered the beast that had become Cherry Hill High School East in the highly unsettled and experimental 1970's. This was a school of over 3500 students with one graduating class numbering over 950 students. Imagine the skills necessary to train staff in a myriad of areas to manage a graduating class of that complexity, especially in a community that demanded excellence, loved ceremony, and prized extraordinary academic achievement. His tenure in that school, with its extremely high demands and complex challenges, is deserving of being memorialized. He moved to Haddon Heights, a smaller community but one with equally high expectations, with the promise of assuming the role of chief school administrator. Here again he thrust himself into the fray, and, as principal, advanced the capacity of that high school many times over. Like Catherine, he refused to hide the truth, exposed the warts and tried to cure them and was denied the top spot. His loss was truly a blessing for the community of Delran, who welcomed him as superintendent! As we have seen, Bernie brought a touch of class to everything he did, brought the district into modern times, raised the school out of bankruptcy and laid the foundation for Carl Johnson and the "golden age" of that school system. Bernie had very definite ideas about commitment, dedication to excellence, and leadership, and, decided to move to another career when he decided the system was broken and not likely to recover, and, moved into a new career, as Director of Hampton Hospital School.

Bobby Boose, called my "twin", was my first "Mr. Inside Mr. Outside partner". Bob was superbly prepared professionally, maintained a can-do attitude throughout his career, and was very astute politically. He was able to take my sometimes not completely baked ideas and sell them at the highest levels so that they became institutionalized. While this caused a lot of pressure to be placed on me, it always worked out. Bob was a success at whatever he tried and he is always listed as "among the very finest" whether it was as a bureau chief, assistant commissioner, director of the state school for the deaf, county superintendent, a commissioner of a state agency or college president. It was to the everlasting loss of New Jersey that the last two assignments, in which Dr. Boose had tremendous and wide reaching impact, were completed in New England. Bob is one of the people who always evoke great memories in me.

Max Baumgartner and Jim Garban, while not working directly for public education establishments, taught me a great deal about program and staff development, command, leadership and responsibility. They may have been the best educated, in terms of quality and appropriateness, best trained and hardest working officers of the United States Armed Forces that I ever encountered, either as a serving officer or a civilian management consultant. These extremely important traits carried over in their personal lives and subsequent civilian careers. Both gentlemen abandoned the potential of flag rank in the US Navy to retire and save their families from being uprooted several more times, not exactly the kind of sacrifice most officers would offer to their loved ones, but these two officers were always very special indeed. I never met any other serving officers in over two decades of service that built military organizations on trust and respect for the worker, a true Drucker like human community. They taught me a key lesson, the importance of substance over style, in a truly institutionalized bureaucracy. Not surprisingly, they assumed civilian positions of great significance and continued to make great contributions. Max and Jim have been well respected in their local communities for many years now, including K-12 local school establishments.

Bill Shine is another of my favorites. He was always a gentleman and I think was able to maintain that posture because he was always the most senior or second most influential person wherever he was employed, at least during our time together. As county superintendent of Burlington County, he ran one of the largest establishments in New Jersey, bringing a sense of organization and leadership gleaned from his many years as a senior officer in the United State Marine Corps. He earned a reputation for brilliance in problem solving, advocacy for his constituents, and taking action. As Assistant Commissioner for Curriculum and Instruction he engineered a complete resurgence in the capacity of the state education agency to fulfill its leadership mandate in these areas, and, perhaps most importantly, the staff he trained still holds key positions throughout the state. When the abomination known as "Thorough and Efficient" became law and the cumbersome monitoring system replaced Shine's emphasis on quality in teaching, he became one of the most admired superintendents in the history of Cherry Hill, placing him high on a list of some very distinguished people. I shall never forget his courtesy in calling me on my first day in that cherished district. In the same calm voice that commanded so much respect, he offered his opinions as to why this assignment would be a symbiotic relationship, and he was right on, as usual. Bill was speaking to me from his last position as superintendent of schools of Great Neck, Long Island, which was the community that enticed him to leave New Jersey. One more time, Bill Shine had an opportunity to work his magic.

When I get to Heaven, I intend to ask God to permit me to spend a considerable portion of the next million or so years hanging around with Abraham Lincoln. The Great Emancipator is my all-time hero, and, in my opinion, the most selfless person in history. Once I meet Mr. Lincoln, I shall have then become acquainted with two of the most unselfish persons, Honest Abe, and, our next hero, Steve Barbell. Steve is one of two all time effective board of education members I have encountered. Dr. Barbell got his start as a member of the Cherry Hill West Home and School Council, to which he was quickly elected president. Steve had gotten involved because the school had fallen on hard times. A fantastic staff needed leadership, the building needed a lot of work, and everyone needed a few bucks more. I could mention a lot of people who got their start in just this manner but Steve was already demonstrating that he was something special indeed. Steve of course was an articulate and effective spokesperson. He quickly proved his ability to influence people and to build a constituency, a powerful combination for anyone seeking to change public policy. Again, it is not a unique development to see someone performing this way when they are motivated by a mission, and, often this influence becomes very parochial or even self-serving. Steve was quite a different case; he *ALWAYS* used his influence in a beneficial manner. While his focus was certainly on High School West, he was careful to achieve his ends not by causing other schools in the district to suffer, in what is unfortunately a common model, but by building the capacity of the entire district. Steve was extremely skilful at building a following, person by person, meeting by meeting. I have never met a board of education member who invested so much of himself, who worked so hard, with such a sense of vision. Working in a very demanding community, he brought others along to a realization of the resources needed to maintain excellence in every aspect of the district. Steve was elected to the board of education almost by acclamation and soon was elevated to president of that body. He achieved consensus where quite diverse interests were primed to force divergence. He refused to allow his powerful intellect to interfere with the district administration, preferring instead to concentrate on monitoring a system of goal setting and measurement.

During his term, the district achieved its golden age and it was beautiful to behold. We were blessed by his presence, most particularly because he possesses extraordinary empathy, the gift of putting himself in the place of another, experiencing their feelings, understanding their motives and desires. Steve relinquished his position when capable others were ready to assume the responsibility. A noted dentist in the area, Steve was persuaded to become a candidate for a position on Town Council, to which he was elected repeatedly, retiring only when he had achieved his stated objectives. A few years later, Steve was called on again to head a massive effort to raise funds and build a most impressive library and media center for the community, replacing an earlier structure that had grown obsolescent. Long may this building stand as a testament to the vision and dedication of a distinguished citizen.

We have read a great deal about Fred Burke, my all-time favorite chief state school officer. I once read a comment about the great tenor, Mario Lanza, after his death. The writer stated that Mr. Lanza was a flawed human being, as are we all, but was a gifted artist who lived life "with a song in his heart", the title of a famous Lanza song. Fred Burke lived life in the same manner, knowing he was brilliant but always careful to allow the rest of us to catch up, and was never arrogant about his accomplishments. Fred accomplished a great deal and, had circumstances permitted, was poised to accomplish a great deal more. His failure to win reappointment, much like Carl Marlburger, was based on the fears of several constituent groups that some of their power might become eroded as the Burke movement gathered even more momentum. Fred, a master political scientist, needed all of his skills and all of his courage to accomplish what he did. He traded years of a comfortable existence on the public dole for his beliefs and was himself a victim of the political intrigue that came to characterize all but the administration of Governor Florio, moving forward in time. We can now only mourn both his passing as well as his unfinished work.

Dan Bevilacqua is one of the great human beings of my lifetime. I met Danny when he was a graduate student at Temple University. Dan had been drafted for the Vietnam War after completing most of his course work for a Master of Science degree at the university. After a three year career as a distinguished officer of the US Army [Dan always served with distinction!], he returned to Temple only to find the new program managers expected him to complete new requirements, an incredibly short-sighted view, which I can state with relief was rare during my three decades plus with the University. I volunteered to work with Dan and we became fast friends. As we have read, Dan joined the New Jersey Department of Education and was instrumental in my subsequent employment there. Whatever Dan touched for the rest of his career became noteworthy. Wherever he worked, people came to appreciate his service. Whenever he left for a new assignment, children had profited from his passing through their lives. A giant Bravo Zulu, Danny!

David Adler was a tremendous local superintendent of schools and eventually was promoted to the position of county superintendent. David had the good looks of a leading man and a bit of the thespian in him, and was extremely intelligent, qualities which easily thrust him in leadership roles. I most admired him for the resolute manner in which he always pursued what be believed to be the proper course of action. I recall one sweltering late afternoon in the State Board Conference Room, when we were being berated by a staff member of DEP [the greenies] as to the importance of forcing every school district to promote water conservation during a drought, as if such a thing could be forced. Dr. Adler had tried to lead the gentleman to an understanding of the importance of leading staff and students to this position when the DEP type remonstrated, and yelled "What have you done today to promote water conservation?" To this David replied, "Well I prayed for rain this morning", at which time a tremendous downpour began, as David continued, "and, it looks like God was listening!"

Basan Nembrikow, as we have seen, was a tremendously successful board member and later, president of the board, in Howell NJ. Basan is one of the many people I have come to miss as I grow older, knowing that what was once shall never be again. When we met he was hardly a supporter, Basan wanted to be convinced of a person's worth before he offered his support, which is what he had experienced growing up. When he came to accept you, you could not find a more worthy or more formidable ally. He represented the interest of his particular ethnic group by insisting on only the very best for every child in his care. Years later, about midway through my tenure in Delran, I came to meet an assistant principal who had grown up in Howell. She came by to introduce herself and said, "Mr. Nembrikow said I was to trust you." Thanks, Buzz, for your years of friendship.

Terry Kraft was a cohort of Buzz in Howell and had no need to seek a seat on a board of education: his children were brilliant and needed no special protection. Like Buzz, Terry sought neither political advancement nor any special privilege for his own employment. He was comfortable financially, owning a substantial trucking company, and actually lost money as a consequence of his commitment to the district. He served with distinction, often having to overcome extreme pettiness, in serving the children of Howell Township, New Jersey. The time we spent together was just great Terry!

Don Beineman was absolutely the finest superintendent the county of Camden ever experienced and one of the finest anywhere, anytime. Don was knowledgeable, unafraid to support his constituents as they battled ever more challenging bureaucratic nonsense from state sources, and had an engaging sense of humor, a rare yet important commodity among his peers. I first encountered Dr. Beineman with the state education agency. In that capacity he was responsible for building the finest curriculum development and support network I have ever seen. His dedication to excellence, his commitment to quality and his willingness to follow the correct path rather than that which might be propitious endeared him to all who were fortunate to be touched by his guidance. Don should have been a commissioner of education but he was ready for the assignment too late, i.e., after the job became a political football. A Burke-Beineman handoff would have been just fabulous; another missed opportunity that I can now only lament.

Here is a set of twins that could only be recognized as "good guys", Karen Davis and Mary Genca. Two of my favorite people, they were highly effective board members in Delran because: they had the common sense to know what was best for the children, they put in the effort to learn all they could about key issues, they were smart enough to know crap when they saw it, and, they were courageous enough to try and do the right thing, even though they had a great deal to lose. How much? Well, each had four children in school yet they never hesitated to insist on quality from the teaching staff and, at the best possible price for the taxpayer. Great moms who worked hard on behalf of all the children of the community. Well done, ladies.

Hal Melleby was someone I met on my arrival in Cherry Hill and it was immediately apparent that this was a special individual. Hal was part of the terrific group of people at High School West, probably the best large student body high school administrative staff I have ever seen. He was insightful, highly creative, and most innovative, especially with programs of instruction, built broad coalitions among the staff, had a huge constituency among the parents and was widely respected by everyone in town who knew him. Hal did a terrific job as principal of the special needs high school and was being widely recruited when I left the district. The fact that he was permitted to leave is a testament to the quality of leadership in place at the time and his departure, while a God send for several other communities where he completed future assignments, was a grievous loss for the citizens of Cherry Hill. He is one of the brightest lights among the current administrative population in the entire state. I was privileged to serve as the external university professor for his dissertation study, which was completed at the University of Pennsylvania. In an age of mail-order doctorate degrees, his PhD is based on a strong academic background, a distinguished residency and a research oriented thesis. At this writing he is starting his tenure as superintendent of schools in the Eastern Regional High School district and already achieving great things. It is sad indeed that so many other communities, and their children, have to settle for so much less.

Joan Katz was a partner of Hal's at HS West in Cherry Hill. As principal, she was the chief architect of this once wonderful place. She was a gifted leader, indeed my second book, Total Quality Leadership, was dedicated to Dr. Katz. Another product of years of training and advancement through the ranks at Cherry Hill, the concept I believe that made the district great. She was exposed to people like Bill Shine and Jack McKeon. She had an uncanny ability to mold strong personalities into a team. Her science department head, and the best I have ever seen, Harry Zakarian, was a brilliant teacher and fought fiercely for his programs as science department head. He would back away from no position that he thought benefited his staff and students, and yet he worked harmoniously with Joan. Barbara Banks, Dennis Davidow, Reds Jordan and Hal Melleby were all strong personalities and yet under Joan they were a seamless team, one capable of great things. Above all, Joan was a role model, for her staff, for her students, and for everyone connected with the school district. I felt privileged that my own daughter was exposed to the Joan Katz magic. I still recall the angst felt by hundreds of mourners during Dr. Katz' memorial service. Joan, I miss you every day and West, unfortunately, has never been the same.

Joyce Tully was my colleague and dear friend during my years in Cherry Hill. It was an interesting organizational set-up, very large in scope and with hundreds of staff, yet, most days it was just the two of us dealing with a wide range of problems. Joyce is an uncommonly bright person, with keen insight, and the ability to cut to the chase. I used to say I could send her to run any building and that she would probably do a terrific job, because she had courage as well as smarts. She could not stand people in positions of responsibility who waffled before making decisions, always seeking a public criterion to cover themselves. I used to tell her such was the way of the bureaucracy and that it was our job to counter such behavior with decisiveness but she remained unforgiving. She had one trick I always admired. One of the endless bureaucrats would call for permission to do something simple. Joyce would answer the phone, keeping it open for all to hear, and come to my doorway and state, "It is Mr. so and so on the phone. He probably wants permission to go to the bathroom." Enough said. There is a postscript here. I never paid much attention to my birthday but Joyce always did and threw a great party, just inviting the blue collar types, knowing I was always most comfortable among them . Thanks again, Joyce!

Joseph Carbone, Carmen DeFelice, Dennis McCawley, and Ernie Luccarini, were key individuals responsible for facilities, housekeeping and maintenance in Cherry Hill. They were amazing, not just for the quality effort they delivered consistently, but for the manner in which they stretched a dollar to do so. Miss you guys, especially the half-days on Saturday we "donated" to the district each week to get a head start on the following work week.

Denise Wiltsee and Kaye Peterson were school librarians extraordinaire. They combined outstanding library science skills with exceptional teaching ability and they were two of the most caring people I ever encountered along this long trail. I used to describe them as the kind of people who returned $100 of value to the children for every dollar in resources they were given. Well done, ladies, I miss you!

Joseph Chiaravello is a risk management manager for Utica National, our comp and liability carrier in Delran. I have never met a more caring person working in this capacity. Although a senior manager, he kept to the field as often as possible to maintain as realistic as possible outlook on the challenges facing clients. He worked closely with Delran, because, as he put it, I worked out of the box and never shrank from a difficult challenge. To whatever success I may have achieved, people like Joe are mainly responsible.

Dr. John Rocco was an educator and a ranking member of the New Jersey Assembly. We graduated from the same high school in South Philadelphia some years apart but never connected until the 1990's, when we needed dire relief from ill-advised legislation, and John came to the rescue. The governor had signed a bill that actually penalized districts for raising large amounts of cash through cost-efficiencies. John took the effort to investigate the damage being caused and although it impacted on only a few districts, managed to ram through what he called the "Delran Amendment". It gave us immediate relief and we even got a large check from Governor Whitman, my only pleasant memory of the woman. John's work in many areas was characterized by the same caring attitude. We needed more like him.

John Flynn and Gus Ruh have been close friends for decades. We spent years together in the state education agency and they provided support for every one of my crazy ideas and then thanked me for getting the job done. Their foresight and courage led to many of the improvements of the Marlburger and Burke eras, and, they held things together for quite a while in the convulsive period that followed Fred's departure. Gentlemen, it was a wild ride.

Ralph Lataille already has had a lot of ink in these pages. Smart as anybody, loyal without limits, he had an uncanny sense to see through nonsense AND provide a script for corrective action. In a bureaucracy run wild, he insisted that people do their jobs, do them well, and, he made sure there were no extra bodies around whenever possible. Once Ralph decided someone was worthy of his support, it became a very enjoyable and profitable relationship.

Marge Roukema is one of only a few members of Congress that I have met. She took a concerned young man, convinced him his testimony was eminently necessary to correct a system run amuck and made sure that his reputation was only enhanced by the effort. She owed me none of these things. Thank you Congressperson!

Ruth Mancuso was the longest serving president of the state board of education during my time. She was magnificent, the highest ranking child advocate I have ever encountered and no one did it better. She deserves her own memoir. To those of us running the agency during her time, the question "would Mrs. Mancuso approve" was always the criterion employed in making key decisions.

A life long friend, Dick Wright, deserves mention here, for his own unique leadership style and for the lessons he taught me. A superbly educated person, The George School, Lafayette College, and the Wharton MBA program, Dick held a number of senior civilian positions such as vice-presidencies for Revlon and Tiffany. You might expect a person with such a background to be a bit snobby or standoffish but Dick was a real hands-on leader, spending most of his time with those who did the real work, developing products, serving customers, etc. His Navy career is just as interesting. He rose to the rank of Commander in a very difficult specialty area, cargo handling. With his education and performance record he could have had the cushiest jobs but he chose the most important, billets involving hundreds of enlisted personnel and they loved him, why: he lived among them, had mastered all of the technical skills necessary to the task, and, spared no effort in supporting them and making their lives easier. His units became the benchmark against which all others were measured.

Among the plethora of outstanding university professors I have observed, Dr. Stuart Schmidt stands tallest. Stuart worked harder than anyone I knew in this environment. His commitment to excellence in teaching, creating superb learning opportunities for his students, his outstanding and very pertinent research and the cocker expressed for each and every student, whether beginning freshman or doctorial candidate became legendary. He would have earned the sobriquet "leader' just by these examples even if he had not served as a multi-term department head. In that capacity, he was equally generous with his time, serving as a resource to each and every faculty member fortunate to be placed before students at Temple University.

Finally, kudos to my dear friend from our Navy days, Robert Kelly, the Camden County Engineer and director of public works. Bob is the antithesis of the popular perception of the civil servant. As labor costs occupy an ever larger share of a shrinking budget, he must do more with less, and does. He is a master motivator, working in a very challenging public dole environment, and is just extraordinarily creative in finding smarter ways to get things done better and less costly. He gets it done every day!

John McKeon and Ronald Napoli were my two greatest mentors. Their intelligence, commitment to excellence, and their courage were without peer. I was fortunate that they came along at different times to keep me from ever hesitating. Gentlemen, the best of what I accomplished is owed to you.

Well, heroes, here's to you. Shame there were damn few of you!

NO ONE CARES ANY LONGER

"I dream things that never were and say: Why not?"

George Bernard Shaw

FINAL ACT

Is there no one interested in cleaning up the pigsty that now characterizes public education in this country? As of this writing, the conventional wisdom still states that almost thirty percent of high school students drop out and that college is out of reach for almost two-thirds of high school graduates, not because of cost as much as for the simple reason they are unprepared for even some of the glorified high schools now passing themselves off as "colleges". In 2004 less than half the high school graduates have met the course requirements for college. I can recall sitting in a board meeting in New Jersey listening to a report of their terrific SAT prep course sequence. Yes, I said "sequence" for the children were getting credit for taking TWO courses designed to prep them for the exam, which I always understood to be an exam of how much they had learned cumulatively in their quest for a college education. The course had been constructed in a comprehensive fashion and there was every reason they would succeed in boosting SAT scores, but is this the purpose of high school, to clean up the mess of negligent performance? Kind of reminds me of the transition courses that were so popular for years. A transitional kindergarten, followed by a transitional first grade, then second grade and finally, third. It became a cause celebre for me at the time as I welcomed the opportunity to publicize the fact that this trend pointed to twenty-six years of potential public education for students condemned to this jobs program for teachers. There were no data to support the concept, just the announced statement by the local teacher unions that having slower children in these grade levels would "slow down" the progress of the brighter children. Of course the staff wanted slower children pulled out, as if you could even scientifically discern children who should be classified at that early age, let alone those deemed "slow" by teachers eager to teach only to the middle Thus alarmed, the parents started a witch-hunt because as one said at a board of education meeting: "...unfortunately, everyone knows who these children are and while our hearts go out to them, they must not be allowed to hold down the 'brighter' children". Wild applause for a crusading mom, one more parent who thinks she begot another Einstein. The solution, why of course: group them together in an environment designed to slow them down even more. However much this approach might satisfy parents, show "cooperation" with teachers and create more jobs, calling it a "win-win" approach as many do, does not take into account the welfare of the children involved and the irreversible damage they must endure. Need another example? How about the alarming, to me at least, trend of paying teachers to tutor children after school in order to help them pass statewide tests designed to measure student proficiency in the same subjects they cannot master during the regular school day, thus necessitating paying the same teachers to teach them some more after school.

When I was associated with the New Jersey Department of Education, there seemed to be a fresh movement every year to BROADEN the number of areas to which a child could be classified. The joke became soon no child except those of the teaching staff would remain in a regular classroom. In one district in New Jersey, the teachers held information sessions for the parents as to how over-burdened they were and the unfortunate negative impact they might expect their children to suffer. A few parents, but only a few, outraged by this behavior and the cost of their proposed solution, told them to get off their derrieres and start working for a living. Unfortunately, such is not a prescription for success for the children of parents who speak thusly. The herd knew better and began immediate propaganda warfare for the proposed solution, "classroom management aides" for every kindergarten class, and then for every first grade class, and then for every second grade class. I am pleased to report that under the pressure by the taxpayers, this insanity stopped with the third grade. I used to call it the *caddy approach*, you know, for each teacher there would be someone to follow them around and carry their chalk. After all, these are the same people who brought you the pull-out program, you know the one where they used federal funds to hire specialty teachers and then yanked kids out of the regular classroom to give them "help" with basic skills while they were missing all of the instruction their classmates were receiving at that time, the delimiting factor normally being the short work day of staff.

Here we have a great example of what industry refers to as the "rework syndrome", i.e., if you cannot get it right the first time, do not fix the system, as that involves labor accountability. Instead, extra labor is hired to rework the product. I once was asked to consider a consulting assignment for a former MBA student, who had taken a position as a quality control guru for a car assembly plant, and it was a marquee American brand. I was reluctant, as I was booked solid and was concerned that I may have taught him too well and he was off on a mission he could not complete. I did agree to visit the plant and it was incredible. They had all this modern equipment and little of it was being used properly. I actually saw one vehicle leave the paint shack, which was operated via computer driven robotics, with three of the four fenders painted a different color. The dome light installer had gone home ill and took the keys to his parts locker with him so there was a swarm of supervisors climbing over the front seats trying to install the lights by hand. A few screws went through the roof of the vehicles being fitted, as they were not the proper part, and then the supervisor climbed aboard to sand the screw tip flush with the metal roof and apply touch up paint. The best part was the rework portion of the assembly line where a small army equipped with hand tools was trying to fix what the sophisticated line had installed improperly. More than 25% of the resources available to this plant had to be expended in the rework area, fixing what was not done properly in the first place. Then there was the "yard", as it was known, where the vehicles were divided into three categories: those ready to ship [cars with less than 15 defects, which the dealer was supposed to deal with]; those not ready to be shipped because the number of defects exceeded what the dealer was expected to deal with; and, those so badly manufactured they were ready to be scrapped. In fact there was an insurance shack in that section of the yard and the agents just wrote off the cars. It is a shame parents cannot buy insurance for a lousy job by the schools, sort of like travel insurance when the tsunami ruins the trip, only here there is no fix for a ruined life.

Educators hate accountability, in fact they remind me of teenagers who erupt when parents barge into their rooms, stating, *they* are the "professionals" and therefore *they* know better, and, "how dare you interfere", Mr. and Mrs. Parent. If that is so, that is, if they are so "professional", how come it is so easy to enter the "profession, especially in a place like Philadelphia where the district was forced to admit how many of its staff was not certified to teach the subjects to which they were assigned. If they know better, how come in Pennsylvania, a "union education" state in 2004, nearly 200,000 students were eligible to transfer from 'failing" high schools, under the No Child Left Behind statute. In New Jersey, the same year, in a state with a far worse reputation for hiding the sins of its educational establishment, less than 400 students were able to transfer to better schools under the same law. Perhaps there are just not enough good schools to qualify for the program, perhaps administrators make it too difficult for parents to get information let alone force the transfer, perhaps the boards of education have stooped to ruses to avoid busing costs, all the while only 34 percent of the students entering ninth grade end up being ready for college on graduation day. If the professionals know so much, how come tutoring is one of the fastest growing businesses? If they are so proficient, how come nationally in 2004, over 200,000 children were provided with outside tutoring services, unfortunately only eleven percent of those eligible! Right now the car assembly plant is doing much better.

BARBARIANS AT THE GATE

In the late 1980's, the story of the breakup of the once proud RJR Nabisco conglomerate dominated the news. The company still appeared very strong on the surface but the leadership, headed by its chief executive officer, F. Ross Johnson, knew that troubled times lay ahead. You see, the tobacco business was by far the stronger of the two; yet, public sentiment was beginning to build as the evidence of the dangers of nicotine addiction presented by the anti-smoking factions tended to outweigh the vast financial resources of the tobacco lobby. In addition to foreseeing the beginning of the end for the tobacco industry, albeit the light at the end of the tunnel was still well into the future, RJR had invested a fortune in a smokeless cigarette, which if it was lit with a sulfur tipped match tasted like, well think of a combination of manure and rotten eggs and you have a pretty accurate image. It is worth watching the very fine HBO production to see Mr. Johnson, portrayed by James Garner, gagging the first time he lit up. I remember the company giving away thousands of these cigarettes in the cities, asking smokers for their opinion, and seeing the surveyors struggling to light the cancer sticks with a lighter to prevent the inevitable reaction. The company hierarchy was doing all it could to hide the problem from even the board of directors. I believe the new line of smokes was called Premier, and Ross Johnson knew they were the start of something very bad indeed.

The food division was perking along at a very strong clip, with earnings maintained at a very profitable margin. The resource base of this division was strong, assets that could be sold off to help pay the cost of a leveraged buy-out of the tobacco division so Johnson decided that he had better buy the company himself, sell the food division to pay off the debt service and live happily ever after, according to the standard to which he had become accustomed, which included a private jet to ferry his German Shepherd around. Once word of the Premier debacle became known, RJR would be put into play and for Johnson, buying the company became a struggle for personal survival, despite the numbers of jobs that would be lost. The case was part of the MBA case book at Temple and the movie did a great job portraying the greed involved in the entire process. Once RJR was put into play, Johnson had to confront Kohlberg, Kravitz and Roberts, the kings of LBO's, and the game began. To bring an overly long example to closure, the group headed by Johnson, which included Jim Robinson, CEO of American Express, offered substantially more per share than KKR, but those who knew of Johnson's plan to divest Nabisco, had leaked the magnitude of Mr. Johnson's personal compensation and benefits plan, and the result was outrage. The company employed a Chairman of the Board, who functioned as a separate entity from the CEO, and served as the principal officer evaluating the proposals. It is said that he was so offended by the magnitude of what Mr. Johnson planned to pay himself that he exclaimed, "Now I know what the "F" in

F. Ross Johnson means." The KKR proposal was accepted, even though they offered a substantially lower per share price, because everyone was offended, indeed outraged, by the "piggishness" displayed by their own corporate officers.

What is the purpose of this example? Well, my experience of over three and one-half decades in a leadership position, has led me to postulate that the boorish behaviors of the unions involved with public education is not only dangerous to the welfare of the children supposedly in their charge, but also, in a comparative sense, more "piggish" than even the redoubtable F. Ross Johnson, who incidentally ended up having to be satisfied with a $53 million severance package. Think I am being too tough, then consider these examples.

Please note: as with all examples in this book, these are real events with which I have first hand knowledge, yet they did not necessarily happen in districts in which I was employed, or during my time in a particular district. As our reputation for excellence grew, I became acquainted with hundreds of districts in several states.

A superintendent once asked me my advice concerning a problem that seems both too obscure as well as too bizarre to have really been an issue; yet, it almost cost the district a huge and very necessary reconstruction project, one designed to rid an entire school of asbestos. I was well aware of the problem he was facing, the floors were composed of vinyl asbestos tile, which had been crumbling. Air testing had taken place frequently as the staff was rightfully concerned, with some claiming the tile problem for every ailment that had ever cost them a sick day. For example, one teacher, with 27 years service, and *not a single sick day accumulated during that span*, eventually filed a complaint charging a 'sick building syndrome', and demanded pay for 270 days of work she had missed because the building had made her ill. I digress a bit but she dragged the district through every jurisdiction possible, failing each time, indeed, she never ever made a strong enough case to even warrant a formal investigation let alone a hearing. Even her pulmonary specialist was forced to admit she had never exhibited symptoms, she had complained of them, supposedly every day at work. Here is where the good guys won ONE. As reported to me, while she failed in her attempt to take advantage of a situation and win over a year of pay, her efforts were brought to the attention of the state disabilities board. Ever watchful of an opportunity to save pension dollars, the board placed this teacher on partial disability retirement, which was significantly less than her regular pension would have been, and the district was rid of her, a resolution that should reaffirm everyone's belief in the existence of a deity.

Back to the main topic here, it turned out that complaints over the dangers presented by the floor tile were not at all the issue. The almost continuous air testing had yielded no findings even approaching a problem. The issue upsetting this superintendent was the teachers' concern with, you guessed it, MONEY, and his distress was based in the fact that he was unable to figure out how to give it to them. This is another illustration of a syndrome I witnessed all through my career: when the union accommodating superintendents had a teacher dominated board of education, they were quick to use that board to support rationale after rationale to forgive transgressions or justify extra pay. On the other hand, when they had a board of education that took a more critical look at the affairs of a district, they were quick to try and devise justifications by which items could be resolved without formal action by the board.

For another, I was once asked to become involved with a case involving a demand for pension payments to be made on behalf of selected teachers. The chief school administrator was all for getting it done, "…just add them to their payroll checks", he exclaimed. Now ordinarily someone in my position would be expected to get involved with an issue involving pensions but in this case there was much more involved. First of all, the individual pension accounts are a matter between the member and the pension system, with the payroll folks responsible for completing certain data etc. In this situation, there was documentation that some of the teachers had deliberately waited too long to have the deductions for pension begun that they never responded to the requests to complete the data sheets and eventually they were forcibly enrolled by the pension system. Added to this was the normal occurrence of the vagaries of the postal system and a few people who never intended to enroll because they never intended to stay with the system very long. These were all normal situations.

What makes this case unique was an increase in the required contributions of the members during the time while several of the members were procrastinating and they demanded payment of the differential involved. Well, this was at first extraordinarily amusing because the pension system does not allow payments to be made on behalf of members and two, I had no interest in helping to reward ever more obnoxious behavior of some of the staff. I certainly was not going to cooperate in making a payment without the knowledge of the board of education. My position was that the solicitor should seek some basis of settlement, for the sake of "labor peace", and then the board of education could decide whether to approve the payments. I only relented to this because of a terribly nefarious development: I was told that the union intended to try and affix blame to a former payroll clerk who had died in service. This was a lovely woman whose work had always been impeccable, through countless audits and had succumbed, painfully and slowly, to a terrible disease. The purported position of the union was reported to be dementia on the part of the employee in her final weeks on the job, and so, I promised not to block any settlement. I did draw the line at the attempt to having all this occur behind the scenes so there were a few fruitful and satisfying moments when members arrived demanded a check for their "settlement" only to be asked if they could produce an approved board of education resolution mandating a payment, specifying the amount, and providing a basis of calculation.

But back to the floor tile [I am sorry but there are so many tales of abuse to relate!]. The district always provided movers to minimize any disruption to the staff during construction in the classrooms, whenever the normal room packing expected each year had to be exceeded. The district provided boxes; they provided the tape and other accouterments. All the staff member had to do was drop the material to be packed into a box and leave the box in place, which would then be the responsibility of the professional movers. After the construction was completed, the process would be reversed. Sounds pretty neat does it not, and it cost about twenty grand a school just for the movers! As an interesting aside, other districts were forced to begin employing movers because of what I refer to as the jungle drums, the behind the scenes network in which an advance or benefit that occurred somewhere, became a demand used everywhere. Whenever a district gave in, whenever they made a mistake, then that advance became the standard to be used against other employers. I actually had a situation in which a district adopted completely out of bounds salary increases over four years for their teachers, a contract approved by a teacher dominated board incidentally. This contract was met with howls from surrounding districts as having raised the bar to a bankruptcy standard, which was in fact accurate. Of course the other districts were then bombarded by demands for the same salary increases and a few gave in. I am sure you already knew the end of this story, as the contract for the original district was in its final year, the union naturally began demanding the same range of increases, pointing to the fact that a few other districts had just adopted the same magnitude of raises in the last few years. Soon the superintendent and some board of education members were moaning that the "trend" was still for five plus percent increases. Everyone involved refused to be reminded that they had started the cycle!

Please never forget one of the principal findings of my career: "there is more than enough money, it is just how it is being spent; that is the issue".

The answer to all of this of course is to remove the human resources role from these completely vulnerable local boards of education. State education agencies throughout the country have removed much authority from boards of education, almost as much as have the courts, because the boards "cannot be trusted" to set standards, spend funds, etc. On the other hand, under the guise of maintaining local control, these same jurisdictions refuse to tackle the issues of contracts, salaries and benefits. Why? Because, to do so, to make a valid effort to right the ship, would involve taking on the teacher unions, something they are simply unwilling to do.

Once again back to the floor tile. Well, the teachers had decided that being asked to pack their rooms, which all of them were supposed to do each year anyway, was just too much effort and they deserved a reward, they wanted a $500.00 stipend per teacher as compensation. The superintendent was seeking my advice as to how to justify this when I asked what had happened to the rule that the rooms are to be packed up very year. "That practice has become obsolete", was the reply, which means in English, we do not enforce that anymore because it upsets the teachers. In an interesting twist, the union used, as a justification, the supposed fact that another, nearby district that was to undergo construction, had given their staff an extra week of pay to get the job done. When I checked with a friend in that OTHER district, I was told they were upset because they were told my district was providing $500 and movers. I had to confirm the movers; I disclaimed the $500 stipend. When I asked about THEIR program of providing an extra week of work, I was told that no such thing was going to take place. 'Just get the work done on your own time' was the slogan of the other district quoted to me. Of course I was told their superintendent could give in to the pressure at any time also.

When the $500 would not fly, the teachers moved to a demand for the aides to be given six days of extra work to do the packing, yet the movers were still on the scene. Just like Jackson standing, "… like a damned stonewall", at the Civil War Battle of Bull Run, I insisted that no extra compensation be provided, using the new restrictive spending rules as a rationale.

There is an interesting corollary to this story. In the district in question the annual retirement dinner for retiring teachers, which was supposed to be sponsored by the union, had to be abandoned for lack of attendance. They simply would not come on their own time to honor their peers. Likewise, the annual afternoon cocktail reception had to be abandoned. The solution, take the last paid work day and have a half day [or more] retirement breakfast. When the taxpayer began footing the bill for the hours spent at the party, attendance soared to almost one hundred percent! For the year in which the floor tile had to be removed, the teachers who could not possibly complete the required packing of their rooms without movers, stipends and aides, all went to the party and were given most of the afternoon off. I know because I was told they returned from the party at noon to demand their last checks as they were allowed to promptly leave for the summer.

You have read that I worked in a situation in which the ops mgmt people generated large amounts of savings as cash each year, which, for a time was spent in support of improvements for the children of the community. In a succeeding administration, with a philosophy of labor peace and a teacher dominated board of education, the cash began to be used to fund ten month positions into twelve, extra summer days for most, stipends galore, in effect the most ambitious jobs program I have yet seen in my career. This was all done under the guise of program improvement, yet the leadership collected not a shred of data to document increases with productivity, indeed the test scores declined during this period.

Despite this, one year, at the height of this crisis, there were several members of the board of education who told me they were seriously considering the offer of their local union affiliate to extend the current contract, and its ruinous salary guides, stipends and other provisions. This incredible scenario was to repeat itself several times, each time I found myself making a speech against the insanity involved. You should immediately see the flaws in such a system, especially since there was absolutely nothing to gain for someone in my position from sticking their head in such a noose. It is almost laughable to think that even the person responsible for internal control should be expected to provide a conscience for the leadership, especially if they are not tenured, yet the practice of conferring tenure is being described by the politicians as the bane of progress in improving the public schools! You can also well imagine the effect this had on the handful of employees on whom the district depended to run everyday, the non-affiliated, who had been paid half the prevalent scale in raises the previous summer, and had to endure the public humiliation of being described as the best of the district staff; those who now had to accept much less in order to send a message to union employees! An act of fiscal responsibility it was deemed, but it certainly seemed to be a strange time to find religion. It should be noted that, when confronted with this fact, several members of the board of education actually denied the event, indeed these were the same people who committed the act, tried to force the superintendent and business official to accept responsibility for the affair, met with the staff involved, in an incredibly draconian scene, repeated their message and then tried to deny that the affair had transpired as everyone involved had witnessed.

I know of a district that faced a worker comp case filed by a teacher who coincidentally had had orthopedic surgery, was out for a while, and had burned a great deal of sick time. Now this person freely admitted having a goal of retiring in little more than a year and she seemed anxious to embark on what we used to call in the Navy, her sunset cruise, a milk-run to occupy the final months before going over the side. On her return from medical leave, which she complained was premature because of the leave issue, she suffered a fall, according to the claim she filed, blaming the contractor who provided the cleaning service, which included floor maintenance. This story is not at all unusual. Like many states, New Jersey provides special protection for school teachers at the elementary and secondary levels, with an incredibly lenient allowance of one year at no loss of pay or benefits. In many years of affiliation with teaching, managing and consulting in the field of HR, I have never seen such a beneficent approach to providing security for a protected class of employees. In some cases, teachers past their prime may have even been encouraged to ride out their last year via a comp case. The attitude expressed by some of the people willing to permit such an approach is that "no one gets hurt", except perhaps the taxpayer, and even perhaps the children, who fall victim to the trend of ever more lax standards of discipline among those in whose charge the children are placed. It is also interesting that most of the cases similar to this one involved deep tissue injuries, which are difficult to verify and, there are seldom any witnesses to these slip and falls.

While questionable, what I am describing is unfortunately not unusual. What makes this case somewhat unusual and perhaps most disturbing is what follows. With astonishing speed, this teacher filed a series of legal actions well before her case was even closed. She took it upon herself to return to work on the advice of her physician, without prior clearance from the comp carrier, and then filed suit to have her attendance record cleared of any sick leave, despite the fact that the law required the district to mark her absent when she was not present, and, that partial days are not compensable. She hired an attorney to file suit against the cleaning contractor and, there is much more. The district had a program of offering its staff the opportunity to cover classes for a fee. No particular staff member had a guarantee of such payments and they certainly could not earn any extra money if they were not present for duty in the first place! This staff member filed paperwork demanding the extra class coverage stipend for each day that she was absent. She also had been assigned to cover a student activity, for a stipend of almost a thousand dollars. She also filed a demand for payment of this stipend, while acknowledging that her injury prevented her from completing the activities planned, and she had the support of the principal, at least according to the superintendent who reported that, "unfortunately the standard had been met". When asked for an opinion, I inquired as to how many days the teacher had missed, and was told she failed to work a full day since October of the previous fall, for the remainder of the school year. I responded with a question, if that was the standard for considering a club activity to be completed then the district should seriously consider dismantling its entire program of student activities because it was a jobs initiative for teachers not a beneficial program for students. I suggested further that not to challenge this lunacy would be a complete abrogation of the trust placed in the leadership by the community. Now, the administration feared the new, somewhat antagonistic, board of education almost as much as the teachers and seemed relieved when I suggested that the matter be allowed to proceed to arbitration, which her union promptly filed, another sign of an immature labor union. I made this suggestion with the full knowledge of the abusive nature to which the arbitration process has degenerated. However, a compromise position was needed even if ultimately injustice would be rewarded yet again. By the way, our teacher was not done. She filed a demand to have her social security taxes returned for the days absent that had been marked as sick leave, even though the other items of litigation that she initiated prevented her case from being closed. Finally, although theoretically still "out on comp", she somehow convinced the powers to be to provide her with three days pay for a summer program, that qualified her to be paid as a mentor for newly hired teachers. Pretty good when you do not even have to report for work and are still being paid. How much is enough? It is never enough whenever more is available.

When I worked with districts that were represented by a joint insurance fund for worker compensation, the examples were just incredible. One district had a teacher who incidentally was also a board of education member. She represented herself as a "specialist" when in fact she taught basic skills, a sinecure for some districts because they are able to move a weaker teacher to a position in which they can cause less damage, and they get a full share for working with a handful of children a week. Well, this person came to the attention of the JIF because of still another worker comp claim that she had filed. This time she claimed she damaged her back by simply working with the children, and taking full advantage of the most lenient comp laws I have ever encountered, stayed home with full pay for a year. When I asked how the district could possibly manage this case in such a cavalier manner, that is, basically give the person a free walk to a paid sabbatical, they reminded me how "politically wired" the person was and how everyone was better off with the teacher out of the district. How about the taxpayers, who never realize how politically wired they can make themselves? Ought they not to deserve better?

Of course, when discussing situations such as these, I cannot get the meatball king out of my mind. You remember the teacher caught stealing meatballs by the cafeteria manager and then made physical contact with the women, only to rebuke the principal who wrote him up. He is still going strong, safe in the knowledge that his union would challenge any affront to his "professionalism".

Another of my favorites is the one about the teacher who exposed himself to his students and wound up urinating in the trash can. Of course, his local affiliate filed a grievance when the board of education tried to remove him from the classroom, an action I defy any parent not to support, the board that is, certainly not the union.

Where do people turn to for relief? Most governors need the teacher union endorsement, witness the 2005 Corzine campaign in New Jersey. The chief state school officers are an artifact of the political process and the state boards of education are political appointees. Some states, including New Jersey, have adopted strong ethics laws, only to see case law and in some cases, the decisions of their school ethics commissions water down whatever positive impact these laws may have delivered. For example, the school ethics commission in New Jersey adopted a series of opinions over the years that give teachers serving on boards of education full access to the process that established the cycle of ever escalating salaries and benefits. These are the people who brought you the doctrine of necessity, in which, whenever the number of people with direct conflicts of interest are too numerous to enable a quorum to act for necessary business to be conducted, the notion of conflict of interest is simply waived, regardless of the impact!

Writing in the Philadelphia Inquirer on July 3, 2005, columnist Stephen Smith, known for his courage and hard-hitting journalism, wrote a piece on a recent episode involving a baseball player, Kenny Rogers, who had been having a rather rugged first half of the season. While the name may invoke the seemingly mild mannered country singer and sometime purveyor of fried chicken outlets [not "fast food" but "good food served quickly"], Mr. Smith was in fact speaking of a baseball pitcher who had, on national TV no less, attacked two camera persons, pummeling one sufficiently to force a cameraman to the hospital for treatment. The news videographer, someone who had the permission of the league and the team mgmt to be on the field filming the players as they warmed up, or whatever it is baseball players do before a game. The videographer was not a journalist in the sense that his assignment, indeed his livelihood, involved the simple act of exposing film through a lens, capturing the rather mundane act of grown men making millions actually playing themselves out of shape as a baseball season progresses. Thus, he did not even question Mr. Rogers about his somewhat sub-par season, he just filmed him walking around [I hesitate to pour fuel on a fire but perhaps a bit of practice should have been occupying Mr. Rogers at the time]. For this simple act of filming, the man and his camera were thrown to the ground repeatedly by Mr. Rogers. The player was also charged with simple assault; and, in a manner reminiscent of teachers and parents mounting a charge at a board of education meeting to "defend one of their own", the team, other players, media and some fans were livid in their arguments to the videographer to drop the charges. As an interesting side note, on the day Mr. Rogers voluntarily gave himself up for arraignment, he again threatened photographers at the court house.

Mr. Rogers was given a 20 game suspension and a small fine, $50,000, even though this was not the first offense of the season. The obstreperousness of the players' union so limits the ability of the chief executive that Mr. Rogers shall be paid his full salary during his suspension. The player, through his agent, issued an apology that I found to be perfunctory. It was the inability of major league baseball to display effective leadership that Mr. Smith decried; the inability to come to grips with this incident and many similar that preceded it; a leadership with a reputation of ineffectiveness. The suspension of Mr. Rogers, which was immediately contested by his union, was announced the day after a teammate, Frank Francisco, was sentenced to a work–mgmt program as well as anger mgmt classes for assaulting a fan last season. He actually broke a woman's nose after hitting her with a chair. He was also suspended, with full pay, showing that his punishment was so insignificant that other players such as Mr. Rogers were not in the least deterred. The lenient disposition of such acts was a failure of the very senior most mgmt to display courage according to Mr. Smith, and he took pains to provide illustrations that showed the contrasting firm determination of major league basketball and major league football to act decisively and notoriously, despite the presence of active unions, whenever their players tended to stray from an already broad avenue of tolerable behavior. To show how little regard the players have for behaving decently and how little they have to fear for abhorrent behavior, Mr. Rogers' teammates have sworn to stick by him until he is absolved of any blame!? This is the same player's union that insists testing of its members for illicit drugs is a violation of their civil rights and privacy rights, unless of course the requirements are negotiated with the union. What of the rights of the fans? What of common decency? Incidentally, Mr. Rogers was granted, and got to keep, a $50,000 bonus for making the All-Star team. A role model for the ages!

In addition to finding myself in complete sympathy with Mr. Smith's hypothesis, I found myself even more interested in a little noticed aspect of the same story, that, despite the fact that millions had witnessed the incident, and despite the fact that Mr. Rodgers had apologized, his union, in an act of immaturity reminiscent of teacher unions, appealed the fine and suspension and threatened to file a grievance for the "unprofessional" manner in which their constituent had been treated. One of the recurring themes of this book has been the negative impact, on all concerned, when a union acts immaturely, i.e., when it keeps pushing the envelope to expand the safety zone of conduct for its members. Combine this with ineffective organizational leadership and you end up with a combustible mixture, unfortunately, one that often smolders undetected for some time until you end up with the chaos that has become major league baseball or the mess that now characterizes public education. What excuse did the union give for the player, that he was provoked of course! This little old man with the camera "provoked" this big strapping player who then pummeled him!

So, if we trust the judgment of Mr. Smith, and he makes a lot of sense to me, then people like David Stern and Paul Tagliabue, the respective commissioners of the National Basketball Association and the National Football League, score aces for their leadership ability, while Bud Selig, the much maligned guru of Major League Baseball, lays an egg. Messers Stern and Tagliabue have displayed great courage in the administration of discipline to wayward players. They have a reputation for being fair, because they are consistent. Their "employees" know the rules beforehand, as well as the penalties for being recalcitrant. They applied the same characteristics, as their management style, to negotiating contracts, which they have done successfully. They are the Carl Marlburger and Fred Burke of my youth. In baseball, the leadership has not been up to the task, one disastrous contract after another was negotiated, and Mr. Selig became the laughing stock of professional sports. His stock was hardly helped by his disastrous approach to the issue of substance abuse, primarily steroids, that infected his sport to this day, a performance so weak he almost single-handedly invited Congress to intervene to control the problem, thus reversing over a century of benign neglect by the government into the affairs of baseball. He is the modern day school superintendent, helpless before the union, which controls the parents, influences their brothers and sisters who are members of the board of education, and, often hold seats on the municipal councils of these little bergs. Please recall that we have already made the point that one of the great faults of the system of public education is that the leadership is not required to have any training whatsoever in management. They make great curriculum people, but that is hardly the stuff that CEO's are made of. By the way, Mr. Selig could not even see his way clear to remove

Mr. Rogers from the American League All-Star Team, an apparent accommodation to the mgmt of the Texas team, which worked the fans the way the teacher unions work the parents.

Jack Welch, the noted CEO of General Electric, was trained as a PhD in chemical engineering as well as management. He thus brought the best of both worlds to the task of leading a large and complex organization. In Straight from the Gut, [Warner, NY:2001], Mr. Welch states that he always considered himself a teacher, "...finding and building great people as the core competency of GE". Now no one could ever accuse "Neutron" Jack as being soft on standards, and, his insistence on establishing Six Sigma as the sine quo non of the organization certainly established his bona fides regarding performance. Yet, he saw himself as a teacher, first and foremost, and as a leader all the time. He popularized the notion of the four Es of GE Leadership: very high *energy* levels, the ability to *energize* others around common goals, the *edge* to make tough yes-and-no decisions, and the ability to *execute*, to deliver on their promises. Does not sound like many of the educators described herein does it?

I once received a complaint from a head custodian, someone who had been with me for a while and was known to be capable, trustworthy, and, most importantly, extremely patient in dealing with the never ending demands of the teachers assigned to his building. He has been through the grinder for many years and I thought, foolishly, had become immune to their depredations. Boy was I wrong! On the day in question he had dutifully shoveled the sidewalks and entry ways and had proudly displayed his work to a supervisor who was traveling around the district to ascertain building readiness to receive staff and children. While the two were talking, two teachers arrived and began vociferously berating the custodian. His crime? Well it seems that in shoveling all of the walks, he had neglected to shovel a path up a *grass covered hill*, thus preventing the teachers from saving 12 linear feet of travel by cutting across a corner. He wanted me to know about the incident and expressed concern that after I had moved on to another assignment, the superintendent would be free to act aggressively to support sanctions against people like him whenever those "idiot" teachers complained. Why was he so sure of this? In the previous storm, several teachers violated the prohibition of arriving early, which was put in place to allow unfettered plowing to take place. When asked to move their cars, they became so outraged at being inconvenienced they not only refused to move their vehicles but also filed a grievance against the staff operating the plows. Boy o' boy, wish I was driving a plow that day. Aren't you starting to feel the same way? By the way, guess what happened to the teachers who violated this policy. Absolutely nothing. In fact, it was quite amusing to see the leadership falling on themselves trying to justify their behavior.

BESPRIDEL

This is a Russian word, which refers to a certain emptiness, leading to anarchy, caused by fickle leadership. They have a proverb that advises: "Be right, be wrong, only don't be indecisive." Why were these teachers so emboldened to act in such a priggish manner? Why, because, like the baseball players, they knew they could do with complete impunity; their union would protect them, no mater what.

Leadership must start at the top so let's close this section with a recap of some of my experiences with chief state school officers, the 50 supposedly top people in the country who bear the responsibility for the welfare of millions of school aged children. Given my education and experiences, I am more than just a casual observer of this group of people. I have worked with them in meetings. I have worked on assignments of national interest with them. I have lectured to them as an expert presenter at their conferences. I have sat and enjoyed social experiences with them and even served several of them as a staff member. In this capacity I can only identify a few whom I believed made a significant difference. Let's not lose sight of the fact that they are political animals. In this capacity, John Pittinger of Pennsylvania and the oft mentioned Fred Burke of Rhode Island and New Jersey were just extraordinary. They achieved much, avoided political suicide without ever compromising their commitment to children, and they stood for something.

Remember the scene in the movie, "And Justice for All", in which Al Pacino lectures a disgraced judge, played by John Forsythe, and says, "You are a judge; you are supposed to stand for something!" Well, these people stood for something and they earned my eternal admiration. Prior to Fred in New Jersey, there stood Carl Marlburger, and, as we have seen, he was something else also. Poised, self-confident, a superb planner, he set a course and was advancing toward his goals when the NJEA decided that they would use an innocuous point as a test of strength and, in a vote that forever disgraced the NJ Senate in my eyes, Dr. Marlburger narrowly failed re-confirmation for another term and the children of New Jersey lost a great advocate. As an interim, Edward J. Kilpatrick was a gentle man, who kept the ship of state afloat but was most anxious to begin his retirement. To his great credit, he refused to allow his many years of associations with power brokers and political groups to influence his judgment and thus he kept the wolves away until Fred Burke, 'Rhode Island Red', as he was nicknamed, came to the fore. Fred was many things but first and foremost a political scientist. He accomplished much until the office was politicized to such an extent that even a political scientist could not register for two political parties simultaneously and thus it was time for him to go. This complete prostitution of the office was managed by Governor Tom Kean, a likable individual whose PR exceeded his performance record. It was so strong that I voted for him, and then I saw how he gutted the New Jersey Department of Education, stripping it of all its heart, of all its dignity, of all its staying power. His appointee, Saul Cooperman, came to be known to many on the inside as a vindictive man, who claimed Fred's near finished work as his own and then appeared to run out of ideas before his term too came to an end. This began the great decline of the office, the cavalcade of mediocrity that exists to this day, as political appointee succeeds political appointee, each coinciding with every change of administration, until we have reached the point where it has become difficult to even find candidates for the job. This then is what passes for leadership in the top educational post in the State of New Jersey.

To show you how it can be, consider the following, which I hope is an isolated case, but fear is not, simply because, school districts, for one reason or the other, tend to ignore problems, particularly with personnel, if at all possible. A district with which I am familiar hired someone at a director level, who had an assistant superintendent type between himself and the superintendent of schools. The person was known to the district and came with a good recommendation. It turns out that he had some really interesting, let's say, personality quirks, that became known to his own staff fairly quickly, and became more damaging to the organization as time went on. The prior employer knew of these behavior quirks and it looked like a clear case of negligent hiring, which the district did not pursue, both because it feared the negative publicity and because the prior employer claimed that they had no way to measure these behaviors and they were "personal" in nature. What makes this case really intersecting is that, by a number of first person accounts, the director was able to insulate himself from any harm by aligning himself with the superintendent of schools, whose only ultimate excuse was, "I have to listen to everybody." After some time on the job, the director was becoming ever more abusive to his staff, conducted his affairs without regard to the district supervisory model, and seemed determined to subvert the district supervision mode. The latter became such a significant problem that his assistant superintendent, who had no idea of how bad things had become, wrote to the superintendent and board president disclaiming any ability to supervise the director. Shortly thereafter, a number of staff began confiding to the assistant superintendent that his director was boldly claiming protection from any disciplinary action because he had forged a coalition with the superintendent, with a focus on "getting" the assistant superintendent. The matter only came to a head when the staff of the director would no longer tolerate the abuse, which included being assigned dangerous tasks for any who complained about the director. Still, the superintendent and board president took no action and only the threat of involving law enforcement and civil suits caused the matter to be resolved. Can you imagine something like this happening at IBM or GE? Indeed not, as that would represent a complete failure of their leadership mode. Those organizations are not responsible for the welfare of children so why should school districts be forced to accept such decrepit leadership?

Assuming the federal government rightfully does not belong in the business of running the daily operations of the nation's schools, and then some other solution must be found. In the forthcoming sections we shall see that a political solution must be brought to the forefront and that parents must become the focal point of that movement. This political control must be exercised over the states with the following goals to be pursued: property taxes must be eliminated as a source of school district operating revenue; the states must foot the bill and then they may set whatever standards they can sell to their constituents. This would end most of the scapegoating. Local boards of education have got to get out of the business of negotiating contracts. With state assumption of the cost of public education, then regional control of salary increases and benefit packages is the next logical step. This prohibits superintendents more concerned with survival than professionalism from giving away the store just to cater, on an increasingly short-term basis, to the teacher unions. Such a system would also allow local boards to concentrate on policy and would remove more objections to teachers serving on boards in their home communities. Sounds amazingly simple doesn't it? Well, read on.

A NEW CIVIL RIGHTS MODEL: THE POWER OF US

It is time to ask, "What's next?" In June of 2005, *BusinessWeek* published an issue with a cover story entitled, "The Power of Us". The focus of the article was the explosion of communication among ordinary people, an influence so powerful that it threatened not only the traditional forms of media, including transcending the internet; it might even precipitate a new economic system. The latter may become possible as millions of bloggers meet online to merge their opinions, critique products and services, and debate salient points. Why not apply this same strategy to organize parents to fulfill their primary role as advocates for their own children? Over the protests of teachers and administrators, parents fought for and won the right to be able to access such key data points as: homework assignments, curriculum packages, and even their child's grades. District websites contain a great deal of information: meeting agendas, philosophies of boards of education and superintendents, test schedules and even permit some interaction. What they do not allow is a role for the parents, the people the districts most count on to pay the bills and carry their baggage at budget referendum time, especially against the fears of those on fixed incomes. In spite of this, these key figures are basically without franchise. They may even run for a board of education and win yet still be told they have little choice but follow the dictates of their leadership.

It is the parents who have to organize themselves to hold power, the educational version of the power of we the people. The civil rights movement did not get the attention of the US Senate, which had been shamefully pigeonholing any reforms, following the lead of segregationists who claimed the real issue was states' rights not racial equality. This stance may have cost Lyndon Johnson the Democratic Party nomination for President in 1956 and it surely cost Adlai Stevenson the campaign. The civil rights legislation was not passed until the public put faces to the tragic murders in places like Mississippi and Alabama that had all been buried by the print media. It was the public who refused to allow the eastern and midwestern senators to continue to propagate the sanctimonious crap of people like Richard Russell and Herman Talmadge and gave the Justice Department the power to enforce the Supreme Court decisions, and, it followed, the authority for the executive branch to employ the military to enforce the new laws. How about freeing the children from their bondage? The southern segregationists swore they would never allow the races to be equal and they were defeated but only after the status quo was toppled and a new establishment was created. So too now must we march, and this time for our children.

I have written in these pages that I do not begrudge the teacher unions their power because each advance in their arsenal was earned because of the abuses heaped on them by boards of education, administrators, and various jurisdictions of government. However, that was a long time ago and the balance beam has not just swung too far, it is leaning precipitously on the precipice of disaster, a disaster for our children. If we are paying for a yearly activity, then the children deserve more than six weeks. If they attend school for thirteen years completing grades K through 12, they should not be shortchanged by more than a year of instructional time during their public school experiences because teachers have negotiated extraordinarily short work days, etc, etc. I recall a friend of mine mentioned previously, Bob Swissler, who tragically lost his first wife and was left to raise two small children. As far as I know, Bob was the first person to pioneer the "little john" theory, lavatories for small children exclusively with private areas where the little ones might be attended by a parent. He was a respected lobbyist and a person of significant influence. I was with him when he approached a senior member of the state legislature with his brain storm only to be told, "Children do not vote".

Our children may not vote but they need a bill of rights. Parents vote and they need to step up NOW to protect their children. The entire structure must be brought down and rebuilt only this time with a focus on serving children, not the agendas of parents turned board members, the comfort level of superintendents earning millions across countless small towns, and heaven forbid, certainly not the continued self-aggrandizement of the teacher unions. We must begin anew and we should have started a long time ago. Time is running out. Remember, the children are owed the privilege of growing up with a decent education. Indeed, a case is now being made in some quarters to relax the post 911 immigration rules because the Untied States needs the skills of those foreign trained students. Would it not make sense to not abandon the potential of our own children, to force the moribund educational establishment to fulfill its commitment and enable us to fulfill our promise as parents? There is a concept known as the "wisdom of the crowd", that is, many people turn out to be smarter and capable of solving many more problems than individuals. Let's get started thrashing that single minded educational establishment and start working with the purpose of children first!

We are in a battle where the stakes are too high, a battle we cannot lose. Yet, despite the worthiness of our cause, history shall pay scant attention to our efforts unless we are successful and we shall not be successful until we realize the potential of parents aroused and committed to the welfare of their children, parents who are prepared to play politics to safeguard the birthright of their heirs. Play politics we must and we must play with the same ruthless abandon as those who would deny our children their posterity display everyday in safeguarding their fiefdoms. We must demand relief from union members safeguarding the rice bowl of their fellow union members; we must demand leadership that holds people accountable for performance, at least in terms of valid and reliable indicators of student achievement in the classroom and student support in the ancillary areas such as guidance, etc. Most of all, we need politicians to fear us as parents and to appoint people in charge with the authority to make decisions. I was struck by this last point because, as I wrote these words, Mayor Blumberg had won reelection and he would be returned for a second term. Many New Yorkers are wondering if they shall ever see a resolution to the absolute mess that surrounds the so-called planning for the ground zero memorial and replacement buildings and express hope that the Mayor shall find time to deal with the problem now that he is safely back in power. This situation has been hanging on for four years and each time some committee recommends a plan, some group objects to some aspect and the whole enterprise recycles again. Consider the same city in the middle of the twentieth century when the legendary Robert Moses created authority after authority to build numerous bridges and expressways, all in record time and at modest cost. Mr. Moses was in charge and HE ACTED LIKE IT. He did not consult with labor unions before he decided to build, he just built. He did not bypass constituent groups before he built; he listened, told them why certain ideas would fly and certain others would not, and then moved on each project. Doesn't this sound like the kind of person we should have as State Commissioner of Education? Well, it is the kind of person I was exposed to, when things were getting done. The current state of affairs is even more depressing when you consider that the chief state school officer in New Jersey is supposed to be among the powerful in that role, in the nation.

It should be obvious that the current system is so corrupt that we may not count on boards of education and their superintendents to always pursue the best interests of the *children and taxpayers.* What of labor peace? Well, in December 2005 the City of New York was hit by a massive and illegal strike by transit workers that paralyzed the five boroughs the week before Christmas. Among the key issues was a proposal to change pension benefits for *future workers.* Mayor Blumberg stepped up, criticized the transit workers, who are obviously a huge political constituency, and said that the era of labor peace had to take a rear seat to the reality of today. That his administration was beset with finding solutions to programs of labor aggrandizement and that tomorrow had arrived and the financial coffers were empty!

It does seem like this is an uphill fight, and it shall remain so until more folks join the battle on the side of the children. Like the woman who appeared every week while I was at Howell, we must report ourselves to be: "Appalled, Aghast, and Alarmed", and, ready to do battle in state capitals. Recall Mathew: "They that endureth to the end shall be saved". In this fight, that which is to be saved is our children, and, throughout all the years reported on herein, I never forgot that I was acting from the perspective of a parent.

As for me, was it all worth it? You see, it has always been a question of honor, given my training and the standards by which my service has been judged, either military or civilian. I was trained to stand watch every few hours on board a Navy ship, a watch that came with a promise, that no harm would befall the many hundreds of souls in my charge during that watch. With respect to the public schools and its children, for me that watch lasted well over three decades.

LAST THOUGHTS

"Never Has So Much Been Spent on So Little"

Joseph Picogna

With all due respect to Sir Winston, this phrase has been the mantra for much of my professional career. Sure, there were successes, but, with the entire structure so weak, it was impossible to have very much impact on very much of the establishment. When I worked in my last school district, the ops mgmt folks developed such a strong reputation that people from all over New Jersey who came to learn, seemed to leave impressed. Their response is what prompted the bonus section of this book, which I call a tool box for bureaucrats. This may be the only real constant in my career, developing marketable products and strategies for those in the public domain. It characterized my work with the Feds, with the state education agency of New Jersey, where I spent ten years, and others for which I worked: Pennsylvania, New York, Rhode Island, Florida, and North Carolina, every one of which contained truly excellent and dedicated people. While this was certainly professionally gratifying, we never seemed to have a true impact regarding change, innovation, and risk taking. For example, in my last years, we had little opportunity to impact at all on productivity and especially accountability. As our work grew in quality and more and more dollars were saved via ever increasing productivity standards, the result was that more and more money went into maintaining the status quo of staffing trends and ever increasing salary and benefit requirements. Perhaps, we were really at fault. Perhaps, had we not been so successful in generating dollars, the public would have come much sooner to the great reckoning that seems to have pervaded the system beginning in 2004-2005.

This quality seems to characterize my work over the years. If you continue reading to the appendix, you shall see that I was troubled by the same trends in my latter years as a Naval Reservist, when, as a senior officer, I was employed almost exclusively in performing organizational development audits. In this and every other assignment throughout my career, I met many fine people, most dedicated to their work, and some highly committed to excellence. However, we were too few, too far from the real sources of power, too committed to production to embrace the political realities: that status quo is the best many would ever aspire to as the new millennium dawned and that parents, were ever increasingly devastated by taxes and perceived poor performance of the schools, were powerless to change the fundamental structure of a system committed to "local control", a cover for what actually may have been legal, but which probably was the biggest rip off ever of the taxpayer and the greatest impediment to our children.

I never wanted to wear the mantle of "hero" as bestowed on me by the Newark Star Ledger, or appear as a government witness in a congressional hearing drama. Like most, time spent with family and the ability to earn a living, working at something satisfying, was something to aspire to. As I stated at the beginning, when I was a young boy, growing up in South Philadelphia, everyone wanted to work for US Steel, live in the suburbs, e.g., Levittown, in Pennsylvania or New Jersey, and earn $10,000 a year. How far have we come? Well, not very far when it comes to offering a quality education at a manageable price, to ALL of our children.

Even the people described herein as the very best of the best, knew that their efforts had to be tempered by initiatives that fell short of requiring political suicide as the children would fare far better having these people working on their behalf, even well below what they might have delivered, than trying to go too far and facing the distraction of surviving professionally.

People have often asked me why I spent so many years continuing night after night, year after year, teaching my MBA classes. Well, the answer is twofold: I truly enjoyed the experience, and most importantly, I needed the experience of being a resource to people who had to strive mightily to improve each day on the job, in order for me to survive the next day, on the public dole. The money was darn good also. It allowed me to continue working in school districts and kept me around people who put their talents on display everyday, people not afraid to put themselves at risk to achieve something.

On October 11, 2004, *BusinessWeek* published an editorial on innovation, highlighting the quote, "Risk taking is the fuel that powers the process of change." Pretty basic stuff for even undergraduate management classes, but let's not forget that few if any in public education have taken those courses. Even if they had, the system would make them so risk adverse as to obfuscate their training.

In this book I have presented a memoir of working through more than three and a half decades through the labyrinth we have come to know as "public education". I have tried to present an accurate picture of some really promising practices, a few impressive successes and an awful lot of disappointment, as well as some suggestions for overhauling the system.

In addition, we have studied quite a few examples of people who were thrust into positions of leadership in public education and the success that they enjoyed or the circumstances that prevented them from fulfilling their ambitions or potential. We have also examined a number of theoretical constructs that have received popular support as being "meaningful" in any search for the perfect profile of effective schools. If we have learned anything, it is that there is no magic formula or prescription for success and that the current program is quite flawed, perhaps to the extent that it is not fixable. But mainly this has been a book about examples and I would like to finish with just one more, my "favorite" educator.

I once attended an award's ceremony in which a yet to be named individual was to be honored for his role in building an organization. One fellow, in particular, had been quite unabashed in telling everyone who would listen about his role in building that organization and how he, "quite modestly," believed that he was the intended recipient of the award. Well, he was so carried away with himself by the time of the dinner that, at the moment of the announcement, he arose with a kind of "gee whiz" expression on his face, just as somebody else's name was announced! The scenario was so similar to the final scene of the movie, "The OSCAR", that I thought that I would have a stroke because I was laughing so hard. This is NOT my hero but I thought of the situation because of the way in which this behavior contrasted with that routinely exhibited by my all time favorite.

Mr. John McKeon is the individual to whom I would ascribe the sobriquet of being the finest "leader" that I have ever encountered in the public domain. A former Naval Officer who served in combat theaters in World War II, Mr. McKeon was an educator who served the Cherry Hill, New Jersey, public schools for twenty years, retiring as the Superintendent of Schools in 1986. This fine gentleman consistently displayed all of the finest traits which I have attempted to describe throughout this book. He was extremely knowledgeable in a wide variety of areas, he was genial, and his affability put people at ease almost immediately. Mr. McKeon served in an organizational setting in which appearance often counted for more than substance, politics more than performance. The pressures to conform to this expectancy set have often contributed to the downfall of even the brightest individuals who choose to pursue a career as a school district administrator. Mr. McKeon was an exception. He had the courage to persevere, because it was the right thing to do, when so many of his contemporaries preferred to dwell on building a political network and therefore cement their next contract.

McKeon displayed skills that are all too often lacking in the public domain. He developed a vision for his organization and communicated it freely and with such a sense of imagery that others were quick to grasp the significance of his goals. He never hesitated to change direction when a plan failed to live up to expectations, learning as much as possible from the experience and training, always training his staff to profit from what had gone before so that the next evolution might exceed expectations. Finally, he had an extraordinary ability to motivate others and, what was most impressive to me, the uncanny ability to excel in this vital area was the most natural of his talents. People naturally found something to admire in John McKeon. His was a referent power, the ability to influence simply because others so admire that for which you stand. He was modest, almost to a fault, in his acceptance of praise, and he proved routinely that he had the courage to stay the course and face pressures which would overcome most public servants. McKeon was a master at adopting an informal air, concentrating on issues, and making sure that those who had earned the privilege of serving as his assistants earned their keep by dealing with the decisions necessary to run their departments. He served as a role model for staff at all levels of the organization. He valued what others had to offer and even when he disagreed with others, they knew that their efforts had been welcomed and they had been treated with every courtesy. Even those who might be considered his natural enemies, officials of the various unions which negotiated with his organization, saw him as a natural leader, someone whose credibility was unassailable.

On his retirement, he was paid, what to me, is the ultimate compliment. One of his staff, who was employed in the lowest levels of the organization, said, with great fondness, "He was so competent that he never hesitated to credit others for all his successes." I doubt that we shall see his like again.

AFTERWORD

In March of 2005, *BusinessWeek* published a comprehensive article relating the transformation of GE from the six sigma, constant expansion days of Jack Welch to the creative, innovative spirit being developed by his successor, Jeff Immelt, each in turn acting in a complimentary manner, each building productivity, e.g., the capacity for the company to continue to excel. Staff development and performance assessment programs had changed dramatically, employee mobility patterns had been altered dramatically and much of the previous emphases had been amalgamated into a much broader effort. Each, in turn, had served to build the capacity of the organization and each must be recognized as an essential ingredient in the continued success of this corporate giant. What an exciting time to be involved with GE, at least from the prospective of an old organization development specialist. Yet, consider how foreign are these twin towers of strength, measurement and innovation, when considered from the perspective of the world in which billions of dollars are invested in the people who must prepare our youth to service the next generation of development of entities such as GE!

When a field of endeavor, I cannot bring myself to say "profession", can attract such people as Carl Marlberger, Catherine Havrilesky, D'Alan Huff, Carl Johnson, Donald Beineman, Arthur Merz, and John McKeon, then indeed all is not lost. These are people who were effective, who were too smart to let their idealism cause their political suicide, and, in most cases, were successful to some degree, despite the odds. In effect, each developed their own system to beat the larger system, the artifact that is choking the capacity out of the public school system. Dr. Marlberger deserved another term and the triumph of a political foe that engaged in an exercise merely of muscle flexing was the loss of opportunity for tens of thousands of children and the shame of a political administration. Catherine was, and still is, a remarkable human being. Her insight, basic goodness, caring nature, and selflessness are unprecedented among those I have encountered during my voyage on the public dole. She is one of the few that did not seek the position of Commissioner of Education after the departure of Carl Marlberger, and stood as a giant among the ants who scurried around overestimating their importance, and more tragically, failing to note their limited capacity to spur productivity. Catherine made others think, she encouraged them to set higher goals, and she was not afraid of the consequences once she made up her mind to pursue a course of action. Can you imagine a better profile for a civil servant? What a missed chance in not having had Catherine as a chief state school officer!

D'Alan Huff served out his time and was missed by many he touched with his kindness, brilliance and loyalty. I never saw another like him at that level ever again among "THE FEDS".

Donald Beineman, Art Merz, and Walter Keiss, took what they found made it better, and left their mark. Each is spoken of for the benchmarks they established and remembered fondly for their patience, skill, and achievements. Each is due a special tribute by parents everywhere for their capacity in rebuilding systems that had become broken.

Carl Johnson was absolutely brilliant in forging coalitions, but, these were unique entities in that they were composed of people who believed in HIM because they trusted him. His easy going style, ability to listen, and, his refusal to let minor matters fester into crises made him a superb leader. He also possessed a superb sense of what I shall call realization, e.g., he was supremely aware of his surroundings, a result of working the crowds so well, and he never tried to persuade a Chevy community into buying a Cadillac. One of his predecessors used to talk of building "world class school districts" and never realized his constituents stopped listening right then and there as they were more interested in pinching pennies than most other things in life. Carl never uttered the phrase yet accomplished so much. He was also a master of understatement, which is probably why he was so admired by the staff. When the best among his people became depressed over still another incident of insanity, he would calmly note: "After all, they are not our children, and they are only entitled to the level of education that their parents are willing to pay for". Thanks to Carl the children in his charge always enjoyed value far beyond the cash and emotional investments of their parents.

What more can possibly be said of John McKeon. Short of being cloned and disseminated throughout the public school establishment, he should have been headmaster of a school for superintendents. Then we would have seen something!

The heroes written of herein all accomplished great things, islands of dignity and achievement in a sea of despair. Each took great satisfaction from their accomplishments and moved on with their lives after their term of service was concluded. It is left to people like me to bemoan their passing, to stress the unfulfilled impact imposed by the cancerous and destructive system under which they endeavored and to only imagine what might have been. Was it all in vain? Perhaps I have become the "Man from the Coast!" It was left to my dear friend and benefactor, Catherine Havrilesky, to suggest a quote to place this material into the perspective intended. It is from General of the Army Douglas MacArthur: *"And in the end, through the long ages of our quest for light, it will be found that truth is still mightier than the sword. For out of the welter of human carnage and human sorrow and human weal the indestructible thing that will always live is a sound idea."*

TOOL BOX FOR BUREAUCRATS

"I have had flattery enough to make me vain and success enough to make me confident."

Horatio Nelson

ESSENTIALS

This section contains a description of many of the award winning procedures, programs and protocols that were developed during the GOLDEN AGE of the Delran Public Schools, e.g., the time of Carl Johnson. The descriptions give some idea of the techniques used to generate so many millions of dollars in tax savings, and, which were the topics of so many training and demonstration efforts we hosted at the request of numerous state and local agencies. Parents may wish to ask their local districts if these cost efficiencies have been implemented, taxpayers shall certainly continue to look for these and professionals seeking some pre-packed OJT should read on.

People are always looking for advice as to how someone could "survive" as long as I did in the "business". Well, my less secure colleagues, it is not about "surviving", it is about being a contributor and thus a dominant force that becomes first invaluable and then indispensable. The worst strategy one may pursue in search of the magical status of being tenured is one of accommodation because, you may remember, "their demands are insatiable". Spend one day fixing something that is not really your business and your reward shall be to face two such problems tomorrow, especially in a district with a board of education dominated by teachers and/or a superintendent committed to "hitting home runs" with the union. For example, it is not your job to provide secretarial support to track the benefit issues of staff, that task is reserved for the broker of record and the initiative displayed by the staff member, especially in this era of privacy rules. "What, you want me to take care of this?" I often heard an indignant teacher say, then to be told, "Only if you want your problem solved". Your job is to make sure people are enrolled and that the premiums are paid in a timely basis. This means: choose the broker wisely, hold your position and be firm in your resolve not be drawn into every little episode of the lives of the staff, a soap opera that may often reach epic proportions. Learn to ignore things that are not critical to operations management, depend on the staff you have trained, work to make sure they have the resources to excel, and shield them from the potentially severe political fallout that often exists with superintendents working to get reappointed through a policy of appeasement of the union, which often holds a majority of seats on the board. In some districts, there is absolutely no value in working in central office as a non-affiliated administrative support staff member. Their raises were half those given to their colleagues who were represented by the teachers' union and their responsibility was far beyond anything faced by those snugly grouped within the blanket of a collective bargaining agreement. This is so incredibly short-sided as to defy belief, but it is happening in several districts just in Burlington County New Jersey and there is now a "rep" for the districts in which applicants ask if a position is "in the union" before they would ever consider applying. It is up to the business administrator to make sure the office staff members are cared for and rewarded properly, and that is a day to day task, always trumpeting their achievements and extra effort and never failing to illustrate the consequences to the district should those folks not be treated fairly.

Another bit of advice, that should be quite obvious by now is that there is no substitute for leadership. I recall being asked to serve as a consultant to a New Jersey township, an interesting place that had possessed a strong dedication to their schools and a community with increasing enrollment at the time. Thus, there was a need to build more facilities, hence my involvement. I was meeting with the chief school administrator, who had come out of retirement from another state to lead this district, when a BOE member barged right in and threw a banana on his desk and complained that rotten bananas were being served daily. This took most of our time and when she finally left, he turned to me and said, "She likes to see me pirouetting on something every day, today it just happened to be a banana." He then asked me for advice and I told him, he should have stayed retired if he allowed himself to be subjected to such treatment. If you resemble this person in any manner, then seek a job in a bank, or some other less stressful environment, for this cauldron is not for you. Also, use care in looking not just at the job but also the superintendent and the board of education. The superintendent may be interested primarily in "Labor Peace", in which case you shall become an after-thought whenever you attempt to employ sanity in finances. Throw in a teacher dominated BOE and you also face the scepter of becoming a scapegoat, if you attempt to do more than just follow orders. Unfortunately, for the children and the taxpayer, too many of the brethren and the sisterhood chose the safe course, at best a boring existence and one that usually shall fail both in satisfaction as well as long-term survival.

You must also use care in plotting the career of the chief school administrator as well as your own. Should the person who hired you retire either very early in your tenure, or, later when you are established, you may well face the scenario in which a new chief may be more comfortable bringing in someone else if you are not tenured, or, feel to need to undercut your position in favor of his own, if you are tenured and established with a track record of excellence.

I had to learn this the hard way although I was rewarded handsomely for my pain and suffering.

Parenthetically, to learn more about the traits that seem to be essential ingredients of leadership see my first book, Personality Sex and Behavior. For a practical lesson in building leadership capacity, see my second book, Total Quality Leadership: A Training Approach, and, for practical examples of leadership traits that work and sometimes do not, see my third book, Command Personality.

Having a good county superintendent cannot hurt either. By "good", I mean a person experienced in the business with the courage to be innovative and the chutzpah to defend his or her constituents from the wrath of the public and their own state education agency. At this writing Walt Keiss is still working his magic in Burlington County, New Jersey.

Walt knows his stuff and works quietly among the diverse groups seeking to dominate public education to achieve consensus wherever possible. He does not hesitate to intervene where the welfare of the children is concerned and always supports the districts with regard to his masters. Where have you gone, Gus Ruh, Don Beineman, Howard Hunt, Pete Contini, and Art Merz? We no longer see the likes of you in these key jobs. These outstanding educators made a difference. There are a few names I could add here, but not nearly as many as you may think, and that is over three and one-half decades!

This section is intended to serve as a primer for those charged with operations management of school districts: keeping the bills paid, the lights on, the heat working, the buses rolling and the doors open. It is designed to illustrate the unique programs developed by the Delran Public Schools and to recognize the work of some very special professional services vendors. Readers with specific questions are invited to write to the author at jlp@picogna.com for access to specific programs and strategies described herein. Best Wishes!

TECHNOLOGY

Automating your processes is the essential ingredient of success. No business services operation can serve, at least in order to concentrate on really important tasks, without office automation. Establishing capacity for scanning and retrieval of records, automating all of the situation specific payroll inputs, forcing people to communicate via email, prevailing on them to check electronic bulletin boards for important notices, etc, all are keys and require a great deal of developmental work, in a technological sense, but also the intestinal fortitude to tell the superintendent and board president that regardless of the protestations of the teacher union reps that this is not the way it used to be, moving ahead to create a more productive work environment is something that must transcend their normal fear of upsetting their association. You are dealing with folks who have no conceptualization of the importance of making their organization more productive and staff who have no stake in sharing in this enhanced capacity. If you disagree, just take the trouble to check out the type of "Baldrige" process many districts have adopted. They choose the newer models designed for the public domain to begin with, e.g., those that require far less of a quantitative case being built, and then water down even those parameters. The district garners some positive PR for the embarking on this productivity improvement program while in reality collecting no data nor asking anyone to put anything at risk. This latter point cannot be emphasized too strongly as none of the applications that people traveled miles to see and learn about in Delran would have come about had they not been developed when the district had the right combination of superintendent and board president.

What are some of these applications? I would consider your first priority to be the automation of selected payroll inputs. Having principals place an electronic signature on a form approving overtime for eligible staff and all of the occasional teacher payments, such as chaperoning, class coverage, etc. is an incredible time saver, makes them accountable for scheduling and approving these payments, and creates an automatic audit trail for those "spot checks" your auditor should be completing during the course of the year. In addition, it makes it much easier to generate reports about which staff are receiving which payments and hopefully then having the superintendent confronting the principals to ask why certain staff seem to be favored as to type and or quantity of these extra assignments as well as preparing reports for the public that document what incredible sums are involved, monies that otherwise would be virtually invisible to the taxpayer. This is also the only real way to establish budgets with automatic top-stops, which act to control the seemingly endless stream of cash flow.

Another application that worked well was the combination of improvements in payables. The first was simply an internal matter, streamlining the manner in which the accounts payable files were constructed and processed. Modern scanner technology allowed the inevitable paper records to be affixed to an electronic file and retrieved as a file to be printed for the hard-copy required by the audit process to easy transmittal of files, queries, etc, among the district, vendors, banks, and even interested citizens posing those inevitable inquiries into district affairs. I have found that districts using several different types of Department of Education approved accounting software all profited by adopting these processes and few had much of an adaptation chore. The cost centers [each school, transportation, special education, curriculum and professional development, etc.] were on-line with the district computer networks and completed the purchase order [PO] on line, along with the ability to add a business registration certificate, and, other needed documents such as quotes, directly into the system. If the vendor being employed already was in the system, the purchase contract number, quotation result, and existing businesses registration cert were all available to be affixed from a master file. We were fortunate indeed to have available to assist us a great visionary, Earl Johnson, of Global Frontier Resources, a true technical genius and a very talented consultant.

From here, things really got going! The vendors were on-line and so processing the purchase orders [PO's] became much easier, and, when the control person for the transaction sent an electronic approval to the Business Office signifying that the material or service had been provided and payment was authorized, the dollars flowed from our bank to that of the district, all without touching much of any paper. This was one of the most popular projects to be adopted by other districts. A particularly fine installation was achieved by Bruce Benedetti, the business administrator for the Florence Public Schools, a fine professional and one who would be a perfect mentor for the aspiring to excellence dole member.

Another key aspect of your technology program should be online ordering of as many goods, supplies and materials as possible. Many years ago, Delran brought an outfit called Educational Data Services to South Jersey and the result was a run-away hit. We needed a partner to justify the amortization of the initial cost, actually only a few thousand dollars, and I chose Burlington City because my counterpart there was the widely respected William Ryan. Bill, who has since moved to the insurance industry, one of his many strengths, was a consummate professional, laboring in the nightmare of what came to be called a Special Needs District. You need to live through this to get a feel for what I am describing here but such districts unfortunately seemed to have a hard time attracting top talent, which really made Bill the exception because there were few finer in his time. Bill was not an educator and so he brought legitimate training in ops mgmt to the job, a fact that was readily recognizable and he was just the person to partner with us. EDA was created by a very articulate and intelligent individual named Alan Wohl. Alan blended great vision with a strong sense of marketing as we not only became one of his clients; we began piloting numerous progressive improvements with him. The process of refining operations at EDS is a never ending task, particularly as they do so in strong concert with their clients, probably the major factor in their continued success. The capstone of their products in my time was the online ordering system and the model for this system was that which had evolved during my time as a Naval Reserve Officer, as a logistics specialist with the Naval Supply Systems Command. A ship at sea could call up what seemed to be an almost endless series of catalogues and place orders with literally thousands of vendors and time the deliveries to coincide with budget cycles and ship arrival dates. Thus, a warship on a short turn-around would find the material waiting for them on the pier. This is what we piloted in Delran and Burlington City with EDS and what was eventually brought to the client school districts.

In our version, the schools, acting as cost centers, with various departments as subunits, along with transportation, maintenance and the other typical entities who order things, could call up the catalogues of numerous vendors, all of whom had been pre-qualified via comprehensive competitive bidding, and place their orders. Let's look at this from the usual lowest level entity, the classroom. The principal would assign a budget to the individual classroom teacher, for example, in the areas of supplies and materials. The teacher would be able to view photos of the product lines, prices and other pertinent data from the vendors. There were also online and telecon HELP contacts to assist with questions. Best of all, each teacher had been assigned a budget and EDS took all of the guess work out of the process by not only posting the budget, but debiting the account, on the screen, as the ordering progressed. The system also provided a warning for those who persisted in ordering even after the counter reached zero.

What used to be a seven month operation requiring the movement of mountains of paper could be reduced to usually no more than a month, about the time it took the staff to get around to spending a few minutes online ordering. The orders were placed, electronically of course, with the vendors as soon as the district budget was determined and the deliveries for each commodity, over 10,000 annual transactions for Delran alone, could be individually scheduled as to date, time and location. The system also benefited by another EDS innovation, their system took care of the ordering and provided whatever kind of media the client district needed to provide a hands-free entry into the accounts payable system.

Once this online program gets going, there is no limit to the amount of applications that may ensue. For example, the state forced districts to adopt a horrific system of logging dozens of cost applications for work required to maintain its facilities, I assume in order to support their requirement that buildings be maintained at a certain level of spending. Not to digress too far, but by way of background information, the districts had, for years, been allowed to permit their buildings to slip into decay as dollars became tight, spending became capped and labor had to be appeased. Even the proud Cherry Hill schools suffered the embarrassment of having a stairwell in one its high schools collapse in its own footprint. If that could happen there, imagine the condition of buildings across the State!

The problem with the requirement however, is that I never met anyone, either at the state, county or local levels, who admitted to ever using the data. We did in Delran for several reasons. Years earlier we had begun collecting such information into a computer file, along with a record of depreciation of fixed assets, as part of our resource allocation program and as substantiation for our insurance program, which included depreciation and maintenance programs as part of its cost renewal basis. Thus, years before it was required, we were using these data in part to hold down the cost of insuring the buildings. Later, we began a system of much tighter inventory control. For the major line-items, and there are thousands, we kept high, safety and low levels of inventory control data. As items were allocated for repairs, the computer inventory was updated. When the safety level was reached, then a reorder message was cut. The difference between the safety and low levels was the time required to process an order, receive and stow the material before the low level inventory might be expected to be expended. Kind of neat, huh! The introduction of the state program forced us to develop bridges to our other applications and caused some problems and introduced some limitations [some cost benefit analysis should be done here and the same might be said for most of the DOE software applications I saw in my career] but they were mostly overcome and we eventually added online work order requests to the program. We now received the requests electronically, which made sharing the data among the key parties very simple and the scheduling of work, updating of inventory and filing of required reports became possible. As with the payroll inputs, the use of electronic signatures from accountable parties was implemented along with various other security controls, including a very important component, daily onsite and remote backups of key data. I cannot emphasize this latter point too strongly as the systems shall crash, frequently and without warning. I once was without my computer for several weeks preceding the generation of the preliminary budget. Without the remote backup there would have been some serious consternation.

Also, do not overlook the damage that may be caused to the district, and the aggravation that may be caused to you, should other aspects of operations dependent on technology lag. For example, in Delran, the application for state school aid was managed by the folks who were charged with the collection and maintenance of daily attendance records, compiled into the registers. For a few years we had a very dynamic, young and terribly creative assistant principal by the name of Scott Oswald in the district. Scott established a tremendous capacity in this area and neither the ASSA nor the registers were ever faulted during their respective audits. Scott eventually moved on to a much better position, as talented people should do, and the district was never able to replace him. Sure, there was a body in place, a much more expensive one at that, but, that individual and eventually the staff, never saw themselves as being responsible for such mundane tasks, and, the result was a real problem, a significant management issue that dragged on year after year, until the superintendent intervened personally.

The framework described here easily leads to other applications as the "strings" are already in place. Items such as online scheduling of buses, asset management, scheduling and movement of shared district resources, signoffs for key billing records such as cell-phones, facility use requests, even online completion of the aid-in-lieu of application for reimbursement of parochial school transportation related costs. The compilation of minutes, the screening of same by the board of education prior to adoption and the publication of same became a snap. Some districts were even experimenting with electronic meetings, a system in which I truly regret never having participated. The management of records retention and retrieval as well as filing requests for public access under the Open Public Records Act can be handled as online applications, very easily and expeditiously, and at little cost. The real cost benefit analysis of all of this is the accuracy and speed by which these tasks may be conducted, thus freeing the staff for even more dramatic improvements in the manner in which business is conducted, a true productivity improvement capacity, something almost unheard on the curriculum side of the house.

There were two other individuals who deserve the major credit for these accomplishments, Ed Kulshinsky, Principal of Century Consulting, and, Steve Struthers, the senior technical officer for TekConnect. They worked in the district for years and I am proud to say their achievements were so note-worthy that other districts began to retain their services and the network of promising practices spread from place to place.

Ed was a senior systems engineer for IBM. Big Blue was going through a difficult period and the clients noticed their difficulties more than anyone else. For example, we had to constantly work via salespersons to get to Ed and they were not very knowledgeable. They were persistent; I could not get one of them to address my needs because she was trying to market everything under the sun direct to the staff in the schools. I finally solved the problem by contacting a very senior person at IBM by the name of Louisa Foster, the spouse of a friend who was a wonderful Naval Reserve Officer and a major tech weenie himself. Louisa was not only brilliant, she was especially creative and flexible, and always represented the interests of IBM in a fine manner. She saw our programs needed to be handled by a different protocol and so Ed came to work continually and consistently on our system 36 and ultimately on the series of AS 400's that we employed over the years. The sales rep did not react well to the news, she created a scene in the district that resulted in my having her escorted from the premises and then she sped so recklessly from a school parking lot that I asked the local police to ticket her. We solved the problem and set a standard for our relationships with professional vendors for years to come. IBM began cutting back and charging more and more and so we convinced Ed to begin serving us directly, which turned out to be a mutually beneficial suggestion as Century Consulting was born.

Ed was instrumental in working with the Gloucester County Education Management by Computer Center [what a moniker!], an outfit you read quite a bit of in the earlier chapters. They performed in a manner that was satisfactory to almost everyone, except us, as they were always reactive instead of proactive. Replacement software was available but hugely expensive and the transition period for a new roll-out was involved more than a year, closer to two. A much cheaper solution was to push the envelope with Hog-Heaven [our pet name for GCEMCC], and we needed first Ed and then Steve Struthers to accomplish this. Imagine how accomplished they had to be to allow this hugely bureaucratic organization to "let them in". TekConnect is a large, multi-site organization that I credit Steve with building, at least from the vantage points of product bases and customer satisfaction, and their target audience was schools and other public domain entities. They employed incredibly talented people and during the Johnson years they worked closely with Carl to implement computer networks, where there had been none, and with me to create an array of ops mgmt automated capacities that were the envy of the region. I was always most impressed as to how they could translate Carl's vision into action and did so in a very economical manner. The new administration had been charged to change things to "make them better" and hired technicians who may have failed to impress other districts. This was the model we sought to avoid in the Johnson years: the district could not afford systems types, only techs and where TekConnect had numerous area specialists available constantly, even after hours and weekends; our new people worked a regular day, had ample sick and vacation leave, and seemed to get themselves buried with "pressing matters". They changed everything they could, sometimes without rhyme or reason and even tried to intrude on what we had built.

I finally put an end to this by informing the superintendent and the BOE president that we could not afford to have an educator and two techs trying to override the work of qualified systems engineers and my "bona fides" were the records that indicated we had been paying more to TekConnect to fix some of the work of the techs than we would have spent had we not employed two new colleagues. When you add the cost of their compensation, it was a powerful tool. I guess the fear of having such data "go public" superseded even the "let's support the new regime" focus and common sense prevailed, at least on the surface.

Let's not overlook the paperless office, e.g., the storage of records on electronic media, which not only saves space but greatly eases not only records retention compliance but also retrieval, the latter being especially important in a time in which we are faced with the odious requirements and penalties under the Open Public Records Act. A related application is report generation and thus, enhanced analysis capacity. What were once useless data sitting in cabinets now become an effective tool for trend forecasting. One of our toughest projects and most useful, was the integration of the district policy and regulation manuals into an online system, that could be queried from the district in-house lotus notes capacity or via the district website. What prompted this effort was the realization that only one set of manuals in the entire district was even close to being up to date, the ones in the business office, and even a cursory glance indicated that the manuals in the possession of the members of the board of education were in the worst shape, not a promising governance model. We were dealing with thousands of pages of text, with interesting border and section markers that made scanning problematical. Our friends at TekConnect worked with the policy service, Strauss-Esmay, particularly one of my favorite all-time people, Judy Esmay, and eventually the text was available, edited, by yours truly, and ready to roll. It greatly simplified the task of keeping these vital documents current and accurate, helped build responsible behavior on the part of the staff as they were required to access the material and comply with the provisions in their routine work, and, it spurred investment in the district website. The latter was a true benefit as we moved to all kinds of staff notices, such as COBRA coverage, pension information, HIPAA waivers, etc. It took quite a while for the teachers to get used to working with the materials on the site and using the links. In fact, the only reason they did, I am convinced, is that we stopped baby-sitting them and forced them to use the technology, a set of skills I hope transferred to their teaching because I have seldom seen a worse bunch of adults when it came to computer literacy. "I do not teach computers" [sic!], was a very common response in the early days of this initiative.

FINANCE

Dollars of course make the world go round and this is especially true in the public sector. In Delran we had an especially great run, at least while Carl Johnson was superintendent. During his eleven years, dubbed the "Golden Age" of the district, our program of cost efficiencies and value engineering yielded on average two million dollars a year, one of which was spent on improvements to the schools and the other, was spent on tax relief. Not that the latter seemed to be either noticed or appreciated by anyone. Carl was noted for many outstanding leadership characteristics and one of the finest, in my opinion, was his untiring effort to fill in the gaps in his professional preparation. This included management, human resources, and operations. He did not try to become a finance expert, rather he learned how to best use dollars earned, which was indeed an unusual circumstance for a school district in two ways: first, to improve the district and second, to avoid getting the district in trouble by mis-spending the "extra" funds. That is why the extra money was spent on THINGS rather than PEOPLE. The rationale should be obvious; things benefit the children immediately and create no recurring funding burden. People, on the other hand, when they are bought with monies available on a one-time only basis, create tremendous debt in succeeding years, each budget cycle in turn being impacted by a geometrically exacerbating magnitude until bankruptcy hits.

When Carl left, the district entered, as you have read, the "let's hit home runs with the teacher union phase". The extra dollars kept flowing, for five incredible years, in which the amount grew in unprecedented sums. Even when the same BOE members who used to publicly praise our efforts turned their backs on those who worked daily to create this safety blanket, as if such effort was the norm, they still kept the spigot to the unions running. The impact of S1701 finally burst the bubble as the costs associated with the teaching staff members broke the bank. Consider the phrase, "if you see a teacher they are being paid" and imagine the beyond the salary and benefit package financial burden: stipends for class coverage, for tiny assemblages of students in activities, the fees for after school work, the after the fact bills submitted by principals for non-approved extra activities completed by teachers, who used to provide many of these services without regard to the clock or extra incomes and you begin to get an idea of a system run amuck, one driving itself and the tax payer to bankruptcy. Remember the story of the music teacher who created phantom "commissions" in his own mind and attempted to bill the district? Or, the one about the teacher who was absent for most of the year yet still demanded the stipend for supervising a year long student activity club? Well such occurrences are not that unusual, and, such outrageous claims are normally paid unless there happen to be people willing to risk the peril of standing alone to stop them. Carl Johnson realized that in a community that refused to pay for facility improvements and was loathe to providing even computers for their children, the extra dollars were essential to providing these vital capacities. The alternative use of the funds was to line the pockets of the teachers, exhaust the funds and leave the district in a state of extremis. You must grasp the dangers of this approach and if you cannot do not waste your time reading the following material involving the technocracy of running a first class financial operation in a school district. In Delran, for five years, they were warned in writing that this might be the end of the line, the projections were uncannily accurate but the funds kept saving them until the excess exceeded all parameters of prudence. Never once did they attempt to stop the flow of extra staff, the stipends, and the vast outflow of monies. Never once did they attempt a staffing study, never did they heed the warnings that their enrollments simply did not support their expenditures on teachers. Instead, they blamed the legislature and various assorted public officials.

For example, for the fiscal year 2007 budget, years after the new state staffing models and spending limits had been invoked, the Delran Board of Education was still pursuing its program of labor cost escalation, funded for years by the extraordinary gift of cash, some two millions of dollars each year, to exceed its legislative spending limits. Now, it is not my intention to suggest that what they did violated the existing regulations for budget development. Indeed, they were free to earmark ALL of their assets to teacher salaries and benefits. Included with these warnings was the annual doomsday prophesy, a warning that soon they would face a scenario in which the spending plan would include a shortfall that exceeded even the extraordinary performance of their Business Office and yet they routinely adopted a budget that required over several million in cash and cash credits to reach their spending threshold.

Once the district abandoned its program of using cash to soften the tax burden and buy things for the children and switched to allocating millions for the new program of labor peace, then the seeds of ruin were sown. Makes you wonder that in a world of incredible oversight how such a thing could be considered allowable.

While other considerations may seem to pale by comparison, there is still a technocracy to be served in the area of finance. One of the key aspects of generating so many excess dollars was the online asset movement system for investment maximization, another not completely baked idea of mine that was explicated and implemented by the remarkable Mrs. Carol Hearn. Carol was making about nine grand when I arrived in Delran but it was immediately apparent that she was not only significantly underpaid, she was significantly underutilized. Her dedication to excellence, her enthusiasm to try new approaches, her creativity and her determination to put forth maximum effort to better the lot of the children she saw herself serving were outstanding traits that the district put to good use. Carol worked up the specifics of moving money constantly, often several times a day, to take advantage of the very best of opportunities. There was a significant technology aspect to this achievement and, even more importantly, there was a human relations aspect to this process. After all, she had to convince banks, investment houses and the like to take seriously someone from a school district in New Jersey, no mean feat! She was successful, as she was in all of the crazy projects we attempted together, and the district profited handsomely. Carol was so successful at this that, when the State changed their funding formula in the 1990's, they neglected to consider the use of accumulated free balances in calculating revenue CAPS. A rather remarkable member of the State legislature and Chair of the Education Committee, Dr. John Rocco was informed of our accomplishments and actually took the trouble to meet with Carol and reviewed her work. To his considerable credit, Dr. Rocco authored what became known as the Delran amendment and these funds became part of the official formula. All because someone hired as a clerk in a once backwater district was given an opportunity to show her stuff!

Delran also went on to lead the league in purchasing cooperatives, jointures for various areas and one unique achievement, value engineering, a term that came to be used throughout the State as a money generation tool. Cooperation among districts in transportation and special education is certainly nothing new and our programs were extensive and complex and the savings were once valued as a consequence of the work invested by the staff. Our accounts payable supervisor, Judy Napoli, became ferocious in requiring the teachers and principals to look twice when placing an order and was ever alert to something that smacked of a gratuity for the person placing an order.

Our natural gas purchasing cooperative has been described as one of the most successful anywhere, once serving over 20 districts. We were able to buy fuel at a critical pricing period much more cheaply than the county cooperatives that tried to mirror us, primarily because we had no extra bureaucracy to fund. I served as the non-paid executive director, handling admin details, the attorney, Ron Ianoale, did a superb job keeping something by nature extremely complex, very simple for districts to implement, and the dollars saved graphs kept rising. For example, at one time we purchased natural gas at several dollars per decatherm less than the Township of Delran, from the same vendor, Amerada Hess! They were buying the gas via the county cooperative, and paying a great deal more. Delran was also one of the founding districts in an all-lines joint insurance fund. I found myself visiting other districts and speaking at meetings to convince them to join. It worked well for a while and still does for many districts. In Delran, we refined our risk mgmt techniques to such an extent that we were subsidizing other districts to a fairly significant amount and saved significant dollars moving to our own program.

Another program that worked well for us came to be known as "value engineering". This was a rather simple procedure that is, at least conceptually, because it came to involve a great deal of work. In essence, we constantly reworked projects during the long planning and design stages and the even longer construction stages. The architect firm, which was always KDA associates [Gary Kanalstein, Principal], and our long serving construction mgmt firm, New Road [Scott Weitz, Principal], were involved heavily along with district staff, to constantly search for more effective and cheaper ways of completing the projects. As new developments became known, as new techniques were developed, we changed gears, built better projects qualitatively and often more quickly and saved money. Without Kanalstein and Weitz we never would have gotten through this. Incidentally, these two just happened to be in every district in which I was privileged to be employed. They brought in every project early and under budget and NEVER was there a problem with any monitoring agency. Talk about luck, having seasoned, caring professionals such as Gary and Scott was certainly a stroke of good fortune. I should mention that we always tried to reciprocate with such great professional services vendors by providing references and promoting their work throughout our professional communities of business managers.

I have to say the advent of the Economic Development Agency and it successor, the School Construction Corporation, killed this effort. It became almost impossible to motivate people to do all this extra work when every dollar saved was swept up into the sink-hole known as the State of New Jersey, especially after the SCC was shut down during the Codey administration due to charges of financial malfeasance. This idea was spreading rapidly through the state when the EDA came along, an agency that was widely ballyhooed to "end corruption" in school construction. Well, we now know for sure who was charged with corruption. The EDA staff treated us like garbage, created mountains of paperwork that left us numb and certainly killed value engineering. Without Gary Kanalstein, Scott Weitz and Ron Ianoale, we never would have gotten through this nightmare. Thus witness another great money saving initiative of the early 21st century!

BANKING

There is only one simple, over-riding consideration in the banking area, that is, IF you are prepared professionally and academically to handle a contemporary banking program and that is to select the best possible financial institutions. I cannot even remember how many banks we dismissed over the years in all the districts I served. It was a continuous search accompanied by a consistent failure to achieve the performance levels I expected. This was true only until we encountered Commerce Bank, which served all of our needs to a level beyond the appreciation of their competition. This incredible financial institution came to us in bits and pieces, as they were just beginning their expansion of the client base and scope of services. As we began becoming comfortable with outstanding people such as Sharon Hammel, John Hall, and Jackie Hershberger, the bank itself was beginning to experiment with explicating its philosophy of comprehensive customer service, to them a concept that was a living, maturing, entity, with outstanding benefits for the customer. We were able to join with them as they embarked on their journey and so we were able to marry our goals with their capacity and the result was new products, services and ever increasing staff capacity that was soon disseminated to their other clients, especially school districts. When the State allowed only its own agencies to finance purchases, entities such as municipalities and school districts were forced to add a second round of competitive bidding to their procurements that related to financing the purchase. Many simply ignored the requirement until they happened to be caught, and the taxpayer once again suffered heavily as the vendors selling the equipment also arranged usurious rates for the privilege of financing the purchase through them. Commerce was ready to step into the gap, when dealing with districts who had exhibited outstanding financial acumen and management, which usually meant having a hefty surplus, and they developed the concept in Delran, which became know as a "master lease". This was a solicitation for an open line of credit that was bid for a fixed time period and since few could compete with the financial muscle of Commerce, we soon had something going in which we could literally buy things on a signature, and usually pay off the financing before interest was due, given the outstanding results we achieved with our capital investment program described earlier. This is one of many examples of what turned out to be an incredible array of cooperative efforts with this outstanding bank and its wonderful staff. Many were given an opportunity, including all the top names, but only one was found capable, Commerce. They provided service, of an unparalled effort, they worked to the very limits of the capacity of the client to develop creative approaches to financial challenges, and, they earned their way by the performance of their people, not with lunches, trips, golf outings or the other ploys of the competition. Since this is undoubtedly my last opportunity to recognize a colleague from those halcyon days, I wish to take a moment to recognize John Hall. This incredibly talented professional, a true gentleperson, worked tirelessly to develop great ides with us. As a consequence of our relationship with John and Commerce, we had numerous situations in which we had to finance items in the short term, while investing surplus in the long-term, actually making a profit on the purchase of the services or commodities thus financed!

AUDITS

I have never failed to be appalled at the number of absolute idiots who conduct audits in school districts, and get away with it year after year because they are supposedly "wired" politically. If I had a dollar for every colleague who told me "I hate my auditor", well, you know… I really was blessed, almost, by the number of fine auditors I worked with in my career. There was, of course, the group in one district who seemed competent, seemed cooperative in working with me to correct some interesting abuses and then who bailed when I was no longer in a position to recommend their reappointment. I can say no more than what is reported in the transcript of the subsequent trial. It kind of says it all for me and makes interesting reading.

In Delran, we had Rob Inverso, absolutely the perfect person: knowledgeable, creative, hard-working, customer service oriented, with a focus on serving as a resource to the district. Just the kind of person I wish I had to prepare my income taxes. Rob was a partner in Inverso and Stewart and I had the pleasure of recommending him to a number of districts, all of whom expressed great satisfaction working with the firm.

Together we developed several rather simple operational steps that make the audit evolution a truly worthwhile endeavor for the district. It began with the ASSA time period, in which we had the firm audit the process, records and application between the initial and final district submissions, in order to identify any errors, which could then be legally repaired prior to the deadline. We also got that portion of the audit out of the way and made the firm responsible for the accuracy of our reporting. In a similar fashion, we had the firm audit the food service records while the data base was being developed and periodically reviewed student activity funds, the enterprise fund and the registers during the year. The other peak period happened in the spring when the "pre-audit" took place. Again, any records that needed to be explicated were managed at this time and everyone got a head start on those payables that were to remain open at the end of the year, funds that had to be re-established, etc. The main audit evolution, usually took place in October in Delran. We were heavily automated and the records were reviewed on a regular basis so we held a position of honor in being near the end of the time-frame, because our audits usually went smoothly and much more quickly than some. Rob was a great partner to the office staff and together they were error free during the time that team was together.

ATTORNEYS

Ah, the blood sucking lawyers! Actually, I seldom had that problem. With the State Education Agency, I got to work with some great deputy attorneys general, in Howell, the Bathgate firm was very capable and responsive. In Cherry Hill, well, you should read the court transcript and form your own opinion. Let me say that my experience had been about the most and worst anyone in my position could hope for. It was in Delran that I really got lucky! Have I got two for you: bright, capable, articulate, able to find a way to support your needs but always conscious of the canons of ethics, John Barbour and Ron Ianoale. John was the solicitor in Delran when I arrived and our professional relationship took off immediately. I recall that the BOE from time asked whether we should look at screening for possible successors, some lame idea of the State School Boards Association, and they actually did once, only to unanimously re-embrace John. He worked so hard specializing in the subject matter most pressing to the needs of public school districts and his briefs were well researched and so persuasive that we were able to win decisions in areas in which no precedent existed, against both county and state jurisdictions and we did so with regularity. I recall that we chased the Clifton Board of Education for ten years on a case involving the education of a homeless child. A long chase because the place you go for justice, the Office of Administrative Law, is notorious for concentrating on high profile cases, shuffling others to the dead letter bin. There are time limits for the OLJ's [office of administrative law judges] to respond and they can simply declare themselves overworked and slip the deadlines, thus a ten year fight over what should have been a quick fix. I truly believe that our adversaries anticipated this sort of ally and thus refused to face their obligations. In most districts, the attorney fees would have been prohibitive and the business official too occupied to continue the fight. Not so with a bulldog at the helm and a talented, patient and resourceful staff attorney available.

Similarly, we fought West-Windsor/Plainsboro and Nutley along with their county superintendent and, remarkably enough, our own, and won, a case our critics said was hopeless. Just reading this decision, which was so definitively supportive of our position, was a great restorative in the belief of jurisprudence. Carl and I found that the burden of cases that were coming our way required more and more attention. It seemed, ala the hydra, whenever we chopped off the head of one potential profiteer, there was another hoping to get lucky. Using an analysis of trend for a five year parameter, it became obvious that a cost-effective solution was to place John on staff. We profited greatly by the extra time commitment he provided, his compensation was known as a fixed entity prior to the start of the fiscal year, and the district had the benefit of the stability inherent in a long-standing relationship. John also began handling negotiations for the district, bringing his usual high standard of professionalism and I can only say that things would probably have worked out much better for all had he been given a freer hand in producing the contract.

I have known Ron since we were both in high school, from age fourteen. Like John, he is just a superb human being, sharing John's expertise, personal habits that are beyond reproach and commitment to excellence. They both held important positions in their community, with Ron serving as a Trustee of Rowan University, and John holding several key lay positions in his church. Ron was a former school business administrator, acquiring a subject matter doctorate in the process before completing law school. He was the best known bond counsel in the State, albeit because of his success, and his work on behalf of municipalities and school districts became legendary. His competence, along with his conciliatory nature made him an ace in the hole heading into tough negotiations with the department of education or a planning board. You could almost sense the attitude of accommodation his adversaries brought to any negotiation involving Ron. These two gentlemen were key players in our success, especially since they were able to take my not completely baked ideas and give them the substance necessary to carry the day. From a technical perspective, giving them access to all of the electronic data bases of the districts as well as the legal and policy services that routinely emailed us updates proved invaluable, much more so than the modest investment required to build the system. Perhaps their best collective achievement was their work with me on privatization and the many cooperatives we developed, which are described below.

Anyone who tries to accomplish anything is going to trample on some toes, which I always thought was easier to survive than an abrogation of all you stood for. Nevertheless, you are going to need legal talent and this is another area where NJASBO shined. I was privileged to be able to call on Frank Campbell, Esq., a fine attorney and an even finer human being. I recall the first time we spoke, he told me that I had extended a courtesy to him many years before, which I did not remember at all, and that was the beginning of a lasting friendship. Frank was patient, explored areas in depth for me and stood by in support each time I felt a stand had to be taken. His advice was always succinct, on point, and never challenged successfully. I found that just showing the name of such a renowned attorney on the bottom of one of my "battle letters" often had a very positive effect on getting the matter resolved to my satisfaction. Without people like Frank, a lot more of us fighting the public dole types would be tempted to follow the path that cause cowards to die a thousand deaths.

ARBITRATIONS AND MORE

The causal reader or the beginning bureaucrat might be asking, "Why not just depend on the binding arbitration process that has worked so well over the years?" Well, let me tell you a bit about this. First of all, processes such as these, including worker comp and civil actions relating to HR, should have an employee bias, in my opinion, as any sort of judicial process should speak for the potential victim. The arbitration process was once a major pillar of this system and labor today, especially the teacher unions are quick to extol its virtues, as the system is now all too easy to manipulate. In my early years at Temple University, I had the chance to work with many fine students whose goal was to become empanelled by the American Arbitration Society, and thus begin to function as an arbitrator. Some of those students went on to work for the State of New Jersey as mediators, a process that while not unrelated to grievance resolution, has a different perspective and goal, to engage in conflict resolution process to make sure the opposing parties fully understand the motivation, resource base and limits under which each is operating. I had occasion to work with state mediators only a few times during my career and found that they were all too quick to act as quasi fact finders and non-binding arbitrators, rather than mediators. Their goal was clearly to achieve a settlement, cost not withstanding. These experiences included one occasion when one of my former students was involved and, in a private moment after which I had advanced some criticism over how the process was progressing, he confided in me that their huge case load precluded anything more than trying to get matters resolved and that boards of education had resources, were loathe to tolerate work stoppages, had little support in the community when faced with strikes and "they were school people and did not know better as all they wanted was a public criterion to get out of their potential mess." He made it clear that this was unofficial policy not his position.

Back to arbitrations: given the rolling system of increases whereby teacher dominated boards of education set a higher standard, which is used in the following set of negotiations and so on, unions always have available a precedent to use to show that their demands are "fair" when considered in light of other settlements. Also, the arbitration process itself has become prostituted, that is, arbitrators have to maintain a balance between decisions favoring unions and management or they simply are not asked back to work. Two examples: there was an arbitration involving one of my districts in which the arbitrator let it be known he was ruling for the staff members, "...because he had to as it was *their turn*", but was sure the matter would be reversed in favor of the district as "...the issue was so clear cut". Second, unless you were on a raft lost in the mid Pacific, you have to be aware of the traumatic events surrounding the union grievance filed on behalf of Mr. Terrell Owens against the Philadelphia Eagles of the National Football League. The original matter was heard by a very experienced arbitrator, Mr. Richard Bloch, who was of course, acceptable to both sides. The mutual consent aspects represent both the boon and bust of the process as it is a necessary precondition to any arbitration but also the reason why the arbitrations must have a "balanced" decision history. When the pending arbitration was announced I tried to examine the record of the arbitrator to ascertain whose turn it might be and it looked like a pretty even split. Apparently, in the opinion of the arbitrator, Mr. Owens' behavior was sufficiently disruptive to warrant a very severe penalty. Subsequent to this, a second grievance was filed when the team attempted to recoup a portion of the original signing bonus, purportedly a provision of the extant contract. The union chief, a Mr. Eugene Upshaw, who had been roundly criticized for the collective bargaining agreements under which his constituent labored, immediately announced that Mr. Bloch would not be welcome as the arbitrator and that he was banned from all future arbitrations of this type. Some system, eh? What do you think the chances are that the next arbitrator shall be given any future work if Mr. Owens's loses a second time?

INSURANCE AND BENEFITS

This is another key area and for me, the solution was working with fine professionals, completely dedicated to customer service, even when the clients of the customer, the teachers, were extremely difficult to cope with. Time after time I had seasoned insurance executives in for information sessions with our teachers and many returned to me with the same complaint, that they had encountered a certain level of arrogance they had not seen before and each immediately attributed the situation to the entitlement mentality that permeated the staff, especially since they knew who was running the show.

Nevertheless, we did accomplish some interesting things. By way of convenience, let me discuss this area in two sections, property/casualty, with worker compensation and health benefits.

Many were called and many were dismissed before we found our dream team, Tim Irons of Haines and Haines/ TC Irons, and Ed O'Malley of Commerce Insurance Services. Both of these fine professionals served us and many other districts well. They "worked" the account and were extremely successful in their efforts with the teaching staff, taking each snide remark and even the insulting behaviors as just another challenge to be met and they did. It took some doing to build this network; probably a lot of readiness was necessary on our part before the district matured to the point that we were ready to maximize our benefit from dealing with Tim and Ed, and their absolutely terrific staff.

When I arrived in Delran they were being insured by the NJ School Boards Association Insurance Group [NJSBAIG], a very fine operation that had reconstituted itself after a series of scandals had damaged their credibility. The rep for our district was a great guy by the name of Gene Hollownicky. NJSBAIG saved Delran, even though the district was paying in excess of 225k for insurance in 1990, the best indication I may give as to how screwed up the program was at the time. There was simply no risk mgmt effort at all in place, yet the district would come to win a prestigious award in this area before my retirement. Just before my arrival, the district administration had decided to transport some 12 custodians to a school for a special event "set-up", what is called in the Navy as an all hands evolution. Would you believe they transported these staff on folding chairs set in an empty panel van? Well, they did, and as you may have guessed, they traveled exactly one block to a stop sign before disaster struck. The worst part was they seemed to not learn any lessons from this and they moved from episode to episode with no prior thought. Training was non-existent, etc., so the district was lucky to have NJSBAIG and Gene did a commendable job in trying to help the place straighten itself out.

While I was grateful for the time NJSBAIG bought me, it was obvious they were not the final solution. In those days, at least, a district was dependent on group experience, to some extent and could never get to the point of earning really low rates based on its own performance with risk mgmt and losses. Also, I was not thrilled with the insurers for NJSBAIG and both the agency and their sponsors were a bit too arrogant for me when it came to trying out some new concepts. Again, they probably grew to this paternalistic attitude given their experiences with many districts, for which they worked well, especially as the districts did not know any better. To give you an example, some years after we left NJSBAIG, we were owed money. Their director at the time decided to trumpet the fact that these over-reserves were in fact not refunds but dividends, based on some almost dazzling accomplishment on the part of NJSBAIG! They insisted on presenting these checks with a plethora of fanfare and publicity at the annual tri-association conference held each October in Atlantic City, of which you have read in an earlier section of this book. We said "NO" as it was almost a fraud, would be an insult to our current agents and carriers and just plain inappropriate, specially since our district took what was valuable from the conference but never made a big deal about attending. The alternative, they said, was to invite their reps and the press to a BOE meeting, where they would put on a commercial and make the grand presentation. Again, we said "NO" and they threatened to withhold the check. It was amazing what a drafted complaint to the State Insurance and Banking Department, with individual complaints targeted against the licenses of the specific people involved accomplished. Well, we got the check but this kind of sums up where we had come to with NJSBAIG. Still, it does work well for many districts.

We needed an all lines approach, something that would permit us to influence a small group of quality districts and reap the benefits of group rates, especially for reinsurance purposes, while having the benefit of being small enough to have solid performance count. The answer was what became known as the Burlington County Joint Insurance Fund. This "JIF", as they were known about the State, were basically self-insurance groups, with copious reinsurance and were successful if they were managed properly and it seemed as though our JIF had decent representation, both in its Board of Directors and the agency involved, the Cashan Group. The JIF had been in existence for some years, as a worker comp only entity and it took quite a bit to move the districts to all lines coverage. I can still recall the amazement I felt as I visited different board of education meetings to make a pitch for the JIF, the amazement coming from often ridiculous arguments for the status quo, especially when some of my adversaries were not only board members but people insured by the very agents they were trying to protect! I must say I never had that problem in Delran, and never really in Cherry Hill, Carl and John McKeon simply would not tolerate anything like that. Plus our numbers were always too good to be quarreled with.

The JIF worked well at least for a while for us, for the risk management program in Delran was getting stronger and stronger. This was also about the time I was introduced to Timothy Irons. He came very highly recommended; indeed, the districts that he served uniformly spoke of him with the highest praise, and related many examples of his professionalism and outstanding customer service. Tim never tried to sell me anything. We got together from time to time and it was readily apparent that the scope of services available from his agency exceeded even that which we can come to welcome from the JIF. For example, I had for some time been investing in professionally managed fixed assets appraisals, both for our inventory control and equipment cycling needs. We had a great software package but no ability to use the data for insurance purposes until Tim began working with us to develop what eventually became the model now required by DOE.

I have never hesitated to recommend this particular JIF for districts who have neither the ambition nor the skill to manage their own risk program; they could not be in finer hands.

The JIF board did all of the work. The member districts could and did profit handsomely from this administrative paradigm. The members did tend to feat themselves once a year, a bit too lavishly for my tastes but well within the parameters extant at that time, and, some received stipends for their work, which were also appropriate but not the kind of thing we had employed with our natural gas consortium. I guess we came to a parting of the ways for two reasons: first, even though we were saving a great deal of money [really big bucks!] from our time with NJSBAIG, we were still subsidizing the other districts to the tune of 25k a year; and, two, Cashan's fee was based on the size of the premium generated, which was not unfair, but, we seemed to be embarking on a shopping spree to enjoin other districts. One of which was Willingboro, which, despite the many fine and dedicated people affiliated with the district, had come onto some challenging times. Their worker comp multiple was very high and they had just tried to demolish a building with their own staff, to save money, and a member of the staff was killed in the attempt. We foresaw our premiums continuing to subsidize others and some of the others taking us back to a virtually uncontrollable member pool.

Tim Irons became the solution. He matched us up with a few other districts of similar bent regarding cost controls and management oversight and we saved even more money, with long-term guarantees and were able to afford, within those savings, even more insurance. For the first time we had the coverage we needed, strict control over our own cost factors, and services well beyond our expectations. Tim worked with us to generate far more capacity and capability from our Safety Committee. He arranged for multiple building inspections throughout the year, each accompanied by remedial training and system sessions for our staff, and a regular program of improvements. Perhaps most importantly, he brought us a number of fine staff but always worked the account himself, and, his patience with some of our more challenging teachers became legendary within our office. For a district such as Delran was at the time, Mr. Irons and his services were a perfect fit. How good is he? Well, it is safe to say that without his assistance, we would have never won any awards for the effectiveness of our risk management program; and, our worker comp multiple was .647, one of the lowest anywhere and simply outrageously low for a school district. For the uninitiated, worker comp insurance premiums are based on the size of the payroll and experience. Of the two, the payroll should be the easier to control but with superintendents and boards of education giving away five percent plus raises to their unions, the only way to hold down costs is to maintain a very strong loss control program, really a challenge if you read some of the case citations in the book. The premium is based on assigning experience relative to a factor of 1.00, with most school, districts well above one. Therefore, 0.647 represents a significant discount.

Ed O'Malley came to my notice about the same time. You have not lived until you have tried to manage a health benefit program for public school employees. Those who survived this experience probably have performed sufficient penance to last a lifetime. At the risk of slighting Ed, but to save the reader some tedium, every character and professional trait that I described for Tim, also applied. Ed is quite simply, another very fine person, wonderfully prepared in his chosen field, with a strong commitment to excellence.

We had been represented in this area by Frank B. Hall, actually in several of my districts, which worked fine as long as one of their key staff, James De Marco, worked on our behalf. While Jim obviously did not enjoy his contacts with our teachers, he was a fine professional who worked his contacts for good rates and provided a much wider scope of services than I had ever before experienced. We stayed with Jim who opened his own agency after Hall was assumed by other interests and when Jim sold out we needed a person and there was Ed.

Much like Tim, Ed, had made his presence known for a while, not to sell us anything but just getting to know me and we found that we shared many similar ideas about additional products and services that would benefit both districts and their employees. It was about that time that the on-line enrolling, modification and monitoring system that Commerce eventually built became popular. When it became time to replace Jim, there was absolutely no hesitation in turning to Ed, even though there were a few other quality people known to me. No one could begin to match the scope of services and low cost available from Commerce, and this package came with Mr. O'Malley, absolutely the best person I have ever seen working through the maze of grief that is known as teacher negotiations.

Commerce Insurance Services, through Ed and two really terrific members of his staff, first, Jennifer Finnelli and then Diane DiPietro, brought us incredibly low commission rates, especially in light of the scope of services offered, while at the same time using their influence base as the representative of a huge constituency to manage our contacts with carriers in a highly effective manner. We got all of the benefits of being a member of a large buying group but, like Tim, Ed, always made us feel as though we were his only client.

Ed is a visionary and knows his business like no one else I have encountered. We increased our coverage and saved a bundle through such strategies as minimum premium programs combined with catastrophic insurance thresholds and premium stabilization funds. Each concept was new and therefore had to be worked through the various state bureaucracies and Ed was there to help. Whether dealing with Horizon, Aetna, Delta Dental or the other behemoths whose service was never known to be sterling; whether dealing with the NJEA; whether problem solving for a staff member; or, whether analyzing the demands presented at the negotiating table, Ed O'Malley was there and made his presence felt. Again like Tim, I have never seen either of these gentlemen give offense even though they NEVER failed to represent the best interests of the tax payer, even when the district administrators were eager to give away the store to achieve labor peace.

People like Tim and Ed do not come along every day and I welcomed their service to my districts and would gladly welcome their services had I the opportunity to do it all over again. The same can be said for Gary Kanalstein, Scott Weitz, Rob Inverso, Ron Ianoale and John Barbour. I never regretted for a moment the time I invested in providing references regarding their outstanding work on my behalf.

BUDGETING AND REPORTING

Here again we developed systems that were widely adopted throughout the region. We worked closely with Steve Struthers and Ed Kulshinsky to examine and actually field test applications and finally selected Lotus Notes as the vehicle to satisfy our requirements. One of the major delimiting factors was the budgeting and accounting software in place in many of the districts, that provided by, again the outfit with the amazing handle, the Gloucester County Educational Management by Computer

Center [GCEMCC]. Snide comments aside, this organization did provide a valuable service, especially to small districts, since the 1970's, in fact I provided a chunk of federal and state program development funds to get those folks up and running while I was with the state education agency. The problem was their limited capacity for R&D and their tendency to be reactive rather than proactive. I am sure they would argue strenuously as "everyone is satisfied with our services", the common refrain I received whenever I asked them to develop something new. Indeed, most were satisfied with their efforts and you know the old saw about good enough being the enemy of excellence. In this case, I am not even sure that "good enough" applies.

Fortunately we had Steve, Ed and of course, Carol Hearn, who seemed to have almost unlimited vision and capacity to implement new strategies and programs. Lotus Notes was a God send as it was very effective, comprehensive in scope, easy to use [always a concern when working with school people], and, we could marry it, albeit with some difficulty, to the extant school budgeting and accounting package. Here again, having Carl Johnson at the helm was invaluable. Carl had worked very hard to learn all he could about organization management and I can think of few other superintendents who would have taken the trouble to invest himself so heavily in such a project, with the vision to see the positive outcomes, and the courage to deal with all of the complaints from people who were ignorant of anything we were dealing with and completely resistant to change. You see, your normal curriculum guy or gal may refer to themselves as a CEO once they become superintendent, but they simply do not have the skills and experience to manage an organization, at least not to the level in a contemporary environment. Marry this with a rotten political system and you get what we have today, a mess.

Here is just a quick synopsis of what resulted. Our cost center directors, principals, directors, et al, could look at current budget status on an almost real time basis, each day. I say almost because, due to EMC limitations, the data were as accurate as of the daily closings, which were updated overnight. The data arrays were comprehensive and even analyses of trend were possible. The data fields also included descriptions as to their spending plan for the year, for each account. Each line item had a corresponding screen in which the staff members preparing PO's, could use a calculator that listed the PO and debited the account, a great feature for the time period before the close-out and re-establishment of funds cycle was completed. By switching screens, the users could examine data for comparable reporting periods, for every year that the system has been in existence! These data could have been made available to the general public via the website, which was a direction the powers to be chose not to follow.

It was with budget development that this system really shone. We achieved a paperless budget development process. Each year in early January, the cost center directors were given fresh screens, for the following fiscal year. These were kept open for a month and already included stock descriptions of the materials and supplies ordered, the texts to be published for the next cycle, etc. By clicking on an account line on the screen, a writing pad was immediately displayed, where by the person preparing the budget could insert descriptions of her or his intended spending for the coming year. When combined with the on-line ordering capacity described earlier, you can easily see how we created a system that removed a lot of the drudgery for all concerned. The superintendent and the BOE members could easily review the budget inputs by dialing in via any machine in the district, or off site, if they so chose [few did]. Again, a click of the mouse brought up the comparative budget page, which provided ten years of data [as of this writing] for each budget location.

The best part, we could lock out the system and automatically roll it over to the EMC software! Then the budget was ready to go and the cycle repeated. This worked so well that I never heard a complaint and that from people for which complaining was a joie de vivre.

FACILITIES AND GROUNDS // FOOD SERVICE // TRANS-PORTATION

I am grouping these three areas, not to diminish, their importance, but, to emphasize their commonalities. These were the first three areas that we examined for privatization and outsourcing and all three efforts were hugely acclaimed as successes, and widely imitated. Not every district was successful in adopting these programs because they tried too many adaptations and ruined the central focus, primarily for two reasons: they lacked the technical acumen in operations mgmt to make this work and, they lacked the courage to deal with the political ramifications of the situation.

As to the latter, when some districts tried to move any of these areas to vendors, they gave in to what was a very considerable political initiative by the various unions. For example, trying to privatize yet guaranteeing the current salary and benefits of the employees whom were then guaranteed work with the vendor was an obvious prescription to disaster yet was a fairly common occurrence among the more timid central office types and boards of education. Even in Delran, we had a near riot when the employees who were the targets of the privatization effort stormed [in a physical sense] the board of education. I can still remember the one individual who dived across the board table to unplug the communications system as the key vote was taken. That board stood tall and carried the day. Of course, the professional preparation had been superb. We used John Barbour on the labor side and Ron Ianoale on the all important contractual documents to great advantage. The bottom line for any such initiative is the "financials" and here is where the technical background in ops mgmt is key. A neighboring district had a real jerk for a superintendent at one time, a person, who let's say, never impressed me with his veracity. He was under considerable pressure to privatize and obviously had not the slightest idea of what he was doing. Now this guy was being monitored by a tax watch group that actually impressed me a great deal when I got to meet them. You see, they came to Delran, because they had heard a great deal about our cost efficiency efforts and our policy of splitting the savings between improvements for the children and tax relief. Privatization was a key item for this group and we met with them at length, carefully explaining the program and processes, while taking great pains to avoid any comment that might embarrass our "colleague" in a neighboring district. I can still picture Carl Johnson patiently meeting with these folks time and again, sometimes even downplaying our achievements to keep this person from the scrutiny he certainly deserved. Well, we came to understand that our "colleague", when he could not deliver, began stating that "...the savings being advertised by Delran had to be a lie." At that point, all bets were off, we gave them ALL of our savings data, provided a workshop on the technical skills required to do the work, and then letting them draw their own inferences about their own leadership.

To make this work, you need people who are trained in the twin concepts of core competency identification as well as the generation of essential elements of work, not the kind of skills usually learned by educators. Basically, you end up with a quantitative model that generates only the essential elements of work that really are important, and that is what you place out for bid. In addition to evaluating the proposals, you have a grid of criteria to price the projects, demonstrate savings and monitor the work of the contractor, and, make deductions when the services specified are not provided. You see, when you start with a blank sheet and add only those items critically important to the task then you have very specifiable elements by which to evaluate the entire effort, and to calculate savings.

This is obviously a gross oversimplification. For more information see my paper presented to the Greater Philadelphia Industrial League, presented at the Navy Inventory Control Point, Philadelphia, November, 1995, sponsored by the Philadelphia Region Supply Corps Association; or, the final report to the Navy Supply Systems Command, of the privatization of the Fleet Industrial Support Center San Diego, April, 1996. These papers shall give you a detailed summary of what the concepts truly mean and offer suggestions as to models and the necessary consultants to make this work.

These three areas also lend themselves to the technical protocols described earlier, especially as to record keeping, report generation and financials. All were immediately infused into the on-line ordering system and with great success, especially with respect to the quality of goods received, the speed with which they appeared, and the savings enjoyed.

Another pleasant [to me] aspect of this program is the fact that these people are not members of employee associations that refuse to recognize superior performance. While the NJEA shall never tolerate performance bonuses, having the type of work elements described earlier enabled very specific judgments to be effected regarding the work of contractor personnel. Thus, we were able to employ bonus and recognition awards for contractor personnel that exceeded their performance goals.

Nowhere was this more successful than with respect to food services, obviously a key area. I worked with several food service management companies during my career with the public schools, and used many more in my work as a management consultant and Naval Reserve Officer. Never, ever, did anyone come close to Nutri-Serv, of Burlington County New Jersey. They won almost every competition in the districts, at least where the competition seemed to be honest, and their reputation for customer service was excellent. They provided us with two truly outstanding individuals, the people who really made the program work, Bonnie Horner, a regional supervisor without peer, and Fiorangela Hummel, a caring, talented and absolutely gifted district manager. Their tireless work in bringing the best for the least investment was just magnificent to see and their employees always met or exceeded their performance goals, and were granted recognition awards.

They were so good that we never had to exercise our prerogative for first right of refusal of any staff member assigned to Delran. This was one of many special provisions built into the key contract documents, including special liability sections, hold harmless clauses etc. Those documents are in the public domain and should be available via the Delran business office, unless my successors have wiped out all vestiges of my tenure.

ETCETERA

Keeping a careful eye on the ancillary areas, especially when you are privatized, is also a key consideration. Strong bid specs, comprehensive contract language, measurable performance indicators and even stronger vendor monitoring are essential. Having a top flight lawn and landscaping service is a nice hedge against the never ending challenge of field maintenance, and, they can also be used to handle any overflow snow removal. However, a poor contractor and a lack of proper supervision can prove to be a financial drain and an administrative nightmare. We were fortunate for most of my years in Delran, a firm called McHugh's Landscaping, owned by a local, Jim McHugh, someone with strong ties to the community always won the competitive bid, sort of like icing on the cake. While the preceding attributes were useful, Jim was well trained in both the technical aspects of his business as well as operations management. He knew what he was doing whether driving a tractor or a computer spreadsheet, and, he made sure he recruited staff that never were a problem for us. We had similar success with our building maintenance, HVAC, electrical and plumbing contractors. Another key area: copiers, faxes, document handlers, type writers and the like. We hit home runs with Chuck Hahn's Stewart Industries and our personal account rep, Fred Greenberg. The Stewart's people were always on the cutting edge equipment wise, offered the best pricing and, were the most responsive people I have ever seen regarding service, which kept the thundering herd, teachers, principals and parents, not quite grateful, but mainly quiet. Their superb technology also allowed us to make important advances in office automation, especially given the manner in which they were able to network everything including classroom instructional applications. Fred also exhibited the patience of a saint, which was very important in working with our constituents.

REFLECTIONS

"The sun never shined on a cause of greater worth."
Thomas Paine

Obviously all of this can only serve as a synopsis for your own further research and personal development. You can contact me for detailed information, if I am still among us, enroll in the challenging but very rewarding MBA program in operations mgmt at Temple University [which also offers great security from the fickle world of the dole], or hook up with some of the great ones still in the business. As of this writing, people like John Knorr, Bob Oldt, Frank DeBernadinis, Bruce Benedetti, Mike Gersi, Rob Wachter, Peggy Ianoale, and Jim Hager, all were still achieving great things in their assignments. Talk about great achievements, I could not possibly overlook John Amato, with decades of service in a number of difficult situations. Buying them lunch could reap real benefits. Another great source is the New Jersey Association of School Business Officials. As a long-term business school professor in organizational development, I do not hesitate to offer my professional appraisal that NJASBO is without a doubt the leader of the pack, in terms of the so-called professional associations in the business of public education. Years of dedicated service by people like Ed Meglis, Eugene Keyak and John Donoghue created an entity that well represented their constituents, brought sanity to the mess annually created by political quackery, and developed and managed the very best professional development and licensing program I have ever seen on the dole, and they have terrific lawyers! In recent years, a truly gifted business administrator by the name of Frank Hicks joined the staff and made a great organization even stronger. Frank would be high on my list to contact if I were just beginning the trip that shall hopefully lead to retirement.

Of course, you also need to find a way to recruit and retain great staff. The administrative support positions in Delran were all defined during what I refer to as the Golden Age, the 1990's, with salaries set to match the accountability assigned and superior performance rewarded. There were few transitions and each time the outgoing nurtured the incoming team members. Another great attribute was their willingness, nay eagerness, to cross train and sub for one of their own. People like Maureen Bartlett, Carol Hearn, Judy Napoli, Pat Tracy, Mary Minko, Joyce Vaughan, Pat Latacz and Barbara Edwards, were just astonishing in my opinion. They not only displayed incredible commitment to excellence, they redefined that standard on an annual basis. They made each day interesting despite the culture that fostered tedium and never indicated any infection with the malaise that seemed prevalent among their colleagues in other venues. It got tricky when their performance stopped being recognized and rewarded adequately. I never saw them falter and they seemed intent on maintaining their performance standards. Incidentally, having someone experienced in HR making decisions here certainly helped. We hired for capacity and then built productivity, a true prescription for excellence.

What more can I possibly say of Carol Hearn, who was my "partner in crime" as we developed strategies to stay ahead of e state education agency and the legislature. As a tribute to Carol, let me repeat what Carl Johnson said about her on his departure, "Carol is surely the one truly indispensable staff member in this organization." Let me add that, together, they were something special indeed, yet each was quickly forgotten, perhaps so as to not embarrass the district as to the circumstances of their post-employment period.

Carol was to go on and build an incredible reputation for excellence but outside the district. There was at one time, a board of education that recognized her efforts, compensated her according to her performance and created the title of Assistant Board Secretary and Controller to justify her new status and importance in the district. That came to an abrupt end with the swing to the union emphasis; after all, Carol was part of the group that was warning of the consequences of the out of control spending and therefore came to be ignored officially. By the time she retired in 2005, this tiny woman who contributed so much to the children of Delran was all but forgotten, except by all those she had touched by her incredible commitment to excellence. Instead of the traditional salary boost for high performing staff as they entered their last year, Carol was part of the group deemed to be used as an example for "future financial austerity" and her last salary increase percentage was less than half that awarded to administrative support personnel nested comfortably within a union, people for whom the terms performance and accountability were unknown. The climate, and everything that goes with it, was changed forever in central office. There was one other interesting phenomenon. I volunteered to give up half of my raise that year, the difference would not have made a significant difference in my life, and the board of education almost fell over themselves accepting. The proviso was that the funds were to be given to the office staff. The staff continued to work beyond expectations, even with the inevitable turn-over, so strong was the office culture. But, they all made it clear that they were working that hard for me, not the district. That single gesture earned me more good will than a life-time of trying to build close relationships with key staff, thus the overriding value of the dollar as a motivator. I guess the message is once again that having people micro-manage things in such a finite manner really becomes a problem when they have little qualification to do so.

There is potential for great staff such as these folks in all school districts, just as the number of successful administrators exceeds those listed above. What differentiates the people named from a lot of their peers is that these staff demonstrably succeeded in spite of a system designed to inspire failure, and, they took considerable risks in doing so, for in many cases representing the best interests of the children and the taxpayer placed them at odds with the political establishment. They, and others like them, are the people who make things work in the land of nod, verbiage, and hubris; and, their stories are the best teaching tools available. They are truly the heroes fighting the public dole syndrome every day. To these, Sir Winston could have attributed the phrase: "Never have so many owed so much to so few."

30

OTHER WORKS BY JOSEPH PICOGNA

Personality Sex and Behavior: *a comprehensive analysis of the traits that have been proven to be essential ingredients of leadership.*

Total Quality Leadership: A Training Approach: *a detailed review of theoretical constructs vital to leading others in building productivity; and, selected case studies in building leadership capacity.*

Command Personality: *differing perspectives of multiple examples of leadership traits that work and sometimes do not, presented from a historical perspective, featuring vignettes of noted individuals in leadership positions.*

Growing Up Immigrant: *Tales of Guys, Girls, God and Good Times. A work in progress that examines of acculturation of growing up in the fifties and its impact on the transformation of life for the baby boomers some sixty years later.*

511889

Made in the USA